MAKING SPACE FOR THE GULF

✺ WORLDING THE MIDDLE EAST

Making Space for the Gulf

HISTORIES OF REGIONALISM AND THE MIDDLE EAST

Arang Keshavarzian

STANFORD UNIVERSITY PRESS
STANFORD, CALIFORNIA

STANFORD UNIVERSITY PRESS
Stanford, California

Printed in the United States of America on acid-free, archival-quality paper

Epigraph from Behbahani, Simin, Farzaneh Milani, and Kaveh Safa, "Eight Poems by Simin Behbahani," *Iranian Studies* 41, no. 1 (2008): 91–96. 2022 © Cambridge University Press, reproduced with permission.

ISBN 978-1-5036-3334-6 (cloth)
ISBN 978-1-5036-3887-7 (paper)
ISBN 978-1-5036-3888-4 (electronic)

Library of Congress Control Number: 2023057985

Library of Congress Cataloging-in-Publication Data available upon request.

Cover design: Michele Wetherbee
Cover painting: Houshang Pezeshknia, *Fishing in Khark*, 1958. Reproduced by permission from Houshang Pezeshknia, *Companion of the Wind* (Tehran: Nazar Art Publication, 2017); © 2017 by Nazar Art Publication. With thanks to Niloufar Pezeshknia.
Typeset by Newgen in Arno Pro 11/14

For Greta

The world divided by a line is a dead body cut in two
On which the vultures and hyena are feasting

SIMIN BEHBEHANI, "The World Is Shaped Like a Sphere"

Contents

Acknowledgments

Due to no fault of anyone other than myself, this project has taken long to complete. If not for the support, inspiration, and conscientiousness of many, it might not have been realized at all. Because the project went through so many reconceptualizations, I am sure to forget many who have helped me track down sources, shared their knowledge, invited me to present my work, and commented on my writing and presentations. But several colleagues have been important to the genesis and culmination of the project. I acknowledge and thank Begüm Adalet, Ismail Alatas, Aslı Bâli, Houchang Chehabi, Kaveh Ehsani, Yasser Elsheshtawy, Mahnaz Fancy, Lucia Gomez Robels, Manu Goswami, Adam Hanieh, Natasha Iskander, Wilson Jacob, Mehran Kamrava, Firoozeh Kashani-Sabet, Laleh Khalili, Azam Khatam, Zachary Lockman, Noora Lori, Karuna Mantena, Shana Marshall, Ali Miresepassi, Amin Moghadam, Harvey Molotch, Pete Moore, Lawrence Potter, Laura Tapini, and Helga Tawil Souri.

In the past few years my students have done a lot more than listen to and entertain my curiosities. Through their reflections, writings, and own research agendas they have elucidated and taught me much. I have tried to cite them where appropriate in the body of the book, but let me acknowledge my debts to Roham Avandi, Alex Boodrookas, Jeff Eamon, Mehdi Faraji, Nadia Khalaf, Matthew MacLean, Bita Mousavi, Ada Petiwala, Brian Plungis, and Gabriel Young.

Lori Allan provided expert editorial assistance. Her perceptive reading and constructive suggestions on the entire manuscript were invaluable. Azba Wahid provided much-needed support with bibliographic citations. Throughout the project Guy Burak has been an invaluable resource for navigating library holdings and tracking down sources. I completed this manuscript while chairing my department, a "challenging" responsibility that was eased by our indomitable department administrator, Kieran Lettrich. I am very grateful to the Center for Humanities at New York University for their generous support both in defraying publishing costs and in hosting me for a fellowship.

Kate Wahl demonstrated why she has such an impeccable reputation as a thoughtful and diligent editor who magically manages to care about authors and readers all at the same time. I am thankful to the entire Stanford University Press team who astutely shepherded the manuscript through review and production. In particular, I appreciate Charlie Clark and Martin Schneider's meticulous copy editing of the manuscript. Erin Greb and Michael Izady were generous and helpful when it came to designing maps for the book. I thank Mahmoudreza Bahmanpour, Nazar Publishing, and the family of Houshang Pezeshknia for allowing me to reprint his painting on the cover.

I owe an enormous debt to Naghmeh Sohrabi for her friendship, kindness, and brilliance. She has taught me so many "true things" and was always patient as I muddled through questions about space and time and so much more. Leila Pourtavaf and Hamed Yousefi have prodded me to keep working and through their intellectual curiosity and analytical rigor extended the horizons of this book. Leila, Naghmeh, and Hamed made me a believer in Zoom writing, accountability check-ins, and writing retreats, just to name a few of the items on the long list of lessons they taught me.

Over the years Mona El-Ghobashy modeled intellectual rigor and clarity of thought. This book owes so much to her rich comments and incisive questions that stimulated me to think more systematically and write in a more reader-centered fashion. I am forever appreciative for the countless hours she devoted to reading "memos" and drafts of chapters. I am sure I did not meet the high standard she sets, but I hope she sees at least some of her understanding of politics and ethics of scholarship in the pages that follow.

Children are wonderful, yet they don't really "help" with writing a book, nor should they. I am very thankful for Leo and Minu being in my life and displacing my thoughts about the Persian Gulf with their own love of geography, music, book writing, (outer) space, and football. None of this would have been possible without Greta Scharnweber, who has waited for this dedication and these acknowledgments for too long and with boundless grace. Although it was not titled *Gulfography,* here it is. I dedicate it to you, with loving gratitude.

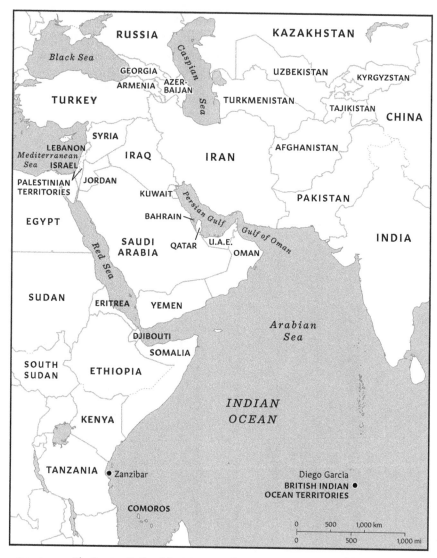

IMAGE 1: The Persian Gulf and the Western Indian Ocean. Map based on Michael Izady, *Atlas of the Islamic World and Vicinity* (New York: Columbia University, 2006–present); https://gulf2000.columbia.edu/maps.shtml.

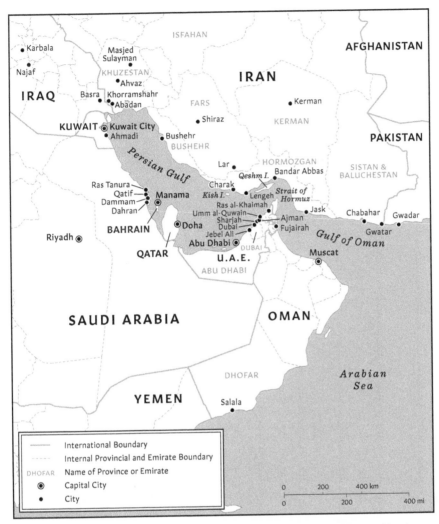

IMAGE 2: The Persian Gulf. Map based on Michael Izady, *Atlas of the Islamic World and Vicinity* (New York: Columbia University, 2006–present); https://gulf2000.columbia.edu/images/maps/Gulf_Administrative_Units_lg.png.

MAKING SPACE FOR THE GULF

REGION-MAKING ACROSS SCALE AND TIME

MODERN CARTOGRAPHY DEPICTS the Persian Gulf as a two-dimensional space, an indigo oval surrounded by land on three sides (see Image 3). It is roughly the size of the United Kingdom or Uganda or the US state of Indiana, 1,000 kilometers at its longest. It opens to the Gulf of Oman and the Indian Ocean through the mere sliver of the Strait of Hormuz. This satellite's-eye view of the sea encourages us to apprehend the waterway and its environs as an undifferentiated place, smooth except for the ribbonlike coastline almost perfectly encircling the sea. Despite the fixed, ahistorical picture that maps give us, land erosion and the silting of riverbeds reveal the impermanence of geography. The Gulf's northwestern terminus is a good example of this with the marshes and mudflats of the al-Faw Peninsula, created by the confluence of the fabled Tigris and Euphrates rivers, making for unstable terrain and a treacherous river route. Although changes to the landscape are not what most consider when they think of turbulence in the Gulf, the shifting ecology has posed serious obstacles to people and ways of life in the estuaries that make up the borderlands of Iraq and Iran as well as far-off urban centers assaulted by the increasingly habitual dust storms.

As is more widely known, it is the Gulf's political meanings that are contested, with antagonists using nomenclature to argue over it. In this perennial battle, simply uttering its name can raise temperatures in a conference hall or generate endless social media indignation. By calling it the Persian Gulf, the

IMAGE 3: NASA Satellite photo of the Persian Gulf, November 28, 2007.
Source: https://earthobservatory.nasa.gov/images/8354/the-persian-gulf.

Arabian Gulf, or using the pragmatic dodge of "the Gulf," citizens, scholars, and nationalists convey and claim different histories, identities, and alliances.[1] States take part in these naming duels by affixing their preference to currency, stamps, and textbooks to stoke and deflect nationalist fervor. Kuwait's coastal road is named the Arabian Gulf Highway, while the Persian Gulf Highway wends its way from Tehran down the center of the Iranian plateau. In 2014, when the UAE named its soccer league after the Arabian Gulf, Iran's football federation blocked one of its best players from joining an Emeriti team and renamed its own competition the Persian Gulf League. These fracases are the product of contemporary geopolitics, nationalist zeal (and fragility), sectarian strife, and the polemical nature of discourse in the age of the internet. For diasporic communities, most of whom have never set foot in its tepid waters, debating the Gulf's national features is also a means to participate in "long-distance nationalism," a common mode of imagining political community.[2]

These claims have histories. The push and pull of the "Arabian Gulf" can be traced back to the 1950s when it was increasingly adopted by Arab nationalists and leftists. Naming it the "Arabian Gulf" was as much a challenge to British colonialism as it was a critique of Iranian chauvinism and hegemonic posturing. Except for Saudi Arabia and Yemen, the rest of the peninsula was made up of British-protected states until 1971. Taken up by Egyptians, Iraqis, and others, the term "Arabian Gulf" denounced Pahlavi Iran's alliance with Western powers as well as Gulf Arab shaykhs' collaboration with empire and their unwillingness to join the reawakened Arab nation. More than simply a matter of naming and identity, the desire for Arab solidarity that was conveyed in the term *Arabian Gulf* extended to demands for redistributing revenues earned from subsoil treasures, or "Arab oil," crude oil being yet another slow-forming substance that has taken on an ahistorical sheen.

This Arab-Iranian and intra-Arab rivalry was in part a contest between sympathizers and detractors of European imperialism. While Iranian officials expressed concern in the 1920s that their Gulf had become a "British Lake,"[3] a Lebanese-American political activist with Pan-Arabist sympathies, having traveled to the Arabian Peninsula, concluded, "The Gulf should be renamed: it is neither Persian nor Arabian, it is British."[4] Several decades later, a historian of modern South Asia extended "the British Lake" so far as to envelop the entire Indian Ocean and the "wide arc of territories" built in the nineteenth and early twentieth centuries.[5] Yet amidst this desire to valorize the

Gulf's importance for Empire was the quip made by the British foreign minister that George Curzon, champion of British imperial expansion into the Gulf, was "prancing around the Persian Puddle."[6] Characterizing that body of water as a mere puddle would probably annoy Arabs and Iranians no end, but it was meant as a jab at those in London and Calcutta who advocated folding the waterway and its coasts into its imperial project. For many decades now, naming the Persian Gulf has not been politically neutral. Few can imagine an innocent discourse about the Gulf.

Not all attempts at claiming the Gulf have been through naming. "The American Gulf" is rarely evoked, even after decades of continued US military presence in the Gulf or just "over the horizon" stationed in bases in the Indian Ocean, the Red Sea, or the Eastern Mediterranean. Despite the term never gaining traction, the Gulf has been vital in the plans and mental maps of US policymakers and strategists since at least World War II. In 1981 Secretary of Defense Casper Weinberger told Congress that it was "the umbilical cord of the industrial free world."[7] Whatever the preferred nomenclature, the Gulf has emerged as a contested site caught up in the colliding currents of the past century and a half.

Despite the different ways that the Gulf was depicted by powerful forces— as the domain of Persians, Arabs, Americans, or the British or a puddle of an umbilical cord—they all imply that it is a bounded, immutable body that can be encompassed as a single geographic scale. It is defined either as a national space and an extricable rooted in the Persian or Arab nation or as a place of imperial domination on a geographic scale "above" or "beyond" the national. Out of various geographic imaginaries and imaginative geographies,[8] the Gulf has been construed as being unstable, cosmopolitan, or pivotal for British Empire, for national self-determination, or for global capitalism. When people argue that the Gulf should be contained, secured, stabilized, or held in the bosom of a single nation or a part of the free world, they are building this on a host of assumptions about geography, society, and power.

The Persian Gulf is treated as a world region because these prevailing representations of the Gulf insinuate that whoever has the upper hand over this quasi-inland sea has access to and dominance over its littoral, the surrounding hinterlands, and a significant part of the globe. By the time US Secretary of Defense Caspar Weinberger addressed the Congress, the stakes had swelled to encompass "the industrialized free world" or what today would be called "the global economy."[9] Attempts to define the Gulf as a region are linked to different hegemonic aspirations; they evoke and promote visions for what the Gulf should become and who should control it. Debates about who should or does control the Gulf typically also rest on the premise that it has a timeless essence or else a seamless linear trajectory from a local body of water to a British lake to a US-protected global lifeline. If empires and global hegemons conceive of history as a calling to fulfill their Great Power destiny, for Persian and Arab nationalists history is something to purify or escape.

Battles over the proprietorship of the Persian Gulf index a particular understanding of space, scale, and time. These contests mobilize a view of space as fixed, homogenous, and existing primordially or prior to human action. As the influential Dutch-born émigré geopolitical thinker Nicholas Spykman concluded in 1938, "Geography does not argue; it just is."[10] This abstract view of space, one that strips it from social complexity, symbolism, and multiplicity, has been buttressed by modern cartography and aerial views that make territory more quantifiable and concrete. It obscures societies living in the Gulf, placing them behind a veil of mathematical calculations that determine with precision the measurement of the land and the sea. It also owes much to classical geopolitics or the nineteenth-century study of relations between nation-states struggling to survive with different geographic endowments.[11] Within their claim to being "scientific," geopolitical thinkers take geography for granted, with the analyst as occupying the detached "god's eye" view of "the world."[12]

The Gulf is abstracted as a frictionless surface easily traversed or a unified territorial object ready to be enclosed and captured, a compelling expression of what Henri Lefebvre described as "Space . . . becoming the principal stake of goal-directed actions and struggles."[13] Such a formulation encourages a view of the Strait of Hormuz as a chokepoint rather than a gateway and its shoals as a barrier rather than a porous membrane. Thinking about the waterway in this fashion "evokes the image of something physical and external to social context and to social action, a part of the 'environment,' a context *for* society—its container—rather than a structure created *by* society."[14] The Persian Gulf region is a two-dimensional plane emptied of people.

Practitioners and observers have come to know and grasp the Gulf as a region—a single bounded object and one of the homogenous parts of the globe. In the rush to devise ways to project power or bring stability, left unasked are questions about how and why this body of water and its abutting lands have been regionalized in the many ways that it has, through concrete social relations and abstract representations. And what these region-makings (and un-makings) tell us about the world. In raising those questions, many apparent contradictions in the representations and realities of the Gulf appear. It is depicted as a regional whole but also fractured and deeply divided politically. Many represent the Gulf as an encased territorial unit, even though it is indispensable for transregional circulations. How the Gulf is defined—whether as a region, a "world region," a gateway, a transnational contact zone—by policymakers, urban planners, migrants, university deans, and patrons of think tanks matters to how wars are fought, how citizens and immigrants live, how faculty are hired, how political issues are defined as problems or solutions. To disrupt the essentialized, closed, and abstracted representations of the Gulf requires alternative conceptual tools and ways of writing about space and time that make change and contestation visible in all their complexity.

RELATIONALITY AND REGION-MAKING

Making Space for the Gulf tunnels underneath these naturalized understandings of the Persian Gulf region as a location on maps or an abstract enclosure. I examine processes of region-making, or what I term regionalization, as they have unfolded from the mid-1800s to the present. I call for unmooring our perspective away from the position of a detached observer strategizing for territorial control or national honor and instead surveil the many investments in space necessary to sustain political power and capitalist accumulation or navigate struggles for upward mobility. By tracing how the littoral societies of the Persian Gulf were bound up with far-flung places via sea-lanes and credit lines, I document how they were gradually and unevenly integrated into and left their mark on the circuits of international capital and the designs of geopolitical strategists. The Gulf then comes into view as a mutable, created space that does not exist as a passive stage but is assembled out of human actions and relations as well as being constitutive of struggles. The societies of the Persian Gulf were not a backwater or latecomer but a site for purposive participation in the making of global capitalism. Spatial politics of the Persian Gulf are not a competition over a single object but a feature of layered and multiple, sometimes incommensurable, regional formations. The textured topography of the Persian Gulf has been overlain by histories of region-making and unmaking. I show the fault lines of Gulf geography were the outcome rather than the determinant of politics. Methodologically, the Persian Gulf does not function as a divide but rather a kaleidoscopic lens allowing us to view more than the sum of its parts; a social space and a world of a region.

Conventional understandings of the Persian Gulf as a "region" evoke a sense of a place that has unity and an interior logic, making it one of several key regions that make up the modern world.[15] Certain images of "the Gulf" depict it as embodying specific cultural and environmental characteristics. Other representations portray it as a coveted destination for investment, migration, or military command. Politically, these depictions of the Persian Gulf as a world region paved the way for it to be possessed, monitored, and compared with other regions. They underwrote a maelstrom of collective or individual projects: British colonial presence in the Gulf through 1971; the massive investments on behalf of US policymakers and private firms since World War II; migrating laborers and businessmen casting around for fortune on one coast or another; political mobilizations in the name of decolonization and internationalism; the jockeying for regional dominance by Iranian, Iraqi, and Saudi Arabian rulers even as their critics accuse them of being "subimperial" clients or traitors to the cause or of national self-determination.

These standard narratives of the region comprise a common contradiction, namely insisting on the Gulf as a regional whole and uniform space that can and should be secured, contained, and filled, while treating the waterway as either a transportation artery or boundary between empires, states, Muslim sects, and alliance blocs. It is in this manner that the Persian Gulf region has taken on coherence in our consciousness but has also been continuously treated as vulnerable and unbridgeable. Some of the best works on the topic highlight this in their titles, such as *Insecure Gulf: The End of Certainty and the Transition to the Post-Oil Era; Troubled Waters: Insecurity in the Persian Gulf;* and *The Unstable Gulf: Threats from Within.*[16] In these and other works, the focus is on the Gulf's "security architecture," identifying how "security dilemmas" unleash vicious dynamics between rival states. Political maneuvers take place in, on, and over the Gulf, but the region itself is an empty chasm between peoples or states.

The ambiguity of regionalism is often deployed strategically. Invoking this tension between, on the one hand, the wholeness and fragmented nature of the Gulf or, on the other hand, its appearance as a fixed container or a fluid channel can be used for one project or another. Similarly, countries such as Iran and Iraq can drop in and out of "the Gulf" depending on balance of power considerations. The Gulf can have clear boundaries defining what is inside or outside of it, but it also can be viewed as open to the world. The ambivalent nature of the Gulf as a region is reflected in its being imagined as an imperial, national, or energy frontier as well as a boundary, zone, and circulatory pathway. Often these portrayals occur in the same breath as much as in the same instance from different vantage points. In the mid-twentieth century, as the US government sought to organize the region in Cold War terms, increases in oil revenues increased the stakes for rulers, Fortune 500 firms, central banks, and foreign policymakers alike. But alongside this a blend of dreams and debts have compelled people to search for work in the Gulf. Responding to the growing demand for labor of all sorts, the scale of labor recruitment to the Gulf multiplied as "Gulf-goers" (*khaleej boro*) followed historic pathways to its shores.[17] But so did workers channeled by recruiters in "sending nations" and subcontractors in the "receiving countries."

With this multiplicity in mind, we must think of the Gulf as a shared space and explore what is socially constructed within the seeming contradictions of the Gulf. The plasticity and ambiguities of the Gulf cannot be sorted out because states, firms, travelers, and others are committed to not settling on a single definition. The frictions cannot always be smoothed out, and uncertainties are often manipulated in the process of defining the nation, maintaining public support, extracting surplus, silencing critics, justifying foreign policy, and tolerating dire work conditions.

By recalibrating our lens on social arrangements involved in *producing* the Gulf, we treat it not as "a formless void *between* societies but rather a unique and specifically constricted space *within* societies."[18] The chapters ahead bring to the fore the interactions of seafarers, migrant workers, rulers, smugglers, engineers, urban planners, pilgrims, tourists, and investors. Through their labors, speculations, and plans over the past century, they conquered distance, leaving in their wake a well-trodden, uneven terrain connected to an array of places and practices. We will scrutinize why the Persian Gulf has been such a fraught space for so many decades. The Gulf region is a locus and outcome of politics, a contested arena, and the object of imperial ambitions, national antagonisms, and migratory dreams. By "fraught" I do not mean wrangling over who is its rightful proprietor or litigating a "stable" or "true" meaning of the Gulf. Instead, this book contends that the roots of these clashes lie in the competing ways that the Gulf has been regionalized through concrete social relations and abstract, but interest-laden, representations.

Building on a tradition that conceives of space relationally, this book treats geography—like region—as the product of histories of struggle over administering spaces, regulating movements, and inhabiting places.[19] These histories involve technological innovations (such as steam engines) alongside social processes (including privatization of communal land, colonial governance, or citizenship regimes) to map how society shapes space and vice versa. This relational approach expands our analytical purview to explore what sorts of regionalization have unfolded in the past century. Relational theories of space have helped explain why capitalism repeatedly addresses crises of wealth accumulation by moving from one place to another to address shortfalls in profit; these "spatial fixes" are responses to declines in profitability as well as investments in particular locations, a set of spatial processes that we register as gentrification, rust belts, company towns, offshoring, and infrastructural hubs.[20] The combination of fixed investment and mobile capital generates conflicts and implies that places must continually adapt to conditions that are beyond their borders and hence out of their control. Thus, space is not just the built environment or piece of territory but a source of revenue, an object of consumption, an object of political struggle, and an instrument of state control.

By situating the Persian Gulf within processes that extend well beyond its borders, these familiar depictions of the region recede—of it being peripheral to world history, an endemic zone of conflict, an energy depot for expanding industrial capitalism elsewhere, or a bastion of traditional tribalism and petro-monarchies. What comes into view is the gamut of forces that have constituted the Persian Gulf as a spatial effect of political struggles across multiple scales. This includes geopolitical, imperial, and interstate rivalries, but equally decades-long negotiations between rulers and merchant capitalists or battles between labor recruiters seeking to turn displaced agriculturalists into oil workers and pearl divers into "migrant" laborers.

The field that has come to be known as critical geopolitics picks up these themes and telescopes them onto international relations.[21] More an approach than a theory, critical geopolitics emerged in the late Cold War to explore the spatial structure of political thought, particularly in security studies and popular foreign policy discourses. Drawing on poststructural, Marxist, feminist, and postcolonial works, this scholarship reads discourses closely to investigate the assumptions about geography, power, and society that go into defining world politics. Assumptions about states or civilizations as the units of politics are questioned, as are treatments of geography as a preexisting set of facts and essentializing ideas about race and culture. Critical geopolitics has illustrated that thinkers and practitioners tend to simplify the intricacies of society and neutralize the politics of space. This approach recognizes that classical geopolitics and early international relations theory were collectively a byproduct and legitimator of imperialism, challenging nationalist and state-centered conceptions of space and time—or methodological nationalism. Scholars in this field de-essentialize spatial politics by exploring the constructed and contested nature of nations, states, and borders. My own approach builds on these insights by pushing back on the tendency to focus on the North Atlantic world and the representational strategies encoded in texts. An examination of the making and remaking of the Persian Gulf in the past century challenges critical accounts to grapple with political economies in sites of imperial rivalry and rule.

If regions are never hermetically sealed, then the challenge is to trace vectors of social relations across space and through a thicket of porous borders. Social encounters and space are brought together as a "power geometry" in which discrete places are tethered to one another in highly unequal ways.[22] I analyze the Gulf as an uneven and differentiated region, a process that takes into account places that are ordinarily left in the shadows, skipped over by capital and overlooked or held at bay by political authorities.[23] While networks may facilitate movement, the way they coalesce into nodes generates friction, meaning that geography continues to matter despite the prevalence of "flows" and fantasies of a world flattened by globalization. To capture these fluctuating vectors of mobility, I attend to (1) boundaries and bordering practices that regulate motion and situate (or emplace) people and things hierarchically; (2) differential experiences of the Gulf—including its relationships to empire, globalization, capitalism, and the nation—depending on where actors are situated physically and socially; and (3) historical events and outside forces that affect locations and polities in the Gulf differently. I insist on approaching the Gulf as a region that fluctuates over time and depending on where one stands.

Geographic scales should also be thought of relationally.[24] Regions are extroverted spatial instantiations of accumulating wealth and control that depend as much on what happens "outside" of them as "inside" their borders. One implication is that the regional scale is yoked into other scales rather than being positioned as one of several self-contained units hierarchically ordered from the global down to the national and local. The regional is jointly formed and co-constituted with the urban, the national, the international, and the global. This is what I mean by a multiscalar approach to regionalization.

In doing so we disrupt notions of scales as mutually exclusive and neatly clustered hierarchies. Geographical scales are commonly imagined as objects nestled like Russian matryoshka dolls with "the global" encasing "the regional," which in turn covers "the national," "the urban," and "the local." The theoretical implication is that these hierarchically ordered scales are autonomous from each other, with some form of control running up and down different levels with the global being superior to or dominating the local, for example. That the regionalization of the Gulf is an accumulation of spatialized relations and strategies moves us toward a multiscalar perspective, rather than one that treats them as bordered spaces. By "multiscalar" I do not simply mean that we should examine phenomena and events from the vantage point of several scales; I mean that these distinct scales are "interdependent and intermingled" accretions.[25] As Ayşe Çağlar and Nina Glick Schiller aptly describe it, the multiscalar is "an understanding of scales as locally, regionally, nationally, and globally mutually constituted, relational, and interpenetrating entry points."[26] This enables us to glean how the Persian Gulf is situated in relation to various scaled political economic projects across the Long Twentieth Century. The Gulf's regionalisms are not restricted or bound only to the regional scale—either in their origins or their expression. The histories of the Gulf's regionalization do not happen as part of the Middle East or "in" it, but because they are connected to and in dialogue with the continual remaking of the Middle East, the Persian Gulf becomes a place to explore the Middle East and other scales.

To argue that scales are co-produced and to study the regionalization of the Persian Gulf as multiscalar does not, however, mean that scales are meaningless or can and should be collapsed into one another. If spatial relations should begin with social relations, then the distance over which they operate matters. Each geographical scale has its own organizations, rules, and decision-makers that cohere in and sustain specific territorial formations. *Making Space for the Gulf* claims that the multiple genealogies of the Gulf region happen differently and in consort with the making of empires, nation-states, cities, free trade zones, international regimes, and categories of citizenship.

In short, regionalizations are aspirations to create homogeneous geographic units, but like so many ambitions they are prone to frustration and incompleteness. Yawning gaps exist between geographic imaginaries and realities. It was hypothetical enough for different actors to project their hopes and anxieties onto it, What we have today is a consequence of decades of these colliding and collaborating attempts to create the Gulf as an abstract and homogeneous geographic unit or tightly bound international regime of nation-states, on the one hand, or a global seam for circulation or hierarchically order urban space, on the other. These very attempts at ordering Gulf space into an abstraction invariably entail differentiating between insides and outsides, allies and enemies. Coordinates on a map are turned into meaningful locale and distance into relationality by such forces that valorize and give meaning to only parts of the Gulf. The fragmentation and splintering that accompany the ordering of the Gulf region have cleaved people and places apart and rest on political alliances that do not comport with the reified depiction of a region as static staging ground or a geography that "does not argue."

BOUNDARY CROSSINGS

This relational approach to regionalization offers a new account of the Persian Gulf that brings together in the same frame what is held apart in popular understanding and existing scholarly treatments. Each chapter ties places in Iran, Iraq, and the Arabian Peninsula together through narratives and by historicizing moments often treated as ruptures—the discovery of oil, the Iranian Revolution, or the rise and decline of the British Empire. With a mixture of comparisons and connected histories, this framework enables narratives to be populated by a more diverse range of social actors—humble migrants and ruling families, pearl divers and star architects, striking taxi drivers and dethroned rulers, protectors of British India and stewards of globalized American universities. In doing this I braid together specialist literatures on the political economy of oil, late British imperialism, US hegemony and primacism, Iranian studies, Gulf studies, and global cities while making use of largely unnoticed research and primary sources.

Narrating the modern Persian Gulf as a region encompassing the Iranian and Iraqi societies confronts a tsunami of knowledge production about what is usually conceived of as a narrower and more impermeable Gulf. For much of the past four decades, Iran and Iraq have been treated as the constitutive outside of "the Gulf" or as forces disrupting regional order. Until the 1980s, it was common to find English-language books and conferences on the Persian Gulf including papers on Iraq, Iran, Yemen, and beyond.[27] But with the 1981 founding of the Cooperation Council for the Arab States of the Gulf (usually referred to simply as the Gulf Cooperation Council, or GCC), the Tanker War at the end of the decade, and the first Gulf War (1990–91), academic and public discourse oscillated and turned the waterway into a separating expanse. This was manifest when the late Shaykh Issa of Bahrain told a vice admiral of the US Navy: "Your men and women, the ships and aircraft of the Fifth Fleet, are a mountain of fire that separates us from the Iranians and the presence of naval forces is what has given us peace and prosperity."[28] He was pointing specifically to the US military's role in the Gulf in the 1980s, but his comments can be extended to the broader maelstrom of actors that has rendered the Gulf "a mountain of fire" between places, peoples, and polities. In this rendering, on one side are Bahrain, the rest of the GCC states, and the United States as their protector, and on the outside are Iran and Iraq and other forces destabilizing the Gulf. Considerable intellectual labor and material investments have been dedicated to portraying the waters of the Persian Gulf as a boundary and aligning military, academic, media, and cultural institutions to represent it this way. Think tanks have been founded, university chairs endowed, annual conferences held, and junkets for journalists and celebrities organized as part of branding campaigns marketing the Gulf as global, tolerant, futuristic, and full of possibility. Replacing "the territorial trap" of nation-states is a naturalized regionalism or methodological regionalism in which "the Gulf" is a ready-made entity.[29]

The consensus within what is now described as Gulf Studies in contemporary Anglo-American scholarly and policy orbits is more or less committed to this formulation. Another scholar critical of this representational narrowing is Sheila Carapico who has illustrated how twenty-first-century Gulf Studies in the United States has reduced what used to be "Arabia" or the study of the entire Arabian Peninsula to a focus on a narrow set of questions related to the lands north of the Tropic of Cancer. This erases Yemen from analysis and replaces it with a focus on the GCC. Analytical "centers" and "peripheries" that are subjective constructions have been naturalized as empirical realities in *realpolitik* conceptions about oil and logistics. Categories typical in political science have the same effect by labeling complex social assemblages and diverse polities with static terms such as the Gulf monarchies, oil monarchies, rentier states, or simply Gulf States.[30] These discourses are institutionalized through scholarly journals, academic organizations, and university curricula, dovetailing into overly rehearsed debates about the name of the Gulf, geopolitical alignments, and typologies of politics based on nation-states. Carapico incisively concludes, "The Gulf is where American interests lie," and calls for the disruption of what counts as the field of Gulf Studies by opening up research horizons to a wider array of actors, temporalities, and concepts.[31]

Informed by this critical epistemological stand, I not only analyze the Iranian and Iraqi littorals alongside of and in dialogue with eastern Arabia but also consider the Persian Gulf in the fashion that Sunil Amrith approaches the Bay of Bengal, as "linked by journeys, memories, and the sinews of power . . . [so that] we can see beyond the borders of today's nation-states, beyond the borders imposed by imperial mapmakers and immigration officials, to a more fluid, more uncertain world: a world that resembles our own."[32] In this pursuit, my research is based on a mix of field and archival research and marshaling emerging, yet still disparate, secondary literatures that write about the Gulf region as straddling our conventional "area studies" units.[33] This work and others have illustrated that the societies of the Gulf are not mere products of modernity but participants in its making even if via noncapitalist modes of production that are sometimes brought forward by capitalism.[34] Working with new archives and posing new questions about individual countries, cities, or topics, these writers examine a range of geographies, worldwide processes, and historical junctures.

Once we approach the Persian Gulf as a product of relationships, we can unearth alternative regionalizations across a more expansive historical canvas. The Persian Gulf went from the periphery of empire to a frontier of capitalism; from a threshold between nation-states to a central seam of globalization. This is the historical sweep that the book reconstructs, through narratives that maintain an open sense of place, allowing for what Doreen Massey calls "the coming together of the previously unrelated, a constellation of processes rather than a thing."[35]

A KALEIDOSCOPE OF SCALE AND TIME

Mirroring its subject matter, the chapters of *Making Space for the Gulf* have a spatial structure. To push against a teleological rendering of how the Persian

Gulf was made into an abstract region, I have written the book as a set of interlaced analytical histories. The chapters connect and counterpose regional projects that have their own histories and intersect with other processes, including imperialism (chapter 2), nation-state formation (chapter 3), "globalizing" capitalism (chapter 4), and urbanization (chapter 5). The book's structure emerges almost organically from a framework that holds that meanings and historical processes change depending on the geographic scale. To maintain a relational approach to space, these chapters are built like a kaleidoscope, revealing different features as we realign the angles of our prism. Individually, each chapter is a portal, demonstrating the interconnections between regionalization and other patterns of scale-making and spatialized politics.

This organization helps us see the history of the Gulf recursively. Historical episodes such as the making of modern absolutism and the founding of oil sectors appear in more than one chapter but look different in light of the geographic scale and specific actors that are foregrounded. Across these chapters, I necessarily examine certain issues in detail and neglect others altogether. By layering the chapters in this fashion, we more vividly notice the simultaneity of spatial politics and the sedimented manner in which the Gulf was regionalized. "No space ever vanishes utterly, leaving no trace," comments Lefebvre.[36] The metaphor of sediments captures the gradual building up of the Gulf into a differentiated region with the past submerged but not dissolved. An example of this is how British colonial administration, commercial activities, and extractive economies (selling dates, pearls, and oil, for example) were dependent on these preexisting translocal mercantile families, labor bondage, and racialized hierarchies. British and then US policymakers at once condemned and upheld views of the "tribal" and "primitive" nature of the region. Tribes were a source of backwardness, inefficiency, and political instability that required western disciplining, while shaykhs and traditional practices were cost-effective instruments by which to rule and extract resources from a distance. Events of the past and historical dynamics reappear later memorialized in heritage sites or ingredients of national myths as they are called on to mark national belonging and "un-belonging."[37] Chronological junctures are less unforgiving that some histories claim. Also, the narratives that follow are alive to the many temporalities at play—from geological time associated with crude oil, to seasonal patterns of debt and labor, to the acceleration involved in containerization and the logistics operations. Just as I interpret regionalization as a spatial accumulation, so time features similarly as cumulative and as spiraling. Thinking in terms of accretion and erosion disrupts typical conceptualizations of time as either cyclical or linear, progressing from one period to another.[38] By adopting this narrative structure, I am consciously encouraging the reader to think with me nonchronologically and recursively. What are too readily viewed as inevitable or natural, wars and definitions of belonging for instance, become puzzling products needing to be deciphered anew. My narrative about the Gulf's region-making works dialogically through multiple scales as the chapters fold onto themselves to braid space and time together.

* * *

On the cusp of the nineteenth century, the waters of the Persian Gulf were a social bridge, not the political boundary it would come to be seen as. Chapter 1 demonstrates this by describing the environmental, socioeconomic, and political conditions of the Persian Gulf prior to the advent of industrial capitalism and the breakdown of the land-based Qajar and Ottoman empires. Maritime life and labor fashioned a densely knotted society enveloping the southern reaches to the Iranian Plateau, the Arabian Peninsula, and eastern Africa, enjoying inroads into large sections of the Indian subcontinent.[39]

This synthetic history, built on a host of works on specific towns, commodities, empires, and companies, paints a picture of an oceanic world that is spatially expansive and socially interdependent. It foregrounds the ecological conditions and social relations—in particular, around pearling and long-distance trade—that were disrupted by subsequent modes of regionalization. These sea-facing peoples who appear in Chapter 1 recognized the Gulf's waters as having a multitude of functions with people bound together through necessity and obligation but also coercion and exploitation. Ports, wind-powered vessels, caravan routes, kinship ties, and credit lines worked like hubs and spokes to establish intimate and long-distance relations, often across several generations. Despite the waterway being central to the people living there, from the vantage point of competing land-based empires of the time, the Gulf was a frontier where authorities overlapped and ebbed and flowed.

Chapter 2 examines how this unbounded arena of mobility and cross-fertilization became both valuable to and a challenge for the British Empire and then US-centered capitalism. The geopoliticized conception of the Persian Gulf that continues to haunt discussion of the region today emerged in the late nineteenth century. Geopolitical imaginaries and new technologies were marshaled to fashion the Gulf into an enclosed space. Geographically inflected imperial strategists and capitalist investors in infrastructures directly intervened to access valuable assets in an "empty" terrain protected from "outsiders." In the process they differentiated between friends and foes, drew boundaries, and defined territories and their rulers. As such, this geopoliticized Gulf was the product of new territorialities or political projects that defined spaces in order to organize it through inclusion and exclusion.[40]

Focusing on two eras of geopolitical region-making, this chapter explores the establishment of geopolitical imaginaries over time and opposition and obstacles they generated. In the first era in the quarter century before World War I, geopolitical thinkers (such as Halford Mackinder) and colonial officials (including Lord Curzon) were becoming concerned with maintaining control over British India in the face of brewing challenges to the British Empire. Championing empire in the face of resistance and competition in the colonies and criticism at home, classical geopolitics combined with the growing capital investments in fixed assets and the new cartographic technologies to demarcate and represent the Gulf as a defined territorial space between the Raj and London. Nearly a century later, US officials were depicting the Gulf as a central pivot of global power, a process crystallized in the 1980 Carter Doctrine. Despite a number of crucial differences between these two historical moments, policymakers convinced themselves and others that the Gulf was an abstract geometric zone demanding intervention and incorporation to counteract its inherent instability and to address crises of capitalism.

Chapter 3 illustrates how rulers and aspiring state-builders made the Gulf their own by parsing it into national spaces and articulating specific conceptions of sovereignty. It explores the concrete ways that extractive capitalism and empire—and resistance to both—were catalysts for state formation on the shores of the Gulf. By juxtaposing the histories of state-formation in Saudi Arabia, Iran, Iraq, and the British-protected sheikhdoms of Arabia in the first half of the twentieth century, we see how nation-states are co-constituted along with regions and imperial praxis.

During the first quarter of the twentieth century, imperialism was reinvented as internationalism. Despite the continuing hierarchies of power, internationalists envisioned a world project based on juridically equal, nominally independent states represented in new international institutions, such as treaties and the League of Nations. Within this framework colonial officers, oil firms, local business interests, and ruling shaykhs and shahs forged a Gulf region of sovereign territorial states. However, sovereignty did not translate into governance by the citizens. Instead, treaty arrangements divided authority between British colonial officers and Gulf rulers, who in some cases were "protected" by Britain. Whether shaykhs, shahs, or prime ministers, these internationally recognized executives positioned themselves as trustees of a society that they kept at arm's length. Like so many other parts of the world, decolonization of the Gulf was hollowed out by handcuffing self-government to British tutelage and preserving the sanctity of contracts held by western companies, giving them privileged access to resources and markets. These unaccountable executives woven into the fabric of the geopolitical conception of the Gulf generated resistance with political movements targeting this impoverished sovereignty and demanding self-determination.

The coupling of territory and sovereignty explored in chapters 2 and 3 did not end with the founding of sovereign nation-states. Spatial politics found new expression in supra-national imaginaries and sub-national scales. Chapter 4 unearths the political economies of two early articulations of footloose capitalism and global neoliberalism in the free trade zones of Iran's Kish Island and Dubai's Jebel Ali, both founded in the 1970s. I show how states and corporations collaborated to construct Kish and Jebel Ali to connect the emerging global factory centered in East Asia to far-flung consumers on many continents. These two zones in the Gulf were part of the logistical revolution of the past half century, in which "corridors and gateways" or "pipelines of trade" were requisites for a frictionless economy of just-in-time production and globalized supply chains.[41] These juridical-spatial enclaves, which freed capital from a slew of national laws, combined with innovations in shipping to create new monopolies. The result was the splintering the Gulf into distinct but related regional and global channels.

Sovereignty was reworked in seemingly paradoxical ways in Kish and Jebel Ali. Based on field research and the examination of Persian and English archives, Chapter 4 illuminates how the region was transfigured for commodity and capital circulation by creating enclaves that were connected to but distinct from state boundaries. Iran's shah and the Maktoum ruling family of Dubai used them to project sovereignty as the British withdrew from the Gulf and oppositional movements formed. Despite their differences in origins and outcomes, the free trade zones of Kish and Jebel Ali thickened national boundaries as markers of difference and sovereignty. As deregulated enclosed places, they also became conduits for transnational coalitions of capitalists to accumulate wealth. This chapter corrects the widespread assumption that global capitalism erodes national boundaries and weakens central authorities, showing how national governing elites turned the Persian Gulf into a site for the making of global capitalism.

Chapter 5 pivots to the urban scale to explore how the built environment and social formations of cities have expressed and constituted different forms of regionalism since the beginning of the twentieth century. By juxtaposing and tracing the swing from the port cities of the first quarter of the twentieth century to the nationalizing cities of the middle of the twentieth century to the globalizing cities of the past three decades, Gulf cities are historicized and regional patterns differentiated. Across these three phases, both the urban models and social processes necessary to construct the urban fabric ricocheted well beyond the borders of the cities. The chapter shows the constant importance of migration, transnational circulations of urban design, and capital accumulated by global markets for pearls, oil, and finance. These movements of people, ideas, and revenue were not flows but structured channels that brought peoples and places together and complicated or even sabotaged notions of a seamless globalism. Port cities were imbricated in broader commodity movements through shipping lanes and caravan routes. In the middle of the twentieth century, legal distinctions between citizenship defined who could migrate, own property, and secure work in the newly built company towns. As some of these port cities became capitals (Kuwait City, Manama, Abu Dhabi, Doha) and others became provincial cities (Basra, Bushehr, Qatif) separated from the seats of power in Iraq, Iran, and Saudi Arabia, the nationalizing processes of building markets, road networks, and property regimes defined the relationship between cities, the nation, and uneven global development. This urban fabric was constructed by laborers, who in turn were rendered "permanently temporary" in law and practice.[42] The global cities paradigm sought to break the mediating role of nation and region by positioning cities as the prime portal and force in organizing life globally. Dubai, Doha, and Abu Dhabi adopted these polices and symbols in their "Gulf Cities" branding campaigns as futuristic blueprints for all humankind. But some of the Gulf's private firms and public investors built new regional alignments and vehicles to profit from urbanization elsewhere and to sustain their own cities through cheap food, labor, and capital. Yet historic patterns have not been erased, and contestation in and over cities abounds.

Tacking between different geographic scales, historical moments, and alternative coastlines allows us to see the Persian Gulf as simultaneously globalized through transnational relations, regionalized as a geopolitical category, and cleaved along myriad juridical divisions and spatial enclaves. Spatial forms and social processes meet as a series of agglomerations with different degrees of completeness. These pages will tease out the lessons gleaned from examining region-making as process-driven and using a more unbounded, networked, and plural understanding of regionalism. Sleek "global cities" and tuckered-out coastal towns are brought together within the same field to consider how places and identities are made and unmade in tandem. It is about coming to terms with the Gulf belonging to many different and differently positioned peoples and political projects. This polyphonic story of regionalization that rests on social relations offers an alternative to a metaphysical notion of a unified Gulf manifesting a single identity or culture. There is no theoretical answer to which Gulf region is more correct or will win out— "it is determined through political contestation and struggle and, hence, a relatively unstable determination."[43] This is essential for interpreting the past and fashioning alternative futures for the Gulf and the many places enfolded within it.

BOUNDLESS REGIONALISM

THE PERSIAN GULF'S WATERS are quite shallow, averaging fifty meters of depth. Its deepest areas are along the northern shore; it is shallower along the Arabian Peninsula. This has meant that the Iranian littoral has tended to benefit from better anchorage and ports, while the most abundant oyster beds have been found in the warm salty waters to the west and south, especially near the Bahrain archipelago. Under the right conditions grit in the mollusks produces pearls, around which fact a social world fanned out across the waters of the Indian Ocean and reached late nineteenth- and early twentieth-century Europe and North America. In the first half of the twentieth century, as oil explorers began to discover profitable fossil fuel reserves, it became clear that the distribution of crude oil and natural gas was in a similar way unevenly distributed under the Gulf's water and adjacent terrain. This geology and topography had a huge impact on the port cities, the entrepôt trade, the pearling industry, and the oil towns in the Gulf. The materiality of the Gulf has presented opportunities and constraints on how society has been organized along its coasts and how wealth has been accumulated near and far. In turn, by the early twentieth century this remade nature into something increasingly interpreted as resources, shipping routes, and manpower.

Recursive relationships between nature and society rebounded upon one another to leave an uneven and dynamic geography centered on the Persian Gulf and stretching out in many directions. This social geography shaped politics in ways that constrained the grasp of power by governing authorities and refracted the ways capitalist modes of production and accumulation unfolded. The regionalism in the eighteenth and nineteenth centuries was outward-facing, networked, and polycentric and as such superseded a conception of space as abstracted and inert. The Persian Gulf and its littorals were a quintessential frontier, where authority was "neither secure nor non-existent [and] open to challenge" and "order and chaos assume many guises."[1] The Gulf was not a place that was empty or devoid of society, but one in which political and economic power was incomplete and ever-changing. In the weakly institutionalized setting with state and capital only penetrating the littoral society in a patchwork manner, the Gulf acquired its meaning not by being an enclosure defined by borders but by its permeability.[2]

WATERS AND ITINERARIES

As with oyster beds and oil, the Gulf's limited quantities of freshwater have also been unevenly distributed. With little rainfall across the region, freshwater was almost exclusively found in the Upper Gulf, where the Tigris and Euphrates meet to form the Shatt al-Arab, or Arvand Rud, as it is known in Iran. It is here that under Sassanid rule (224–651 CE) complex irrigation systems were devised and laboriously maintained for grain production. By the nineteenth century a thick forest of date-palm groves signaled the region's main cash crop.[3] Despite the unstable contours of the rivers caused by silting, the fields have been worked by settled peasants on either side of the river delta for centuries, and animal husbandry has persisted to the present day. On the Arabian Peninsula water is restricted to isolated oases, leaving much of the area barren and uninhabitable to large populations. A significant exception in eastern Arabia, however, is the archipelago of Bahrain and the neighboring al-Hasa region of present-day Saudi Arabia. These societies were made up of many generations of cultivators living alongside pastoralists and town-dwelling traders and fishers. East and south from the Shatt al-Arab, the Iranian coast consists of a strip of land nestled between the shore and the Zagros mountain range that runs parallel to the coast down to the Gulf of Oman. Mountain runoff and ancient underground irrigation systems (*qanat*), a technology adopted in the mountainous regions of Oman and the UAE as well, make more extensive agriculture possible in foothills and valleys. The built environment was designed to respond to this harsh climate. Those who could afford it constructed windcatchers (or windtowers) to direct breeze down to pools of water to cool their homes. Others depended on narrow streets with high walls to produce shade.

This uneven distribution of water has meant that water-poor towns in the Arabian Peninsula have depended on importing water from the Shatt al-Arab and northern littoral. Up through the first half of the twentieth century, this water was transported by *dhows*. These were ships of various sizes built from wood imported from long distances, since timber was not locally available. In towns such as Kuwait, water carriers, many of them Persian laborers, dispensed water to townspeople.[4] This scarcity contributed to the prejudicial way that Iraqis refer to Kuwaitis as "people who drink sea water."[5] More recently, there have been attempts to sign agreements and build underwater pipelines joining the northern and southern shores.[6] Although these pipelines aroused the ire of Iranian nationalists and environmentalists and were ultimately not built, the initiative sought to cultivate diplomacy while addressing the dependency of Kuwait and Qatar on costly and ecologically destructive desalination technology—a process that generates a salty brine that is returned to the sea with the effect of increasing the energy requirements of future desalination. As we enter an age when climate crises generate more conflicts, it is likely that unequal water distribution will become more contentious.

In addition to being an instrument for transporting drinking water or raw material to desalinate for consumption, the sea was the basis for a mixed economy built on commerce, shipbuilding, and pearling. Residents of coastal towns and the hinterlands were reliant on ecological exchanges structured by dhows, their large triangular sails keeping time with the metronome of monsoon winds.[7] Throughout the nineteenth century the cyclical pattern of these weather systems allowed for regular trading routes to develop connecting eastern Africa, the Persian Gulf, South Asia, and beyond. Some of the main goods exported from the region were pearls, mother-of-pearl shells, horses, salt fish, tobacco, opium, and dates. These goods were sold primarily to traders in Bombay and Zanzibar who then distributed them to other destinations on the Indian Ocean littoral, East Asia, Western Europe, and the United States. Some commodities, such as grains and pottery, circulated more narrowly among ports in the Gulf and the western Indian Ocean. Dates were exported from Basra, while tobacco, dried fruit, ghee, cooking oil, sugar, and carpets made their way from Bushehr and other Iranian ports. Ports on the Makran Coast of the Gulf of Oman and the subcontinent of India exported and re-exported many essential commodities—textiles, cotton piece-goods, cattle, tea, sugar, rice, teak, and metal products. "Only a monsoon apart," eastern Africa, specifically Zanzibar, was the source for slaves, ivory, mangrove poles, and cloves.[8] Aden, at the entrance to the Red Sea, provided coffee, gold and silver coins minted in the United States and Europe. Some goods multitasked. Dates were not only central to trade; they also steadied ships as ballast and were a unit of measure: the capacity of a one-hundred-ton vessel was described as two thousand packages of dates.[9] For a millennium, the Gulf's waters were part of a "maritime silk road" that aided the spread of settlement and socioeconomic exchange.[10]

Trade occurred at every port, where vessels picked up and dropped off cargo and passengers. Besides prearranged deliveries, sailors would sell their cargo based on information about commodity prices that they gathered at sea.[11] The relative efficiency of sea, as opposed to land, transportation produced ongoing circuitous routes. As late as the 1930s, a prominent southern Iranian merchant based in Kuwait operated a business transporting Shia corpses from Iran to Iraq's Shia shrine cities via Kuwait.[12] These routes and voyages were shaped by price differences and arbitrage, as much as topography and trade winds. The truism that value is created by imbalances between prices worked in tandem with nature.

Caravans carried goods from these ports over taxing terrain all the way to the Levant or through narrow mountain passes reaching into the Iranian heartland. This is how in 1903, one could find products from India, Oman, Arabia, Birmingham, Germany, Bombay, and Manchester in the marketplace of the ten-thousand-person Iranian port of Lengeh (also known as Bandar Lengeh) at the Strait of Hormuz, where the Persian Gulf empties into the Sea of Oman.[13] When King Abd al-Aziz Al Saud (ibn Saud) built his palace in the new Saudi capital of Riyadh in the 1930s, he could transport six thousand mangrove poles from the Swahili Coast via Bahrain.[14] Well into the twentieth century, towns deep in the Arabian interior were dependent on the coastal trade for subsistence and surplus.

Beyond the economy generated by traded goods and the seasonal and year-long employment for sailors, crewmen, and stevedores, shipbuilding created its own set of mobilities and interconnections. Sailboats were built in several towns on the Arabian and Persian coast, with Kuwait being a notable example—in 1912–13, for example, 120 pearl boats were built there.[15] By the early twentieth century much of the actual manufacturing of dhows had been transferred to South Asia, which is where the Malabar teak and coir (coconut fiber) for cordage (ropes for ship rigging) had always been sourced. But ships were a translocal creation; it was unremarkable for a sailboat to be built in Oman, owned by a Persian, and registered in Kuwait, just as it might be built on the Malabar coast, financed by a Bahraini merchant, and captained by a Kuwaiti.[16]

Steam engines introduced new actors and re-spatialized relations without completely eradicating these patterns. With steamships came a host of other necessary investments and infrastructures, most importantly coaling depots, anchorage requirements, and stabilizing ballasts, which favored certain ports, companies, and trades more than others.[17] The largest-scale infrastructural project and arguably the most consequential for the political economy of the late-nineteenth-century Indian Ocean was the construction of the Suez Canal, which allowed steamships to radically reduce the time, risks, and cost of transoceanic travel while increasing the volume of trade. Steam power and the canal reduced the voyage from the United States to the Gulf by a third, a quintessential example of Marx's dictum that capital tends toward the "annihilation of space and time."[18] It cut the length of journeys between London and Mumbai, Colombo, and Singapore by 41 percent, 36 percent, and 26 percent, respectively.[19] Total transits through the canal increased from 486 ships in 1870 to 2,026 in 1880 to 3,441 in 1890 and over 4,500 in 1910. As the quantity of ships transiting Suez increased, so did their tonnage—which was 45 times higher on average in 1913 compared to 1875.[20]

A year after the opening of the Suez Canal in 1869, the British India Steam Navigation Company established a biweekly service binding Karachi to Basra via Muscat, Bandar Abbas, Lingah, Bushire, and Manamah.[21] Dubai was added to its itinerary in 1904, an indication of this city's rising status as a port and mercantile node. No longer dependent on monsoon winds, carbon-fueled transportation became cheaper and faster, fostering new scales of consumption and forms of cultural hybridity. This is how Arabian dates (wrapped in bacon) became a popular delicacy for American Thanksgiving dinners at that time.[22] Large numbers of men and women left their homelands on these steamships in search of financial returns elsewhere. Spiritual rewards via pilgrimage to Mecca also gained a fillip with the British India Steam Navigation Company dominating the port of Jedda and pilgrimage travel from South Asia, eastern Africa, and Egypt thanks to their access to capital from British banks and government subsidies for delivering the mail.[23]

This intensification of traffic cut into the profits of wind-powered dhows handcuffed by the patterns of the monsoons but did not completely displace them. Allan Villiers recounted these changes with much empathy in his 1949 travelogue documenting his ten-month voyage from Aden to the Rufiji Delta and back north through the Strait of Hormuz to the Kuwaiti hometown of the captain. During both world wars, when Gulf societies were ravaged by shortages and famine, new "smuggling" routes emerged to and from port towns, such as Dubai, to circumvent British export bans; dhows were repurposed both for this grey economy (including selling arms, gold, and slaves) and transporting Allied troops and equipment.[24] Centuries of nautical charts and scientific inquiry continued to help dhow captains negotiate shallow sandbanks and craggy coastlines that were completely unnavigable to large steamships. As Nelida Fuccaro concludes,

> local shipping maintained a solid profile sustained by pearl trade with India and by the exchange of goods for local consumption with Iran, Iraq, and the Arabian Peninsula. The continuation of intercoastal trade was also assisted by the size of British ships, which could only approach large harbours. Native shipping was also able to support the bulk of regional trade in the late 1920s and early 1930s, when the collapse of pearling and the depression in the world markets restrained the circulation of international commodities.[25]

Prior to that collapse, however, the tiny pearl gems were a staple of the nineteenth-century economy, and pearling created social and economic networks that extended across the globe. The pearling sector ensured that the lives of people in these coastal societies were tightly interlaced with one another and reliant on actors and markets on land and across long distances stretching from the communally owned pearl beds nestled off Gulf coasts to merchant houses, financiers, and conglomerates in Bombay, Paris, London, New York, and Tokyo. Pearls were the main source of surplus on the shores of the Gulf on the cusp of the twentieth century, when global demand generated an exponential rise in the value and production of this labor-intensive commodity from 1880 to 1930.[26] At the height of the boom, an estimated "one-quarter of the male population along the Arabian shore worked in the pearl industry in one capacity or another."[27] In 1910, the British vice-council felt it necessary to provide two different population figures for Lengeh, one for the summer (8,000) and one for the winter (12,000), when the pearling fleet returned ashore.[28] Pearling activities dominated Kuwait's productive life with the number of residents increasing from 6,000 in 1840s to 35,000 at the start of the twentieth century and 50,000 in 1914 during the pearling boom years.[29] In the lower Gulf, pearls were almost the only economic activity, and almost all men were employed in pearling ships.[30] Even though pearling was concentrated on the Arabian coast, it was also central to the economy of certain places on the Iranian shore. In the 1920s, about three-quarters of the population of Lengeh were directly or indirectly engaged in the pearling sector as traders, divers, investors, shipbuilders, and the like.[31] Ruling authorities benefited by levying taxes on divers, boats, and traders. Workers and boat owners paid them seasonally in cash or kind, often with bags of rice. Rulers also occasionally supplemented their income by forcing captains to buy their provisions from them directly.[32]

In short, the pearling sector produced surplus for an array of people and places at an increasing rate in the second half of the nineteenth century and the start of the next. Based on Lorimor's *Gazetteer of the Persian Gulf, Oman, and Central Arabia*, the estimated value of pearl exports from the region multiplied fivefold, with exports reaching 1.5 million British pounds in 1905, up from less than half that in 1873. The values of pearls only rose during the roaring 1920s, as the appetite for them increased among the expanding bourgeoisie of Western Europe. Even the oyster shells made for lucrative business as they were repurposed for mother-of-pearl with the remains used to build out the shoreline in early forms of land reclamation (see Image 4). There was great volatility in prices during these years as new actors, especially from France, sought to circumvent Indian trading houses and buy directly from Gulf-based merchants and captains. Speculation in pearls as well as exports of opium to China exacerbated boom-bust cycles and generated more debt than people could repay, leading creditors to pass on risk in the form of higher interest rates. These profits left their imprint on the urban landscape of Paris, for it was wealth from Gulf pearls that was plowed into building the Arcades.[33] Profits transformed coastal towns driving opportunities for consumption as

IMAGE 4:   Oyster shells outside the office of Wönckhaus and Co., Bahrain, circa 1914.
Source: *Times History of War,* 1914, v. 3, p. 94. © The British Library Board.

well as reinvestment in shipbuilding, commerce, plantations, and properties throughout the Indian Ocean.

LABOR AND BONDAGE

Pearl fishing required a substantially larger workforce than these mercantile towns could provide, so both free and unfree workers were recruited for the summer months. The grueling and dangerous work of diving for pearls in waters replete with shark and jellyfish was done by seasonal workers drawn from many quarters of this maritime world. Divers were eastern Africans and bedouins from eastern Arabia, while the pullers were often Persian and Baluch.[34] Supervised by the ship captain and with only the most rudimentary equipment, divers plunged up to twelve fathoms (seventy-two feet) to the bottom of the sea dozens of times a day for roughly a minute each time, while pullers worked to ensure that the diver, the stone weight, and baskets of oysters attached to ropes descended and ascended swiftly and with synchronicity.[35] To pass the long hours at sea, captains would hire musicians to sing, drum, and lead the crew in refrains as the boats plied the waters.

Sometimes pearl divers were able to finance their own boats or create cooperatives, but the typical practice was debt peonage. Captains, who themselves were often indebted to Arab, Persian, and Indian merchants, would extend advances to crewmen at the start of the pearling season to provision the boats on their four-month voyages and aid the families of laborers while they were at sea. The expectation was that debts would be repaid after the culmination of the catch, sale of pearls, and distribution of shares among the crew.[36] Divers and pullers could not work on other boats without clearing their accounts with captains and securing a document issued by the captain releasing them.[37] This system was predicated on sales and on merchants and captains making payments quickly, rendering it vulnerable to the vicissitudes of markets and environmental conditions but crucially also to the string of loans made through the supply chain of intermediaries. If profits from the season's fishing did not cover debts—a very common occurrence—they could be transferred to other family members in cases of death or flight. Conceptions of honor and family obligation helped clothe debt as a form of profit-sharing, rather than wages paid by capitalists to laborers. At the same time, because debt was so endemic there was little stigma attached to it.[38] Yet these financial liabilities generated a series of dependencies throughout the pearling hierarchy. While conducting fieldwork in the mid-twentieth century, anthropologist Peter Lienhardt recorded the sentimental tales of the merchants, who paternalistically cared for their pearl divers in the off-season and paid off the debts of compatriots facing financial setbacks.[39] Nostalgia for this system survived even after the oil boom of the 1970s.[40]

Not all debts were settled, and not all laborers were free to seek alternative employment or pay back debts. Specialized pearl-diving courts in such places as Abu Dhabi and Ras al-Khaimah suggest that there was a proliferation of disputes over payment and other issues.[41] And reports about people absconding to escape debts were not uncommon.[42] In 1849, the rulers of Abu Dhabi and Dubai "came close to war" over the unpaid debts of two men who had fled from the former to the latter. An Abu Dhabi–based moneylender sought to mobilize the ruling family to intervene, but he was unsuccessful despite a series of tit-for-tat attacks on shipping vessels.[43]

Debt peonage coexisted alongside more stringent forms of bonded labor. Although Britain declared it illegal during the mid-nineteenth century, a highly profitable slave trade swelled alongside the expansion of the cash economy. Ship hands, divers, and dockworkers or "coolies" included enslaved people and recently emancipated men from eastern Africa and Baluchistan. Rather than laboring in the homes of elite families, as had been their primary role, slaves were sent to work in pearl beds and date palm fields after international markets for both commodities developed. The shares from pearl-diving expeditions were paid to their masters.[44] Keeping costs low and labor disciplined was the cornerstone of the profits reaped by brokers and agents. It also made trade in human cargo and the kidnapping of people lucrative. In short, while profits were being made across this globe-spanning system, the allocations going to workers was cyclically redirected from the families of laborers to the lenders of money and the owners of slaves.[45] This is the profitable, yet brutalizing, way the region was integrated and peripheralized into the capitalist system; this was the Gulf iteration of Marx's observation that "capital comes dripping from head to toe, from every pore, with blood and dirt."[46]

As the pearl trade bred a system of bonded labor across great distances, it also produced a class of mobile business families that accumulated wealth and political influence across many ports of call.[47] A medley of merchants and moneylenders financed shipbuilding and provided loans for captains to cover seafaring expenses. Using their own accounts, even as they cooperated with other merchants across borders and occasionally the politically powerful, they covered costs of commercial expeditions drawing on extended and tribal families based in desert oases and port cities. They identified as Muslims, Hindus, Armenians, and many other sects and castes. They traveled across the Indian Ocean world for months at a time, occasionally spending half or more of their lives away from their places of birth. It would be anachronistic to describe them as multinationals and inaccurate to think of them as vertically integrated firms, but they were ethnolinguistically and religiously diverse business networks adept at shifting portfolios from pearls to grains to enslaved peoples to shipbuilding and so forth.

The merchant families had multiple branches based in myriad port cities and involved in many diverse trades. James Onley describes one such family, the Safars, who operated in Basra, Bushehr, Shiraz, Manama, Muscat, Mocha (on the Red Sea), and Bombay during the nineteenth and early twentieth centuries.[48] Establishing multiple commercial centers was good business because it enabled these families to forge trading partnerships and kinship ties with various communities to guard against the risks associated with volatile markets and politics. Like merchant capitalists elsewhere they relied not so much on competitive production as on their capacity to arbitrage the supply of goods across disjointed markets—to buy cheap and sell dear.

This pre-oil mercantile economy was fused together via letters of credit and legal mechanisms underwritten by colonial banking institutions based in Iran, Iraq, India, and Europe.[49] The merchant families paid only nominal taxes but lent funds and gave gifts to rulers and officials. To attract merchant capital, customs officials competed by reducing their duties or even establishing "free ports."[50] The Safar family parlayed this pivotal status into gains when the Bahraini ruler granted them a 1 percent concession on customs duties and control over some of its pearling fleet.[51] Merchant families also had influence over townspeople through philanthropic ventures providing for the needy and maintaining mosques, hospitals, schools, and cisterns (also see chapter 5). Through these activities and by indirectly employing larger numbers of people, trading families enjoyed a paternalistic status in these coastal communities.

Although this diverse array of big and small merchants made investments in land and property that would subsequently turn into markers of residency and belonging, their capital and social acumen were highly mobile and responsive to shifts in customs regimes. For instance, in the early twentieth century, since there was no custom tax on women's jewelry, a great deal of wealth circulated on female bodies. As one woman who lived between Lengeh, Karachi, and Dubai recalls, when she was a child this practice extended to pinning jewels on her dolls to help transport the necessary sums for her family's sojourns.[52]

LITTORALS AND DIFFERENCES

The Persian Gulf, like other bodies of water, was more a bridge than a border. It brought people together, rather than kept them apart, and in doing so sustained a rich social diversity. Michael Izady's map (Image 5), which centers the Persian Gulf's nineteenth-century social world, demonstrates the "symbiosis of land and sea" rather than treating the shoreline as a boundary delineating separate realms.[53] The interrelation is found even in the mental maps evoked in nomenclature. Although not as evocative as Swahili, which literally means "shore folk" or "people of the shore," the Persian *bandari* refers to the people of Iran's southern shores as "port folk" or "people of the port."[54] Both *ahl al-bahr* (or *ahl bahriyya*) and *khaliji* in Arabic draw a strong connection between the inhabitants

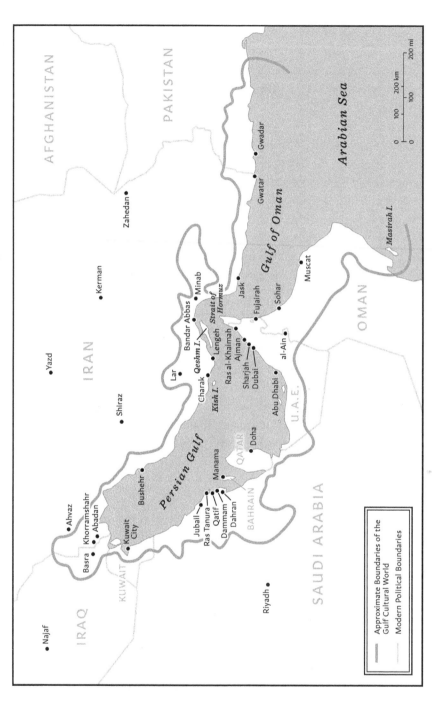

IMAGE 5: The Persian Gulf Cultural-Historical Domain. Map based on Michael Izady, *Atlas of the Islamic World and Vicinity* (New York: Columbia University, 2006–present); https://gulf2000.columbia.edu/images/maps/GulfCultralWorld0804_lg.png.

and the sea or gulf (*khalij*).[55] In all these cases the sea basin is treated as an integrative center, rather than a national edge. Being of the sea and the shores implied a shared fate that may not have erased other distinctions and differences but sketched a mutual vista.

In the nineteenth century, our contemporary distinctions between the "Arab" and "Persian" sides of the Gulf made little sense. Not only was migration common, but people of the littoral spoke many languages and dialects and identified themselves at one and the same time as members of a kinship network or tribe. In the heyday of the pearling economy, familiarity with Arabic, Persian, Hindi, and English was a prerequisite for commercial and political success.[56] This perplexed the future viceroy of India and foreign secretary, George Curzon, who after traveling through the Persian Gulf in the 1880s concluded, "Surely a more curious study in polyglot or polychrome could not well be conceived."[57] A half century later, Allan Villiers described the crewmen, passengers, and port towns he encountered as "half-Persians," "half-Arabs, or "half-Malibari" and ultimately a "cosmopolitan Eastern crowd." Historians have used court records and cultural practices to paint a world of shopkeepers drawn from various shores, bedouin moving between communal pastures and seasonal work on boats, and conjugal relations across waters, sects, and master-slave ties. Dhow captains often spent long stays in a port, waiting for the next monsoon. These were not fleeting stopovers. They could and did turn into second and third domiciles, complete with local wives and children, which the captains would visit periodically or rarely.[58] Unlike the notorious "one-drop rule" in the United States, Islamic law provided for "ascending miscegenation," which served as an avenue for upward mobility through marriage.[59]

Remoteness from historic centers of religious authority made the coastal region a refuge for heterodox religions and people practicing multiple religions or the same religion in different ways.[60] This was particularly true in the more mountainous regions of present-day Iran, Oman, and Yemen. Both Sunni and Shia preachers and communities traveled to the coast seeking refuge. Hindu temples existed in coastal towns well before the large numbers of South Asians were recruited to fill the demand in labor after the 1970s; one early example was constructed in Bandar Abbas in 1892. It had an attached *zurkhaneh*, or traditional gymnasium, with Sikh iconography, which suggests that it was used by British Indian soldiers of Sikh background.[61] This pluralism and plasticity has been characterized as "hybrid," "transnational," "dhow culture," and "a brotherhood of the sea," with identities so layered *and* localized that they can usefully be depicted as "anational."[62] The flow of people and things, particularly their social connectivity and intricate horizontal histories, constituted this sociability.[63]

Narratives of a prenational, cosmopolitan Golden Age celebrating a single hybridized culture, however, can gloss over the inequalities and hierarchies that underpinned the regional economy. Social stratification mattered and was blunted less by tolerant attitudes than cross-class and communal joint work that engendered obligations even as they enforced a multitude of distinctions and exclusions. Different identities and social positions mattered. For instance, merchants from India, both Hindus and or Ismaili Shia (Khojas), were often moneylenders because they had access to capital in the subcontinent, but because they were "less well-placed than Arab colleagues" they were less capable at recouping their debts.[64] While at the scale of individual towns, urban segmentation preserved ties among people from the same regional or tribal background, endogamous marriage and markers of distinction, such as dialects and dress, differentiated people (see chapter 5). People moved not only out of individual choice or the operation of free markets but also due to compulsion and coercion. Mobility was both a form of punishment as well as a socioeconomic resource. While both Sunni and Shia communities existed on all coasts, there were inequalities and prejudices both in Shia and Sunni majority regions. Not only were men and women kidnapped and put into servitude, but "troublemakers" were also regularly deported to one place or another. As late as 1917 people were deported from Iran to Dubai as a form of punishment.[65] What Jill Crystal calls the "outward orientation" of Gulf societies did not preclude forced movement, internal regulation, and the recognition of difference.[66]

POLITIES AND EDGES

The Persian Gulf has been both a center and an edge. Societies of the Gulf Basin are part of a relative and relational space, a mutable product of cross-fertilization between place and power geometries of intertwined scales. The ecological barriers of deserts and mountains held Gulf societies apart from inland powers—the Qajar rulers of the Iranian plateau based in Tehran and provincial capitals such as Shiraz and Isfahan; the Ottomans headquartered in Baghdad, Basra, and along the Red Sea; the Saud family based in Najd. Well into the late 1800s, it was easier and safer to travel from Tehran to Abadan via Baghdad or even via Baku, the Black Sea, the Suez Canal, and then around the Persian Gulf. These land-based empires had a tenuous, fluctuating hold on these peoples and lands. They ruled over them indirectly through pledges of allegiance and payment of tribute by local representatives, be they tribal bedouins, trading families, or landed households. They commonly were drawn from families from other parts of the littoral regardless of ethnolinguistic or religious difference, as in the case of the Omani Arab family al-Madkur in Bushehr. These notables had their own interests and enjoyed varying degrees of local authority and efficacy. Merchant families and nomadic tribes had too much to lose from ceding complete control to the powerholders in provincial capitals such as Shiraz and Basra, let alone in imperial centers farther away. The power of clans and individual rulers ebbed and flowed depending on the strength of alliances and on the willingness and capacity of the Ottomans or the Iranian rulers to intervene for greater returns on their tax farms and leases.

Maintaining this delicate balance between regional rulers, local landowners, and mobile traders was crucial even after Portuguese gunboats entered the Gulf in the beginning of the sixteenth century. Less than two decades after Vasco da Gama's voyage to India by way of the Cape of Hood Hope, the Portuguese began to establish fortressed trading outposts in the Indian Ocean, including a small garrison inside the mouth of the Gulf, on the island of Hormuz. The Portuguese used their superior weaponry and navigational aids to force local leaders in key islands and coastal towns to pay them tribute. Although it sought to monopolize the spice trade and even block the Red Sea to direct trade through the Strait of Hormuz, the Portuguese ultimately had to compromise with local rulers and become "assimilated" as one of several "players profiting from perennial patterns of production and exchange."[67]

In the seventeenth century, the Ottomans, Safavids, and Portuguese were confronted by three new institutions active in the lucrative spice, silk, and textile trade: the Dutch East India Company, the English East India Company, and the Muscat-centered Omani maritime sultanate stretching from Bahrain to Mozambique. To reestablish Iran's upper hand over the southern Gulf, Safavid ground troops in 1622 allied themselves with the navies of the Dutch and English East India companies to wrest control of the island of Hormuz at the mouth of the Gulf and expel the Portuguese. In return, Iran's shah issued a royal decree to extend privileges to the East India companies, including giving them exemptions on duties to engage in trade within his realm and the court itself. In 2005, the date April 30 (the tenth day of Ordibehesht in the Iranian calendar), and the capture of the island or Hormuz became more important to the cultural imagination of Iran. The date was adopted to commemorate National Persian Gulf Day in Iran.

With the Portuguese repelled from the Persian Gulf, the recently founded Dutch East India Company enjoyed supremacy over its English rival until the mid-eighteenth century. It maintained a trading headquarters in Bandar Abbas and, later, further north at Bandar Rig to export silk in return for spices from Southeast Asia. The Dutch and English East India companies were in the midst of inserting themselves into and became bound up with preexisting Asian economic networks.[68] Pepper, cloves, timber, silver, silk, calicos, and more were cornerstones of a complex intra–Indian Ocean trade extending to Japan and northern Europe. While inland trade from the sixteenth to the eighteenth centuries was dominated by regional rulers, landowners, and traders, the European companies gained the upper hand on the seas thanks to introducing "armed trading" that used naval power to outmuscle competitors and pass the cost of protection on to buyers.[69]

English commercial interests in the Gulf were initially less developed than their Dutch counterparts, even though the East Indian Company had established a Persian Agency in Jask in 1616 to oversee its commercial interests on the coasts of the Gulf. The Company focused on establishing a few fortified trading settlements (or "factories"), including Basra, but did not expand until the mid-1700s when the English edged out the Dutch, who by century's end had withdrawn from the region. The East India Company transferred its post from Bandar Abbas to Bushehr, bringing it closer to its "factories" in Shiraz and Isfahan; it was refigured in 1763 into the main British Residency of British-India in the Gulf, where it remained until after World War II.

Both the English and Dutch firms had to contend with royal courts as well as navigate local rivalries and bedouin raids against vessels and caravan routes in their predatory pursuit to feed industrial capitalism back home. Meanwhile, an Omani imperial formation stitched together coastal and inland settlements in southeastern Arabia and eastern Africa. As Fahad Bishara has elegantly shown, authority in this oceanic polity was forged through trade, religion, and jurisprudence with the circulation of paper documents as the material manifestations of complex social and economic relations, which despite being deeply invested in properties and maritime infrastructures was devoid of a fixed territorial domain.[70] Although British colonial officers understood it as an "empire," Omanis themselves did not use the term until the 1950s, a century *after* Zanzibar was separated from the rulers based in Muscat and during the last outpost on Makran Coast, the port city of Gwadar, being ceded to Pakistan.[71] These separations and accessions came to represent *territorial* loss and implied a spatial homogeneity and sovereign unity that before the twentieth century had not existed.

The layered and fragmented political control over eastern Arabia and Southern Iran in the eighteenth and nineteenth centuries meant that there were opportunities for several tribal confederations to carve out space and make their own political claims. The most prominent tribes that migrated from Najd in central Arabia in the seventeenth century formed settlements in towns along trading routes and the coast, sometimes even crossing the Gulf to settle in Iran.[72] Tribes, or collections of clans that recognized themselves as sharing a common ancestor, grazing lands, and set of customs, were organized to exert political control. These real and fictive kinship relations generated obligations and mobilized protection from rivals within tribal confederations and from interlopers threatening pastures, caravan routes, and towns. Leadership succession was typically organized through intricate consensus-building rather than a mechanical transfer of power from one generation to the next. Family ties shaped labor recruitment, and kinship was also the basis for mutual aid in times of war and natural disasters. (This does not mean that kinship and family do not also generate conflict and even violence.) Specific norms and practices, such as endogamous marriages, payment of tribute, and assumption of the debts of the diseased, were public displays solidarity as well as a means of forging reciprocal obligations within and across family groups. This pattern of rule was routinely contested from within by tribal rivalries and family schisms and from without by forces arriving from beyond the mountains, deserts, and waves.

To wield influence over the many clans, tribal leaders or shaykhs needed command over resources. The support of nomadic tribes was critical for any power that sought to maintain authority. Pledges of allegiance by bedouins meant that they would not raid caravans or intercede in shipping and would pay tribute and provide fighters necessary for warfare. These bedouin allies secured routes and staved off attacks on towns and villages, especially when men were absent during the pearling season.[73] In return for their loyalty and services, tribes involved in trade were given access to town markets and water wells.

For their part, merchants provided financial resources in the form of taxes and loans to ruling tribal families and local governors representing the Qajars and Ottomans. Jill Crystal has mapped the financial circuit as follows: "Merchants extracted revenues from pearl divers rather than peasants, and gave a portion of these revenues to the ruler through customs duties, pearl boat taxes, and personal loans." Crystal concludes, "Their political power grew from their economic strength. Their ordinary input into decision-making came from the social institutions of marriage . . . and *majlis* [councils] . . . which gave them informal but daily access to the rulers."[74] This relative balance between merchants and rulers explains why these polities are best characterized as "city-societies" rather than "city-states."[75]

The wealthy merchants enjoyed significant leverage over the monarchs. They had a foothold in more than one port and trading houses could move, or threaten to move, in the event of changes to customs duties and policies. In response to authorities seeking to levy higher taxes, merchants from Lengeh relocated to Dubai in 1905, and in 1909 merchants and pearl boats moved from Kuwait to Bahrain. The migration of merchants from southern Iran to Dubai was precipitated by the Qajar's inviting Belgian tax collectors to assist in centralizing the administration of customs to generate greater revenue for Tehran.[76] After they fled, the merchants did not return to Lengeh. In the Kuwaiti case, however, the merchants returned two years later, after the ruling al-Sabah family acquiesced to their demands to reduce duties.[77] More than just their mobility, what empowered the Kuwait-based pearl merchants was their ability to organize support for their cause, with one pearl merchant promising to destroy his accounting ledger and forgive debts if sailors and divers supported the resistance against the shaykh. While this option to exit empowered merchants in their dealings with centralizing state builders, it also reflected and inscribed the networked nature of port cities.

By the first half of the nineteenth century, the series of tribal confederations that had settled near the coast had consolidated a modicum of authority after defeating or subordinating rivals, including forces based in southern Iran and Oman. Different branches of the Bani 'Utbah were based in Kuwait and Bahrain, known as al Sabah and al Khalifa, respectively. The Bani Yas gained a foothold in the lower Gulf; rulers of the present-day UAE trace their roots to its roughly dozen branches (including the al-Nahyan family in Abu Dhabi and the al-Maktum family in Dubai). Competing with the Omani rulers and sitting astride the Strait of Hormuz was the Qasemi clan that enjoyed a presence in ports and islands on both sides of the entrance to the Gulf. Meanwhile, other historically significant tribal confederations were defeated at this time, most notably the Bani Khaled; they had been a significant force in eastern Arabia and Iraq but were unable to recast themselves into a ruling dynasty.

By the nineteenth century, the Portuguese and the Dutch had receded from the scene, and the British Indian naval and mercantile forces had become an integral part of the Persian Gulf, generating its own struggles and countervailing forces (see chapter 2). In December 1819, the East India Company called on British warships to intervene and protect shipping from the Qasemi and their bid to collect tolls.[78] Accompanied by Omani forces, a fleet of British vessels and three thousand men were sent to confront "the Arab chiefs of the pirate coast" or, more precisely, bombard the Qasemi stronghold of Ras al-Khaimah. This was coupled with the Bombay-based British Navy burning Lengeh to the ground in the same year and East India Company cruisers bombing the Red Sea port of Mocha.[79]

The subsequent General Treaty of 1820 regulated shipping and empowered British naval surveillance to restrict all activities and vessels that fell into the category of "piracy." The coastal region extending north from Muscat became known to the British as "the Trucial coast." As will be discussed in greater detail in the next chapter, the treaty and the creation of the Gulf Residency (1822–1971) marked a turning point in Britain's overseas adventures and the steady development of a colonial apparatus straddling the waterway. The future viceroy of India, Lord Curzon, recalled this naval expedition in his *Persia and the Persian Question* by underlining the territorialization of the sea: "The pacification of the Persian Gulf in the past and the maintenance of the status quo are the exclusive work of this country; and the British Resident at Bushire is to this hour the umpire to whom all parties appeal, and who has by treaties been intrusted with the duty of preserving the peace of the waters."[80]

CRASHES AND REALIGNMENTS

"[I]f pearl beds were to fail, the [Bahraini] Shaikhdom would shortly be reduced to comparative insignificance."[81] This prediction was made by J. G.

Lorimer, an Oxford-trained civil servant of the Raj, in his famous *Gazetteer,* which was published between 1908 and 1915. In the space of the next two decades this was no a longer hypothetical proposition and not isolated to the Bahraini archipelago. The market for Gulf pearls crashed in the late 1920s due to global market convulsions. However, counter to Lorimer's prophecy, Bahrain, Kuwait, and other pearling areas did not become any less significant to British officials and firms.

Beginning with World War I, Persian Gulf pearls began to hemorrhage market share to recently developed Japanese cultured pearls, which were far more abundant and were produced at a fraction of the cost, as well as natural pearls fished off of Venezuela and Colombia.[82] Coinciding with the Great Depression and the tumbling of demand for gems, French banks ceased lending to jewelry firms; this decision proved wise when shortly thereafter, several jewelers and pearl dealers went into liquidation.[83] To the shock of many, some traders in the Gulf ports took to selling cultured pearls as natural pearls with two merchants in Bahrain receiving a seven-year prison sentence for their deception, which only contributed to depressing prices further.[84] British colonial officials, meanwhile, were caught between their interests in preserving profits from this Indian Ocean trading network and dampening the threat of massive unemployment and impoverishment in these pearling communities. They sought to protect these pearling societies through a series of haphazard but consequential decisions. They banned new technologies—inboard motors and wet suits—that could have reduced demand for labor and increased costs for investors, but these new methods had the capacity to introduce non-British firms into the region.

Between 1929 and 1931, Bahrain's pearling entrepreneurs, including some of the most prominent families, lost two-thirds of their capital due to poor sales.[85] Merchants were left with pearls without buyers, and people in the region faced massive impoverishment, starvation, and death. Some captains simply could not go to sea during the pearling season. Lacking credit or demand for pearls, Bahrain's fleet of 970 ships in 1910 dropped to only 340 in 1934, with records showing a similarly precipitous decline in Kuwait's fleet.[86] During both world wars, pearling boats were refitted for trade and transporting soldiers and equipment.[87] With little prospect for pay, pearl divers and haulers refused to go to sea. The Kuwaiti ruler cajoled the merchants to extend "something to the families and ordered the ring-leaders of recalcitrant divers 'to be flogged and cast into prison.'"[88] It was left to Kuwait's first leg-islative council in 1938 to address some of these grievances by formalizing and reforming labor relations in the pearling and long-distance trade.[89] The crisis extended to shopkeepers, who were not able to maintain stocks of rice and flour or recoup their sales on credit. Observers commented on "a new and pathetic feature . . . in the form of gangs of beggars," who drifted through the towns.[90] The upshot was that populations of towns shrank by almost half in several cases. Adding to the demise of pearling was the decision of the newly independent state of India to prohibit the import of pearls from the Gulf to stem the flow of currency out of the country.[91] Just like that, the pearl economy was mothballed, only to return a few decades later as a marker of national heritage (see chapters 5).

In same period, the date economy was undercut by the same forces of trade, finance, and consumption. The global depression cut available credit from traders and reduced worldwide sales of the sweet, sticky delicacy, but by then so did competition from a new producer—California.[92] The palms in Southern California's Coachella Valley traced their origins to the same infrastructural and commercial networks built in the nineteenth century to transport dates from Basra and the Batina plains in Oman through the Suez Canal to the East Coast of the United States in time for Thanksgiving and Christmas. Instead of continuing to import the fruits, American traders gained support from the United States Department of Agriculture to trans-port the saplings of the palms; the same array of dates would then be grown and harvested domestically, replacing the Gulf's largest export market with homegrown fruits by the 1920s. Shortly thereafter, the local high school in the Coachella Valley adopted "The Arabs" as their mascot.

People did not passively accept these economic and social convulsions as their fate. Gulf-based merchants responded with both exit and voice; some migrated, and others mobilized politically (see Chapter 3). Pearl div-ers and crewmen launched protests targeting the municipal authorities and food stores, directing animosity at Persians and Indians, who were dispropor-tionately represented in the sectors profiting from the shifts in the economy. The very real hunger and suffering was catalyzed by new political ideas and notions of governance that circulated among the population via dhows and steamships along with the commodities, printed materials, rumors, and dis-sidents from what we would today call the decolonizing world. We do not know which ideas led a group of divers to jeer and expose themselves to the brother of the Shaykh of Bahrain as he sailed by, but it shook him enough that Bahrain's British advisor was informed and Indian soldiers were duly sent to attack the meeting places of divers.[93] Together, the colonial advisors and their local interlocutors fashioned a system to regulate the movement of labor during this moment of crisis.[94] This set of practices carried with them the seeds of a fuller regulation of mobility by establishing sponsors over a and populations conceived of as temporary guest workers.

Yet the pearl crash was not all misery and privation; for the region's enslaved people, it was something of a mixed blessing. On the one hand, the rapid collapse of the pearl industry in the 1930s reduced the demand for slaves. The definitive factor putting an end to ships with enslaved passengers was transactional calculation, rather than moral apprehension or legal enforcement of the 1833 ban on slave trade.[95] Some slaves took this opportunity to take their masters' boats and flee or gain manumission,[96] and others turned to British political agencies to gain emancipation.[97] The ruler of Bahrain formally banned slaveowning in 1937. Qatar, Saudi, and Oman did not follow suit until 1952, 1963, and 1971, respectively. The fossil fuel industry provided employment for the newly manumitted slaves, cash-strapped sailors, pool of indebted divers, and enslaved people who worked in the oil fields on behalf of their owners.[98]

Economic dislocations also realigned the political architecture of these littoral societies. The earlier era of Ottomans, Iranians, Omanis, and East India Companies jostling for market share and the spoils of war was being overwritten by a new era of imperialism and statehood that we will examine in the next two chapters. The British colonial flag followed trade, but initially it was only to specific outposts. Until the mid-nineteenth century British-Indian officers and firms had clung to the shoreline and cared little for what was occurring further inland. As the nineteenth century gave way to the twentieth, new treaties were signed by the British government of India with local potentates whom they recognized as autonomous rulers of distinct principalities. They were no longer considered to be mere agents of the Ottoman Empire or one shaykh among equals. These exclusive treaties that the British signed with shaykhs in Bahrain (1880 and 1892), Oman (1891), the Trucial States (1892), and Kuwait (1899) represented the beginnings of territorial divisions as well as the recognition of particular lineages as sovereign. In the nineteenth century, crossing the Gulf did not entail transgressing a legal or political frontier, but in the opening decades of the twentieth century this was beginning to change. This also marks one of the means through which the regional world of the nineteenth century Gulf was unmade and regionalized anew. But we are now trespassing on histories and new scales of separation and connectedness that will occupy the remainder of this book.

CONCLUSIONS

The Persian Gulf's nineteenth-century regionalism was forged out of specific material conditions and lived practices with their attendant interpersonal relations generating a shared space. Environmental factors and topographical conditions insulated communities, but they did not wall off these societies from each other or deprive them from the outside world. The conjuncture of historical forces that brought people together cooperatively, coercively, or by coincidence were not direct geographic byproducts or ecological requisites but a set of social organizations and practices across many scales—family, town, tribe, mercantile network, and empire. As a set of trestles holding up a lived and unbounded regionalism, they combined the coercion and debt of servitude with the affection and obligation of kinship. This made the Gulf more like an arena than a system.[99] The power of imperial formations and commercial coalitions was highly mediated and arrayed as overlapping formations, rather than engineered as an interlocking structure. Regional coherence was built out of social heterogeneity and economic difference with whatever political borders and social boundaries existing being highly porous and relationally produced.

The cords that held the Persian Gulf together became overextended at the beginning of the twentieth century. Commodity crashes reverberated through society to expose the fault lines accompanying the web of connectivity. New layers of accumulation and sovereignty submerged this nineteenth-century social world, although without erasing the influence of key social groups such as tribal leaders, merchants, pearl divers, and bedouin populations. The waters of the Gulf began to lose their social centrality and acquired geopolitical resonance in representations of the region and the enclosing of space.

TWO

IMPERIAL ENCLOSURE

AN EARLIER REGIONALISM unfolded by way of monsoon winds, family genealogies, interconnecting debts, differently bonded labor, and well-worn trading routes. By January 4, 1980, it had been overwritten by an enclosed geometry devoid of any markings other than spartan state borders. On that evening, a small globe sat to the left of Jimmy Carter when he delivered an address to the American nation (see Image 6).[1] The globe was carefully positioned to display the northern part of the Indian Ocean with the Arabian Peninsula, Iran, Pakistan, Afghanistan, and the Soviet Union. Beginning by referencing US hostages in Tehran, the president pivoted to address "another very serious development which threatens the maintenance of the peace in Southwest Asia. Massive Soviet military forces have invaded the small, non-aligned, sovereign nation of Afghanistan, which had hitherto not been an occupied satellite of the Soviet Union." Challenging Soviet claims and imputing nefarious motivations, Carter said, "It is a deliberate effort of a powerful atheistic government to subjugate an independent Islamic people."

The content of the speech and the careful placement of the globe reminded viewers of the status of the United States as a great global power. As he outlined the implications of Soviet troops in Afghanistan and the threats it posed to the entire region and "peoples throughout the world," a rectangular map was displayed on the screen. Iran, Afghanistan, Pakistan, and the USSR appeared in primary colors, and gradually the camera zoomed out to

IMAGE 6:   President Jimmy Carter's address to the nation on the Soviet invasion of
Afghanistan, January 4, 1980. Source: Screenshot from https://www.youtube.com/watch
?v=u2Y4t0-_9MY.

display neighboring Iraq, Saudi Arabia, India, and others appearing in beige.
Although only the words "Arabian Sea" were marked, the camera eventually
centered on the vivid blue waters of the Indian Ocean and the Persian Gulf.
Those viewers who had somehow failed to notice the globe could no longer
miss the regional configuration at stake. Brushed aside was the nineteenth-
century social world of the Persian Gulf that spilled out in many directions
and extended across distance and time. In denying these sociabilities, the
map masked the very thing that actually turned the Persian Gulf into a coher-
ent region, a region that was unbounded and fluid but interdependent.

The ease with which a sitting president could deploy cartography to ar-
ticulate politics captures how natural it had become to think of the Persian
Gulf world as a regionalized abstraction. But this was the product of a century
of intellectual labor and political strategizing. Contested processes aimed at
making the Gulf region a homogeneous whole and an object over which

control and claims could, and in fact must, be projected. First led by the British political agencies and firms and then by US ones, intricate processes of capital accumulation and imperial formation gave rise to this container-like geometric regionalization that aspired to supersede the previous nodal and networked regionalism.

As Ann Stoler has cautioned, thinking in terms of empires as "clearly bounded geopolities," "fixed realities," or the "rise and fall" of a series of world powers is historically inaccurate and imposes a misleading uniformity on both British and US hegemony.[2] "Colonial empires," Stoler insightfully reminds us, "were always dependent on social imaginaries, blueprints unrealized, borders never drawn, administrative categories of people and territories to which no one was sure who should belong."[3] This multiplicity and obscurity are reflected in the adoption of concepts of "informal empire," "covert empire," and the "Arabian frontier of the British Raj" to navigate how imperialism was enacted and experienced by the littoral societies of the Gulf and Arabian Sea.[4] Gearóid Ó' Tuathail draws attention to how geography is "not something already possessed by the earth but *an active writing of the earth by an expanding, centralizing imperial state. It* [is] not a noun but a verb, a *geographing,* an earth-writing by ambitious endocolonizing and exocolonizing states who sought to seize space and organize it to for their own cultural visions and material interests."[5] Thinking about geopolitics as an active "writing of the earth" reminds us how politics happens through space and not just on it. At historically specific moments, meanings and social relations between places are made and remade.

The notion that the Gulf could be marked and internalized as part of the British imperial formation accentuated the ways that imperialism, regionalism, and the building blocks of state sovereignty have been intimately intertwined. This chapter explores this phenomenon by first tracing how ideas about geographies and state power (otherwise known as geopolitics) and "technologies of force" (surveys, maps, and laws) in the last quarter of the nineteenth century combined to spatialize the Persian Gulf into a bounded region.[6] While British global hegemony waned and ultimately needed buttressing by US military and financial assets, Britain's dominance over the Gulf and its shores was carried forward by the formation of independent nation-states and by the transformation of the Russian threat into the Cold War–era fear of the communist bloc and its "satellites" across the Third World. US power was less tutelary than the British and was articulated through defense agreements, special relationships, and interpenetrating economic arrangements that in the self-conception of American decision-makers protected "the Free World Economy." Unlike Europe and East Asia after World War II, the United States invested little in institutionalizing regional organizations in the Gulf or the Middle East.[7] Across this century and a half, the Gulf gained meaning as an imperial or global frontier that denoted strategic importance but was also seen as vulnerable and fractured and therefore demanded intervention to counteract its inherent instability. These incremental accumulations and imperial tinkering informed how the Gulf was perceived, administered, and positioned in the world.

In part this is a story animated by geopolitical thinking and how regions are naturalized by a deterministic understanding of physical and human geography. In equal measure, technological innovations and methods of accumulating wealth and military power reworked the material terrain and shaped the ability of policymakers, investors, and local rulers to see the Gulf as essential in new ways. "Geopolitics," Deborah Cowen and Neil Smith usefully remind us, "was never only about the state's external relations, but rather . . . involved a more encompassing 'geopolitical social' that both crosses and crafts the distinction between inside and outside national state borders."[8] I am not approaching geopolitics as a way to explain the world but as a thing within it and with powerful consequences. Geopolitical thought coupled with attendant material forces has been a marker and maker of the Persian Gulf's regionalism.

"THE PERSIAN QUESTION" AND A REGIONALIZING RESPONSE

The British Empire cast a long shadow over US thinking about the Persian Gulf and the Indian Ocean.[9] It did so both in terms of the material infrastructures it left behind as well as the polities it cultivated. But it also became an avatar for dominance over the region. In the midst of World War II, Nicholas Spykman, the Dutch-American political scientist, argued that Great Britain's empire expanded precisely because its Royal Navy ruled the "girdle of marginal seas" that encircled the Eurasian continent.[10] These seas were the conduits for projecting British influence and control onto remote shores— something that Spykman called upon Washington to replicate. Britain's achievement from the perspective of midcentury US analysts was its ability to police the border between the external and the internal and to do so for its own advantage as well as the world's.[11] This image of the British Empire as a ballast to counter the Gulf's instability has roots in the last two decades of the nineteenth century, when the science of geopolitics was being pieced together in northern Europe.[12]

Geopoliticians were mapping imperial rivalries and vulnerabilities by adopting the position of the "detached viewing subject surveying a worldwide stage."[13] This geopolitical approach sought to measure physical geographical attributes—territory, population, location, and natural resources—claiming that it affected relations between states and specifically enabled domination of some polities over others. The field of geopolitics emerged in the cross-fertilized world of social Darwinism and scientific theories of race.[14] Alfred Thayer Mahan, the American strategist of "sea power," justified British and American territorial annexation of the Transvaal and the Philippines, respectively, by claiming that inhabitants of both places were similarly "incapable of statehood."[15] European knowledge of the Middle East was still cursory, highly mediated, and often inaccurate, enabling racial theories to flourish with abandon. Notions of racial difference and hierarchy permeated almost all Western writing about Iran and the Gulf region and left an indelible fingerprint through its articulations of modernity, backwardness, and nation.[16] Geopolitical thinking was not just built out of abstractions articulated in imperial metropoles. The advent of geopolitics as a recognized field of study and form of expertise at the end of the nineteenth century was an outgrowth of a whole new set of ways of experiencing and visualizing space, distance, and power that ultimately imposed a geography on the Gulf.

A series of technical breakthroughs in transportation and communications generated new opportunities and challenges for colonial officers and capitalist investors. The building of the Suez Canal enhanced the importance of the Gulf for British rule in the subcontinent in the 1860s, as did the beginning of steamer mail service and the laying of two telegraph lines along the Persian Gulf coast—an underwater and an overland cable—giving Britain near-instantaneous communication with India. Having just experienced the 1857 Mutiny—also called the Indian Rebellion of 1857—the British government established the Indo-European Telegraph Department to expedite reporting between the subcontinent and Europe. The telegraph lines were paid for by the Iranian government with materials purchased from England, but the telegraph was administered by British firms in exchange for an annual royalty.[17] British telegraph workers were extended elaborate extraterritorial privileges under the Anglo-Iranian Convention of 1865. Almost in tandem, steamship companies also shrank geographic distances and created hubs for passengers, mail, commodities, and the delivery and loading of coal. Using government subsidies and monopolistic positions, shipping magnates, most notably William Mackinnon's British India Steam Navigation Company, established increasingly intricate shipping lines to and from Gulf ports.[18] It was through coastal outposts that British interests extended into what was often described as the hinterland.[19] These were bridgeheads for Victorian explorers, merchant capitalists, and colonial officers to "discover" and increasingly map the non-European world for personal ego as much as control and profit. Newspaper articles, books, and lectures exposed the British public to this age of exploration.

Some of the readers and authors of these late Victorian writings were certainly in the audience for Halford Mackinder's 1904 lecture at the Royal Geographical Society when he declared that "the map of the world [had] been completed."[20] In "The Geographical Pivot of History," the director of the London School of Economics at the time forcefully argued that exploration and technological breakthroughs had ushered the world into "the post-Columbian epoch." From his vantage point in London and his limited travel in Kenya, Mackinder saw steamships, railroads, and telegraph lines as the necessary lubricant for colonial expansionism and the filling of empty spaces on maps. As frontiers were closed, he posited that the world was made more compact and system-like:

> From the present time forth, in the post-Columbia age, we shall again have to deal with a closed political system, and none the less that it will be one of world-wide scope. Every explosion of social forces, instead of being dissipated in a surrounding circuit of unknown space and barbaric chaos, will be sharply re-echoed from the far side of the globe, and weak elements in the political and economic organism of the world will be shattered in consequence. . . . The attention of statesmen in all parts of the world, should shift from territorial expansion to the struggle for relative efficiency.[21]

Territorial expansion may have ended geography, but Mackinder argued that a new era of imperial reform was needed at home and abroad to counter the ill effects of connectedness associated with the shrinking and enclosing of the globe. Economic wealth and political power could no longer be generated through geographic conquest without triggering inter-state or inter-imperial conflict. Rather than turning against empire, however, Mackinder was calling for imperial renewal, with Britain leading all Anglo-Saxon people by way of an "Empire of the World." This was a highly uneven terrain, with Mackinder at that time developing a notion of "racial geography" through the charting of blood lines, skull size, pigmentation, and "relative nigrescence" as essential components of human geography.[22] The struggle for this new efficiency, or what Lenin would call capitalist development, expressed itself in tariff protections and imperial preferences that Mackinder supported and simultaneously were taken up in the United States and Germany.[23] Lost in all this was any possibility that "weak elements in the political system" or colonized peoples might strive for self-rule, as they had been doing with mounting frequency and intensity. This would have required Mackinder and other geopoliticians to approach space and societies of all parts of the world very differently.

The specifics of Mackinder's arguments about the importance of the Euroasian "heartland" as "the pivot region of the world's politics" or the fundamental clash between land power and sea power set him apart, but his contemporaries in Germany and the United States were simultaneously taking up similar projects to govern the relationship between geography and power. It is in this context that geography in general and geopolitics, in particular, galvanized the attention of the political class. Geographical knowledge had always been a science of statecraft, but in this late Victorian Age of Empire it attracted many self-assured admirers.

A Splendid Highway

The geopolitical lens was configured to address conflicting approaches to Britain's imperial formation in the Persian Gulf. It had taken the better part of a century for the East India Company and the British navy to use a mixture of gunboat diplomacy, alliances with local shaykhs and merchants, and technological superiority to ward off "pirates" and establish British outposts on various parts of the coastline (see chapter 1). British imperial policy in the Persian Gulf was informed by the views and interactions of a whole host of institutions (e.g., the Treasury, Parliament, the Board of Trade, the Admiralty, the Foreign Office) and officials divided between London and the government in

India.[24] The office of the British Residency in the Gulf embodied the multiple and sometimes incompatible interests at play. The Residency was at once handpicked by the government of India and answerable to the Foreign Office in Whitehall.[25] Even the financing of the post was a point of conflict between London and Calcutta.

In spite and because of this "chaotic pluralism of British interests" in the final two decades of the 1800s, questions were raised both "at home" and in the dominions about what steps should be taken to maintain control over territories, to address the financial and moral expenses of empire, and to manage social conflicts that reverberated through capitalism as it was internationalizing.[26] This was an era of many questions, including the more sweeping "Eastern Question" that had been posed throughout the era of European imperial expansion and rivalry. One version of these discussions was the "Persian Question."

It is not surprising that within the empire's institutionally decentralized context and with limited knowledge of the region, there were multiple understandings of the Persian Problem and multiple answers to the Persian Question.[27] In the late nineteenth century, for instance, prominent Foreign Office officials such as Henry Drummond Wolff "looked upon the exploitation of Persia as a basis of friendship, not conflict" with Russia.[28] Yet his argument that Britain should in fact give a port to Russia[29] was mocked by others as a "gratuitous surrender."[30] As for gentleman capitalists and speculators, they viewed Iran as a market of high risk and low returns.[31] Shaped by, among other matters, the bloody and costly Second Boer War (1898–1903), public opinion in Britain had also become more skeptical of imperial adventurism. Economic panics seemed increasingly regular occurrences in the late nineteenth century and an increasingly organized society demanded provision of social welfare at home.

Yet for others the Persian Gulf was an ill-defined frontier leaving British India as vulnerable to imperial forays by European powers and sabotage by locals. Influential in advocating a more proactive "forward policy" toward the securing of India was Lord George Curzon (1859–1925). Curzon and Mackinder attended Oxford at the same time and were both members of the Conservative Party; in addition, they were colleagues who went on to collaborate in formulating Britain's anti-Bolshevik policies.[32] Mackinder is remembered as a classic geopolitical thinker, but his analysis depended on the work of practitioners who were administratively, rhetorically, and politically engaged in far-flung regions of the Empire as well as in Whitehall. As Viceroy of India (1898–1905), the president of the Royal Geographical Society (1911–14), and the Foreign Secretary at the end of World War I, Curzon is a quintessential example of such a figure. Curzon's actions and writings produced evidence for Mackinder's beliefs as much as the other way around—the latter providing theories for the former's praxis.

Before all this Curzon had earned his post-Oxford spurs as an explorer and by cultivating many contacts with British and European officials in Iran and Central Asia. An avid geographer and student of classics, he traveled to Iran for three months in 1889 while he was a Conservative MP. The fruits of his sojourn were a series of newspaper reports and, ultimately, a 1300-page book titled *Persia and the Persian Question*. In elaborating how he understood the problem facing Britain, he explained that a lot more was at stake than profits. Persia should not merely "be consigned to interested hands" but should be viewed "from an Imperial standpoint, and in its due relation to the broader question of Asiatic politics as a whole, of which it constitutes no unimportant part."[33] He continued by coining a long-standing geopolitical trope as described how he viewed Afghanistan and Persia:

> To me, I confess, they are the pieces on a chessboard upon which is being played out a game for the dominion of the world. The future of Great Britain according to this view, will be decided, not in Europe, not even upon the seas and oceans which are swept by her flag, or in the Greater Britain that has been called into existence by her offspring, but in the continent whence our emigrant stock first came, and to which as conquerors their descendants have returned. Without India the British Empire could not exist.[34]

The chessboard was the ideal metaphor for geography being a single expanse upon which to strategize. Persia was an object—one of these mere chess pieces—that took its meaning and value from its position on the vital frontiers of Britain's worldwide empire. Curzon held this belief through his long career but emphasized the importance of travel and colonial service in developing "national character" via "types of manhood thrown up by Frontier life."[35] After his term as Viceroy ended, he beseeched his Oxford audience, "The Empire calls, as loudly as it ever did, for serious instruments of serious work. The Frontiers of Empire continue to beckon."[36]

Persia became a question for these late imperial strategists, however, because they understood Iran as threatened and sitting on empire's edge. Among other things, they pointed to the French opening a consulate and a coal depot in Muscat in the 1890s, Germany appointing a consul to Bushehr, and Russia expanding its political and economic involvement in northern Iran. Curzon and Henry J. Whigham, the author of the less frequently cited *The Persian Problem* published in 1903, had no doubt that these powers were more than just a challenge to Persia, and its government, which Whigham described as "perhaps, the most inefficient in a hemisphere of inefficient Governments."[37] Iran's political vulnerabilities were a problem for Britain because Iran was conceived as critical for "the peace and security of our great Indian dependency, the safety of the splendid highway from Gibraltar to Shanghai."[38] This charge was echoed by Curzon, who accused policymakers in London with "criminal reign of masterly inactivity" for not recognizing the importance of Persia.[39] Whigham warned that if Russia won a port in the Gulf, it would lead India to "become instantly vulnerable, and the people of Great Britain, the long-suffering taxpayers, would find themselves face to face with a constant menace to their Indian Empire."[40] Whigham was prefiguring Mackinder's opposition of land power to sea power and his fascination with Russian dominance over the Eurasian heartland.

Racial thinking helped bridge the imagined civilizational divide between Persia and Britain. In the midst of arguing for an imperial view of Persia that places it squarely within the Indian *and* British orbit, Curzon reminds his readers of the "racial" bond between Britain and both Persia and India. Hence, the shared Aryan "lineage" or "stock" makes it only natural for an Englishman to be interested and concerned with Persia, even if it was "remote and backward and infirm" and its people suffered from craftiness, supineness, and cowardice.[41] Curzon's tome endeavored to explain Persia's "efforts to accommodate herself to the ill-fitting clothes of a civilization that sat but clumsily upon her."[42] This combination of racial pedigree and social maldevelopment made Persia an excellent candidate for what Curzon believed were the civilizing virtues of British Empire and statecraft. Narratives about Persian and Ottoman political weakness and socioeconomic backwardness combined with the specter of European imperial competitors, primarily Russia, to legitimate arguments for the waterways and lands surrounding India as essential to British supremacy.

Mapping for a "Monroe Doctrine in the Middle East"

Part of what made Iran a puzzle for colonial officials and British "Eastern travelers" was that it was a land shadowing maritime channels and communication pathways necessary for the defense of India. Curzon, Whigham, and others were in conversation with the realities of Britain's maritime empire and proponents of "sea power," such as Alfred Thayer Mahan, the popular American naval strategist. Advocacy for sea power found its way into geopolitical theories stressing the importance of what would later be called "rimlands" by cold warriors such as Nicholas Spykman and George Keenan. They argued that Persia, although having value given its relationship to the sea, should be treated as more than a mere coastal zone between the Russian "heartland" and Britain's overseas domains. This ambiguous relationship between land and sea belies geopolitical writing that summons a stark binary between them, and therefore perceiving the Gulf as a space between the sea power of Britain and the land power of Russia. Conveying the melding of sea and land is the official title of the British Resident: "Her Britannic Majesty's Political Resident in the Persian Gulf and Consul-General for Fars and Khuzestan."

This bleeding of sea and land was expressed cartographically. Unlike travel writing, maps "convey the image of the world without the active mediating hand of the cartographer."[43] Once created, late-nineteenth-century maps operated as "the elaboration of mental spaces" that British-Indian strategists were expressing in prose.[44] Maps precede territory or space-making and actualize geography by making the world knowable, but they do so by hiding concrete techniques and labor needed to produce them. At the beginning of the nineteenth century the British Empire was manifest as a series of discrete locations—coal depots, ports, and trading posts—constituting a maritime world of corridor-like shipping channels and ribbonlike coastlines. Except for these nodes dotting the landscape, the focus of colonial concerns in the Persian Gulf region had been almost exclusively nautical. The British Indian navy was a "prolific producer of charts" and hydrographic surveys of the coastal regions of the Persian Gulf as well as the Arabian and Red seas.[45] By the 1860s surveyors adopted new methods of triangulation to massively improve their accuracy and to claim that there was an equivalence between the map and the real world.[46] With funding by British India, these cartographic techniques were primarily focused on archipelago-like constellations of isolated but interlinked outposts and shipping routes.

The focus of surveyors and mapmakers thickened to include greater swaths of land. The drift toward the land was necessary for extending and protecting telegraph lines as well as engaging in military battles; the Anglo-Persian War of 1856–57 was pivotal for intelligence gathering and mapmaking.[47] Additional knowledge about the physical and human geography of places unknown to the colonial administration was required for colonial expansion. Civilian and military personnel undertook the necessary surveys, drew the maps, and printed the images to represent the Gulf along with larger stretches of land on the Iranian plateau, the Arabian Peninsula, and the Tigris and Euphrates river valley. By zooming out, these modern maps reflected and reinforced a "view of space as a geometric expanse."[48] Cartographic scale became a mathematical expression of the relationship that mapmakers and their patrons wanted to make between the map and the real world.

Surveyors and cartographers literally measured and inscribed the earth, but their maps and data became the ingredients for the more abstract and deductive science of geopolitics. These late-nineteenth-century surveys and maps visualized the Persian Gulf at a regional scale, rather than a waterway or discrete coastline. "The seaman's view gave way to that of the landsman," is how Daniel Foliard has recently described it.[49] Rather than studying detailed charts of seabeds and coastlines or itineraries traveled, cartographers selected scales and perspectives to highlight the waterway's proximity to South Asia.[50] This is exactly what Curzon did in his 1892 *Persia and the Persian Question*, which included a full-page "cartographic accomplishment," meaning a map complete with a delineated border between Iran and British-India.[51] Subsequent maps of the Gulf, including ones commissioned during Curzon's tenure as Viceroy and Governor-General of India (1898–1905), opened the aperture to include the Arabian Peninsula.[52] These Anglo-Indian maps were "not just a reflection of an increasingly accurate topographical and geographical image of Arabia, Persia, and Mesopotamia. They conceived, promoted, and substantiated a distinct set of assumptions on what the East meant to the British Empire and to India in particular."[53] This long process of technological innovations, administrative developments, and policy debates placed all the land borders and shorelines onto a single geometric plane and within a contained region. But it also engendered alarm among British policymakers. This new cartography and the mental maps that came with it helped overcome the physical distance between the decision-makers in London and the colonial officers trying to persuade them to consider the Iranian plateau and Arabian Peninsula as appendages of the subcontinent. These maps operated as "the elaboration of mental spaces" that British-Indian strategists were conveying in prose.[54]

To ensure the maps were read in particular ways, colonial officials and strategies deployed rhetoric and new concepts to turn the Gulf into a vital site. The incremental technical developments were what rendered the Persian Gulf a "British lake" and led Curzon to describe the British Resident in Bushehr as "the uncrowned king of the Persian Gulf" or opine that "Basra is the backdoor to Bombay."[55] In 1907 Curzon, who presided over the Indian Survey Committee, distilled these ideas into a lecture he gave at Oxford University on frontiers. To explain why societies flourish and political stability is maintained, he outlined a taxonomy of borders. To explain the imperial relations with "the petty Arab chiefships of the southern shore of the Persian Gulf" he evoked a relatively new idea of "sphere of influence" as a territory in which "no exterior power but one may reassert itself."[56] Geopolitical theory and practice met one another in Curzon's remaking of Britain's Persian Gulf.

At this juncture a lasting geopolitical imaginary was coined and circulated—"the Middle East." The exact first use of the term is still disputed, but around 1900 it circulated among British officers and among geopolitically minded journalists and essayists in Britain and the United States. The sudden and multiple references to "the Middle East" suggest the larger urgency to alter the geographical scale in order to fully comprehend what was previously simply referred to as the Persian question, Mesopotamia, the East, or "the road to India."[57] This new segment of the East originally fell between British India and British Egypt and was centered on the Persian Gulf, the Arabian Peninsula, the Arabian Sea, and the borderlands of Iran and India. It took until World War II for "the Middle East" to be fully adopted by bureaucratic and military structures in London and Washington, D.C., to both describe the geography as well as organize knowledge and expertise. As the subsequent variety and shifting boundaries of the Middle East illustrate, the Middle East was not confined to an agreed-upon and specified set of places; at this foundational moment the term was tethered to the representation of the Persian Gulf as a frontier region and marked the culmination of several decades of defining the Persian Gulf and its immediate environs as an imperial Achilles' heel.

Thanks to the circulation of geopolitical writings and visualizations as well as Curzon's practice of spreading rumors of foreign meddling in the Indian Ocean, the British government issued a warning against any attempt to break its monopoly in the Persian Gulf. It was at this juncture in 1903 that Lord Lansdowne, the secretary of foreign affairs, declared that the British government would "regard the establishment of a naval base or a fortified port in the Persian Gulf by any power as a very grave menace to British interests, and we should certainly resist it with all the means at our disposal."[58] Along with MPs referencing Curzon's *Persia and the Persian Question*, the foreign secretary justified this new position by reminding parliament that Britain was "supreme" in the Gulf and British Indian subjects were the lone "real traders there."[59] Lansdowne underscored the critical position of the waterway for the defense of India, offering a moral claim to convince skeptics, "it was our ships that cleared those waters of pirates; it was we who put down the slave ship, it was we who buoyed and beaconed these intricate waters." The Persian Gulf had become a space to be patrolled, a territory to be protected—but also ordered anew.

British as well as US media covered Lansdowne's declaration by describing it as a "Monroe Doctrine for the Persian Gulf," clarifying for readers that just as the United States had drawn a line in the sea to repel European imperialism from the Western Hemisphere, Britain was declaring a protective boundary to guard its South Asian frontier and keep rivals at bay.[60] Curzon allegedly described Lansdowne's declaration as "our Monroe Declaration in the Middle East."[61] Lansdowne's proclamation that Britain, and not just the Raj, was committed to maintaining dominance over the western Indian Ocean marked an oscillation away from the focus on straits and channels necessary for the circulation and connections connecting an archipelago-like world empire. While for centuries it had been world-spanning, Britain's overseas empire had no territorial integrity. As Washington had done in Latin America, London now marked a sphere of influence that it intended to guard and treat exclusively even if their colonial status was legally nebulous and in practice incomplete. Strikingly, it was America's imperial posture that was the model for British Empire, not vice versa. By conjuring up a linear geography, Curzon and others drew parallels with the Monroe Doctrine to re-characterize the British Empire as in a "kindred travail" to US settler expansion.[62]

In the wake of the foreign secretary's statement, Curzon embarked on an extravagant vice-regal tour of the Persian Gulf to actualize the thickening of ties between British India and the Gulf. Up until November 1903 many in London were critical of Curzon's proposal to cruise through the waterway on an official visit and worried that it would draw war-weary Britain into conflict with Russia, France, or Germany. Only after the Second Boer War in South Africa was the Viceroy cleared to board the fleet that aimed at demonstrating both British sea power and the new relationship between the government of India and shaykhs in Muscat, Kuwait, and across the region. To an audience of notables and signatories of treaties, he declared:

> We were here before any other Power, in modern times, had shown its face in these waters. We found strife and we have created order. It was our commerce as well as your security that was threatened and called for protection. . . . The great Empire of India, which it is our duty to defend, lies almost at your gates. We saved you from extinction at the hands of your neighbours. We opened these seas to the ships of all nations, and enabled their flags to fly in peace. We have not seized or held your territory. We have not destroyed your independence but have preserved it. We are not now going to throw away this century of costly and triumphant enterprise; we shall not wipe out the most unselfish page in history. The peace of these waters must still be maintained; your independence will continue to be upheld; and the influence of the British Government must remain supreme.[63]

Maps of Construction and Modernization

Abstracting the Middle East region from social processes entailed defining national territorial boundaries and delimiting political authority within them. Surveying and cartography played a crucial role in this process as well. While Curzon's motivations for writing and publishing his two-volume work were clearly the strengthening of British imperial resolve and the mapping of the *external* relations of Persia, he treated his audience to hundreds of pages focused on the *internal* fabric of Iranian society and the Persian psyche. Curzon couched his arguments for control and intervention in the language of Persian independence or "the preservation, so far as it is still possible, of *the integrity of Iran* must be registered as a cardinal precept of our Imperial creed."[64] The goal was to help Iran, in ways economical, infrastructural, and political, to take its place among the family of nations as an independent, yet thoroughly pliable state and accessible market. It was this logic that led to the founding of the Imperial Bank in the late nineteenth century to extend loans to the Qajar government to alternatively keep it afloat and out of Russian clutches.

These arguments about the integrity of Iran or the need to develop and open up national markets for imports and surplus capital implied a "shift from maps of exploration to maps of construction and modernization."[65] The surveyors and mapmakers who represented the Persian Gulf as the fulcrum of the Middle East were in fact tasked with specific ends. The building of telegraph stations and the extending of transmission lines required the signing of conventions, the defining of concessionary areas, and agreement on the maps in their identity as plans.[66] In these concessions the Iranian government gave monopolies to British and other firms over fixed areas for specific numbers of years. Surveyors were needed to produce supporting spatial data and materials for international treaties and the planning of infrastructural projects. These agreements brought private and public British interests in direct confrontation with the overlapping and noncontiguous forms of authorities described in the previous chapter. Sorting out and constructing territorial jurisdictions was no simple matter, with the Omani oceanic sultanate maintaining outposts on islands and southern Iranian ports and the Qasimi dynasty based in Sharjah and Ras al-Khaimah leasing various ports and islands in the Strait of Hormuz region (see chapter 1). Defining the rights and responsibilities and assigning them to specific pieces of land was crucial to surveyors as well as investors and operators of infrastructure and trading houses, but it required clarifying and building up sovereign territoriality.

As the ostensible authority over the Iranian plateau, the Qajar Dynasty of Iran was Britain's principal interlocutor, even though in southern Iran there were a host of local authorities and lease agreements with families in eastern Arabia, which had bridged the Gulf for several centuries. These intra-Gulf arrangements were gradually replaced by more centrally administered, clearly defined and policed borders and customs institutions. The construction and maintenance of telegraph lines across Iran, for instance, led the British to align itself with Tehran to drive the Sultan of Muscat from the Makran coast by 1872 and demarcate the border between Iran and what would become Pakistan. Within a decade, Bushehr, Lengeh, and Bandar Abbas were no longer under the authority of the Governor of Fars and became directly controlled by Tehran, with tax collection at the southern ports farmed out by the government until 1898, when the central customs administration was managed by Belgian officials on behalf of the Qajar.[67] The British came to understand that to extend the telegraph lines that bound India to England, they needed Iran's cooperation and they also had to settle border and territorial disputes. By viewing these infrastructural projects alongside questions about boundaries and authority, borders appear like membranes that on the one hand block the authority of "outsiders" while simultaneously facilitating the movement of telegraph signals. The physical building and fixing of infrastructure were necessary for certain flows even as they helped territorialize Tehran's authority and anchor profit-making by British businesses.

These sorts of British-infused boundary-making also took place on the Arabian Peninsula, although they centered around defining the place of sheikhdoms in relation to the Ottoman Empire. In 1913 a British-Ottoman agreement established a "status of limits" that defined Kuwait as the town and everything within a radius of 40 miles in all directions.[68] A few years earlier the Kuwaiti ruler had secured permission from the British to tax imports from Ottoman Basra as if they were from overseas.[69] At the same time, in the midst of debating who should be the next ruler of Dubai, the British officials who had the final say on questions of succession made their approval of the new shaykh as contingent upon the establishment of a telegraph station and other facilities needed by the British Empire.[70] Also, the non-alienation clauses of many of the treaties signed between the British government and local rulers in eastern Arabia in the *fin de siècle* period forbade the shaykhs to sell, cede, or mortgage territory to any foreign power other than the British (see chapter 3). The main object of these provisions was originally to block Russia and France and their pursuit of commercial concessions and port visits by their navies, but the treaty stipulations gained their greatest traction in repelling German interests in turning Kuwait into the terminus for the Berlin-to-Baghdad railroad.[71] Contours of a national economy and markets were beginning to be demarcated by infrastructures, customs houses, and concessionary agreements. With this what had been merely inter-city or long-distance trade was increasingly defined as "international."

Critically, Europeans were not alone in map-making. Iranians and Ottomans adopted boundary markers, legal settlements, and concessionary treaties to exert political control over people and market as cornerstones of what would become sovereign territoriality. The science of cartography flourished in the courts and the earliest secular educational institutions in Tehran and

Istanbul, which were part of the reform of military education.[72] Many of the graduates of the Dar ol-Fanun (est. 1851), Iran's first polytechnic institution for training military officers and civil servants, were the authors and translators of key geographic texts and maps. Simultaneously, with the aid of British mediators, border disputes between the Persian and Ottoman empires were settled beginning with the Treaties of Erzurum (1823 and 1847). Boundary surveys in the last two decades of the nineteenth century defined which people and tribes fell under British protection in places such as Aden (a British colony since the 1830s) and which were the responsibilities of the Ottomans and the Qajars. Woven into these surveying projects were developmentalist agendas around making land more productive and sedenterizing populations, all of which required extending the authority of the central state.[73] The foundational nature of these surveys and maps and the territorial sovereignty they enshrined has not been lost on Iranians and Arabs. The ongoing dispute between Iran and the UAE over three islands near the mouth of the Gulf continues to be fought by Iranians referencing an 1887 map to lay their claim to Abu Musa and the two Tunbs islands.[74] Many current and recently settled territorial disputes on the peninsula have roots in demarcations and treaties that predate World War II.

These processes set in motion forces that neither Curzon nor courtiers in Tehran and Istanbul could foresee, much less fully control. Even if these cartographic developments accompanied imperialism, the new mapping techniques made claims to a *national* space and political rights and responsibilities for people as members of that nation. During the early twentieth century, modernity, independence, constitutionalism, and nationhood were framing devices adopted by people seeking to criticize their rulers or simply organize as workers, as was the case of one of Iran's first unions, representing the telegraph workers. In Iran, on the cusp of the Constitutional Revolution (1905–11) that created a parliament, merchants contested exclusionary concessions handed out by the Qajars, social bandits raided British outposts, and provincial Iranians sent telegrams calling for constitutional rule. As we will explore in the next chapter, the struggles multiplied, targeting British rule, tribal leaders, monarchical authority, and other systems of "injustice" as new demands were discovered and poverty, unemployment, and health became *social* questions rather than matters of morality and charity. This did not mean that nonterritorial forms of sovereignty based on lineage, theology, and kinship were extinguished overnight, but it did mean that territoriality was increasingly fused with effective political authority.[75]

"FILLING THE VACUUM"

The Persian Gulf between 1940 and 1970 had the quality of an interregnum. British power persisted despite being contested and incomplete. Indian independence and partition battered British Empire politically, financially, and morally, but it also unraveled the strategic logic and administrative structure of Britain's role in the Gulf. Nonetheless, new rationalities and formations for imperial retrenchment were layered onto the Persian Gulf as both an energy frontier and a Cold War front line. No longer conceived of as a valuable highway integrating British Empire, the Gulf was becoming a political economic zone vital for capitalism, or the "Free World Economy" led by the United States.

This process began during World War II when British and US troops occupied Iran and Iraq to support the Soviets' efforts to combat the German war machine. This "Persian Gulf Command" included elements of institutionalized regionalism, with the Middle East Supply Center and the United Kingdom Commercial Cooperation regulating trade, shipping, and distributions of basic goods.[76] In setting up the supply chain known as the "Persian Corridor," thirty thousand US troops joined tens of thousands British-Indian soldiers, and fifty thousand Iranians to transship, assemble, and transport almost half a million trucks and five thousand planes from the Persian Gulf to the Soviet Union in less than three years. While the Persian Command outstripped the more illustrious Arctic route in delivering supplies to the Soviet Union, the Iranian and Iraqi labor force and economy was reoriented to achieve Allied objectives. This had dire consequences for the health and welfare of inhabitants of Iran and Iraq, with food shortages triggering spiraling inflation, disease, and famine despite the United States sending food and supply advisors. With war's end, national and transnational regulatory bureaucracies, such as the Middle East Supply Center, were dismantled as the United States pushed for an open door policy and the British sought to reestablish imperial structures. Instead of devising international institutions to ensure cooperative arrangements, as liberal internationalists claim marked US "hegemony" in the twentieth century, in the Gulf rule-making and organization-building was thin and the United States prioritized bilateral agreements and primacy.

Drifting away from multilateral coordinated efforts to organize the Gulf region, Britain and the United States adopted bilateral relations between each

other and with the emerging independent states as a key component to supremacy. However, this form of internationalization came to be viewed as an
invitation for Soviet expansionism into the Gulf and imperiling the aspiration
for a bounded, homogeneous Gulf region oriented exclusively around Anglo-
American interests. During the course of the Cold War, as we will see, the real
and imagined fear of the Soviet Union shaped an array of actions taken by rulers and opposition parties as well as the policies of Washington and London.
One key site of these struggles was the oil fields.

The political economies of the United States and Britain became increasingly interwoven. The 1950s began with Iranian nationalists headed by Mossadeq and the labor movement in Abadan demonstrating that it had enough
power to dislodge the British monopoly over the oil sector and secure a nominal nationalization of Iran's petroleum industry in 1951. The popular movement, however, was not strong enough to withstand the clandestine operations of MI6 and CIA against it. The 1953 coup overthrew the prime minister
and affirmed Mohammad Reza's position as shah, but it also created a new
international oil consortium in Iran that downsized Britain's most important
petroleum holding, while giving access to US firms to Iran's oil fields. By the
decade's end, Iraqis had risen up to overthrow the British-backed monarchy
and completed a protracted struggle that began with the League of Nations
creating a mandatory rule. Besides mobilizations in Iran and Iraq, the rise
of Gamal Abdel Nasser in Egypt in 1952, for observers on the Arabian Peninsula, exposed the popularity of anti-imperialism and the limits of British
power. Nasser even gained admirers in Qom, Iran's leading seminary city.[77]
While galvanizing students, laborers, and occasional "free" Saudi princes, decolonization on the peninsula challenged the troika of oilmen, monarchs, and
colonial officers. The US government came to acknowledge that Britain was
"distrusted and hated" by the people in the region and needed material assistance to resist the onslaught of decolonization.[78]

The British economy earned valuable hard currency from the export of
raw materials from its colonies, and Iranian and Kuwaiti oil allowed British
firms to import oil in its own currency as opposed to dollars. By 1952 the Ex-
chequer had become weary of military expenses associated with holding off
the will of the restive peoples of Asia and Africa. Already reeling from budget
deficits and repeated runs on the sterling, the Suez War of 1956, which led to
the expulsion of British troops from Egypt and the temporary closure of the
Canal, convinced the British government to shed its colonies and accept US

global predominance in return for IMF loans.[79] Even special arrangements to have Kuwait funds deposited in the Bank of England were not enough to shore up confidence in the pound and protect Britain's balance of payments. Thus started the precipitous devaluation of the pound as major oil firms switched from trading oil in sterling pounds to dollars and the sterling zone crumbled.

In the midst of these tumultuous and eventful few years, US officials began to worry that Britain could not "pull its weight in defending the Middle East against Soviet influence."[80] The US government eventually agreed to the persistence of British tutelage over the Gulf. At a 1957 conference in Bermuda, a "division of labor" was outlined, with the United States relying on the British armaments and local alliance systems to police the Gulf on behalf of the anticommunist free world.[81] For instance, Britain continued to deploy military action to defend its oil and commercial interests: a rebellion against the sultan of Muscat and Oman was put down in 1957, and troops were flown in from Aden and Kenya to defend newly independent Kuwait from Iraqi ambitions in 1961. After the loss of the Suez Canal, Aden and its new oil refinery, built in 1954, became a major military base that required defending on several occasions until independence in 1963.[82] At the Bermuda conference, US Secretary of State John Foster Dulles insisted that it was "important that the United Kingdom should have more power" specifically in Kuwait in the event that "things went wrong in Saudi Arabia and Iraq."[83] Britain was the first line of defense in the Arabian Peninsula for what would become the Eisenhower Doctrine of providing economic and military assistance to countries "threatened by armed aggression"—that is, the Soviet Union. Meanwhile, after intervening in Iran to drive out Soviet troops from its soil in 1946 and coming to its aid in 1953, Washington expected Pahlavi Iran to operate within its orbit and signed a Bilateral Security Pact in 1959.[84]

In the same year as the Afro-Asian Summit in Bandung that was attended by Nasser as well as delegates from Iran, Iraq, and Saudi Arabia, the United States and Britain pushed back against anti-imperialism and Third-Worldism. The 1955 Baghdad Pact, or Middle East Treaty Organization, was a crack at stitching together an anti-Soviet front. The pact included Iran, Iraq, Turkey, and Pakistan as well as Britain with its bases in the Indian Ocean and the eastern Mediterranean. The United States sponsored and aided the military alliance but declined to join it, much to the disgruntlement of Whitehall and the shah, who were both currying US support.[85] Dulles, who had been seeking to devise a regional peace settlement including Israel and Palestine, saw the Baghdad Pact as divisive rather than uniting the Arab world; he counseled, "Better to keep it a paper pact."[86] His preference was largely realized. The 14 July Revolution in Iraq in 1958 resulted in Baghdad withdrawing from the pact, forcing the group to change its name to the Central Treaty Organization (CENTO). It remained a largely impotent organization that did little to prevent wars or the spread of Soviet influence in the Arab world or to assist member-states in their conflicts, such as the Indo-Pakistani or Arab-Israel wars or the Iraqi claims on Kuwait in 1961. This reticent experiment in regional security-making throws into relief the imperfectness of the co-presence of US and British power in fashioning some semblance of Gulf regionalism via "special relationships" and bilateral relations with nation-states.

In 1968 the British government finally announced that it would dismantle its imperial system on the Arabian Peninsula (see chapter 3). Local monarchs, the US government, and academics responded to this impending "vacuum" with shock and dismay. Reflecting this fear was the conference organized in 1969 by Georgetown University's Center for Strategic and International Studies under the title *The Gulf: Implications of British Withdrawal.*[87] The conference brought together a disparate set of Middle East Studies notables, including Albert Hourani, J. C. Hurewitz, Charles Issawi, William Luce, and Hisham Sharabi. The chair of the panel and the primary author of the subsequent report was Bernard Lewis. The central messages, which were not shared by all the participants, were that the British withdrawal would "increase instability in the Gulf" and that the "danger of Soviet hegemony" would rise. The report argued in agitated prose against the British withdrawal by arguing that the cost of maintaining its presence was relatively low considering the value of the region. It added, "The defense of Moscow led them to Czechoslovakia. The defense of Baku might lead them to the Gulf." (10) Reflecting the bête noire of its time, Nasser's Egypt is signaled out as having an interest in disrupting Gulf affairs in order to attract greater traffic via the Suez—a curious claim insofar as the canal was closed at the time. Ultimately, due to the entire region being "inherently unstable" (69), the report recommends that Britain and America conduct regular naval visits to deter the Soviets. Despite these arguments and offers from the astonished local shaykhs to pay for the maintenance of Britain troops, London officially withdrew its military and political protection of all colonial states on the peninsula. The decision was driven by the budgetary predicaments and domestic considerations facing the British government.[88] The Johnson and Nixon administrations were both left disappointed—in early 1968, Secretary of State Dean Rusk upbraided British Foreign Secretary George Brown, "For God's sake, act like Britain."[89]

Britain departed Arabia in 1971, having failed to cudgel the rulers into creating a single federation in the eastern peninsula. Bahrain and Qatar elected to become fully independent, and the ruling families of what had been termed first the Pirate Coast and later the Trucial States agreed to join a confederation called the United Arab Emirates. Kuwait had already gained independence in 1961, Aden in 1963 (the People's Republic of South Yemen being founded in 1967), and Oman became nominally independent in 1951. None of these dire predictions came about; indeed, the 1970s saw significant cooperation among littoral states and the signing of multilateral agreements on navigation and pollution and the Iran-Iraq border.[90]

What is often read as the continuation of Pax Britannica through to a moment of rupture with the official withdrawal "East of Suez" in 1971 is better understood as a culmination of a multifaceted (and messy) midcentury compromise with Pax Americana and a layering of two different imperial formations upon anticolonial aspirations. This was not lost on commentators, including the Soviet Union and Marxist political parties in the region. As early as 1950, *Pravda* wrote that the "fate of the Bahrain Islands is a characteristic example. The archipelago was severed from Iran when Britain, in the nineteenth century, declared herself 'protector' of the local princes. Now the American monopolies have completely taken over production of oil in Bahrain Islands. This is the position: the islands are Iranian, the 'protectorate' is British and the Americans extract oil!"[91] As the shah softened his position on the question of Bahrain's independence, he faced criticism from ardent Iranian nationalists as well as communists. Meanwhile, Bahraini oil workers, journalists, and merchants understood that confronting imperialism had to run through the oil fields and ruling families that brokered relations with the outside world for more than century.

The Klondike Mentality and the Gulf Arms Bazaar

Global capitalism and the pivotal role played by fossil fuels reinforced the notion of the Gulf as an objectified space and molded the imperial arrangement between the United States and Britain by placing constraints on their cooperation. As part of its open door campaign of the early twentieth century, the United States pushed for a larger stake in the former lands of the Ottoman Empire. The 1928 Red Line Agreement between oil executives, which inhibited competition among US and European oil companies, was one of several examples of cartelization as a means to control supply and to inflate profits for firms. The consortium structure, which created interlocking ownership structures, helped pool resources for capital intensive investments but gave the major firms leverage over national governments in negotiating better agreements. In all these cases firms recruited public resources and diplomatic leverage of states to reduce costs and generate scarcity. In the process of contracting concessionary agreements, states as territorial formations were hardened.

Energy and security were fused into the bedrock of much of twentieth-century geopolitical thinking about the Persian Gulf. As early as World War I military strategists acknowledged oil's role in war-making, but at that point, it was the United States, not the Middle East, that was the major producer of the fossil fuel for war machines. Although coal was still important for feeding steam engines, Curzon penned the memorable phrase that the allied forces "floated to victory on a wave of oil."[92] As petroleum became an increasingly vital energy source in the first half of the twentieth century, it was Pennsylvania, Oklahoma, Texas, and Louisiana that were sites of global production and sources for exports. World War II was the turning point. The strategic nature of oil gained greater traction as steam engines were powered by petroleum products and policymakers understood that Persian Gulf oil was a "well head" for European and Japanese recovery and expanding US domestic consumption.[93] If politicians agreed that oil was too strategic to be left to market forces, firms understood that return on investments could be bolstered through public support from states where they were headquartered *and* states in which they extracted petroleum. This symbiosis animated apprehensions about what we would today call "energy dependence" and sustained a "scarcity ideology" even if underlying levels of oil production in fact caused firms to be more concerned about oversupply rather than shortages and dire predictions about peak oil.[94]

As the geographic center of gravity pivoted from the Gulf of Mexico to the Persian Gulf, the demand for oil skyrocketed. In 1950 oil accounted for only 30 percent of the energy needs of the United States, Western Europe, and Japan; by 1973 consumption levels were increasing at an annual rate of nearly 8 percent and oil's share had reached 53 percent.[95] The Persian Gulf supplied two-thirds of the world's total imports. The six Gulf members of the Organization of Petroleum Exporting Countries (OPEC) earned $185 billion in 1980, up from merely $7 billion nine years earlier.[96] Around this time grand strategists began to claim that in addition to being important for war-making, oil was scarce and profitable and if "controlled" could be wielded against foes and allies alike. As a strategic commodity for the global economy it required the United States as an international hegemon to design policies to ensure its physical flow and financial profitability. Although having been championed for almost a century, conceiving of oil markets in terms of scarcity and securing has had its empirical shortcomings and no shortage of critics.[97]

When British withdrew its protection for the Arab states of the Gulf, the United States had to directly address its goals of staving off Soviet interests, supporting pro-Western rulers, and ensuring the flow of cheap energy. Already during the Johnson administration, US officials called for an end to wooing Arab nationalists and stronger alignment with Israel and regional monarchies.[98] Against the backdrop of the Vietnam War, rather than directly replace Britain's presence in this geopoliticized Gulf, the Nixon and Ford administrations turned to local "clients" to manage distinct "regional rivalries" in what was known as the "economy-of-force" approach. The United States pushed through rapprochement with Sadat's Egypt in the mid-1970s, including establishing military ties and reopening the Suez Canal after it being closed during the 1967 War. However, with the largest populations and land masses as well as existing close diplomatic ties, Iran and Saudi Arabia were obvious contenders for playing the role of "stabilizing the region." The opposition to "radical Arab states" was a glue that drew the United States, Iran, and Saudi Arabia together. US policy relied on arming the shah and the Saudi royal family to "fill the vacuum left by British withdrawal, now menaced by Soviet intrusion and radical momentum," as Henry Kissinger described it.[99]

The shah desired and maneuvered to play the role of regional hegemon, and he embraced it with gusto. On the eve of the Iranian Revolution, the United States' so-called Twin Pillars Policy seemed to be a success, as the shah unleashed Operation Caviar to suppress a Marxist rebellion in Oman and appeared to have the upper hand over Baathist-led Iraq, an assumed ally of, if not an outright proxy for, the Soviet Union.[100] Saudi Arabia, the other pillar of US security architecture, was less significant militarily, but its large earnings from oil and small population resulted in the prize of surplus capital, or petrodollars, for global financial markets.

Financial instruments were as critical to US-led order as force projection. Beginning in the late 1960s, the position of oil exporters provided succor for financial markets suffering from inflation as well as budget and trade imbalances associated with the United States' war on Vietnam.[101] The post–World War II Bretton Woods monetary system of pegged foreign currencies depended on the gold-backed US dollar as the currency of trade and reserve for the global economy, which in turn required the United States to balance its budgets. This broke down in 1971 as US politicians shied away from taking the electoral risk of raising taxes and neither the United States nor the IMF enjoyed the resources to address balance-of-payment shortfalls. Nixon severed the convertibility of dollars with gold, and a system of floating exchange rates was adopted. As capital controls were lifted allowing private banks to deal in deposits other than in their national currency and for a market for dollars to emerge outside of national regulatory system (e.g., Eurodollars), the internationalization of capitalism entered a new financial era aided by new computer and telecommunications technologies. From 1964 to 1980, the value of offshore holdings rose from 1.2 to 16.2 percent of world GDP.[102]

It is at this moment in the early 1970s that the decisions of US-allied Gulf oil producers played a critical role. The price of oil went through a revolutionary increase driven by three interrelated forces.[103] Oil exporters joined the decolonizing struggles of the time to wrest effective control over their economic resources and break the shackles of concessionary agreements. A group of lawyers, economists, and engineers championed and popularized these arguments while building international organizations to exchange information and learn lessons from national struggles in Latin America and the Middle East and North Africa. It increasingly became clear that oligopolistic powers of oil majors, known as the Seven Sisters, were using the system of concessions to dominate extraction, refining, shipping, and marketing to suppress how much they paid to producers and recouped from consumers. In response to this, oil producers organized their own cartel, OPEC, in 1960. It was built on shared interests as oil exporters rather than being a Gulf organization (Venezuela was a key founding member, and North African countries were early entrants). Second, aiding oil producers in this battle against "the postwar petroleum order" was the appearance of smaller oil "independents" who were willing to offer better terms to host nations so as to gain entry into untapped and more costly fields such as in Libya.[104] Finally, these risky investments made economic sense because of the ratcheting up of global demand for petroleum by energy-intensive industries and lifestyles. These dynamics came together in the early 1970s to adjust the balance of power in favor of oil producers, who succeeded in driving the price of oil per barrel from less than $1.50 in 1970 to over $11 by January 1974; the value of oil exports skyrocketed. What is commonly referred to as an "oil shock" by importers was understood by exporting countries as an "oil revolution." With this revenue, producing countries could buy back concessions and establish national oil companies.

Despite these structural dislocations, the perception and popular wisdom continues to hold that the fivefold increase in oil prices in the early 1970s was triggered by the "the Arab oil weapon" used in the 1973 war against Israel's allies. While this is poor history and an overly voluntarist interpretation of economics, it has had traction because it engages xenophobic stereotypes of greedy and spiteful Arabs and the dominant view of oil as a strategic commodity and the Gulf as a location where oil simply exists, needing to be organized by great powers.[105]

Rather than reduce their own profits, oil firms transferred the higher prices for crude to consumers. This came after a half-century in which industries, cities, and consumers structured their transportation, manufacturing, and electricity systems around cheap petroleum and multiplying uses for petrochemicals.[106] For cash-strapped countries in the Third World, this meant borrowing from the IMF and private banks, a process that would soon lead to the 1980s debt crisis when the United States raised interest rates and plunged economies, especially in Latin America, into austerity and privatization under the auspices of structural adjustment.[107]

For the industrialized economies, the challenge was to ensure that oil exporters had attractive outlets for investing their windfalls by purchasing goods and services. Financial investments via private banks, rather than central banks and the IMF, were a critical pathway redirecting surplus oil revenue into US-dominated sectors, including oil refineries and other upstream oil sectors. As capital controls were lifted, private banks could accept greater quantities of deposits from abroad and outside the United States, while oil exporters made other dollar-denominated investments augmenting capital available for the US government and firms, keeping interest rates low for consumers and helping strengthen the US currency. More intensive and direct effort to attract petrodollars occurred in 1974 when US Treasury Secretary William Simon, who had previously been Nixon's "energy czar," traveled to Saudi Arabia and negotiated a unilateral and secret deal allowing the Saudi central bank to use their surplus oil revenue to purchase US Treasury securities outside of the normal auction, a measure intended to guarantee that that OPEC would continue to price oil in dollars. With the higher global demand for US dollars to purchase oil and OPEC surplus, the United States financed its budget and trade deficits without having to cut imports or raise taxes.[108] The episode captures what Alice Amsden calls "the rise of the financial services sector [and] the triumph of the Treasury over the State Department in foreign economic affairs."[109]

These 1970s financial restructurings paralleled commercial practices that treated the Gulf as a marketplace. As early as the Eisenhower administration, the US government had sought to "absorb" Saudi oil revenues through US weapons deals.[110] Even before the oil revolution of 1971–74, US officials connected the dots between oil revenue, domestic manufacturing, and employment in the United States, with arms sales as a particularly effective vessel: Secretary of Defense Robert McNamara asserted that "Our sales [to Iran] have created about 1.4 million man-years of employment in the US and over $1 billion of profits to American industry in the past five years."[111] By the 1960s, US officials had begun to view the 1953 Iranian coup and other clandestine operations as less effective than investing in Third World policing and militaries as the best method to repel communism and shore up long-term allies.[112] Hence when the shah visited the United States in October 1969, the stage was set to begin a massive arms build-up underwritten by the United States, with some of the deliveries and financing unpublicized and even kept secret.[113]

But this petrodollar recycling became more integral in thinking as oil prices rose. The Middle East accounted for less than 20 percent of US arms sales from 1955 to 1969; by the 1970–74 period it had reached 52 percent, and from 1975 to 1979 it accounted for almost 70 percent, with the vast majority sold to Iran, Saudi Arabia, and other Gulf states.[114] In 1973, the State Department told Congress that the Gulf "is an area which will provide almost unlimited opportunities for the sale of every kind of US good and service.

It is an area which is ideally complementary to high technology and management services that the United States can provide."[115] Petrodollar recycling was driven by increasingly expensive equipment and a phalanx of consultants and service companies, which addressed America's balance of payment problems and buoyed global capitalism through profound sectoral and spatial restructuring. At the same moment that decolonizers had wrested away independence, policymakers in the region and Ivy League professors viewed the process as generating "interdependence" between oil exporters and importers.[116]

Arms sales, consultancies, and advisory missions generated a "frenetic . . . Klondike mentality" among Americans and their Gulf partners with everybody "out to get as much money as they could."[117] The combination of ballooning oil income, the close relationship between US administrations and Mohammad Reza Pahlavi and the Saud family, and Britain's decision to end its presence East of Suez led the Nixon administration to give Iran "a blank military check" in 1972.[118] Military sales to Iran increased from $524 million in 1972 to $3.91 billion in 1974. This included contracts for hundreds of aircrafts, naval ships, missile and radar systems, guided bombs, antitank missiles, and other hardware. Construction of ports and military barracks for local military in the Gulf, such as a USAID project for Bandar Abbas, was another component of the stream of contracts. The actual military efficacy of these sales and arrangements was questionable, though, and the military technology was directed against internal enemies as much as foreign armies. Iranian technocrats based at the Institute of International Political and Economic Studies warned: "The flood of weapons, for example tanks (or helicopters), is likely to result in remarkable waste in two respects. First in stretching the capacity of existing trained crews and decreasing their efficiency, and/or in the inability to maintain and operate these vehicles leading to warehousing, deterioration, or falling into disrepair."[119] Decision-makers in the shah's government turned a blind eye, but many Iranians did not.

The militarization of the Gulf was incentivized from many directions. For military analysts these commercial relationships came with a strategic component in that the provision of weapons and the training of troops by the United States was meant to provide security for local rulers and give the United States access to regional bases in the name of "host country support."[120] For domestic US producers foreign purchases of major weapons systems reduced the cost of the same systems for the US military through savings achieved by mass production. This was a subsidy to the Pentagon's budget and a boon for manufacturers and consultants struggling through the doldrums of the mid-1970s global economy and the unwinding of the Vietnam War. For instance, Iran was the only country to purchase F-14 Tomcats, which "saved the F-14 program by loaning Grumman, its troubled manufacturer, the money to finance the production to fulfill the Imperial Air Force's order."[121] Another example is Saudi Arabia's purchase of AWACS aircraft, which resulted in almost half of the proceeds going to the US Treasury for government R&D expenditures.[122] The formula of "arms sales for oil" became an acid test of special relationships between the United States and Gulf states and a pillar of the national security state centered in northern Virginia.[123] The peace dividend from the withdrawal from Vietnam went to the defense industry via treasuries in the Gulf, but this was not without struggle.

Although he campaigned for president as a critic of arms sales, once in office Jimmy Carter found himself entangled by domestic economic considerations and allied with Barry Goldwater advocating for sales of weapons to the shah and the Middle East. In a government report leaked to *The New York Times*, it was estimated that arms sales supported about 700,000 jobs, especially in the aerospace and arms producers and subcontractors.[124] Arms sales cemented the budding confederation of war hawks, oil executives advocating energy security, advisors from the Treasury Department and financial sector, and advocates for domestic manufacturing. *The New York Times* concluded that despite calls for "energy independence" and considerable congressional opposition, the US arms sales policy "had a life of its own."

EVOCATIVE GEOMETRIES

Just as it became a market, destination, and wellhead, the Persian Gulf by the end of the 1970s reemerged as a place threatened from outside and needing to be stabilized by the United States as the world's hegemon. This came after a decade of vulnerability for the United States at home and abroad. The Vietnam War both demonstrated the limits of US military power and agitated long-standing socioeconomic cleavages carved out by patriarchy and white supremacy that were resisted by civil rights and revolutionary movements in black communities and among feminists. A monetary crisis, combined with a host of other economic dislocations, reduced the power of

manufacturing, and organized labor was blunted by stagflation and retaliation by capital. Meanwhile, Watergate and the Church Committee investigation into the US intelligence community opened the door for Congress to
confront the misdeeds of the presidency. All of this "upended . . . the sense
of abundant prosperity, political stability, and moral righteousness that had
served as the basis for domestic tranquility and Cold War strength since the
late 1940s."[125]

In December 1978, at the pinnacle of the mass movement that would go
onto topple Iran's shah and monarchical rule, US National Security Advisor
Zbigniew Brzezinski sent a classified memo to President Carter: "There is no
question in my mind that we are confronting the beginning of a major crisis, in some ways similar to the one in Europe in the later 1940s."[126] Adopting
the language of the Trilateral Commission, which Brzezinski had co-founded
in 1973 to foster greater nongovernmental cooperation between the United
States and its allies, the memo argued that the crisis in the Gulf region would
reverberate through Europe and East Asia (Japan) and undermine US international hegemony: "A shift in Iranian/Saudi orientation [away from the US]
would have a direct impact on trilateral cohesion, and it would induce in time
more neutralist attitudes on the part of some of our key allies. In a sentence, it
would mean a fundamental shift in the global structure of power."[127]

Brzezinski reasoned that dependence on oil passing through the Persian
Gulf had become an Achilles' heel for the West, given the proximity of the
Soviet Union to the arc of transportation channels and oil fields.[128] In the
midst of Iranians calling for the overthrow of America's shah, he offered an
emphatically geopoliticized rendering of the region:

> As mentioned to you a week or so ago, we are now facing a *regional crisis*. Both
> Iran and Afghanistan are in turmoil, and Pakistan is both unstable internally
> and extremely apprehensive externally. If the Soviets succeed in Afghanistan,
> and [blacked out] the age-long dream of Moscow to have direct access to the
> Indian Ocean will have been fulfilled. Historically, the British provided the bar-
> rier to that drive, and Afghanistan was their buffer state. We assumed the role
> in 1945, but the Iranian crisis has led to the collapse of the balance of power in
> Southwest Asia, and it could produce Soviet presence right down on the edge
> of the Arabian and Oman gulfs.[129]

Within weeks, Brzezinski took his alarmist predictions, including his far-
cical assumption that the Soviet Union was running out of oil, to a press that

was willing to repeat it.[130] In a cover story titled "Crescent of Crisis: Troubles Beyond Iran" from early 1979, *Time* quoted Brzezinski: "An arc of crisis stretches along the shores of the Indian Ocean, the fragile social and political structures in a region of vital importance to us threatened with fragmentation. The resulting political chaos could well be filled by elements hostile to our values and sympathetic to our adversaries."[131] The field of international relations was invested in disassociating the Anglo-American tradition of geopolitics from the German variety, and geopolitics as a concept had lost academic credibility.[132] Yet the deterministic relationship between geography and power were ever present among policymakers in the NSC and State Department officials and interest groups (e.g., Committee on the Present Danger).[133]

"The arc of crisis" lumped together a series of political events that took place in 1977 and 1978. Represented on the cover of *Time* by the image of a stalking bear perched ominously above a crescent-shaped land mass stretching from South Asia to the Horn of Africa, Soviet access to ports and airfields in eastern India, Umm Qasr in Iraq, Aden and Socotra in Yemen, and Berbera in Somalia was rendered as evidence of a looming communist threat.[134] Anxious policymakers and pundits strung these together in their narratives along with the overthrow of the shah by "radical Islamists," military coups in Turkey and Pakistan, Soviet troops drawn into Afghanistan, and improved relations between Moscow and the governments in Ethiopia and South Yemen. Of course, these revolutionary and counterrevolutionary processes did not necessarily mean that the Soviets were involved or effective in all of them or that these episodes were related to one another, but the conception of the arc enabled them to be arranged into in a single chain of incidents capable of raising the level of alarm in Washington.[135]

Time described the arc as composed of "squabbling," "ineffective," "unstable," and "impoverished" polities with the only shared factor being "an innate fragility, a vulnerability borne of being located at the center of so strategic territory."[136] What gave these events meaning and coherence was precisely their shared geography. These politically fragile political units were tethered to critical economic and strategic assets—massive petroleum reserves and transportation routes and chokepoints—that if not controlled by the United States would be dominated by the looming Soviet bear, who had a historic interested in accessing this territory and waterways.[137] Harold Brown, Carter's secretary of defense, spelled out the stakes as follows: "Soviet control of this area would make virtual vassals of much of both the industrialized and developing world."[138] *The Economist* concluded that geopolitical decay ran "straight through the valuable, vulnerable triangle which produces nearly half the noncommunist world's oil, but also lies uncomfortably close to the chest of the world's main communist power."[139]

The geometry of a triangle was less evocative of the Orient, but again the Gulf was the epicenter of a teetering region as an empty abstract space. The *Time* magazine essay used biological metaphors to describe an impending spillover effect: "Instability is contagious, and the opportunities for exploitation are increasing."[140] It is for this reason that a slew of think tanks issued reports demonstrating that "the entire northwest quadrant of the Indian Ocean . . . [was] a region inseparable from Western security."[141] Probably because there was little concrete evidence of grand strategizing by the Soviet Union or direct involvement in fomenting this insecurity, some authors concluded that regional states were made "vulnerable to indirect, disguised methods of aggression often favored by the Soviet Union and its client regimes."[142]

The specter of communist infiltration was employed by local actors to curry favor and shape US policies. In 1979, a Saudi security official stated: "We are not worried about internal upheavals. Our public is calm. What worries us is all those Cubans on our periphery."[143] It is not clear if he meant this metaphorically or literally, but he understood the power of these words for his D.C. audience. The "arc of crisis" may have been a means to represent a whole host of polities as basket cases, but monarchs, arms dealers, and opposition groups were quick to claim vulnerability and convince US officials that these alliances were valuable. By using the same tropes and fears, they contributed to the making of an endlessly applicable geopolitical discourse. As US policymakers, establishment media, and local rulers referenced each other, a "rhetorical economy of persuasion" gained traction and became self-evident.[144]

This understanding of the importance of the Persian Gulf anchored two January 1980 speeches by Jimmy Carter. First came the televised address shortly after the New Year that opened the chapter and was accompanied by the globe and map. Carter drove home the message that the Soviet Union's occupation of Afghanistan was a "stepping stone to possible control over much of the world's oil supplies."[145] On January 21, 1980, the president delivered the State of the Union and announced the Carter Doctrine: "Let our position be absolutely clear:

An attempt by any outside force to gain control of the Persian Gulf region will be regarded as an assault on the vital interests of the United States of America, and such an assault will be repelled by any means necessary, including military force."[146] Observers noted the striking similarity with Lansdowne's 1903 declaration stating the same notion from a British perspective.[147] The Carter administration, along with journalists, academics, and the emerging world of think tanks arrayed a fixed territorial zone where energy sources, shipping lanes, military bases, and arms markets became assets that could be portrayed as vital to the international affairs of the United States. While the regional boundaries had to remain porous, to allow circulation of oil, contracts, and dollars, in order for it to be protect the area had to be contained.[148]

"The Global Zone of Percolating Violence"

The geopolitical concept of the Arc of Crisis was both a description and a prognosis of how the region's destabilization would threaten US national interests. In 1981, the American strategy to confront the crisis was outlined in the annual military statement by the Joint Chiefs of Staff:

> The United States has a number of major interests in the region comprising the Middle East, the Persian Gulf, and the Northwest Indian Ocean. These interests involve access by the US and its allies to the resources of the area, most notably oil from the Persian Gulf States-to include protection of transportation routes for the flow of that oil to North America, Western Europe and Japan . . . In the past year, the United States has taken a number of steps to improve the military balance in Southwest Asia. US objectives call for a greater military presence, a capability to surge additional forces into the region, and access to facilities sufficient to support both peacetime presence and contingency operations.[149]

This paved the way for what Daniel Sargent calls the fashioning of "a regional acceptance of a US military protectorate."[150] The first step in actualizing the Carter Doctrine was to build a new logistics architecture out of existing military investments, much of it left over from Britain's engagements. Although since 1949 the United States shared certain Bahraini port facilities with the British in what was known as the Command Middle East Force, the fleet was small and the logistics platform was limited until the Tanker War in the 1980s in which the US Navy protected oil carriers (see chapter 4). After the 1990–91 Gulf War, the US Fifth Fleet was reactivated to cover the Persian Gulf, the

Red Sea, and the Arabian Sea. In the wake of the Carter Doctrine the United States invested in various ports and airfields in Kenya, Somalia, Egypt, and Masirah, an island off of Oman. In addition to spending $200 million to re-furbish its newly acquired airfields and ports in Oman, the US government spent three times that in four years to expand the facilities in Diego Garcia, which had been a British outpost.[151] As part of a "Strategic Island Concept" advocated by a naval planner, US and British officials collaborated to secretly remove two thousand inhabitants from the Indian Ocean attule.[152] Built by the long-time Navy contractor Brown and Root, the base is seven thousand miles closer to the Persian Gulf than major bases in the United States. Ex-pressing the sense that Diego Garcia was essential to the US security, an ana-lyst commented, "It's the single most important military facility we've got. . . . If it didn't exist, it would have to be invented."[153]

In the early 1980s, the US Navy deployed and maintained two carrier bat-tle groups in the Indian Ocean at a cost of $38 billion, a sum that covered only procurement costs and not operating costs.[154] Meanwhile, the Egyptian gov-ernment, recently coaxed away from its Soviet alignment and brought within the US security penumbra, was pinpointed as a key transit hub for the defense of the Gulf and Northern Indian Ocean. Congress approved $200 million to upgrade facilities at Ras Banas on the Red Sea. Under the Reagan adminis-tration, Washington concluded a major loan agreement with Pakistan ($3.5 billion) that included sales of F-16s and American hopes that this would lead to access to Karachi's port and airfield. These and other military investments integrated air and naval power, making Indian Ocean bases more proximate to sites in the Gulf and the navy's roaming aircraft carriers became launching pads for attacks across mountain ranges and desert expanses. These techno-logical innovations changed the balance of power in the region by recalibrat-ing the relations between time and space and by enhancing the abilities of the US multi-billion-dollar security scaffolding around the Gulf's perimeter.

The second key feature of the Carter Doctrine was the Pentagon's estab-lishment of the Rapid Deployment Joint Task Force. Creating a highly mo-bile force to respond to contingencies of the Cold War had been discussed and debated since the 1960s, when the United States faced and feared proxy wars with the Soviets in the Third World.[155] Not fully accepted by officials in the military, however, the policy was shelved until August 1977 when Sam-uel Huntington undertook a review for the National Security Council and identified the Persian Gulf as exposed to Soviet expansion.[156] It took the geo-political arguments of the late 1970s to implement the proposal under the Reagan administration.

These individual projects and agreements ultimately crystallized into the establishment of Central Command (CENTCOM) by the Department of Defense in 1983, based in Tampa and with a secondary headquarters in Qatar after 2009. This elaborate military complex was critical for the US Navy's participation in the Tanker War (1987–88), for the Reagan doctrine of "rollback" that replaced the "containment" of the Soviet Union in the Third World, for George Bush expelling Iraqi troops from Kuwait (1990–91), and the Global War on Terror waged by multiple US administrations after the September 11 attacks.

The physical and ideological preparation for war and the actual bloodlettings reinforced the geopoliticized understanding of the Gulf. This series of Gulf wars, argues Toby Jones, should be understood as "one long American war in the Middle East."[157] Alternatively, Andrew Bacevich has bitingly referred to this "permanent" or "endless" war as smuggling with it a new round of weapons sales, new logistics facilities, and hiring of associated consultants and brokers at home and abroad.[158] Much of this has been paid for by oil producers after panic-induced rises in oil revenue. With the collapse of communism, the notion of "revisionary" and "rogue" states stepped into the breach to justify the logic. Despite a brief stage in the Iran-Iraq War when the United States "tilted" toward Saddam Hussain, Iraq's ties to the Soviet Union, antimonarchical posture, and territorial claims on Kuwait made it a "revolutionary" impediment to US interests. In 1979, an actual revolutionary regime took over Iran that threatened the regimes of the Arabian Peninsula and offered a radically different understanding in which the Gulf should be guarded *against* the United States and not in alliance with it. The Twin Pillars Policy of Iran and Saudi Arabia as leading US clients crumbled and was replaced by the Clinton administration with the "dual containment" of Iran and Iraq.[159] By this time the Cooperation Council for the Arab States of the Gulf was founded in 1981. Better known as the GCC, it embodies a particular drawing of the Gulf where the Arab states of Iraq and Yemen are not members, and neither is Iran.

The Gulf was conceived of as a key vein in the circulatory structure of late twentieth-century capitalism as well as a boundary marking insiders and outsiders, the former being US allies and the latter pariah states. This tension between being a bordered territory and a circulatory pathway intersected with the interdependence between energy and security. This was martialized in one particular episode in the Iran-Iraq War. Toby Jones argues that by the 1980s oil and war lost their distinction in the Gulf.[160] In the midst of a war between two "outsiders" to the Gulf—Iran and Iraq—attacks on shipping drew the United States into the conflict, ostensibly to protect Kuwaiti super-tankers from attacks by belligerents. Re-flagged as US vessels, convoys of oil and naval vessels traveled through the length of the Gulf as a "water-born infrastructure" protecting "non-communist world oil" from Iraqi and Iranian attacks. This naval mission deepened the logistical and repair needs of the US Navy in local ports (see chapter 4). But there was more to it. The threat of mines was serious, and the value of the oil and the actual ships was immense. Jones discovered evidence that because supertankers were constructed out of heavier and stronger materials than US destroyers and frigates, the naval officers learned to position the mammoth tankers as the lead ship and protector of the naval convoys. Operation Earnest Will blurred the material and political boundaries between military and civilian energy infrastructure. Security and economic interests had become fused to such an extent that the oil tankers were showing the way and protecting military equipment and not vice versa.

Heavily policed, the Gulf has hardly been "stabilized." The military buildup did not save Carter's political fortunes, nor did the bases in Oman enable the United States to rescue the US hostages held in its embassy in Tehran. A US Delta Force operation to send helicopters from an Omani air bases to rescue the dozens of US embassy hostages failed miserably, with the burnt-out carcass of US helicopters symbolically illustrating the limits of US power. Neither did the Doctrine's policy manage, let alone end, crisis or bring stability to this region that Washington continues to view as so critical for global security. In the first decade following Brzezinski's evoking of the Arc, Afghanistan was ravaged by ceaseless war, Pakistani politics were shaped by marshal law and swings between military and civilian rule, Iran and Iraq waged an eight-year war, the Grand Mosque of Mecca was captured by opponents of the Saudi family (1979), and Sudan experienced a series of coups and regional conflicts; the list goes on. These political struggles were not interdependent, as notions of the arc or triangle would have it, nor were they precipitated by Soviet design, but these were exactly the sorts of tumults the White House and the emerging think tanks sought to diminish. Disavowing his own role in its history less than two decades later, Brzezinski described the same region as "the Global Zone of Percolating Violence."[161] The failures and limits of US geostrategic doctrines come with their own remedies—more containment, more militarization—and a greater sense of insecurity and suffering.

CONCLUSIONS

As "convenient fiction[s],"[162] geopolitical imaginaries function as alibis for limiting the territorial sovereignty of other states, redirecting public resources for particular ends, and recasting politics across an entire region. Those who defined the "Persian Question" and the "Arc of Crisis" marshaled facts, assertions, rumors, and fears to shape how policymakers, budget planners, journalists, and public opinion conceived of the world. New geographic terms, such as "the Middle East," were coined to mark the strategic value of regions for maintaining global hierarchies. As policy elites convinced themselves and others that the Persian Gulf was central to the British Empire and the US-led capitalism, the Gulf was articulated as an empty container, an enclosed, asocial vacuum requiring Anglo-American power. This territorialization of the Gulf was a mystification because it suggested that the Gulf was timeless and located outside of empire. Nothing could be further from the truth. Imperial retrenchment required continual investment to maintain a security framework.

The two watershed moments bookending this chapter—Lansdowne's parliamentary speech and the Carter Doctrine—share a similar position in the life cycles of global hegemons. I invoke "watersheds" and "decay" to describe these phases as evolutions and gradual reworkings, rather than ruptures and abrupt breaks with the past.[163] The last years of the nineteenth century and the post-1970 period are both moments of hegemonic decline and a rise of "imperialist activity."[164] Both Britain and the United States had overextended financial systems and deepening inter-state and intra-capitalist rivalries with dissent abroad and schisms at home. Geopolitical activism was as much a sign of imperial rot as vigor. Curzon, Mackinder, and Brzezinski spoke out of fear as much as strength as the terms of imperial engagement shifted but did not evaporate.

Yet the differences between these examples of geopolitical practice reveals much about modern imperialism and its relationship to region-making.

Unlike the United States, the British approach to alliance-building with local actors did not turn to sales of weapons and armaments except for the establishment's select paramilitary forces such as the South Persia Rifles and Trucial Oman Levies. In several key instances before midcentury, such as in Iran, Iraq, and the UAE, the British government even shrank from the opportunity to engage in "development" and subsidize the building of railroads and roads to penetrate the hinterlands and create markets. This frustrated imperialists like late Victorian travelers but also Indian industrialists and Gulf-based merchants seeking to make private earnings from public expenses. British military sales only anchored relations with Arab Gulf states after independence, something that was certainly helped along by a succession of princes attending the Royal Military Academy at Sandhurst. It is a peculiarity of late capitalism and US power in the Gulf that military power and economic power have been fused via the production, sale, and service of weapons to allied states as well as an array of logistics providers and consultants.

A second difference between the policies emanating from Curzon and Brzezinski's imaginaries is the oscillation toward state territoriality and then away from it by century's end. Britain had gained its position of power in the Gulf region after capturing port cities, focusing its attention on securing communication and supply lines, and working with specific merchants and tribal leaders in a world where state sovereignty and boundaries had not yet been firmly inscribed. As British firms and colonial officers articulated a new regional order through concessionary agreements, communication infrastructures, and related bordering projects, a more territorialized conception of the region carried with it other forms of spatialized politics. Even prior to the world wars and the birth of international organizations, the "integrity" of nations and a racialized notion of peoples were deployed by Britain and aspiring sovereigns to conceive of national markets and state-space. As we shall see in the next chapter, nation-states as sovereign territorial polities developed further, and the international state system was elaborated with differing levels of independence underwritten by law.

Hence, the geopoliticized Gulf did not dissolve the region into a single polity, and US hegemonic aspirations had to contend with the checkerboard of territorial projects in the decades after World War II. By the 1970s, however, US geopolitical thinking shifted away from employing state territories to accrue wealth and power and toward employing a constellation of infrastructures ensuring circulation and profits via gateways and corridors. Territorial borders and state-centric international law may have "represented a solution to security projects" in the earlier epoch, but the use of classical geopolitical terminology by Brzezinski came at a time when fears of non-state actors, the geoeconomics of a rising Asia, and attention to ideas about "human security" and "environmental security" were gaining a toehold among grand strategists contemplating a "security 'after geopolitics.'"[165] To stabilize what became known as the "Arc of Crisis," the strategy and its side effects were no longer creating spheres of influence over nation-states but instead relied more heavily on a combination of mobile military forces and bases "beyond the horizon" of the Gulf, some of which was were legacies of the legal and material infrastructures of the late British Empire. Alliances and inter-state relations marked as "special friendships" did not disappear, but as early as 1974 Brzezinski and others had latched onto the idea that "nation-states are losing their centrality."[166] The policies emanating from the turbulence of the 1970s were part of a recalibration away from state space to new forms of territoriality composed of air bases, islands, logistics hubs, and US military advisors seconded to foreign governments buying military arsenals hand over fist. These enclaves articulated a "pointillist empire" of US bases, quasi-independent territories, and patchwork of extraterritorialities.[167]

If the Persian Gulf region was a lifeblood for capitalism, as it had come to be imagined in the midcentury era, it could not be left to market forces or local governments. Oil had to cycle through to benefit the United States' own energy and military industries, two of the most profitable sectors in the country's declining manufacturing sector.[168] Announcing a major increase in the military budget in 1981, Caspar Weinberger, the defense secretary of the United States, vividly captured how US strategy "must still be anchored in certain geopolitical realities. One of these realities is our dependence on foreign energy sources. The umbilical cord of the industrial free world runs through the Strait of Hormuz into the Arabian Gulf and the nations which surround it. That area, Southwest Asia and the Gulf, is and will be the fulcrum of contention for the foreseeable future." He concluded, "We cannot deter . . . [the Soviet Union] from seven thousand miles away. We have to be there. We have to be there in a credible way."[169]

The Persian Gulf was a valuable "umbilical cord" that needed nursing to ensure circulation and the vitality of US-led capitalism. Despite the

differences across a century of empire-making, the geopolitical conception
of the Gulf as a space of instability and an incubator of threats is remarkably
enduring. The British-Indian colonial and inter-state alliance system that
marked the Gulf since the early twentieth century had been repurposed into
a patchwork of air bases, shipping lanes, and port facilities eerily similar to
that which prevailed in the eighteenth and early nineteenth centuries. Even
the role of private armies and extraterritorial instruments (e.g., free trade
zones, outsourced labor, flags of convenience) suspending state regulations
would not be entirely out of place in the earlier age of European imperialism. By the end of the twentieth century, the United States' logistics archipelago was built in part on preexisting British colonial outposts designed for
a more frictionless and less territorially oriented fix to "securing" the region
for US hegemony and the global economy (see chapter 4). In this conception the sea sits outside of society and is an empty plane or what military
strategists today describe as a "maritime domain" and a "vast maritime maneuver space."[170] Harkening back to arguments about sea power made by
Mahan, this twenty-first century securitization of the seas has expanded to
envelop the entire globe, with the US Navy defining its objectives as follows: "Forward-deployed and forward-stationed naval forces use the global
maritime commons as a medium of maneuver, assuring access to overseas regions, defending key interests in those areas, protecting our citizens
abroad, and preventing our adversaries from leveraging the world's oceans
against us. The ability to sustain operations in international waters far from
our shores constitutes a distinct advantage for the United States—a Western Hemisphere nation separated from many of its strategic interests by
vast oceans."[171] The geographer Neil Smith emphasized that the narrative of
America globalism is not simply a temporal one marked by the rise and fall
of "the American Century" but a geographic sea change in which US power
has been re-spatialized.[172]

This making of a geopoliticized Gulf was more a process of assembly
than of forging. It entailed piecemeal moves and spatial contradictions. As
the previous chapter argued, the Persian Gulf's vistas were always extended
well beyond its immediate littorals. Today the Gulf not only encompasses
decision-makers in Washington, Beijing, and Moscow but commanders of
CENTCOM headquartered in MacDill Air Force Base in Tampa, Florida,
and drone operators in Kansas, who geographically extend "the kill chain"

from the Middle East to the Midwest. This swelling of the Gulf intersects with the power of new technologies to obliterate space and the long history of conceiving of the United States as an exceptionalist continental power protected by two oceans. US actions in the Gulf boomerang back and are reflected in police departments becoming armed with equipment from the Global War of Terror and the US occupation of Iraq. The United States, therefore, is both inside and outside of this geopoliticized Gulf. This geographic expansion has been accompanied by the simultaneous narrowing of what constitutes "the inside." If at the time of the Carter Doctrine, it was the Soviet Union that was deemed an "outside force," since then the doctrine has been directed at Iran, Iraq, or both ("dual containment"), who have been labeled rogue actors beyond the "international maritime community." The ensuing policies and posturing displace Iran and Iraq beyond the boundaries of some twenty-first-century Gulf regionalizations. In these inclusions and exclusions are tensions, and debate about who is the cause of instability or who has the right to be in the Gulf bubbles up at every turn. Disagreements are refracted through nationalist debates about the waterway's naming, which are part of the vexed history of enclosing the Persian Gulf.

Throughout the twentieth century, the geopoliticized Gulf did not connote a set of societies or a community of polities but merely an abstract geography to be seized and controlled. Struggles and conflicts within these societies or connections across them were simply irrelevant unless they were detected in threat assessments. To British geopolitical practitioners, instability came in the form of the backwardness of societies and the menace of pirates. To more recent US grand strategists, these ideas and prejudices were newly packaged as failed states and hotbeds of terrorism. Policymakers in London and Washington never considered that the polities of the littorals were interested in or capable of constructing multilateral agreements to address impending instability or foreign adventurism. Geopolitical thinkers are conditioned to see geography as an object of struggle. They draw our attention to space not merely being a place where conflict occurs but also the source of it. Yet they are wedded to a notion of space as natural and inevitable, rather than malleable and variegated, and ultimately one that obfuscates the social. The reminder of the book will explore the multitude of networks unfolding alongside of this history but producing very distinct projects for the Gulf.

THREE

DIVIDED SOVEREIGNTIES

AT THE END OF WORLD WAR I, Lord Curzon was confronted by a new Iranian predicament threatening British hegemony in the Persian Gulf—a region he had helped to conceive. Iran's politicians claimed that as an independent state they should have representation at the Paris Peace Conference for the birth of the new international order. Curzon had once defended Iranian "integrity" as a wedge against Russia; now the foreign secretary, Curzon countered that as a neutral party in the Great War, Iran did not warrant a place at the negotiating table. The disappointed Iranian delegation was sent home, and Iran was denied representation at the Paris Peace Conference. In its stead, London seized on the newly founded Soviet Union's decision to abrogate tsarist-era treaties and withdraw its troops from Iran after the 1917 Revolution, working through an ineffectual Qajar court and cabinet composed of several paid British allies to sign the 1919 Anglo-Persian Agreement.[1] Although it reiterated Iran's independence and extended loans to the shah, the 1919 agreement was a bid to transform Iran into a "veiled British protectorate" by, among other things, assigning Iranian-paid British advisors to the treasury and military and granting Britain exclusive oil-drilling rights in the north as well as south.[2] At this very moment when international law began to define sovereign states as equal, treaties such as this one became the mechanism to maintain primacy and hiving away key zones from self-rule.

The 1919 agreement was a response to the British government's quandary of how to maintain the integrity and territorial sovereignty of Iran to deflect colonial competitors while also limiting the effective power of rulers, let alone Iranian citizens, to make policy that might contravene British interests, which included stakes in the emerging an oil-centered global capitalism and the slow transition away from coal as the dominant form of fossil fuel. This treaty was reflective of a moment in which imperialism was superseded by internationalism, defined as a project based on ostensibly equal and independent states and institutions representing all of them despite the hierarchies of power.[3] Treaties were a disavowal of imperial relations and the geopolitical setting since they were agreements made by sovereign entities—the British monarch and the local ruler, the shah, or the native shaykh. Armed with a conception of the Gulf as a homogeneous region, British policymakers sought to transport treaties that were signed with rulers in eastern Arabia to neighboring contexts. This chapter explores this concatenation of empire, nation-state, and internationalism to trace the ways that struggles over sovereignty articulated a regionalization of the Gulf that was spatially less abstract but geographically more fractured as political-legal instruments shaped power.

From the banks of the Persian Gulf, empire and state are not alternative political formations that appear in sequence but coeval and even interdependent. This chapter will outline this through a comparative telling of histories of treaties, both those that survived and those that were overturned. Even before 1919, international recognition of sovereignty and heads of states was intimately tied to maintaining global hierarchies and fashioning "domestic" sovereignty, or the ability of a single ruler or dynasty to claim and exert exclusive control within demarcated borders. Thus, approaching these treaties from the perspective of the Gulf allows us to draw out patterns and points of intersection missed in national-centered histories or approaches that treat sovereignty as purely ornamental.

Sovereignty surfaced not as a uniform attribute of state rule but a negotiated outcome of political and economic strategies of imperialism.[4] Contrary to the Hobbesian tendency to view sovereignty as transhistorical, universal, and indivisible, the experiences of the Gulf littoral support the contention that the set of practices that make up sovereignty are historically contingent and relational. These histories suggest that international organizations, oil firms, and the persistence of British protected states along the Gulf are actually what determined sovereignty. This regional history illustrates the chasm between defining sovereignty as merely international recognition instead of conceiving of sovereignty as popular self-determination and effective control.[5] The blurring genres of sovereignty are not evidence of empires in decline or the agency of people from "the periphery" but the necessary anchoring of rule by signatories of treaties within national and transnational societies at a specific moment of capitalist development.[6]

Although state formation was relational, it did not transpire in the same way along the Gulf's littoral. In the port cities of Arabia, where Britain forged treaties and agreements in the early nineteenth century, the balance of power had to be calibrated to meet the requisites of the signatories—to wit, ruling families and British-Indian officers representing the Crown. Domains of power were reserved for colonial administrators as well as native rulers in a composite or divided sovereignty. Independence came late—1961 when the Sabah ruler terminated the Anglo-Kuwaiti Treaty of 1899; 1971 for Bahrain, Qatar, and the UAE—and was more granted than seized. Although these colonial arrangements were contested by residents and foreign governments, the jointly constructed pacts gave rulers considerable autonomy from domestic contenders for power. If the British helped manufacture self-rule by "traditional" rulers in some places, in other parts of the Gulf they sought to limit the autonomy of rulers. In Iran, Iraq, and Saudi Arabia the timing and political context of the treaties was quite different. Coming later and during an era of decolonization, treaties and concessions in Iran and Iraq were confronted by emergent mass politics and an understanding of sovereignty as self-determination.

Simultaneously, the chapter demonstrates that the conception of the Gulf region as an abstract enclosed space was interlaced with the production of a whole thicket of boundaries dividing territories, properties, peoples, and even sovereignties. With one of the main characteristics of the treaties being divided sovereignty, or the fracturing of political authority between different entities holding power over distinct domains such as subjects, sectors of the economy, or policy areas. In this process, the Persian Gulf regional whole was simultaneously arrayed as a set of sovereign nation-states with rulers inhabiting this form of regionalization in distinct ways. In doing so these heads of state reconstituted state sovereignty in relation to projects existing at many geographic scales.

EMPIRE BY TREATY AND THE DUALITY OF AUTHORITY

Despite Ottoman and Iranian imperial ambitions and European geopolitical bluster, for centuries no single polity unified the territories and peoples of the Persian Gulf under a single jurisdiction. High degrees of social dispersion were an obstacle against unification, as was the spread of wealth among seafaring communities, pockets of agrarian society, and pastoralists living on the Arabian Peninsula and the Iranian Plateau. Added to this were the mobility and socially networked nature of these maritime and nomadic societies, which made it difficult to tax surplus and concentrate political power. Individuals and entire communities could too easily flee or switch loyalty in response to such attempts. Mobility, communal property, and translocal investments, rather than fixed assets, conveyed political power in these overlapping societies, which were often organized around kinship and tribal bonds.

Even at its zenith at the end of World War I, Britain's empire in India had effective control over only portions of the lands adjacent to the waterway and even then preferred to rule these spaces via bursts of gunpowder and a hodgepodge of localized intermediaries, rather than an integrated administration. In fact, it was the contested and oscillating nature of political authority that both generated British anxieties as well as offered an alibi for constructing protected states, mandates, and economic concessions. Rather than simply bringing about peace, this geopoliticization of the Gulf—the discursive construction of social space into a fenced-in object and target of the great powers—unleashed struggles over demarcating borders, establishing exclusionary agreements, and identifying places as vital frontiers for imperial survival and global order.

"External" affairs bled into "internal" relations when British mercantile interests were reflected in the political agreements. These treaties signed by the British Indian government and "friendly" Arabs focused on regulating pearling and commerce and were expanded to freeze out rivals, initially France and later Russia and Germany. Beginning with the General Maritime Treaty of 1820, a series of treaties initially focused on regulating "the pirate coast" at the mouth of the Strait of Hormuz and ending slavery. In return for maintaining the peace, carrying registration papers, and flying a red flag with white markings, "pacified" Arabs were entitled to British protection. At various moments in the nineteenth century, Britain's Bombay Marine fleet attacked ships it accused of plundering and challenged the signatory shaykhs, who did not or could not uphold their end of the bargain by fining violators of this first treaty. In fact, the autonomous port city of Dubai headed by the Maktoum family traces its history to 1833 when about one-fifth of the population of Abu Dhabi fled as a result of a dispute over succession and the unwillingness of one branch of the federation to abide by the treaty and pay compensation for an attack on a British vassal.

Protections and Exclusions

Britain's treaties with rulers on the Arabian littoral of the Gulf were transactional in that Britain recognized particular families as ruling dynasties in return for shaykhs agreeing to British oversight over trade, concessions, international affairs, and jurisdiction over "foreigners" in their territories, while responsibility for "natives" was handed over to recognized local rulers. Britain's focus at the beginning of the century was the Lower Gulf, which immediately abutted the transportation and communication channels to South Asia and eastern Africa. These maritime peace treaties excluded some powerful tribal groups, yet for the signatory families, the agreements marked them as sharing the same status as the government of Britain. In their implementation, the treaties fused the interests of the signatories and translated this into greater profits for many mariners and traders. The temporary treaties were renewed and became permanent in 1853 with the Treaty of Perpetual Maritime Peace.[7] In subsequent documents signed in the second half of the nineteenth century, the more explicitly enumerated articles turned to preventing "tribal chiefs" or "rulers" from establishing diplomatic and economic relations with other governments as well as protecting British subjects. Individual rulers were obligated to cease raiding British shipping and remain at peace with the British government as well as all the other Gulf signatories; they pledged to return debtors who fled to their territories and reckon with "plunder and piracy," which included slave and arms trafficking. For instance, after the Trucial shaykhs signed a treaty in 1897, each of them became responsible for the debts of absconders who fled to their lands.[8] As raiding was made more risky and nascent forms of sovereign territoriality were practiced, the strategic asset of mobility on land and sea became devalued and even a liability (at least for those unwilling to take on the risk of being labeled as smugglers).

To oversee the implementation of all of these treaties, a more centralized agency system was incrementally elaborated. A British Agent was housed in Qeshm and the office was unified in 1822 under the British Resident in Bushehr with agents in over a dozen other towns.[9] The resident system drew from British officials from the India Political Service, who gradually replaced personnel from the English East India Company. Agents for each designated location reported to the Resident. These officers invariably had experience in India and Iran, but after World War II, they increasingly came from tours in eastern Africa and British mandates in the Arab world. Equally critical were Muslims and Hindus from India and local "native agents" drawn from the Indian Ocean world of merchants, who operated as intermediaries between the colonial administration, the ruling families, and commercial networks.[10] This native agency system that worked in tandem with the British residency came to an end at the turn of the century with more direct British oversight and unmediated collaboration with ruling families.[11] Finally, to police the waters of the Gulf, a naval squadron and port headquarters were based on the island of Hengam until the 1930s, at which point Reza Shah's government removed them; they relocated to Bahrain in 1935.[12] These are the same naval facilities that have been the headquarters for the US Fifth Fleet until today.

The common feature across eastern Arabia was a system of protected states with dual sovereignty parsed out between British officials and ruling shaykhs and shot through with extraterritoriality.[13] While the British officials were given exclusive rights to represent recognized rulers in relations with foreign governments, British subjects, primarily people from India, were bestowed protection from the British military and given access to the British legal system. When the ruler of Ajman, an emirate just north of Dubai and Sharjah, sought to expel an Indian merchant, the latter objected: "We are British subjects of his majesty's glorious empire," as the businessman wrote. After the British navy arrived on the scene, the ruler of Ajman apologetically acquiesced, "I beg your pardon and apologize to you for what happened. . . . I am prepared to comply with any order that you may have for me."[14] Unlike Aden, which was the only full-fledged British Crown Colony, local inhabitants of eastern Arabia were British subjects only outside of their home territories; until 1892 only sailors who were British subjects were permitted to fly the British flag.[15] After World War I, British subjects residing in eastern Arabia were obliged to register with Political Agents. Similarly, the boundary between the sovereignty of the British government and "the ruler" was vague and shifted depending on the degree of leverage enjoyed by rulers and the interests of British officers and firms. Initially, Bahrain and Kuwait were the primary focus of British energies with places like Dubai, Sharjah, Abu Dhabi, and Doha remaining peripheral until the mid-twentieth century.

By the 1880s and 1890s, the treaties developed into what were termed exclusive agreements, which constituted new polities out of Bahrain, Kuwait, Oman, and the Trucial States and turned them into British-protected states. Qatar joined this list in 1916. Notably, these treaties, which often contravened other agreements made by the parties with Ottoman rulers, were secret and not publicly recognized by the British until decades later.[16] The reasons for their secrecy included both parties not wanting to provoke Ottoman ire and also to protect the shaykhs from local criticism. Meanwhile, from the vantage point of the twentieth century, we too easily overlook the potential shaykhs and emirates that sought recognition and either never received it (as in Basra and Khorramshahr/Muhammara); received it, only to have it withdrawn (as in Kalba, which today is part of Sharjah); or gained it after great delay (as in Fujairah).[17] In general the British treaty system privileged tribal leaders in coastal cities over those in the interior.

Treaties became more detailed in the early twentieth century and defined the ways that the British government, British firms, and Gulf rulers gained more financial power over lucrative resources and trade. As the principal British-Indian colonial authority, the British Political Resident of the Gulf had oversight over economic concessions, initially pearling, banking, and later oil exploration and air transportation.[18] While this facilitated British firms and their agents to gain monopolies, such as in shipping lines, colonial officers conceived of the exclusive agreements as a tool to bar rivals, such as German, French, Russia, and US companies, from the region. Oil concessions, especially in the lower Gulf, for example, were not driven by a shortage of crude; there was no lack of supply at this point thanks to operations in Iran and Kuwait. What oil companies such as the Anglo Persian Oil Companies (APOC, later Anglo Iranian Oil Company, British Petroleum, and BP) operating in in the Upper Gulf craved was control to manage supply and inflate prices. The concessions also locked in future streams of revenue for the rulers, who in some cases signed the concessions in the name of their family, rather than the state.[19]

The exclusionary character of these treaties dictated relations between Gulf rulers by drawing a line between neighbors. When the Iranian government proposed that certain disputes could be settled if Tehran negotiated directly with the rulers of the protected states, Britain rejected this option, stating that Iran could negotiate only with the British government.[20] Similarly, in 1900, when the ruler of Abu Dhabi sought to negotiate directly with the Persian governor of the southern province to address activities in Lengeh, British officials in Tehran and eastern Arabia intervened to punish what they deemed a violation of the Exclusive Treaty of 1892.[21] Defining and policing the threshold between "domestic" and "foreign" relations was embedded in Britain's powers as enforcer of these treaties.

These treaties positioned British officials in hierarchically powerful roles but in doing so defined local sovereignty in the person of the individual signatories of these compacts. Administratively it was logical for Britain to identify and deal with a single "shaykh" and their small circle of kin, rather than a collective or council, to govern these societies. "In all matters of communication with the British government," writes the historian of the UAE, Frauke Heard-Bey, "the sole addresses in every state were the rulers. Since the early nineteenth century the status of an incumbent ruler had usually been much enhanced by the importance which the 'High Government' placed on a 'Trucial Ruler' to the exclusion of a tribal sheikh in the interior."[22] Empires always strove to minimize costs, and in response to the 1857 Mutiny, British Crown-rule devised systems of indirect control to enlist "princely states" and shaykhs to manage local resistance and displace responsibilities in more "culturally" appropriate ways.[23]

The shaykhs used these compacts to gain autonomy from land-based imperial powers and local rivals, including other family members. These rulers used their rights to British protection, or even the mere specter of British involvement, to establish political autonomy from tribute-collecting Ottoman governors in Istanbul, Baghdad, and Basra who lacked the necessary funds, communications networks, or local alliances to make their nominal authority effective. British protection gained currency for the rulers of the ports and oasis towns that would later become Kuwait, Bahrain, Qatar, and Saudi Arabia because "it became apparent that it was more steadfast in support than the

Ottoman state while demanding less in return."[24] From Istanbul's perspective, the signs of former Ottoman representatives actively currying British favor constituted an "insidious creep of London's influence."[25]

Succession of rulers was assured only after the new ruler agreed to honor the treaties.[26] At least in parts of the region, by the late nineteenth century the British had the final approval over all successions, and after World War II a formal ceremony was instituted in which the new shaykh would agree to abide by the treaties before being upgraded to the head of state.[27] When rulers ran afoul of colonial objectives, Britain intervened. In 1928, during the struggle for succession in Abu Dhabi, British officials tipped the balance in favor of the younger Shakhbut, enabling him to beat out his uncle and brother to the position of the ruler.[28] Ironically, almost for decades later the British had to step in to remove Shaykh Shakhbut and usher Shaykh Zayed to power in Abu Dhabi. A year earlier in 1965, members of the Sharjah's ruling family collaborated with some of the very same British officials and Trucial Oman Scouts to remove its ruler. Unlike Shakhbout, Sheikh Saqr bin Sultan al-Qasimi, a descendant of the famous al-Qasimi maritime confederation of earlier centuries, was an "enthusiastic modernizer" and was involved in many literary and cultural circles extending to Beirut, Damascus, Cairo, and Kuwait. He was closely associated with Nasserist, Pan-Arab, and Pro-Palestinian politics, however, which was enough to render him a threat to British colonial agendas. British colonial officers and members of the royal family accused him of lacking commitment to Sharjah's treaty obligations and deposed him, placing his cousin in rule.

However, in recognizing a particular person or "tribe" as the authority worthy of protection, geopolitical thinkers and colonial officers made a series of assumptions about local societies.[29] Rather than being pyramidal in structure, tribal societies in eastern Arabia were horizontally oriented, with the multitude of leaders or shaykhs wielding influence over allies and kin rather than exercising power over subjects. Alliances were critical in warfare and the sharing of scarce resources and were forged through marriage, communal pastoral lands, and payment of tribute. This model of tribal leadership implies collective leadership, even if one individual or branch of the family had wrested final authority. Bedouin tribal communities also had little leverage against merchants who enjoyed mobility and access to ports across the Gulf and Indian Ocean. Thus, while tribal leaders could try to collect tolls and taxes by threatening populations in towns and raid caravans and ships, they also depended on merchants and townspeople for loans and gifts. Andrea Rugh astutely reads these cases as indicating that "the British overestimated the abilities of chiefs to enforce maritime infractions. The chiefs increasingly found themselves caught between the forceful demands of the British and their desire to maintain the loyalty of their tribes."[30] This predicament facing the shaykhs is a product of the different kinds of sovereignty at play in the treaties and the obligations they imposed on the signatories.

Moreover, the tribal system aimed at devising consensus, something that was denied by the British system of vertical sovereignty. When shaykhs compromised or made concessions to others, the British presumptuously construed this as weakness and recalcitrance rather than a means to build alliances and strengthen leadership. Although not without violence and inequality, it was a highly negotiated form of power that was overturned by British-sponsored patrimonialism. By designating a single person and its branch of a tribal confederation as the ruler, they made certain figures and groups more powerful than their preexisting resources and social status warranted. By requiring that these rulers remain accountable to the demands of the British Empire and not necessarily the demands of members of their societies, these treaties underwrote authoritarianism.

Put differently, these treaty systems were enormously beneficial to those individuals recognized as rulers by the British. These rulers, or would-be rulers, were currying the favor of colonial officers as early as the 1820s, hoping to secure the benefits bestowed by the British.[31] Rulers such as Mubarak in Kuwait were primarily driven by a desire to accumulate personal wealth from newly commodified land and to collect tax receipts across newly articulated borders.[32] The recognized rulers became protected clients unwilling to challenge and yet able to implement these agreements, which made the shaykhs "No longer 'first among equals.'" With the treaty system, however, "chiefs had become 'pinnacles' of power, and their constituents had lost their leverage to transfer elsewhere."[33] In fact, it was now the British agents and the rulers of these protected states who enjoyed the power to remove people by deporting them or legally erasing them by denying them citizenship.[34]

The rulers and their closest allies in their tribal federation were strengthened by the material gains that accrued to them as recipients of royalties for commercial agreements—ranging from issuing pearling licenses to extending concessions for oil exploration to permitting the construction of aircraft landing strips and refueling depots on their territories. In this regard, states were empowered by the legal principle in the Middle East that subsoil rights belong to the state rather than individual property owners, as was the case in the United States and pre-1917 Russia. This was explicitly understood as a quid pro quo by British officers, such as in 1939 when the British Political Resident in Dubai concluded that "a key reason for the goodwill between the British and the rulers was that negotiations over air [transportation facilities] and oil gave the rulers a square deal which carried a money bag rather than a big stick."[35] The nature of the treaty relation encouraged an unmediated bond. Rupert Hay, the Political Resident of the Gulf (1941–53), described relations between a ruler and his political agent as "those of personal friends and a Ruler is prone to dislike any similar association between his Political Agent and any of his subjects. I remember that the late Shaikh Ahmad of Kuwait once said to me that the best Political Agent he ever had was one who had no dealing with any Kuwaiti other than himself."[36]

The most concrete and momentous implication of divided sovereignty manifested itself in citizenship regimes and the protracted building of national borders. In 1919 the Bahrain Order-in-Council expanded the powers of the British Political Agent, assigning jurisdiction over all "foreigners" to the British agent and placing Sheikh Isa in charge of all "natives."[37] In theory this categorization of persons generated a parallel legal system with the abolition of private courts in 1923 and the founding of a Bahraini state court for natives, while "foreigners" received extraterritorial protection via British imperial courts.[38] During World War II similar orders were issued for the other protected Arab states of the Gulf to clarify which denizens were under British protection and which ones would be treated as natives subject to local rulers. In theory, this categorization of populations was to manage social conflicts and to distribute the responsibility of governance. In the reality of a highly comingled society with increasingly stratified workplaces, such as the oil fields, the courts became a site of conflict between dueling administrators and people seeking state redress for social harm that could not be captured in the neat binary categories of native and foreigner. This was only exacerbated by land laws that both privatized communal lands and tied ownership to citizenship (see chapter 5).[39] The focus of government rule, or governmentality, was as much people as it was territory.

The new legal categories of natives and foreigners had far-reaching ramifications for the circulatory labor migration that had long knitted together the

Gulf littoral. Beginning in Bahrain in the 1920s, British officials created a licensing system in which seasonal pearling laborers who traveled from beyond the immediate port cities were designated as "foreign" and were required to have a sponsor. While debt was a means of control by moneylenders and merchants, this system placed responsibility for a worker's fate in the sponsor's hands, often a ship captain, including a set departure date that would be recorded by the colonial office. These "No Objection Certificates" were the first iteration of what would become the guest worker program, or *kafala* system in the second half of the twentieth century. This method addressed the objectives of British officials, firms, and rulers of regulating migration, ensuring the deportability of these laborers when demand declined or their demands escalated and ultimately wage suppression to enhance returns on capital. The system, which came to be known as kafala, expanded in subsequent decades as millions of workers from within and beyond the Gulf were recruited for the burgeoning oil industry and its many offshoot enterprises.

If the British had jurisdiction over "foreigners," the rest of the inhabitants were subjects of the rulers and members of the political body. As such, defining juridical boundaries was about codifying national difference by setting the boundaries of citizenship. Who counted as local or native could be defined in terms of residency and genealogy. Pinning down people's identity based on location was complicated by the circulatory migratory patterns of the littoral society and nomadic peoples. Nonetheless, the initial nationality laws typically tied citizenship to residency in a particular place at a particular moment. To become a Kuwaiti national one had to demonstrate residence in Kuwait in 1921, to become Emirati one had to prove residence in the Emirates in 1925, and so forth. Not a simple matter, both because of the seasonality and communal nature of residence and the informal nature of documents and records. National belonging was also delimited by a temporal boundary associated with the pre-oil era and the imperative to exclude newcomers from the nation's wealth. Communal attachments were also interwoven with notions of purity, lineage, and tribal allegiance to the ruler or the nation. These categories were always imprecise—allegiances of people to kin and tribes shifted and were up for negotiation. It was unclear who could demonstrate allegiance on behalf of whom and what role notions of Arabness, gender, and religious sect had to do with being a member of the nation.

These questions and all claims to belonging are not empirical ones but rather deeply political questions with implications for who would have the rights and responsibilities of citizenship, who would be rendered stateless or only partially incorporated, and who would be classified as a "guest worker" with no meaningful pathway to naturalization. Without the possibility of becoming citizens, the bulk of the population in the UAE have come "permanently deportable," to use Noora Lori's term.[40] By the end of the twentieth century, the segregation of "guest workers" workers in Arab Gulf states had become a consensus that underpins the nation and for many citizens justified paternalistic rule by monarchs. Similarly, Alex Boodrookas narrates the history of the bifurcation of labor in Kuwait into "national" and "migrant" as constitutive of the history of a "deportation state."[41] This is a past fused with the treaty system and concessionary capitalism.

Discontents and Mobilizations

In his ethnography of Kuwait, Peter Lienhardt recounts how in the 1950s, the notion of a single person as the ruler was still not socially accepted, and the term *shaykh* was reserved for any member of the ruling family and not just the official ruler.[42] This not only illustrates the gulf between the colonial model and political practice but also alludes to the contested nature of the ruler's singular standing. At the time that Lienhardt was making his first field trips to Kuwait and the Trucial States, the fractious relationship between the rulers and the ruled was quite raw, with discontent brewing from the political and socioeconomic dislocations of the previous half-century.

In the 1930s, the power of the British-recognized shaykhs was questioned by residents of Kuwait, Dubai, Bahrain, and other protected states.[43] A blend of merchants, dissident members of ruling families, unemployed seafarers, indebted pearl divers, porters and dock workers, and pastoralists denied access to newly privatized land advocated for courts of justice, measures to monitor state revenues and expenditures, and the abolishment of the ruling family's monopolies. New social groups, including taxi drivers and laborers toiling in the oil industries, joined in demanding what amounted to popular representation in governance. Protesters called for state funds to be used for public services, including investments in education as well as establishing municipalities, something already created in Manama, the capital of Bahrain, in 1920. These struggles against arbitrary power were informed by wider discourses in the Indian Ocean and Arab worlds that circulated at the turn of the century via newspapers, books, organizations (e.g., Islamic Leagues), and visiting dissidents brought to the region across land borders and via steamships.[44] Because the focus of these demands centered on the creation of consultative legislative councils (majles) or assemblies with binding power, they came to be known as majles movements. Councils already existed and brought members of the ruling families into regular communication with merchants and other locals, but these groups were largely informal and their advisory role did not have binding power.

Protestors demanded the establishment of legislative councils in order to address social inequalities and the unwillingness of rulers to spend newly recouped revenues to improve infrastructure, enhance commerce, and respond to unemployment in the wake of the pearl crash. Not unlike Iran during its concessionary era, Kuwaitis, Bahrainis, and Dubaians proposed that these councils oversee and draft budgets based on the revenue resulting from agreements with British firms. The goal was to earmark these windfalls for public works and urban planning, rather than leave them to the discretion of the ruler and their personal purse. It was imagined that the proposed councils would review all expenditures, and only after royalties and concessionary payments went to *state* treasuries would rulers receive preestablished sums for their personal expenses.

The struggles around consultative bodies and political accountability in the inter-war era, as well as again in the late 1950s and early 1960s, constituted a response to how power was distributed under the British. The conditions for dissent were many, including divisions within the ruling families, with some ruling family members participating in these insurrections for accountability and reform. In the 1930s, motivations for upending the status quo were rife. Arab merchants, concentrated in the pearling sector, suffered from the global depression and the relative rise of Persian traders specializing in foodstuffs and textiles. Society as a whole was rearticulated by the restructuring of the economy including the early windfalls from oil and other concessions that were flowing disproportionality to the rulers as workers in the oil sector suffered from squalid living conditions (see chapter 5). Simultaneously, intellectual influences and political threats from neighboring Iraq, Iran, and Saudi Arabia persisted (including a Saudi embargo on Kuwait; see below).

These protest movements were also intimately tied to the nature of these protected states. Despite not explicitly demanding the abdication of rulers or defecting from the trucial order, the protests were products of efforts to shed light on the dark corners of dual sovereignty. At a time of economic depression, when the merchants and mariners faced bankruptcy and indebtedness, the distinction between mostly Indian British subjects, who could claim colonial protection to seek repayment of debts, and traders and sailors who were non-British subjects shaped their plight and political attitudes.[45] Another way that the treaties generated opposition at this time was via the direct British regulation of trade. In response to the declining value of pearls, some merchants turned to trading arms, gold, and slaves, all of which violated treaties and brought them into conflict with the British security apparatus.[46]

Although there was at least one dissident voice among the Maktoum family that "demanded that Dubai be released from her treaties with Britain," the British were not initially opposed to these new demands, and in some instances even recommended "reform."[47] However, British hostility was triggered by the possibility of the councils intervening in their relations with the shaykhs and expanding the majles' ambit to include security and foreign policy issues. Thus, within months, British officials and troops sided with the rulers in their moves to neutralize and then dissolve the councils. In the case of Dubai, what the British resident described as a "democratic wave" was overturned by the mobilization of bedouin forces and British "indifference" and "misgivings" about the movement.[48] In Bahrain, where there was a richer tradition of contentious politics challenging both the ruling family and its compact with the outside powers, the movement had the broadest array of dissidents, but least space to operate.[49] The British position was far more recalcitrant, given that British officials were directly involved in removing the ruler in 1923 and the successor was highly dependent on a newly appointed "advisor," Charles Belgrave, who was "the executive chief and effectively the country's first prime minster for . . . 30 years."[50] Thus, this group of merchants, students, and laborers was stymied on the archipelago.

Despite these consultative bodies being either not created or shut down shortly after their founding, they left their mark in ways that are often denied in contemporary official narratives and forgotten by commentators enthralled by royal lineages. A closer reading of the history is a useful corrective. Mary Ann Tetreault describes 1938 as the font for Kuwait's national myth of democratic opposition, with constitutionalism and democratic ideology being viewed as homegrown rather than "as alien grafts from the imperial West."[51] For Michael Herb, the challenge to the rulers was only settled via the invention of a new form of monarchy, a "dynastic monarchy" that distributed state offices and resources across a larger swath of the ruling family rather than being in the sole control of a single monarch, or emir.[52] This new regime was replicated in other parts of the peninsula in subsequent years. The vistas of political imagination also shifted: "As part of its social reforms, the Majles decided to give financial aid to the disabled and the elderly of Dubai. New terms like 'national duty,' 'country,' instead of the 'city of Dubai,' 'revolution for reform,' which begin to appear in the documents of the Majles, reflected a change in political attitudes."[53] These reform movements were attempts to expand authority beyond the notion of the sovereign as the head of state to one that sought to socialize sovereignty by organizing the body politic and raise the question of who is the subject of sovereignty—the ruler who signed the treaty or something related to the nation or the people.

These would not be the last rounds of popular protest against the British-ruler compacts, as more protests emerged in the 1950s and 1960s.[54] Isolated labor and customs strikes and broader movements adopted new political vocabularies, influenced by communism, Third-Worldism, and both Baathist- and Nasserist-inflected Arab nationalism to galvanize groups other than merchants. In many settings, portraits of Nasser and other public symbols of veneration of the Egyptian president were as prevalent as images of shaykhs.[55] The plight of Palestinians was particularly energizing, for it implicated the British Empire. By 1950, oil laborers, organized by political parties such as the Arab Nationalist Movement and the Popular Front for the Liberation of the Oman and the Arab Gulf, were a powerful constituency suffusing sectoral demands for dismantling the racially stratified work conditions with political demands for representation, an end to British imperialism, and the expulsion of "foreigners" in order to defend the "nation." Once large numbers of men were recruited and migrated to enclave oil towns such as Ahmadi and Awali in Kuwait and Bahrain, respectively, and experienced firsthand the highly hierarchical and segregated working and living conditions dominated by British and American managers, an avowedly anti-imperialist as well as leftist opposition began to grow roots both in the host countries and the sending countries such as Oman.[56]

Given the bifurcated and uneven legal structure of the protectorate, it is not surprising that cultural difference and conceptions of belonging were present in these political movements. With the rupee as the main currency until the late 1960s, economic institutions such as the British Bank of the Middle East (formerly the Imperial Bank of Persia) and Gray Mackenzie were sometimes targeted in the same breath as "foreigners," Indians, Persians, and, in the case of Kuwait, Iraqis.[57] All of these mobilizations in the mid-twentieth century intersected with international developments, such as anti-British movements in Iraq and Iran (see below); the 1956 invasion of Egypt by Britain, France, and Israel; and the rise of anticolonial political parties. As early as 1945, two prominent Lebanese papers called for the creation of an "Arab federation of the Gulf" to replace British rule and to allocate a seat in the newly created Arab League for the federation.[58] Ruling families faced considerable pressure from their own subjects and leaders and publics in the newly independent states of the Middle East, who demanded that the monarchs cease being lackeys of the British and align their politics *and* wealth with the Arab nation and cause. In Kuwait especially, the ruling family adopted Arabism as a means to guard against internal and external opposition to the Sabah's rule; "Kuwait for the Arabs" was the slogan used by the emir to demonstrate loyalty to the Arab nation and desire for independence.[59]

The call for "Arabia for Arabs" did not dislodge ruling families or immediately oust British protection. The popular protests against the treaties between Britain and the rulers were silenced by a combination of intensive policing and collaboration between rulers and British officers, such as when the Bahrain emir paid for three political activists to be imprisoned on St. Helena in the South Atlantic Ocean.[60] But by the time independence was attained, Arabism found legal expression. Constitutions defined "the people of Kuwait are part of the Arab Nation" and inscribed the UAE's confederation as "part of the Great Arab Nation." While earlier legislation had designated citizenship largely in terms of *jus soli*, or emphasizing residence and property ownership, by the 1960s the rights of citizenship in the Arab principalities became restricted to *jus sanguine*, meaning descent, and in particular paternal lineage. Naturalization has remained very rare, limited to those who could claim Arab origin. This ethnonationalism was not a departure from what was taking place in many parts of the decolonizing world, but it was far more consequential in the littoral societies and extractive economies that hosted people from many places and for several decades. As early as the 1950s, citizens, or "nationals," became "minorities" in many places in eastern Arabia and "foreigners" were viewed as a demographic threat.

The quarter century surrounding World War II was a moment of crisis for dual sovereignty, as it was for imperialism more generally; the authority of both the shaykhs and the British was questioned. At all moments of contradiction, outcomes were not preordained, and it was the combination of the world war and the rising demand for oil that solved the challenges in favor of stabilizing the monarchy and its alliance with the British. However, instead of the colonial apparatus and treaties, it was oil revenue and oil firms that began to take on the role of patronizing rulers and guarding state territoriality. By this point the alignment of rulers with British public and private interests had only deepened through the concessionary system for oil exploration that began at the interwar era in the Upper Gulf and reached the Lower Gulf by the 1950s and 1960s. Once oil was extracted and exported, even greater royalties were paid to the rulers. This entangled British agents in the affairs of "natives" more than had been imagined when the treaties were originally penned. "The way in which the rulers dealt with domestic matters was now more closely monitored and, on occasions, severely censored," with the British authorities taking up "inter-tribal strife and the increasing number of territorial disputes in the hinterland."[61] A pillar of this emerging political economy was the expansion of policing, with colonial officers, rulers, and oil companies partnering to deploy bedouin and new police forces made up of Baluch and other "martial races" to suppress dissent. Officers seconded from the Arab Legion and other parts of the diminishing empire created local brigades to police diverse populations distinguished by occupation, "race," and residence.[62]

Oil allowed rulers to accumulate personal wealth and finance political centralization without having to make the sorts of concessions they had to in the past. Jill Crystal's examination of Kuwait and Qatari history shows that the development of the oil industry "led to withdrawal from formal political life of the merchants."[63] Although neither the capacities of merchants nor the reaction of rulers was the same in all places, by the 1950s and 1960s the expansion of the oil industry and the arrival of foreign employees generated a real estate and consumerist boom, which led to new opportunities for merchant capitalists. Rulers were able to realign merchant families, including those specifically involved in the majles movements, by offering them lucrative commercial licenses for importing goods, stakes in infrastructural projects, and carefully parceled out tracts of land just as urban growth was taking off (see chapter 5).[64] These agency agreements created lucrative monopolies but also began to refer to specific national territories rather than the Gulf region as a whole.[65] Mercantile families from southern Iran, Sindh, and elsewhere were also recruited into this political economic pattern. The high volume of exchanges generated transaction fees and customs duties that trickled back into the state coffers. The provision of (national) public goods, such as electricity and telephone services, helped incorporate the merchant class and submerge midcentury popular demands for the municipal services necessary for capital accumulation.[66] Both the sale and purchase of land, some of it reclaimed from the sea, was another means for the ruler to nurture allies in the business community.

Unlike the integrated trading, pearling, and credit systems of earlier decades that united merchants, this new political economy created competition among propertied classes and tied their surplus to the largesse of the ruling family and fixed investments. Many of the merchant families joined the coalition of material interests and political dependencies pivoting around colonial officials, ruling families, oil companies, geologists, construction firms, and a category of people conceived of as "migrant workers." The family-run state administration, rooted in the treaty system, coordinated relations between these actors and to secure land, labor, and markets on the cheap. In subsequent years, a strong discourse of royal protection developed. However, this political discourse was not centered on Britain's role as a guardian but rather the paternal role of the ruling families as protectors of common people from the avarice and exploitation of holding companies, multinational oil companies, and foreign workers. Beginning in the midcentury era but picking up pace in more recent decades, rulers positioned themselves as protectors of Arab purity and "the family" and against threats from "bachelors" and inauthentic newcomers.[67] This narrative articulated the rulers' autonomy as a virtue rather than a vice, as it has been understood by supporters of constitutionalism in the first half of the century. Even though ruling families were deeply enmeshed in global capitalist production, they were positioned as standing apart from "the economy" as well as between the local and the global. At the point of independence, sovereignty was largely defined in terms of the political will of the ruler and his family, who could trace their pedigree back to the nineteenth-century treaties.

STATE INDEPENDENCE AND INTERNATIONALIZED EMPIRE

These nineteenth-century treaties between the British government and eastern Arabian ruling families were the means to more or less successfully carve out autonomous, yet imperially anchored rulers. Part of the tension was carving up a regional swath into discrete national units with recognized sovereign rulers, while trying to maintain a regional configuration led by British imperialism despite emerging norms of international equality among states. The model of treaties, concessionary capitalism, and divided rule displayed other limitations when we examine how it was adopted after World War I in other parts of the Gulf, specifically Saudi Arabia, Iran, and Iraq. In these instances it was less socially tethered and effective for protecting British political economic objectives. In Saudi Arabia, Iran, and Iraq, the endeavor to hammer home treaties neither preserved the polities as British allies nor ensured that their assets would be controlled only by British firms. In a world rapidly engulfed by decolonialism, these more contentious polities made would-be signatories open to counter-alliances and social movements that targeted shahs, emirs, oil companies, and "foreign agents." More so than the protests discussed above, in Saudi Arabia, Iran, and Iraq mobilizations were more class-based and self-consciously motivated by self-determination. They placed limits on Anglo-American attempts to dissolve the Gulf into an abstract geopoliticized regional whole.

The Forgotten Treaty: Saudi Arabia

As British involvement in the political economies of eastern Arabia extended further inland, they encountered the al-Saud family in ways that strengthened their claims to rule over an ever-expanding stretch of the Peninsula.[68] The Saudi dynasts combined conquest of territories and deft alliances with local and global powers to outmaneuver other aspiring families and their Ottoman rivals. The Saud depended on working with clerics and through the tribal system to gain loyalty, mobilize military forces, and secure critical sources of revenue from pilgrimage routes. However, at various critical moments before the founding of the Kingdom of Saudi Arabia in 1932, Abd al-Aziz Al Saud (or Ibn Saud) also received arms and stipends from both Britain and the Sabah family in Kuwait, who were in a treaty relationship with Britain.

The eastern region abutting the Gulf played a pivotal role in the making of the Saudi Kingdom. While Ottoman claims and British protection for local leaders checked the Saudi presence on much of the Gulf for most of the nineteenth century, in 1902 the young Ibn Saud recaptured Riyadh, marking the rise of the third Saudi state. (The first two Saudi-led polities had been founded in the previous two centuries.) Eleven years later the eastern province of al-Hasa was captured by the Saud, allowing them to expand their reach beyond the central province of Najd. The Eastern Province was home to ports allowing access to Gulf trade, but more important, it was a fertile agricultural base for the emerging kingdom. Agriculture and commerce sustained the population and were valuable sectors in the 1920s and 1930s for Saudi taxation in what was still a cash-strapped expansionist project. Without these resources, the expansion of the Kingdom and the seizure of the holy cities of Mecca and Medina would have been far more difficult. As Toby Jones has demonstrated, both before and after the discovery of oil in 1938 it was control over water and the environment that was the instrument to monopolize political authority in the hands of the Saud family and its allies. The discovery of oil only supercharged this process by easing "the financial costs of mastering the environment, turning empire into a state, and securing political power."[69] This included the Saud's forcible settling of nomadic peoples and recruitment of their labor for agriculture or industrial projects.

What is largely forgotten today is that even before the birth of oil economy, the Saud family was not aloof to international politics and during World War I briefly, but decisively, became a British protectorate. Even prior to World War I, the India office developed an interest in the Saud, but a December 1915 treaty recognized al-Saud's rule in central Arabia, including al-Hasa.[70] In addition to promising protection, Britain extended rifles and financial support, including a monthly subsidy to Ibn Saud himself. In return, he pledged to enter into no agreements with any other foreigners and refrain from aggression against any of Britain's protected states. (This last point was eroded when the Saudis imposed a blockade on Kuwait between 1923 and 1937 in the midst of boundary disputes.) With the Ottoman defeat in World War I, support for the Saudis' rivals, in particular the Rashidis and the Heshimites, disappeared and left Mecca, Medina, and Jeddah open for capture. In the interwar context, British energies were focused on recruiting the Saudis in order to maintain the integrity of territories of Iraq and Transjordan. This was managed by the 1927 Treaty of Jedda, which affirmed commitments by the British and Ibn Saud and recognized the independence of what five years later would cohere as the Kingdom of Saudi Arabia.

The trucial experience in what became Saudi Arabia was similar to places like Kuwait, Bahrain, and the UAE in that the treaties were offered by the British as a means of warding off Ottoman claims to Arabia and creating a bulwark against European rivals. They were also reciprocal, in that as signatories the Saud family benefited from Britain's recognition of the family as they strove to entrench their position as the head of an emerging sovereign-terriorial state. Similar to the way in which tribal confederations and families pledged allegiance to Ibn Saud as his forces swept across Arabia, the British signaled their recognition of this reality.

The Saudi Arabian case also points to how treaties require maintenance and mutual reinforcement for them to persist as self-reinforcing alliances. In Saudi Arabia, after the initial utility had passed commitments atrophied as the US oil firms replaced British colonial officers as the primary partner of the ruling family in its quest to monopolize political space in the Kingdom. The 1930s were a challenging moment for the nascent polity. With aid from Britain drying up and the global economic depression cutting into pilgrimage revenue, in 1933 the Saud gave an oil concession to what would become a consortium of American oil firms known as the Arabian-American Oil Company, or Aramco. Five years later Aramco struck oil in the Eastern Province and began exporting it after World War II. During the war the US government extended direct Lend-Lease aid to Saudi Arabia. Robert Vitalis has argued it was not until the late 1950s that Saudi Arabia became more than a federation of tribes and towns and the institutional capacities of the central state became manifest due to its alliance with the oil company.[71] Aramco's adopted the tried and tested method of dividing, paying, and treating laborers based on "racial" differences. Repression targeted Saudi workers agitating over this exploitation, and the American managerial class ensured that the Kingdom's politics would be narrowly defined and wedded to what the US Ambassador to Saudi Arabia in 1947 described as "an octopus"—a firm based on the eastern shores of the Arabian Peninsula but whose tentacles stretched to Riyadh and Washington, D.C., in search for public investments for private gain.[72] By 1950 a 50/50 profit-sharing agreement was struck in which foreign tax credits were extended by the US Treasury to Aramco and Riyadh. The perceived shared interests of the oil company, the US state, and the leaders of the Saud family are what curbed labor militancy, which had gained the sympathy of left-nationalist parties, technocratic critics of Aramco's operations, and the Free Princes Movement of the late 1950s.[73] So while in several ways Britain was part of the history of the founding of the contemporary Saudi Kingdom and muddled through the process of shaping relations with all its neighboring British-protected sheikhdoms, the independent Saudi state rapidly became fully enmeshed in the US energy frontier and web of military-industrial contracts.

Limits of International Recognition: Iran

The treaties and transfer of the oil sector from British firms is also part of the story in which sovereignty accrued in midcentury Iran. However, to understand this and the political stakes of the 1919 Anglo-Persian Agreement, we must go back in time. The Qajar Dynasty (r. 1789–1925) had barely united the lands of the Iranian plateau when it confronted the expanding military forces and commercial missions of Russia and British India.[74] A series of wars with its northern neighbor led to the loss of Iran's nominal claims to the territory of present-day Georgia, Armenia, and Azerbaijan. It also expanded the commercial and diplomatic powers of Russia in Iran, including the Russian navy gaining exclusive rights of navigation in the Caspian Sea and Russians living and working in Iran gaining tax exemptions and jurisdictional immunity through capitulations. By the end of the nineteenth century, other border regions were more clearly demarcated through war and various boundary negotiations (see chapter 2).

On the Gulf coast Tehran's struggles to project authority were with local rulers, many of whom were either tributary allies of or members of tribal federations based on the Arabian Peninsula. In asserting its rule over Bushher, for instance, the Qajar court had to wrest control from the Omani-connected al-Madhkur clan that dominated Bushher in 1850.[75] In another drive to increase tax revenue flowing to the Qajar administration, the lease over Bandar Abbas that was held by the Sultan of Oman ended in 1868.[76] The Iranian authorities in Tehran as well as Fars province had previously sought to cancel the lease and expel the Omanis, but always faced opposition from the British. This was the case for instance, when in aftermath of the 2nd Herat War (1856), Britain sided with the Omanis in their dealings with Iran. But twelve years later, with

Iran's central government badly in need of revenue, the British supported Tehran. The British relinquished sovereignty over coal depots on islands off of Bandar Abbas, thus ending another dispute. By 1887, not only was the customs administration of the ports directly accountable to Tehran, but a new Persian Gulf Ports and Islands governorate had been founded.[77] As discussed in the previous chapter, in these and other cases, British telegraph companies and colonial officers came to see the government in Tehran as the principal authority over the northern Gulf and the Omani Sea coast and their vehicle to accumulate wealth. This was markedly different from the British attitude toward Ottoman claims in Arabia.

By the time Curzon set out on his 1903 voyage through the Gulf (see chapter 2), Iranian sovereign independence complicated Curzon's attempt to treat all ports of call in the sea basin as the same. Curzon's planned dismemberment visit to Bushehr was scuttled in part due to the unwillingness of Iranian officials to follow protocols and diplomatic practices that would designate them at the same level as the Arab rulers of eastern Arabia.[78] This was known in British circles as the "Bushire incident." In local newspapers in Fars, in Tehran, and in Persian publications in India, the voyage and potential compromise by the Qajar were used to criticize British Empire and the Qajar Dynasty.

The Qajars' uneven attempt to centralize power and navigate colonial modernity, however, generated discontent and led a coalition of merchants, clerics, European-educated reformers, and others to call for limits to the despotic power of the monarchy and justice via a constitutional parliament or Majles. Much celebrated in contemporary local history writing, a popular uprising in southwestern Tangestan combined their early twentieth-century struggle to target both Qajar and British tyranny.[79] During the Constitutional Revolution (1905–11), the southern ports became a site of struggle for pro-constitutionalists, who seized customs houses in Bushehr and Bandar Abbas and withheld taxes that had been pledged as security for a loan to the shah from Britain.[80] Like many other towns during the Constitutional Revolution, the port city of Lengeh had its own a political club, known as the Society of Freedom-Seekers of Bandar Lengeh.[81] During the Constitutional Revolution the club briefly morphed into a municipality managing such matters as cleaning roads and collecting property taxes. The British, however, viewed this cross-sectarian society as an adversary; as with the social bandits and rebels that rose up during the first two decades of the new century, British-Indian troops directly confronted them.[82] Despite the brief interlude in 1905–06 when Britain tilted away from the Qajar Dynasty and supported these constitutionalists, London and officials in the Raj realigned behind the shah after emphasizing the need to protect imperial interests in Iran.

In the midst of the Constitutional Revolution and without consulting with the Iranian government, the two powers signed the 1907 Anglo-Russian Convention that carved up Iran into distinct "spheres of influence," with Russia given the upper hand in the north and Britain securing superiority over southern Iran and the entirety of the Gulf shoreline. Echoing the language of Curzon in his lecture in the same year (see chapter 2), the Anglo-Russian agreement was nominally designed to preserve the independence and integrity of Iran, but it quickly became clear that neither power would allow Tehran to extend economic concessions to a power other than themselves.[83] Iran's de jure sovereign territoriality was recognized, but being part of Britain and Russia's "sphere of preponderance" regulated the extent of its sovereignty.

The stakes were high because, as Winston Churchill described it, "fortune" had brought Britain "a prize from fairyland"; this was in reference to Iran's oil reserves.[84] With the help of a kaleidoscope of imperial officers, financial investors, personnel in the foreign office, Qajar courtiers, Bakhtiari tribesmen, and Indian troops, a British mining magnate named William D'Arcy gained a sixty-year concession and in 1908 discovered commercial quantities of oil in southern Khuzestan. The concession was operated by the Anglo-Persian Oil Company (APOC, later AIOC, today BP), which was floated on the London Stock Exchange in 1909. Weeks before the start of World War I, APOC convinced the British government to invest 2 million pounds, a decision informed by Churchill, First Lord of the Admiralty at the time, revitalizing an earlier plan to transition the British navy from coal to oil. British territorial and mercantile priorities were underlined in 1914 when Britain occupied southern Iran.[85] Insisting that the Iranian government impose "order," Britain extended loans to the bankrupt Iranian government and a legation to create a gendarmerie focused on the Southern trade routes.[86]

With the end of World War I, British policymakers turned to the 1919 Anglo-Persian Agreement as an instrument to bind bilateral relations. On the one hand, Iran was denied a seat at the Paris Peace Conference, but on the other hand, Iran became a founding member of the League of Nations, granting it international recognition as an independent state. Officials in London offered the treaty to the Qajar court and cabinet as a recognition their new status. With the central government buffeted by political movements, social turmoil, and a depleted treasury, it signed the treaty. Yet the Anglo-Persian Agreement faced opposition from various quarters of Iranian society, including parliamentarians who rarely acted in concert, but in this case unified against the ill-fated agreement. With the public outraged, the Majles recoiled and never ratified the treaty. Instead, for the next half-century, Anglo-Iranian relations were mediated by the oil industry and a series of British treaties with neighboring states.

A few months before the 1919 Anglo-Persian Agreement was officially rejected by the Majles, Reza Khan participated in a coup (1921) that ultimately led to the end of the Qajar Dynasty and his coronation as the first Pahlavi monarch in 1925. As recounted in the previous chapter, there was at this time a shifting set of conflicts over current and future shares of oil revenues that involved Tehran's emergent military and bureaucratic apparatus, officials of the APOC, various local tribal leaders, and mobilized labor. The British Ambassador concluded in May 1923 that "Persia will never be really independent and orderly until the whole country is brought under a single and unquestioned authority, which must necessarily be that of the National Government, and until the civilian population has been disarmed, so that all physical power rests in the hands of the State."[87] Reza Khan and his allies were able to deploy the state's capacities against local opponents to the central government and bring Khuzestan within its purview. Owning land and property in Basra and Kuwait, Shaykh Kha'zal had positioned himself as autonomous ruler of southern Khuzestan.[88] As such, he was the principal interlocutor of the APOC from whom the oil company leased among other things the island of Abadan which became home to a gargantuan oil refinery, but he was also pivotal in sending his men to break strikes as early as 1914. Not only was he paid handsomely for this aid, but he was also the recipient of a several titles and insignia including the Knight Commander of the Indian Empire. However, by late 1924 British officials were denying that Kha'zal was a British protected person and he was captured by Reza Khan's troops and taken to Tehran, where we ultimately died under quasi-house arrest.

The expansion of Tehran's coercive apparatus into the oil fields, refinery, towns, and ports were welcomed by APOC as a sign of "security."[89] Tehran

now clarified property relations, and the government could be held respon-
sible for social questions including the health of workers and sanitation of
bazaars.[90] As profits increased, the APOC multiplied its facilities in Masjed
Sulayman, Abadan, and Khorramshahr, often by squeezing the mixed Iranian,
Indian, and Arab working population that had swelled due to migration.[91] As
much as the British oil firm, the national government became the target of
labor discontent.

In 1929, Iran became the fifth-largest oil producer in the world. In the
same year, oil workers, supported by shopkeepers and women, went on their
largest strike to date and demanded that the firm improve pay, housing, and
training for Iranian laborers. Building on sentiments opposing British domination of the south during the Constitutional Revolution, the nationalist
press greeted Tehran's greater presence in the oil fields as "a forerunner of
the good news that Iran would soon be able to recover the ports and islands wrested from in in the Persian Gulf."[92] While at first Tehran tactically
aligned with the Iranian workers "utilizing subaltern discontent in the fur-
therance of its own agenda" to expand its geographic and institutional reach,
it ultimately closed ranks against what the APOC described as a "Bolshevik
plot."[93] This was a far-fetched description of a movement that extended well
beyond a cadre of communists and expressed strong nationalist sentiments
published on a regular basis in Persian print media distributed in Iran and
India, which had a long history of diasporic publishing. This rhetoric, however, foreshadowed a tactic deployed for several decades by the British and
the United States on both sides of the Gulf, namely labeling and delegiti-
mating all attempts to extract greater share of profits as tied to communist
"infiltration."

London continued to try to hammer out a bilateral agreement to cement
its role in Iran and protect its interests in within a centralized, yet pliable
Iran. From 1927 to 1935, British and Iranian statesmen sought to conclude a
general treaty to settle the growing number of disputes over debts, Qajar-era
economic capitulations, including the oil concession, Iran's desire to boost
its military armaments, and British naval facilities, in particular on Qeshm
and Hengam islands near Bandar Abbas. The cancellation of the D'Arcy oil
agreement was not a move for nationalization but part of a growing effort
by oil exporters, such as Venezuela and Mexico, for oil deals that were more
"equitable" and "fair."[94]

Part of this struggle to define Iranian-British relations was defining Iran's relationship with the British-protected states in eastern Arabia through physically laying claim to territory and projecting Tehran's authority. This was an era full of disputes over islands in the Gulf, in particular over Bahrain and a series of islands near the Strait of Hormuz.[95] While the Iranian government sought to exercise its place in the international order by referring these cases, including its claim to Bahrain, to the League of Nations for arbitration, the British refused.[96] Iran instead resorted to challenging British authority in the Gulf through pointed actions. Among other steps, Tehran sent physicians to replace British counterparts in the quarantine services at ports, established postal services on islands, stopped vessels sailing off of disputed islands, expelled an Arab shaykh from Hengam when he sought refuge in the telegraph concession area, and bestowed Iranian citizenship on passengers from Kuwait, Muscat, the Trucial States, and Bahrain.

Through these actions Iranian officials claimed that British naval presence in the Gulf, and especially in Iran's territorial waters, was unnecessary. Iranian officials, for instance, sought to impose customs taxes and curtail "smuggling" via the southern ports as part of their ambition to protect the local industries that were so critical for Reza Shah's "development" agenda. To regulate commerce, the Iranian government first purchased vessels from Germany, the first being named the *Pahlavi* and the second (re)named the *Khuzestan*.[97] While the *Khuzestan* was actually used by Tehran to quell Arab rebels in that province, it was purchased by an Iranian resident in Basra who had purchased it from the British. But as had been in the case of Ottoman naval aspirations, building up naval power was easier said than done with Iran lacking the facilities to maintain the ships or instruct the crew. When Britain refrained from assisting Iran to build its navy, Tehran turned to Italy to purchase warships and to train their seamen.

Ultimately, the negotiations over these many bilateral concerns broke down and no treaty was signed. British naval bases were handed over to the Iranians, but territorial assertions and counter-claims over islands and borders were not resolved, with the question of Bahrain and other smaller islands postponed. As for the oil industry, Reza Shah backtracked on his confrontational approach, and a new concession was signed in 1933. By not finalizing an agreement in 1929, the combination of global depression and poor negotiating by Iran's government resulted in an agreement that arguably put

Iran worse off than the original D'Arcy concession.[98] During the negotiations the chairman of APOC publicly declared that the firm had created a "flourishing area of industrial activity . . . in harmony with and for the benefit of the Persian people"; privately, he worried that "the Company had done little or nothing *for the people* of Persia, in return for the natural wealth which it had won and carried away."[99]

Within a decade of signing the concession, British and Allied troops reentered Khuzestan and removed Reza Shah from power in order to shore up the critical Eastern flank in World War II. Military occupation intersected with other political currents, and by 1953 arguments about "economic sovereignty" and "effective control" over Iran's oil resources had become an international lightening rod. As workers in Khuzestan continued their labor struggles, including a massive strike in 1946, in Tehran the political scene was shaped by competing political parties and personalities, notably Mohammad Mossadeq, an international lawyer who had been the leading voice supporting constitutionalism and against capitulations since the 1910s.[100] Although the oil industry was nationalized in 1951, two years later Prime Minister Mossadeq was overthrown by a new Pahlavi monarch, Mohammad Reza Shah, and his backers in London and Washington, D.C.[101] For many Iranians control over oil production, employment in the sector, and transparency as to the oil company's opaque accounting books were essential matters of making oil concessions subject to Iranian law; for executives of what would become British Petroleum and its allies, this was a matter of "sanctity of contracts" and abiding by earlier concessionary agreements.[102] When a British-organized shipping blockade against all tankers exporting Iranian oil failed to convince Iranians to acquiesce to British demands, London pivoted to arranging clandestine activities to remove the nationalist prime minister. Eisenhower's administration became convinced that this was the best path forward. With the coup against Mossadeq's government, this conflict was resolved by breaking the British monopoly over Iranian oil through a new oil consortium agreement that gave major US oil firms a stake in Iran's petroleum production. Only once Iran's new government signed the oil agreement would it receive a major loan based on its future petroleum earnings.[103] The British-US intervention turned what had been a decades-long movement for self-determination into an international conflict against the power of oil.

Even with the demise of British imperialism, the question of extraterritoriality and its reach in Iran's bilateral agreements remained a "crucial signpost along the road leading to the ultimate rupture of Iranian-American relations after the Iranian Revolution of 1978–79."[104] In 1964 a pro-Pahlavi Majles narrowly approved a Status of Forces Agreement (SOFA) that exempted American military personnel and civilian employees of the Department of Defense and their families from Iranian law. Within two weeks the shah accepted a loan from a private American bank to purchase military equipment, but the still-green shah and his advisors faced growing opposition from various segments of Iranian society, who labeled the act as a capitulation similar to those imposed by Russia and Britain in the nineteenth century. This highly unusual and expansive immunity gained by the United States was publicly criticized:

> They passed it [the SOFA] without any shame, and the government shamelessly defended this scandalous measure. They have reduced the Iranian people to a level lower than that of an American dog. If someone runs over a dog belonging to an American, he will be prosecuted. Even if the Shah himself were to run over a dog belonging to an American, he would be prosecuted. But if an American cook runs over the Shah, the head of state, no one will have the right to interfere with him. Why? Because they wanted a loan from America and America demanded this in return.[105]

These were the words of Ruhollah Khomeini, who had gained national fame only a year earlier when he opposed the shah's reformist developmentalist project known as the White Revolution. The shah responded by arresting Khomeini and sending him into exile. He would not return until February 1979 after the shah left Iran for the last time as the Pahlavi monarchy was collapsing (see chapter 4). Khomeini would be the first Leader of the Islamic Republic, which was founded under the banner of "Freedom, *independence*, and Islamic Republic."

A Trucial Pivot from Mandate to Revolution: Iraq

Across the increasingly regulated border with Iran, Britain attempted to exert tutelage over Iraq. Unlike Iran, Saudi Arabia, and the protected states of Arabia, Iraq's political independence was negotiated not bilaterally but through the League of Nations. Forged out of Ottoman provinces and occupied by British and Indian troops in the Great War, Iraq was "held in trust" by the British on behalf of the League of Nations. The mandate was authored by Article 22 of the League's Covenant, which classified Iraq as insufficiently "developed" and "inhabited by peoples not yet able to stand by the themselves under the strenuous conditions of the modern world."[106] Britain's position in Iraq was simultaneously sanctioned internationally and resisted locally.

Britain's administrative approach was divided between those officers and Indian business interests seeking to integrate these lands, people, and economy into the British-Indian government and Arabists and officials in London, who were weary of such direct forms of rule and perceived Iraq as part of the post-Ottoman experiment that they had begun to describe as "the Middle East."[107] The former approach of the "Indian School" was defeated not by debates with officers in London but by an alliance of urban Arab nationalists, Shia religious scholars in the South, and tribesmen revolting against occupation as early as 1920. At least six thousand Iraqis were killed,[108] but opposition continued against British bids to appoint "shaykhs" as tax collectors in rural communities.[109] Facing such politicization, the British military experimented with a brutal and permanent campaign of air power to bring recalcitrant villagers to heel.[110] Dissidents were regularly sent by the British to a coal depot and penal colony founded on the Persian Gulf island of Hengam (or Henjam in Arabic).[111]

The British added another dimension to Iraqi discontent when they decided to recruit a monarch from Arabia who lacked historical connections to Iraq's diverse society. To govern the mandate, King Faisal, a member of the Hashemite family that governed the Hijaz before the Saudi campaign reached the Res Sea, cooperated with British advisors, large landowners, and factions of the urban elite who had roots in the Ottoman provincial administration. These Iraqi leaders sought to square the circle of garnering mass support *and* international recognition to become the brokers between Iraqi people and British power. This alliance produced the Anglo-Iraqi Treaty of 1922 favoring British economic and military interests. "The treaty was the backbone of Britain's indirect rule," comments Phebe Marr. "It provided that the king would heed Britain's advice on all matters affecting British interests and on fiscal policy as long as Iraq was in debt to Britain. A subsequent financial agreement required Iraq to pay half the costs of the British residency and other costs, which not only placed Iraq in a state of economic dependence on Britain but also retarded its development [and that of the oil sector]."[112] As in cases discussed above, the treaty arrangements left little surplus revenue in the public coffers to address Iraqi demands for development, which British officials viewed as "wasteful schemes."[113] Iraqi masses came to view the treaty as little more than a fig leaf for colonialism and treachery by patrimonial rulers.

Facing opposition and mounting costs, as early as 1922 British advisors explored adopting a formula similar to the protected states in eastern Arabia in which formal (or flag) independence was guaranteed in return for exclusive commercial privileges and military commitments. This was opposed by other members of the mandate system, in particular the members of the Permanent Mandates Commission, which sought to "spread the advantages of imperial rule across the Western powers" and complained that Britain was recasting the mandate as a protectorate.[114]

Policymakers in London, Geneva, and Baghdad ultimately elected to disband the Mandate in 1932, and Iraq joined the League of Nations as "the first postcolonial state," in other words gained its independence through the international legal system of tutelage.[115] Indeed, it was the only mandated territory to achieve independence during the life of the League of Nations. As Susan Pedersen documents the resultant deal allowed Iraq to gain political independence in exchange for British control over Iraq's military bases and oil resources. In other words, "Iraq was free to run its internal authority administration much as it liked," including its treatment of its "minorities," although its external affairs, in particular its economy and military sectors, would be internationalized.[116] Other League of Nations members were placated by modifying Britain's control over oil contacts and pipelines and by obfuscating the potential dangers to peoples with minority status, specifically the Assyrians. Additionally, Iraqi negotiators accepted a provision requiring that Iraq to grant most favored nation status to all member states of the League. When Iraq declared independence in October, the British retained treaty rights allowing it to move troops across Iraqi soil, maintain the presence of the Royal Air Force at two air bases, and oversee and train the Iraqi military. The Iraqi Petroleum Company, a consortium of British, American, and French oil companies, meanwhile, enjoyed a blanket concession. As for the "minorities" who had generated moral ambivalence in Europe, they were left unprotected. As Iraqi troops took control, countless Assyrians and Kurds were massacred or fled to neighboring countries.

Yet the autonomy of the new state was shackled by the reserved domains of British control and international debt. If conflict between Britain and Iranians was mediated by exploitation of oil resources, in Iraq it was the tepid investment in the oil industry that fueled opposition by Iraqi leaders and citizens, who wanted greater oil production and financial resources. British policies in Mandatory Palestine helped polarize Iraq's already fractious politics even further, creating the space for coups, reprisals, and local uprisings for the next decade.

Despite volatility in Iraqi politics, key steps were taken to define the nation territorially and in terms of membership. The military rulers who came to power in the 1936 coup negotiated a border and security agreement with Iran, and the resolution of the dispute over the Shatt al-Arab waterway survived subsequent coups. This is maybe less surprising if one recalls that even the champions of Arabism in Iraq maintained that "the demarcation of Iraq's borders was one of Faysel's biggest achievements" and worked with Britain to build Iraq as an Arab state.[117] Nonetheless, Iraq's first Nationality Law, written by the British in 1924, undermined equal citizenship and opened the door for the denaturalization of inhabitants of Iraq, who under Ottoman rule had been deemed either Ottoman or Persian nationals. The irony was that Ottoman subjecthood became the basis of Iraqi citizenship and was taken as loyalty to the new state and the roots of Arabness.[118] Meanwhile, in subsequent decades the category of "Persians" was inconsistently defined as a shifting category that encompassed many Arab and Kurdish-speaking Shia and who concerned British administrators, Iraqi state-builders, and Saddam Hussain alike.

As World War II began, Iraqi colonels took up the nationalist cause to resist the British use of Iraq as a front in the war. As in Iran, Britain responded immediately by reoccupying Iraq for the remainder of the war. When a new Anglo-Iraqi agreement was struck in 1948 to preserve British presence during peacetime, further waves of mass mobilization culminated in the 1958 revolution or coup led by Free Officers that was initially supported by a range of political parties. One of the first items on General Abdel Karim Qasim's agenda was to expand oil production in Iraq, which lagged behind its neighbors as part of the project of the international oil cartel "to produce scarcity." Prime Minister Qasim sought to bring the oil fields, which were untapped and kept off the market by the international consortium, into production while demanding that more Iraqis be trained for management positions and that the Iraqi state be allowed to purchase greater shares in the company.[119] The pillars of British influence—the monarchy, the constitution, and the treaty system—were all disbanded; the Baghdad Pact, a ham-handed 1955

Anglo-American attempt at region-making, was also rejected by Iraqi leaders shortly after the revolution. When time came for the nationalization of Iraq oil industry in 1972, it had the critical support of OPEC leaders to bypass what they described as "the trauma created by Dr. Mossadegh's experience in Iran."[120]

By midcentury, Iran, Iraq, and Saudi Arabia may have been distinct hot-houses of political struggles over how state power should be allocated and directed, yet they all claimed international legitimacy based on rights and practices associated with unitary sovereignty. Like a growing number of what would become known as "postcolonial states," these cases chart a trajectory toward unifying sovereignty over an ever clearer territorial space and seeking to have this sovereignty recognized by European states and international bod-ies.[121] This recognition was not just an end, but political elites deemed it as a necessary attribute for what was being understood as "development" and ef-fective independence at this time. And as Antony Anghie argues, recognition was not granted according to some principle of civilization attainment but as an expedience for colonial powers and struggles by subjugated peoples.[122] Therefore, these developments were incomplete, contested, and enmeshed in the twin processes of colonialism and decolonialization under the interna-tionalization of capitalism.

CONCLUSIONS

There is nothing natural or inevitable about sovereignty accruing to states in general, and this was also true in the Persian Gulf region. The treaties and protectorate agreements were the markers of sovereign recognition, but they were also the means for European powers to "assimilate" the Gulf into "the realm of international law."[123] Despite the pretenses of positive law, Anghie points out that nineteenth-century treaties were unequal in two senses—the material power of parties was unequal and the stipulated obligations and rights were highly skewed. It was in this fashion that the Gulf was brought inside the international and that the rulers-cum-signatories were held respon-sible for their internal affairs. Time and again, however, rulers learned that mere legal recognition or civilizational development was not sufficient to pre-serve all dimensions of sovereignty. As these postcolonial nation-states were hierarchically subordinated within an international order by a global capital-ist division of labor, the limits of international law's claim to universality and homogenization of political authority were hollowed out. The experiences of the leaders in Iraq, Iran, and elsewhere along the Gulf concretized the possibility that they could be removed from power by various combinations of "local" and "foreign" forces.

Yet, this historical process also demonstrates the real limits on the British Empire. Hegemonic decline after World War I and anticolonial mobilizations that ricocheted through colonized societies expanded notions of sovereignty well beyond "self-rule." British foreign officers tried to replicate the mid-nineteenth-century treaties to other parts of the Gulf region, seemingly without regard for the groundswell against empire and the distinct social struggles that the treaties had inflamed. With different iterations, the subject of political sovereignty became the ruler, monarch, or ruling family but rarely the people or their representatives in legislatures. Challenges to this model were expressed regularly and through demands for consultation, oversight of budgets and accounts of oil companies, and demands for public goods and fair work conditions. In response to the universalism of liberal internationalism, the alternative universalisms of decolonization, Marxism, and pan-Islamism gained currency in some quarters, including in Yemen and Oman. Instead of embracing democratic governance by citizens, these unaccountable executives and British-protected rulers adopted the position of trusteeship over a society being held at arm's length and fractured by citizenship laws. The mid-century period is a history of decolonization and national liberation, but it is also an era of reactionary politics and containment by coalitions (shaykhs, old and new merchant capitalists, and multinational firms) against labor movements, meritocratic modernizers, and Marxist internationalism.

The particularism of nationalisms and ethnicities also flourished in the context of this hamstrung sovereignty. It was encoded in nationality and property laws as well as political culture (see chapter 5). Yet its imprint on the Persian Gulf's littoral society was incomplete. In the 1960s and 1970s social mobility for townspeople in southern Iran was beginning to be tied to educational attainment, state employment, and family investment strategies in real estate and land. Yet, short- and long-term migration to Kuwait, Dubai, and the places in between persisted as individual and collective strategies for wealth and status.[124] Like many others who gave up farming to migrate, the people of Larestan in southern Fars, for instance, sent enough remittances to Iran that by 1975 the Lar branch of Bank Melli was the possessor of the largest deposits of all the branches in the province, including the main branch in Shiraz.[125] In many ways, even if many of Shiraz's hotels, restaurants, and supermarkets were owned by people from Lar and its surrounding towns, Dubai remained more accessible than the provincial capital. One sign of their sociopolitical marginalization from Tehran was that it took demands by businessmen for the road from Lar to Shiraz to be paved.[126]

Reflecting these long-standing migratory patterns, Dubai and other emirates, recognizing Iranians as "people of the Gulf," extended them visa-free access for much of this time.[127] While migration has remained unabated, the window on mobilities across the Gulf or between Iraq and eastern Arabia has been regulated. The generalized concept of "people of the Gulf" was being replaced by notions of belonging to Kuwait, Bahrain, Qatar, the United Arab Emirates, Iran, Iraq, and Saudi Arabia. The popularity of Arab nationalism and Third-Worldism in the 1950s and 1960s, for some, conjured up other spatial imaginaries and attachments, such the Arab world. In the process, ethnicities were hardened, becoming "claims to authenticity . . . [and] necessitated by, and increasingly encoded within, the postcolonial state-building projects of the Gulf."[128] Ahmed al-Dailami arrived at this conclusion by tracing how the Hawala, or a community that tacked back and forth between the two coasts for over two centuries, by midcentury had disavowed Persianness, claiming that being a Hawala meant that they were "not not Arab." This process of hammering out a convergence between ethnic identity, political loyalty, and territorial jurisdiction is a ceaseless task and entails more than the writing of laws and history books. In Bahrain, Iraq, Iran, and elsewhere it included the closure of foreign schools, street skirmishes, and deportations. Whole groups of people were classified as "expelled" (mo'aved) or "without nationality" (bidun). However porous and uneven the Gulf remained, state boundaries took on greater political, ethnic, and cultural meaning.

The geopolitics of Gulf regionalization were struggles about encirclement and hegemonic integration of a region as a whole. But it was suffused with other practices of space-making. Empire, internationalism, and capitalism were not orthogonal to state- territory. State-building was not a bottom-up response or a defensive reaction against empire and globalism but a diagonal interlacing of scales. The concrete historical process of coupling territory and sovereignty, or "state/space," show imperial and local logics collaborating and colliding to make land a source of authority and shift the loyalty of citizen-subjects away from juridical sovereigns to the territorial national state.[129] This did not end with formal independence but had to be cultivated through practice. This is revealed in the next chapter by an investigation of the ongoing process of accruing and projecting sovereignty in more recent decades. Paradoxically, by the 1970s and 1980s, free trade zones, enclaves often depicted as offshore or outside the state system, are useful cases to understand how boundary formation is continuous and a means to build zones of contact as well as differentiation.[130] Taken together, we will explore the modalities of carving up sovereignty in the twentieth century; the making of a composite Gulf of states, categories of people, jurisdictions, and enclaves to regulate circulations and accumulation of surplus capital. As borders are drawn, frontiers do not disappear and become sites of concentration of state power.

FOUR

GLOBALIZATION'S SEAMS

UNTIL THE SECOND QUARTER of the twentieth century, the shores of the Persian Gulf were approached either by ships navigating its shoal waters or via caravan trails bringing people and commodities from hinterlands to its wharfs. The invention of air travel changed matters. All of the mud flats, natural harbors, and craggy cliffs could now be viewed from the sky. This verticality offered British officials a new means for surveillance and new methods to inflict violence.[1] Airports, meanwhile, became sources of revenue for local rulers hosting British planes traveling between South Asia and Europe and needing refueling stopovers in places such as Sharjah.[2] Air travel also gave birth to aerial photography. If air travel compressed space by reducing the time of travel, surveying and imaging from the sky overcame the remoteness and environmental harshness of places on the Gulf littoral.

In two specific instances, Jebel Ali in Dubai and Iran's Kish, aerial surveys were used to map and document the Gulf coast in ways bound up with rescaling the nation and globalizing the region; the foothills on the western edge of the emirate of Dubai and the island off of southern Iran were two of the region's earliest free trade zone projects. In 1945, in preparation to drill for oil in the Trucial States, a team of mapmakers from the United States Army Survey Department and the British Survey Department of Cairo deployed aerial photography to comb the region between Qatar and Sharjah.[3] This was after the British-initiated treaty system was ensconced in eastern Arabia (chapter 3) but before the founding of the independent federation known as the United Arab Emirates. The surveying was part of the drive to exploit the newly conceived Persian Gulf energy frontier. Petroleum Concessions Limited, a wholly owned subsidiary of the multinational Iraqi Petroleum Company, hoped that the sort of giant fields that were already being exploited in the Upper Gulf would be duplicated closer to the Strait of Hormuz.[4] As a former British official in Dubai recollected, "Within the Trucial States anything as mappable as linear frontiers was virtually non-existent; and if maps were to be produced for potential oil concessionaries, direct intervention was unavoidable."[5] In anticipation of the El Dorado to come, another British diplomat recalled that when the Political Agency was moved from Sharjah to Dubai, it was because of the hopeful signs at Jebel Ali that the offices were located on the Dubai rather than the Deira side of the S-shaped creek.[6]

Ultimately, oil prospecting in Jebel Ali was fruitless save for quarrying of rock valuable as construction material. Yet as a region contested by tribal federations competing over water sources and aligned with either the ruler of Dubai or Abu Dhabi, the mapping of the outcropping triggered conflicts between rival tribal alliances. Two decades later, exploitable oil reserves were discovered in Dubai, but they were largely offshore and dwarfed by its neighbor and co-member of the UAE, Abu Dhabi, let alone Saudi Arabia, Kuwait, Iraq, and Iran. Nevertheless, the areas surveyed in 1945 proved to be critical for Dubai's rapid economic growth and demographic expansion after the 1970s. It was here that work began on building the world's largest man-made port on to which a free trade zone (FTZ) was grafted. This would become a model for future megaprojects in Dubai and serve as the avatar for so many other places coveting the status of "a globalized city" and a gateway to the global economy.

By the time the state-of-the-art Jebel Ali port and its gargantuan cranes began loading and unloading containers, Mohammad Reza Shah across the narrow strait was being toppled. While the focus of most revolutionaries was on Tehran, six hundred miles away on the island of Kish one of the shah's winter palaces and Iran's own FTZ project lay abandoned. This was an island-wide complex of hotels, villas, a Ladbroke-run casino, and an international airport built by an assortment of Iranian and international firms. The financing came from the Development Bank, which was closely connected to SAVAK, the shah's security and intelligence service.[7] The island was sparsely inhabited, yet the plans necessitated the relocating of villagers to a new model town.[8] On the eve of the 1979 Revolution that would unseat the shah and re-place centuries of monarchy with an Islamic Republic, Kish at once conjured Pahlavi internationalism's vista and symbolized "'western decadence' and the corrupted self-indulgence of the monarchy."[9] Once victorious, the revolu-tionaries debated what to do with Kish; by February 1980 they declared that it would be the Islamic Republic's first FTZ. Aerial photography was enlisted to document the disrepair of the abandoned buildings but also adjudicate the inconsistencies between the inventory list provided by the Kish Develop-ment Organization and what was actually constructed—some buildings were not on the list, while others on the list were not actually built. Confirming the revolutionary critique of the Pahlavi monarchy, the discrepancies suggested bureaucratic negligence at best and graft at worst.

Seeing terrain from above abstracts away the political and spatial com-plexities. Unlike the intimacy of ships and the hustle and bustle of ports, from the sky the shore and the ground below are rendered as an object that can be possessed. Similar to classic geopolitical mapping (see chapter 2), surveying from above is useful for turning land into a resource for economic extraction and taking stock of the built environment. In focusing on tracts of land as ob-jects, the images emptied Jebel Ali and Kish of people and erased the societies that lived and worked on the places below—the villagers displaced by these projects and the tribal groups that laid claims to water wells. Equally invisible in these aerial photographs were the myriad motivations and opportunities that have been part of the stories of Jebel Ali and Kish. The bird's-eye view is also a means to examine the earth's surface without territorial demarcations or political boundaries. We are invited to aspire to a borderless world and think globally. The aerial perspective is a quintessential means to evoke de-territorialization, or the eroding of place-specific practices and attachments, to leave us a seamless surface for frictionless flows.

The reverse is also true. These two cases of FTZ development entail a re-territorialization or a re-scaling of state power by demarcating new political economies as uneven geographies.[10] The aerial perspective fits well with the zoning practices to repurpose the Gulf from an international *boundary* into what over time becomes a thickened socioeconomic *seam* for global circula-tion in early twenty-first-century capitalism. These FTZs aspired to turn the Gulf into a connective tissue between what were beginning to be thought of as the local and the global. They are liminal spaces in that they broker different scales, rather than being an in-between, empty, or interstitial space. In these cases the zoning practices were a method for the Iranian state and the emirate of Dubai to redefine specific places in relation to state territory as well as arranging regional and global economic contours to the advantage of capital allied with rulers. As this chapter lays out, the zoning projects of Kish and Jebel Ali and the multiplication of borders and administrative bodies reformulated state-space and sought to redefine the Gulf region as a collection of hubs and entrepôts to channel and orchestrate movements to and from some places and not others. The "freedom" referenced in "free trade zones" is for some, not all.

These cases are a reminder that state territorialization is an ongoing process. These juridical-spatial enclaves were part of state formation not exceptions to it, part of a strategy to regulate space (territoriality) and define a distinct bounded space (territory). I analyze FTZs as a response, however imperfect, to the related challenges facing rulers in Iran and Dubai in the last third of the twentieth century and the start of the current century. Taken together, we will explore the modalities of carving up and out sovereignty in the twentieth century and the making of a composite Gulf.

Despite their differences, as FTZs and mega-construction projects, Jebel Ali and Kish were places in which sovereignty was reworked in seemingly paradoxical ways. The man-made port and the attendant economic zone were part of the struggle of Dubai's ruling family, al-Maktoum, to govern without sharing power either with rulers of other emirates, especially al-Nahyan in Abu Dhabi, or with its own denizens. Meanwhile, Kish Island became a marker for both the monarchy and the revolutionary republic to project Iranian power over the Lower Gulf. In both cases, the legal regime delimited the state's regulatory powers and situated the enclaves outside the national customs territory—offshoring was a mode of "splitting of the sovereign realm."[11]

FTZs, spaces often depicted as offshore or outside the state system, are useful in understanding how boundary formation is a means to build zones of contact as well as differentiation. These and other zones and port projects were part of a global logistics revolution, which expanded the scale of the economy from the national and were early articulations of states acting with corporations to carve out and secure networks and systems described as "corridors and gateways" or "pipelines of trade."[12] The Persian Gulf did not just participate in or become globalized, but in place-specific ways were integral to globalizing supply chains. This pattern to globalism did not displace the regional scale but came to present a seamless world of infrastructures and patterns of accumulation that left a more disjointed and stratified region. The global hopping and skipping that these sorts of enclaves enabled also estranged them from one another. As we will see, Kish and Jebel Ali histories are interlaced and better viewed relationally, rather than comparatively.

RECOVERING HISTORIES

The majority of FTZs across the world today and in Persian Gulf countries were established after the 1980s. By one measure only 25 countries had a total of 79 zones in 1975, rising to 93 countries and over 800 zones in 1997 and 130 countries with 3,500 zones by 2006.[13] Accordingly, employment in zones grew from less than 1 million to 22.5 million between 1975 and 1997. In 1998 goods and services valued at an estimated $250 billion passed through such zones, and in total they accounted for almost a fifth of international trade at the end of the century.[14] Within the GCC 100 free and special economic zones were established by 2014, with over 20 in the UAE alone.[15] Paradoxically, this growth in specialized zones took place at the same moment that the World Trade Organization was created and mandated the reduction and limiting of trade barriers, which should have made of these zones redundant or even illegal.

Advocates of economic zones have justified them as contemporary variants of the free ports found in earlier centuries, both within the Persian Gulf and beyond—Singapore, Hamburg, Hong Kong, Copenhagen, and Aden are commonly invoked. Yet the scholarship examining the proliferation of export processing zones and FTZs typically frames them as part of the deeper process of enabling capital to become more mobile, while disempowering labor in a post-Fordist and neoliberal phase that started after the 1970s.[16] Several researchers, however, have begun to retrace their origins further back to moments of decolonization and programs for national industrial development with zones deeply interwoven into the developmentalist ethos of protecting the rights of national governments over capital.[17] Patrick Neveling shows that the history of zones in modern times begins in Puerto Rico, Ireland, India, and Taiwan and originates in the "New Deal" and "Point Four" policies of the United States, especially within the United States and its territorial holdings in the 1940s.[18] They were designed less as tax havens and more for the capture of capital. For Ronen Palan and Vanessa Ogle, the rise of these enclaves in British colonial territories are intimately related to the demise of British Empire, tax evasion by colonial firms, and the protection of the British currency through the reestablishment of the sterling zone in 1946, with approximately 40 percent of international trade denominated in sterling as late as the 1960s.[19] Simultaneously, on the heels of war and decolonization, what were typically referred to as export processing zones were championed by organizations associated with the non-aligned movement, such as the United Nations International Development Organization as well as US development agencies.[20]

Legislating the creation of zones has a long pedigree because they are public vehicles for accumulating private wealth. They do this by territorializing, or making particular spaces and locations valuable through legal regimes and infrastructural enhancements. In the case of economic zones, foreign and domestic investment and circulation is stimulated by the combination of modified customs, tax, labor, and other business laws and public investments in enormous infrastructure projects. These offshore enclaves entice international firms and wealthy people to pay a premium in order to relocate or merely appear as if they reside in these new frontiers. These zones are quintessential "spatial fixes" for capital in times of crisis.[21] "Fixed capital embedded in land," or the construction of railroads, fiber-optic systems, and ports facilities, points out David Harvey, is essential for capitalism's needs to move *over* space by fixing assets *in* space. In this model, space is a "fix" in a second sense, in that these spatial practices address capitalism's tendency for overaccumulation. Increasing competition reduces profit rates and leads to cycles of crisis, while territorial mechanisms create new markets to absorb excess capital and downgrade the strains of overaccumulation (at least temporarily and in certain locations).

Resituating the history of zones is critical because the trajectories of Jebel Ali and Kish's development into FTZs reach back to the 1960s and are part of a thicker narrative of "early post–Second World War neoliberalism."[22] This approach disrupts stylized accounts of neoliberalism as a post-1970s rupture in which structural adjustment was imposed by international financial institutions, which hollowed out the state and de-territorialized the economy. Like other projects in the immediate post–World War II years, zoning afforded planners the means to control markets to order to pool and direct capital investments for economic diversification, technology transfer, and employment and to build backward and forward linkages between industries. Despite the circulation of "blueprints" for free ports, tax havens, industrial parks, and more, each initiative had its specific constituencies and historical and geographical particularities. Unlike Puerto Rico, Ireland, Jamaica, Mexico, Taiwan, Mauritius, and India, which were devising their own zones in the 1950s and 1960s, Iran and the UAE were not taking on considerable debt and bidding for capital investment from abroad. These projects were based on diverting growing state revenues into fixed infrastructural investments and feasibility studies to the benefit segments of domestic capital and as expressions of state sovereignty.

COMPLETING THE NATION'S SEAS VIA KISH'S FTZ

In 2015 the *Financial Times* concluded that "with the help of German advisers, the Iranian dream is to create an FTZ reminiscent of Jebel Ali, the highly successful United Arab Emirates hub that serves the Gulf."[23] The article described the Arvand FTZ, an enclave bordering Iraq and at the northern tip of the Gulf. This visualization of Iran as a "bridge" from the Caspian Sea to the Gulf and the markets of Iraq and Russia has a pedigree extending back to the "Persian corridor" built by the Allied powers during World War II to supply the Soviet Union (see chapter 2). Rulers in Tehran have also dreamed of FTZs as devices for redrawing Iran's geography and inscribing its place in the world even before Jebel Ali became the "hub to serve the Gulf." As early as the 1960s, feasibility studies suggested that Minu Island in southern Khuzestan was an ideal site for such a gateway for Arab tourism and commercial activity—a veritable Beirut on the Gulf. It was passed over and in its stead Kish Island near was designated by the Pahlavi monarchy as a Touristic Free Port and Zone and rebranded by the Islamic Republic as an FTZ.[24] What was consistent over time was the thinking that the Gulf was a bridge, an in-between space, and a gateway.

Kish is a thirty-five-square-mile island that resides at a strategic location. A dozen miles off the Iranian mainland, it is close to the Strait of Hormuz and only 70 miles from Dubai. Yet it is far from the industrial heartland of the country and major population centers and fully six hundred miles from the capital city. Unlike some of the other islands in the Persian Gulf that have rich social histories and played a starring role in the commercial entanglements and imperial rivalries mentioned in previous chapters, Kish (or Qais, as it is

called in Arabic) is less frequently mentioned in travelogues and histories of
the post-Safavid era. By the time Villiers sailed past Kish in 1939, a seafarer
originally from the island commented that "the island had fallen on evil days."
This evaluation prefigured the conclusions of a subsequent Iranian historian
that Kish had become a "ruin."[25] Kish had not been a major population center, but migration to the port towns of Dubai and Sharjah on the southern
shore resulted in its small population falling to an estimated 760 people in
the first national census of 1956.[26] This migration from islands, villages, and
small towns in the southern region at the end of the nineteenth and the first
half of the twentieth century was the result of several factors, principally the
increasing efforts of the Iranian central government to regulate trade, extract
tax revenues from commercial activities, and penetrate societies by imposing
such polices as conscription. "New innovations of the new shah" may have
dislodged the inhabitants of the southern coast, but kinship, cultural ties, and
historical patterns of mobility drew them to the port towns on the Arabian
Peninsula. The population of Kish was predominantly Sunni Muslim and
Arabic-speaking like other communities on the southern littoral.[27]

From the perspective of local policymakers and those in Tehran, depopulation was a problem, a sign of territorial vulnerability. In 1940, a committee from the Interior Ministry and Bandar Lengeh, the main port near Kish,
was formed to investigate the decline in population.[28] The following year a
commission was established within the municipality of Shiraz to halt the
out-migration of Iranians from the coastal region. However, there is no evidence that the central government took any concrete actions to address this
situation to solve demographic threats, ameliorate poverty on the coast, and
enhance nationwide development. Meanwhile, the discussion of expanding
Iran's port and warehousing facilities in the 1950s was partly driven by businessmen protesting the high costs and delays in unloading ships due to insuf-
ficient port capacities and bottlenecks in transportation networks. The state's
response was to appoint a brigadier general to head up Iran's customs.[29] Even
then, when an official close to the shah visited Dubai, Kuwait, and elsewhere
on the peninsula, Iranian residents pleaded for the government to invest in
cross-border trade, build airports, and pave roads, and if not, to let them do
so through their own investments and donations.[30]

Strikingly, Kish was absent from the initial discussions of creating free
ports in Iran in the 1950s. At this time a series of consultants and experts on

ports and transportation drawn from Europe and sponsored by the United Nations visited Iran's Persian Gulf region.[31] Iran's second multi-year development plan (1955–62) established a Special Commission on Free Ports, which suggested Bandar Abbas and two ports near Abadan—Khosrowabad and Haj Salbukh/Minoo Island—as possible free trade projects with Danish and Dutch consultants positing Copenhagen's free port as a model for Iran to emulate.[32] Given the existing infrastructural endowments of these cities and their proximity to urban centers, labor markets, and industrial and petrochemical centers, there was an economic rationale for establishing free ports or zones in them.

A few years later Kish Island began to be considered. In 1962 the government purchased land on Kish, which by then had a population of 1,200.[33] The acquisition of the land from private absentee landlords was handled by several officials from the SAVAK security apparatus, which was established in 1957.[34] A couple years later, an official in the Ministry of Economics and Finance stated, "It is possible that Kish Island will be announced as a free port."

Designing the project created opportunities for Iranian and international firms. In 1967 the Iranian government commissioned Taliesin Associated Architects of the Frank Lloyd Wright Foundation to conduct a feasibility study for converting Minoo and Kish islands into tourist resorts. The study, initially based on a consultancy by a retired US Air Force officer, focused on converting these islands located at either end of the Gulf as places to attract Western, Arab, and Iranian business travelers and leisure tourists "through the simultaneous gradual integrated development of the [two] islands."[35] Referencing Puerto Rico and its zone and drawing explicit comparisons with Beirut, the architects advocated for transit-based commerce and tourism to anchor the projects and attract wealthy visitors from the Arab world as well as Europe.[36]

The actual drafting of the proposal by Taliesin was undertaken in collaboration with the Tehran firm Amery, Kamooneh, and Khosravi. Nizam Amery had studied with Wright, the famous American architect, and cut his teeth on several projects in Arizona and Wisconsin.[37] Developing a seemingly close relationship with Wright's son-in-law and becoming a firm advocate of his mentor's "organic architecture," Amery traveled to Iraq in the late 1950s to help lead Frank Lloyd Wright's projects for the Baghdad Opera House and the Central Post and Telegraph Building.[38] The projects were not completed, and with the 1958 Revolution, Amery was forced to escape across

the border to Iran, where he founded his own firm and won a series of private and public contracts. When Iran's Ministry of Interior approached Frank
Lloyd Wright's firm to draw up plans for a Persian Gulf project, Amery re-
joined his mentor as the local partner. Taliesin's proposal emphasized tourism
and sidelined industrial activity, although reference was made to constructing
a free zone and port on Kish and plans to convert Bandar Lengeh into a free
port in order to complement the tourism and commercial center envisioned
for Kish.[39] The plan emphasized that Iran could be a staging ground between
the East and the West and concluded that Minu, with its proximity to infrastructure and manufacturing centers in Khuzestan, was "currently located ad-
vantageously to develop" and therefore to be transformed into an FTZ. Less
enthusiastically, the first report commented, "Kish is currently on the southern fringe of developments in infrastructures, communications, and labor."[40]
Yet, it was the study for Minu that was shelved as the shah's focus shifted to
Kish. The exact reasoning for the decision is unclear, but Minu's combination
of many small agricultural landholders and a rich history of labor activism
and social organization of communities in southern Khuzestan must have
added risk to the sort of accumulation by dispossession needed to actualize
the plans for the island in Khuzestan.

It is a curious coincidence of history that the shah's unrealized attempt to
respatialize its northern access to the Gulf into a new terrain for circulation
of visitors and capital was led by Nezam Amery. He was the son of Shaykh
Kha'zal, the local leader we encountered in the previous chapter aligning himself with the British in order to claim southern Khuzestan as his own principality. His hopes were dashed when Reza Shah removed him from Khuzestan
and sent him to Tehran, where shortly thereafter his son, Nezam Amery,
was born and raised partly by his maternal grandparents, who came from a
wealthy Kurdish family.[41] Amery's own vision for transforming Khuzestan's
Minu Island was abandoned. In the 1960s, the Persian Gulf had circulated
through the architectural scene in Tehran as a place of possibility. A young
Hussein Amanat, the architect that would go on to design the iconic Shahyad
Tower (renamed Azadi Tower after the revolution), first met the shah and
the queen for the first time when he designed a resort on the Gulf that was
awarded the best thesis prize at Tehran University's School of Architecture.[42]

By decade's end a series of studies were completed by the Office of Regional Development and Agricultural and Irrigation Planning, an entity

within Iran's principal development agency, the Organization of Planning and Budget. Echoing Taliesin's feasibility study, the reports focused on the development of ports in the southern islands, concluding that because of the warm climate in the winter, these were ideal for commerce and tourism and complemented the existing summer resorts by the Caspian Sea to the north. It was claimed that these locales on the Gulf "complete the use of the nation's seas." The report, backed by the analysis of the feasibility study conducted by Taliesin, went on to urge the government to invest in the islands and encourage the private sector to do so as well.

With SAVAK purchasing land on Kish and the shah visiting the island along with his close advisor and Minister of the Royal Court, Asadollah Alam, the project to transform Kish became intimately bound up with the court. In his diaries Alam pronounced, "Here we are building a new Imperial palace, and not mere amusement. The island lies at the very heart of the Gulf and for HIM to spend a month or so here each year would have a tremendous impact."[43] To administer the estimated $100 million investment in what was initially described as a "Touristic Free Port," the shah founded the Kish Development Organization. Funded by the Development Bank (20 percent) and SAVAK (80 percent), the organization's board of directors included the head of SAVAK (Nematollah Nasiri), the Development Bank (Houshang Ram), and Minister of Court Alam.[44] However, the Planning and Budget Organization, the most technocratic arm of the Pahlavi state, was not fully supportive of the plans for Kish and withdrew itself from later planning and financing, which was executed by ministries and state banks.[45]

Gaining a stimulus from the oil revolution under way, fresh plans were drafted for a dizzying array of projects on the island of Kish. An aerial mapping and feasibility study conducted by Taliesin Associated Architects demonstrated that however sparsely it may have been populated, Kish had a living community. The village of Masheh was relocated in order to accommodate the building of a winter palace for the shah and a new village named New Saffein was built for the relocated inhabitants of the village. Additional palaces were built for other members of the royal family; luxury villas, several hotels, two shopping centers, a casino, a marina, and a golf course were also built.[46] Kish's airport was constructed to accommodate the supersonic Concorde passenger jet with a planned schedule of twice-monthly flights from Paris.[47] In 1977 the official opening brought the royal family and an exclusive list of

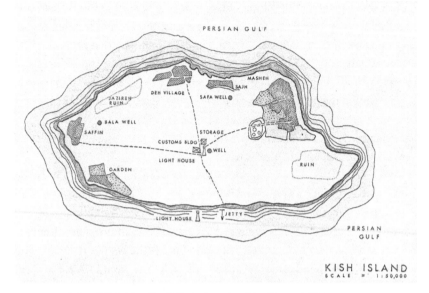

IMAGE 7:   Map of Kish island by Taliesin Associated Architects, 1967.
Source: "Minoo-Kish Feasibility Study State 1, 1967," p. 47, box 8, folder 12, Taliesin Association Architects projects in Iran: architectural drawings and records, 1968–1980. Copyright
© 2024 Frank Lloyd Wright Foundation, Scottsdale, AZ. All rights reserved. The Frank Lloyd
Wright Foundation Archives (The Museum of Modern Art | Avery Architectural and Fine
Arts Library, Columbia University, New York).

European passengers, who arrived on the first Concorde flight from Paris to
Kish. The majority of the development projects were awarded to a French
company at an initial cost of over $52.5 million. The Shayan Hotel, adminis-
tered by France's P.L.M. Company, opened in 1977. The San Francisco–based
landscape and urban planning firm Eckbo Dean Austin & Williams and the
Tehran-based architectural firm Mercury Consultants built the majority of
the project. Mercury as well as the Kish Development Organization were
headed by Mahmoud Stanley Monsef, who was related to Alam. RCA was
contracted to build a radio and television studio on the island; the Israeli
firm IDC was recruited to build a desalination plant, while the German firm
AEG was tasked with providing the necessary power plant. A series of multi-
million-dollar loans were extended by the Central Bank to the Development
Bank. The multinational catalog of engineering firms and consultants aimed
at realizing an architecture that "has a style that combines signs of ancient

Iranian architecture with modern Western building techniques."[48] The shores of the Gulf yet again became the frontier zone of hybrid innovation, but this time it was propelled by technological innovations such as air travel, desalination, and air conditioning and projected by demands and social forces far from the littoral itself.

A "Curious Set-Up"

This grandiose and capital-intensive project fits the model of the shah's high modernist and increasingly audacious projects that were aimed at leading Iran to what the king styled the "Great Civilization." Regardless of the subsequent economic performance of Kish or the political trajectory of the Pahlavi dynasty, the FTZ project in Kish was structured to enrich and garner the loyalty of a small coterie of powerful individuals and international consultants. The British Ambassador from 1963–71, for instance, described Alam and Monsef and their families receiving large sums of money in the "curious set-up."[49]

These types of technologically elaborate top-down schemes dominated by international firms fed the discontent of expanding middle and working classes, and even government officials prior to the Islamic Revolution, which overthrew the shah before his projects on Kish could be completed. These social groups not only suffered economically from the mismanagement of state resources but also saw these grand plans as reflecting the utter unaccountability of the shah. Even prior to the revolutionary mobilization, the project received criticism from technocrats. In one meeting, a consultant to the Ministry of Economics and Finance argued that the project in Kish was "not in the interests of the Iranian people" and "the people's capital should not be wasted in Kish."[50] Put more tersely, an Iranian woman born in Bandar Lengeh, who worked for the shah's government, described Kish as representing the "excesses of the court."[51] In his diary, a British diplomat appraised the venture: "Above all the monument to scandal and cynical exploitation of privilege as represented by Kish Island—that apogee of corruption and near-sanctioned gangsterism (how I wish I nevertheless had seen it—the Last Days of Pompeii). The fellow Mahmoud 'Stanley' Monsef must be shown up as the most unscrupulous and scheming shark of all."[52]

In the weeks leading up to the revolution, Iranian media shed light on embezzlement and waste in Kish, with Monsef and his wife at the center of the accusations. In the heat of the revolution, the shah set up anticorruption agencies to investigate wrongdoing by civil servants and make arrests. Before they could charge Monsef and his wife, the couple allegedly bribed a pilot and flew across the Gulf to Bahrain. From there he and his American wife made their way to the United States.[53]

Focusing on graft and patronage built around Kish, however, abstracts it from its time and place and misconstrues the logics of its founding. It is difficult to explain why the shah's project was located specifically on the island and not in economically more promising locations such as Bushehr or Abadan, which had far better transportation infrastructure, had existing industrial labor force and commercial enterprises, or were closer to larger population centers in Iran. After all, these were the locations the Iranian and foreign consultants had suggested. Furthermore, the timing of the discussions and planning for this project preceded the oil boom of the early 1970s and Dubai's own zone projects.

To account for why Kish was identified in the 1960s as the place for an economic zone, we must afford greater weight to the geostrategic thinking, aspirations, and anxieties of the decision-makers of the time. With a 1,200-kilometer coastline and almost all of Iran's trade, including the vast majority of its oil exports, going through the Strait of Hormuz, control over the strait and its narrow shipping lanes was "vital" to its increasingly oil-dependent economy. From Mohammad Reza Shah's perspective, Gulf security was threatened in the 1950s and 1960s in two distinct ways. First, Nasser's rise to power in Egypt and his calls for Arab solidarity and threats against the "reactionary" Arab monarchies in the Gulf were an obstacle to the political coalition of British firms, political administrators, and ruling families recognized by British authorities but not always by others in their society or even their family. The security system in the Gulf in the 1950s rested on British presence from Aden to Bahrain, monarchies sympathetic to the West, as well as the shah, who had recently been reinstalled in power in 1953. The challenge became more immediate in 1958 when Abd al-Karim Qasem swept aside the British-dependent monarchy in Iraq and brought to power a leadership consisting of a cadre of young nationalists who were allied with the Arab nationalist cause. The rise of a Marxist South Yemen only confirmed this trend. Iranian nationalist insecurities, meanwhile, were inflamed by the new Iraqi government when it began to refer to the Gulf as "the Arabian Gulf" and the oil-rich province of Khuzestan as "Arabestan."[54] All the while, Nasserists drew parallels between Iran and Israel by pointing out that not only did the two states have relations with one another, but they both made claims on Arab lands, Palestine in the case of the latter and Bahrain in the former.[55]

At a more general level, Arab nationalism and Marxism offered anti-imperialist critiques of monarchy in Arabia as well as the shah's clientelist relationship with the United States, but it also presented a palpable danger given the ethnolinguistic makeup of Iran's southern population at a time when many localized movements, such as the Kurds and Baluch, were instrumentalized in international politics. Thus, members of the Pahlavi establishment felt that talk of the Arabian Gulf and Nasser's radio messages sought to foment political unrest among Iran's Arab populations living along the Gulf as well as to generate anti-Iranian sentiment on the Peninsula.[56] Even if Arabs in Iran were not mobilized against Tehran, Pan-Arabism potentially could unify Arab governments and even lead to a powerful single polity on the southern shores of the Gulf.

The second major development shaping the shah's decisions was Britain's surprise announcement in 1968 that it would dismantle its political tutelage and military protection of the Gulf States in 1971 (see chapter 2).[57] Deeply entangled in Vietnam, the United States was critical of Britain's decision and feared Soviet ambitions in the region at a time when Moscow had established close relations with Iraq. For several years the shah and his advisors shared these concerns and pondered British withdrawal but also saw in it an opportunity to enhance their regional status.

With US support, the Iranian regime adopted first a policy of "positive nationalism" and then "independent national policy" as a means to project power and position itself as the regional hegemon by oscillating between military forays and a "search for peace."[58] Military muscle and projection of power included moving Iran's naval headquarters from Khorramshahr to Bandar Abbas at the mouth of the Gulf as well as dramatically expanding the navy's arsenal and more than tripling manpower between 1972 and 1978. Simultaneously, the Iranian military joined the "counter-insurgency" in the Arabian peninsula against Marxist and other dissident groups by sending as many as four thousand well-supplied troops to support Oman's Sultan Qabus, who became the ruler after a British-backed coup in 1970.[59] While the shah's well-funded military intervention, named "Operation Caviar," ensued, Iranian opposition parties sent members to Dhofar to fight alongside their

Marxist comrades.[60] Sharing a striking resemblance to the military base in Diego Garcia, the shah sought to establish an Indian Ocean outpost by purchasing the island of Gan in the Maldives in 1976, but this plan was not realized.[61] At the same moment that the Kish project was being constructed, the shah was sending troops to capture three strategically located and disputed islands at the Strait of Hormuz, allegedly to prevent anti-shipping attacks by guerilla armies.

Interspersed with the efforts to amplify Iran's sphere of influence in the geopoliticized Gulf was a series of significant diplomatic initiatives. Besides being the first country to recognize independent Kuwait, Iran renounced its long-standing claims over Bahrain in 1970 after the shah approved an UN-sponsored survey of Bahraini opinions. This was a departure from both the shah's earlier position and the nationalist government of Mosaddeq, who had included Bahrain and the Bahrain Petroleum Company in their nationalization of Iran's oil in 1953.[62] Iranian-Egyptian relations were reestablished after Nasser died and Sadat took power. Meanwhile, a series of territorial disputes were settled: in 1968 Iran and Saudi Arabia agreed on demarcating Farsi and al-Arabi islands as well as their submarine boundary line; the following year, Iran and Qatar ironed out a boundary agreement; Iran and Abu Dhabi followed suit after recognizing Bahrain's independence when the two countries arrived at an offshore agreement; and in 1974 Iran and Oman agreed to the delimitation of the continental shelf.[63] This was all interspersed with frequent meetings between state officials, and after the 1960s the head of SAVAK's provincial office in Fars was charged with inviting shaykhs from eastern Arabia for hunting trips and medical treatments.[64] The shah and his representatives positioned Iran as a model of development to be emulated by their "neighbors" on the Arabian peninsula and as a leader of the struggle against oil firms for higher revenue.[65]

The development of Kish into a touristic and trade zone marked it as a sentinel projecting Iran's sovereignty and its claim to being the guardian of the Strait of Hormuz, if not the entire Gulf and the northern Indian Ocean. But designed as it was to cater to the wealthy, Kish was also a place for social intercourse and joint planning, as was the case when King Hussain of Jordan visited the island just days before both countries sent troops to Oman.[66] Economic and security concerns, civilian and military infrastructures, and public and private partnerships were as tightly woven together as they would be in subsequent years in Jebel Ali and the Gulf as a logistics space.[67]

Revolutionary Reconstruction

"Today's Dubai," muses Abbas Milani, "is the child of yesterday's aborted Kish project."[68] The connections that Iranians make between Dubai and Kish often emanate equally from pride and insecurity. Statements such as this one overlook that the island's status as a free zone did not end with the fall of the shah. Kish remains an FTZ, and plans and studies to brand it as the "Pearl of the Persian Gulf" have persisted despite the revolutionary hostility to its founding.

The revolution was successful because it unified opposition to Shah and did so in large part because there was agreement that Pahlavi modernism had not fairly and equally distributed the benefits of Iran's wealth and also did not create opportunities for the meaningful participation of all Iranians. In this context, Kish's luxurious and exclusionary projects were anathema. Nasrin Tabatabai and Babak Afrassiabi describe the initial predicament facing revolutionaries as follows:

> On the one hand it represented 'Western decadence' and the corrupted self-indulgence of the monarchy—all of which the new regime despised. But there were also unpaid wages and 250 million dollars of national and international debts plus a huge infrastructure that had to be dealt with. The post-revolutionary government simply did not have the means to absorb its inherited excess. Various ideas were proposed: turning the island into a museum, an exile for drug addicts, a maritime university with a naval base, an international medical center, or simply returning it to the island's indigenous people. Finally, in desperation, the government declared Kish the Islamic Republic's first free zone in February 1980. This would, theoretically at least pave the way for the island to generate income if it engaged in custom-free trade.[69]

In keeping with this decision, the revolutionary council tasked the Kish Development Organization with ending the looting and deterioration of the completed projects and half-finished structures as well as with figuring out ways to generate revenue to pay off debts. It did this by selling off materials from incomplete building projects and items from villas to pay overdue salaries of employees. It was at this moment that the air survey mentioned earlier was needed to adjudicate between the discrepancies between the construction lists and what was actually on the ground.

After the end of the Iran-Iraq War and in the context of Tehran's push for "reconstruction," the administrative body overseeing the island was renamed the Kish Free Zone Organization and was joined by two additional zones—one on the nearby Gulf island of Qeshm and a second zone at the port city of Chabahar located on the Sea of Oman, near the Pakistani border.[70] Unlike the monarchy, which had described the Kish project in terms of creating a playground for jet-setting international tourists, commensurate with its larger populist and revolutionary mandate the Islamic Republic described the goals of the projects in terms of development and industrialization in socioeconomically "deprived regions."[71] In practice, these FTZs were part of the first postrevolutionary Five-Year Plan and the postwar "Reconstruction Crusade (*jihad*)." These were initiated by President Ali Akbar Hashemi-Rafsanjani to dismantle the state-regulated war economy and replace it with one that was friendlier to private-sector interests, foreign investment, and consumerist habits of an emerging post-revolutionary middle class. The basic package of incentives provided in the zones copied those found across the world including 100 percent ownership by foreign firms of any subsidiaries operating in the zones, free entry and exit for capital and profit, a fifteen-year tax exemption on income and assets, and relaxed labor laws and export duties. The express aim of the project was to generate employment, technology transfer, and exports. However, a mix of lack of investments and stiff competition from alternative commercial, logistic, and touristic places has resulted in only modest and erratic levels of job creation, trade, and tourism.[72] Unemployment being a force that exhausts and cajoles workers.

The Islamic Republic, on the other hand, was also attracted to Kish for a combination of international relations and domestic political coalitions. Iran's preexisting geostrategic concerns were augmented in the wake of the Iran-Iraq War that began in 1980. The new regime's leadership found itself needing to develop its port and trade facilities away from the border with Iraq and the northern Gulf region that was militarized after the Carter Doctrine. Kish took on economic purpose at a moment when President Rafsanjani sought to liberalize trade and Dubai was increasing its regional commercial activities. Kish was an attractive conduit for the new mercantile interests involved in the informal and gray economy in the postrevolutionary era.[73] Although not enjoying anywhere near the same partnerships with American and European capital as the Pahlavi monarchy, the Islamic republic has sought to recruit international capital to turn its border region into a discerning membrane to advocate for Iran's place on and in the Gulf. A new economic disposition emerged in the 1990s that was distinct from the social formation that made up the revolution and generated anxieties about the economic and moral corruption of the Kish. Now profit-driven state institutions combined with an array of commercial ventures fueling urban consumerist culture and navigating international sanctions and volatile policies.

An Interlude: Kish, 1979

In December 1978, as revolutionaries were on the cusp of deposing the monarchy, the shah began considering an extended vacation as part of some sort of political transition.[74] *He floated the idea of retiring either to his residence on Kish Island or to the nearby $200 million naval base in Bandar Abbas.*[75] *In the 1970s, while Kish was being transformed into a free trade and touristic zone, other dimensions of Pahlavi internationalism materialized in the nearby naval base at Bandar Abbas with its barracks designed by Israeli architects and its harbor frequented by both US and Soviet warships.*[76] *But in the winter of 1978–79, the shah stopped strategizing about how to be the policeman of the Gulf, and his thoughts were fixated on the Gulf littoral as a place of refuge. Fancifully or desperately, he even suggested to the US Ambassador that he would be willing to retire to a yacht in the Persian Gulf's international waters. Maybe this was primed by the memory of his father, Reza Shah, traveling to Bandar Abbas in 1941 to depart from Iran for the last time after the Allied forces occupied Iran and forced him to abdicate the throne. In the midst of losing his grip on Iran's political reigns, Mohammad Reza Shah, the person that had labored for two decades to be an indispensable guardian of the Gulf, came to view the southern shores as a safe house and location removed from national politics—a place that was so geographically marginal that revolutionaries would accept his presence there as an absence. However, as much as the shah tried to extend his authority to the shores of the Gulf and make it central to Iran's sovereignty, the unrealized plot illustrated that the Gulf retained its peripheral qualities.*

A few weeks after the shah suggested retiring to Kish and after he and his family left Iran to begin his exile in a host of different countries, Kish

was again evoked as a national threshold and solution during the revo-
lutionary situation. This time the US Ambassador reported that the last
prime minister appointed by the shah, Shahpour Bakhtiar, and a group of
generals in the National Security Council had devised a plan to divert the
plane returning Ruhollah Khomeini from exile.[77] *The scheme was to close*
all of Iran's airports and have the imperial air force intercept the plane,
forcing the leader of the revolutionary movement and his closest confidants
to land at Kish's airport. At which point the pilot would be told to depart
and the revolutionary leader and his entourage would somehow be held on
the island until next steps could be taken. Despite this ploy to use the littoral
as a liminal space to bide time, Khomeini's plane landed safely in Tehran
sixteen days after the shah had departed and less than two weeks before the
ultimate victory of the revolution.

Despite all the economic and nationalist investments of the past century,
Tehran's relationship with the Gulf region was ambivalent and contradic-
tory. Islands and shipping lanes were where sovereignty was projected, but
in the midst of revolution Kish became the place for the outgoing sover-
eign to depart and the ascendant sovereign to be kept at bay. Both of these
clumsy and unrealized plans evoked the long practice of exiling criminals
and political dissidents to Iran's geographic and political frontiers, with the
coastal region as a particular stigmatized frontier where judges could send
social pariahs.[78] *Kish, however, had become the border that defined the*
center, the edge of Iran that was thoroughly internationalized. The Persian
Gulf's coastline and its islands were a membrane-like buffer isolating certain
objects while accommodating others. In conception and practice, this ver-
sion of the Gulf is less a national border and international boundary than
a corridor and seam acting as a conduit for some flows and a buffer against
others. This is after all the logic of FTZs that has informed the development
of Jebel Ali into a vital component of the Gulf as a global logistics space.

ZONING FEDERALISM VIA JEBEL ALI'S FTZ

In eastern Arabia the twinned processes of oil exploration and commodification of land in the mid-twentieth century were the conditions for capital's production of space.[79] The property rights regime and Dubai's 1960 urban master
plan were prepared by British consultants but were enmeshed in close working relations among an multitude of actors: colonial officers, British banks,

municipalities meeting growing budgetary needs through permits and fees, merchant families drawn into real estate markets, and commercially oriented members of ruling families.[80] In Dubai, the master plan, drawn up by British architectural firms and unevenly actualized by engineering companies, stipulated that the ruling Shaykh would own large segments of the land.[81] The land owned by the ruler would be his own private asset but would be managed as an asset by the state.[82] In cases where by 1960 there were no buildings or land was reclaimed by dredging, these plots of land could be seized by the ruler, who had the option to "sell the land, lease it, put it to special uses over a set period, or allocate it to the municipality for public utilities. If land is disposed of without charge, . . . the ruler reserves the right to reclaim it at a future date."[83] This was the adoption of the legal principle of *res nullius* and the productivist model, in which land that is claimed to be unused or barren is viewed as ownerless and can be taken over and improved.[84] It was deployed extensively in the eighteenth century for French and British colonial expansion and appropriation of land in order to make it more "fruitful."

Land, likewise, can be claimed as the territory of the state, and hence its control is intimately related to understandings of modern sovereignty. Land development in Dubai's Jebel Ali occurred amidst conflicts as trucial states were being forged into the United Arab Emirates. In 1945, when an Anglo-American survey team combed the Jebel Ali in their search for exploitable oil, neither the surveyors, geologists, oil company executives, nor colonial officers realized that their activities would trigger what the specialized literature of eastern Arabia characterizes as a "war." Between 1945 and 1948, there were a series of tribal raids and border disputes between Abu Dhabi and Dubai, killing over fifty people.[85] The Political Agent in Bahrain stepped into the fray, declaring that the movement of forces violated the "Maritime Truce" of the previous century. Yet when raids and counter-raids ensued, Britain called on troops and applied economic sanctions. The agent cancelled Dubai's delivery of mail by streamers. The British notified the Shaykh of Abu Dhabi that he would only receive a shipment of 250 rifles if he agreed to a border settlement—a rather peculiar offer in the context of a war between two emirates, both of which were protected by Britain and bound in a truce.[86] After several dozen tribesmen were killed, British officials were able to arbitrate a ceasefire. While a border was not drawn, an agreed-upon buffer zone helped keep conflict at bay and sketch a boundary good enough for oil prospecting.

This violence was also an impetus for the creation of the Trucial Oman Levies a few years later, a marker of British interests extending to "the interior" after decades of focusing on the maritime. Over the next quarter century, the Levies would become instruments for managing political conflicts, suppressing labor protests, and engineering coups against wayward shaykhs.

In 1968, when Britain announced that it would relinquish its position as colonial protector, London brokered negotiations among rulers and advocated that they unite to build a confederation out of the series of protected states headed by families tracing their lineage to the original signatories of nineteenth-century truces and concessions. London conceived of the UAE as the solution to the sort of violence and anticolonial mobilization experienced after its colonial adventures came to an end in Palestine, India, Aden, Kenya, and Yemen.[87] Rulers in Bahrain and Qatar refused to join the confederation, but on the heels of Britain ending its treaty obligations, the rulers of seven emirates—Abu Dhabi, Ajman, Dubai, Fujairah, Ras al-Khaimah, Sharjah, and Umm al-Quwain—agreed to enter the political experiment.

Throughout the 1970s, the very survival of the UAE was questionable, with Dubai-Abu Dhabi rivalry being a particular source of conflict that jeopardized the whole endeavor.[88] The question of the border between Dubai and Abu Dhabi was not settled even at the time of the British-sponsored creation of the UAE in 1971, and the boundary dispute was one of the wedges in the disputes over the structure the federation in 1979. The port and zone project at Jebel Ali played a part in fashioning a de facto compromise between rival rulers that ensured the survival of the new state. It was one of the ingredients in forging alliances between local, regional, and international forces rather than negotiating a political compact with citizens or striking class compromise. Indeed, re-territorialization by zoning was at once economically liberal and entrenched the Maktoums' grip on political power in Dubai.

Not just a man-made port and economic enclave, Jebel Ali is where sovereignty was reworked in seemingly paradoxical ways. The port and attendant economic zone were part of the struggle for Dubai's ruling family, the Maktoums, to govern without sharing power either with rulers of other emirates, especially the Nahyan in Abu Dhabi, or with its own denizens. This "commercialization of state sovereignty" also delimited its ability to control and tax movement across its borders.[89] The contradiction was palatable, even necessary, because it moored the ruling family's authority in geoeconomic entailments of accumulation in the late twentieth century. The Maktoum family, which had been Britain's partner in dual sovereignty, had become rulers of an emirate in an independent confederation and used its powers to make and suspend law for constitutional jockeying, pecuniary gain, and the creation of a transnational social base under the rubric of globalization and the science of logistics and transportation.

Infrastructure became implicated in mediating political competition in the confederation. Dubai's Shaykh Rashid (r. 1958–90) oversaw the building of a deep-water harbor and dry dock that initially consisted of fifteen berths in 1971 and by 1980 had expanded to thirty-seven berths.[90] This harbor, adjacent to historic Dubai and its maritime artery, the recently dredged creek, was named Port Rashid and constructed by Sir William Halcrow & Partners and Costain, two of the principal British engineering firms working in the Gulf at the time.[91] Shaykh Rashid personally owned the dry dock along with other enterprises.[92] Benefiting from the closure and lack of investment in Aden's port as well as port congestions across the region, Port Rashid quickly reached capacity, with large numbers of Baluch and Iranians employed at the dock and the ship repair facilities.[93]

Another Giant Step for Dubai

In as early as 1972 work began on an even larger and more automated port facility with initial plans for the construction of 67 berths and 17 kilometers of quays located some 35 kilometers southwest of Dubai's city center; this would become the Jebel Ali port.[94] To this day it remains the largest harbor between Rotterdam and Singapore, and its capacity to handle container traffic has consistently grown, with its 15.6 million TEUs in 2015 more than doubling its capacity in 2005 (the standard measurement for capacity for container shipping, TEU stands for "twenty-foot equivalent unit"). All major container shipping lines call at the port, and feeder vessels connect it to all prominent ports in the Western Indian Ocean.[95]

The project was devised with the consultation of Neville Allen, an engineer with Halcrow and Partners and a longtime resident of Dubai.[96] It depended on deploying new heavy-duty machinery to cut, dredge, and suction a channel into the coastline and to pour rock, concrete, and cement in order to build seawalls for a massive harbor with many wharfs.[97] The port and warehousing complex was the linchpin of a massive commercial and industrial complex, including a dry dock, gas facilities, desalination plant, and aluminum smelter, which in 1985 was converted into a nearly 50-square-kilometer FTZ that is now home to over seven thousand companies from around the world.[98] Several of the merchant families that were powerful at the beginning of the century and gained exclusive import licenses and agency agreements in the midcentury era have expanded their portfolios and listed holding companies active in these zones. Exemplary in this regard are the Ghurair and Futtaim holding companies, which trace their lineage at least back to the 1950s, when they were leading Arab nationalist figures and members of the oppositional National Front movement.[99]

The zone and port facility have primarily been a re-export hub. A manager at a business consulting firm commented matter-of-factly, "It makes more sense to bring products here and then re-export rather than producing here. It is cheaper if the goods are produced in other countries."[100] Indeed, approximately three-quarters of all goods imported to the FTZ are re-exported, and in the past quarter century it has become a re-export center on a par with Hong Kong and Singapore.[101] In the 2010s, Jebel Ali and the FTZ have been integrated into the Dubai World Central complex, a mega-project that includes an integrated residential, commercial, and logistics zone that encompasses Al Maktoum International Airport and an airport-seaport corridor.

Witnessing these trends, residents of Dubai and journalists narrate the creation of the Jebel Ali port and FTZ as born fully formed from the mind's eye of Shaykh Rashid and his sons, including the current ruler (r. 2006–present). Acting as a series of farsighted, benevolent, and "shrewd" business-oriented rulers, these shaykhs oversaw "Dubai pull[ing] itself up by the bootstraps."[102] In this framing, Dubai's economic growth is explained as an outcome of the visionary shaykh's realization that Dubai's limited oil reserves would run out in the early twenty-first century, and therefore they used the windfalls from the first and second oil booms to build a "world-class" infrastructure. In addition, to expand the warehousing and logistics facilities at the Jebel Ali port, the airport was dramatically expanded, and Emirates Airways was established, all in order to take advantage of Dubai's location between Europe and the emerging markets in East Asia.[103] Echoing the assumptions of tribal leadership that anchored treated and dual sovereignty, in these more recent accounts it is as if politics in "traditional," "tribal" societies can be reduced to the will of a shaykh and Dubai's "trading culture."[104]

This fixation with explaining Dubai's economic success has, perhaps inevitably, colored narratives of the Jebel Ali project in overly consequentialist
ways, assigning the rulers attributes of prophetic prescience, with the implication always being that counterparts in Sharjah, Abu Dhabi, Bahrain, Kuwait,
and Iran simply suffered from ineptitude or myopia. This elides the contexts
that made shaykhly power possible and ports and zones responses to the conjuncture facing Dubai's decision-makers. These are the forces operating along
multiple geographic scales and legal registers that deserve examination.

To explain the timing of its founding and location, Jebel Ali has to be situated in relation to multiple productions of space and scale—on the level of
the nation-state, the regional, and the global.[105] Jebel Ali port was not a natural harbor but a colossal man-made port. Thus, the location of the port, although not completely arbitrary or without geological constraints, resembles
a choice. It was Shaykh Rashid and his Arab and British advisors who decided
to build it far from the town center, abutting what would become the Dubai–
Abu Dhabi border; on land that had been claimed by Abu Dhabi and was the
flash point triggering the "war" in the 1940s. Second, the early 1970s were pre-
carious times for the Arabian Peninsula and for the UAE and its fledgling federal project, with border disputes, family rivalries, and constitutional quan-
daries threatening to scuttle the British-backed polity.[106] The conflict between
the Maktoum family of Dubai and the Nahyan in Abu Dhabi in this drama
was central. The construction of the massive harbor at this time was part of
an attempt by Dubai's rulers to strengthen the emirate's commercial standing
and their bargaining power in relation to its neighbor, which had far more
oil resources.[107] The port construction was part of the multifaceted bargaining over the federal structure of the UAE, in which Abu Dhabi relinquished
its territorial claims allowing Dubai to build the Jebel Ali port in return for
the Maktoums' fidelity to the newly founded federation.[108] The stakes were so
significant that Shaykh Rashid concealed his plans from the other rulers and
the press and "simply presented" it to Abu Dhabi's Shaykh Zayed "with a *fait
accompli* at the very last moment."[109] In the process, the previous plan to construct a new capital city for the UAE was abandoned, and Abu Dhabi became
the capital of a federation that was far less centralized than the leadership in
Abu Dhabi wished.

The legal structure of Jebel Ali's FTZ was also produced in relation to the
UAE's federalism. Whereas previously rulers had issued emirate-specific laws

at their discretion, after 1971 there was a push toward codifying and regulation at the federal level.[110] This included commercial laws outlined in 1981
and 1982 that required all foreign-based companies to have a local agent and
all domestically funded companies to have at least 51 percent of their capital
owned by locals. When Shaykh Rashid signed the decree establishing an authority to administer the zone in May 1980, he created the Jebel Ali Free Zone
Authority.[111] Dubai's FTZ law "was passed with the express aim of providing
the [JAFTZ] Authority with greater freedom and exemptions from existing
UAE business regulations."[112] Thus, JAFTZ set an important precedent for a
roster of subsequent FTZs established in Dubai and other emirates, which
circumvented UAE's federal law that regulated markets.[113] In particular, unlike the federal law that restricted foreign ownership, the JAFTZ authority allowed non-Emirati firms to retain full ownership. Export and re-export duties
were reduced, and restrictions on capital repatriation were also eased, while
to the dismay of locals restrictions on the foreign labor needed to build the
project were also softened.[114] A government official acknowledged this: "In
essence, establishing the free zones was meant to overcome deficiencies in
the federal law, which does not meet the requirements of foreign companies
in the UAE in terms of full ownership."[115]

The free zone regime, consequently, was a compromise permitting Dubai's
government to carve out a legally distinct zone from the UAE's federal guide-
lines without having to negotiate with the rulers of the other six emirates
over federal laws, anger local business community protected from international competition, or risk arousing nationalist sentiments among their own
citizens.[116] As in Kish, instead of the state confronting existing local capitalists
and restructuring established sectors, policymakers elected to create *new* sectors via these zones focused on tourism or shipping and logistics.

The development of the Jebel Ali port and FTZ intersects with the place
of the UAE in the emergent regional and international political economy discussed in the previous chapters. The oil price shocks not only resulted in an
economic downturn for oil importing industrialized countries and a massive
windfall for oil exporting countries and firms but also situated oil revenue
in new ways that helped integrate global financial markets. This multilateral petrodollar recycling included the offshoring of oil revenues in dollar-
denominated assets (including investments in treasury markets), mammoth
weapons sales, and more gratuitous and cynical tactics to redirect surpluses

(see chapter 2). In the case of the UAE, the British government, as former colonial administrator, was initially best located to broker economic ties between the royal family and British firms. A 1975 dispatch from the British Ambassador in the UAE dryly captures the sentiment of the day: "We can not change this place. We can only try to get as much of the money as we can, and since the Sheikhs control most of the spending (if not all the money) it is they [and not their modernizing advisors] we must keep on terms with."[117] Later in the same dispatch, echoing frustrations expressed by other British officials, UK firms are lambasted for their inability to move decisively to win contracts and also to coordinate their bidding and activities to ensure maximum profits for large infrastructural projects.[118] Data from the 1970s and 1980s collected by Abdulkhaleq Abdulla suggests that these anxieties were exaggerated.[119] British firms continued to dominate banking, construction, telecommunications, military contracts, and other sectors, with US, Japanese, and Western European activities remaining marginal in the UAE at this time. Despite these concerns it was in fact British contracting and consulting firms, such as Halcrow and Balfour Beatty, that won almost all the major contracts in Dubai,[120] including the construction of the various sites in the Jebel Ali complex.[121] The economies of the Gulf and Britain were woven together by various contracts and investments in sterling securities. As such, private British firms became members of the coalition behind the Jebel Ali project and the Maktoum's political dominance. A buoyant contemporary British commentator concluded: "As we see it, Jebel Ali is 'One small step for the UAE, another giant leap for Dubai.'"[122] The magnitude of the step is captured by population growth in Dubai from less than 60,000 in 1968, a year before oil exports began, to 276,000 in 1980 and over 370,000 five years after that. Much of this new population was drawn from South Asia, whose dislocated rural population was more easily deportable and controlled than migrant laborers from the Arab world and Iran, who were increasingly involved in strikes and mobilized by political ideas and organizations threatening to the monarchy. From wherever the workers were drawn, this was a process of offshoring labor to suppress wages.

A Favorite Port

The development of Jebel Ali fed the transformation of the security regime in the Gulf after 1979 and the fusing of geopolitics and geoeconomics (see chapter 2). With "the territorial model of security" overturned by the logistics revolution and replaced by what Deborah Cowen terms "supply chain security," Dubai and Jebel Ali, which had been hit hard first by global recession and then a decline in oil revenues, were well positioned in the 1980s to profit from and bridge geoeconomics and geopolitics. One direct boon for Jebel Ali was war. Its founding coincided with the Iran-Iraq War (1980–88), the "Tanker War" in which the US Navy protected shipping (1987–88), and the expansion of the US naval footprint in the northern Indian Ocean after the Carter Doctrine and the Gulf War (1990–91). Maritime and commercial activities were redirected from the northern Gulf to its southern shores and away from Jebel Ali's competitors in Kuwait, Bahrain, and Iran. Al-Sayegh writes, "Dubai's dry dock, one of the largest in the world, was busy maintaining and overhauling tankers as well as repairing those damaged in the fighting. Dubai was therefore loath to relinquish its neutrality in the war."[123]

The Iraqi invasion of Kuwait in 1990 and the subsequent US war with Iraq reinforced the position of Dubai as a safer location for maritime activity than the northern Gulf as well as a gateway to multiple hinterlands stretching from South Asia to eastern Africa and from Central Asia to the Arabian Peninsula. With the British departure from the Gulf in 1971 and the loss of Iran as a regional bulwark, the United States, armed with the Carter Doctrine, began to increase its military relationship with the UAE.[124] During Operation Desert Storm, the Emirates provided logistical assistance and some $6.5 billion in financial support. In 1991, the UAE and the United States signed a "loose defense pact" allowing the US military to base equipment in the federation and obligating the Emirates to purchase military hardware from the United States.[125] It is from this moment on that Jebel Ali began to receive as many as two hundred warships a year[126] and became "a favorite port for US Navy ships in the Gulf," indeed, "the most frequented port outside of the United States."[127] Jebel Ali's logistics capacities have allowed it to become the critical node for naval operations despite the United States Fifth Fleet being based in Manama.[128] The importance of Jebel Ali for the Global War on Terror was stressed in a Senate Armed Services Committee meeting in February 2006 on the Dubai Ports World (or DP World) takeover debacle. In the wake of the government-owned port operator and logistics firm's purchase of the British-based firm P&O, Gordon England, the deputy secretary of defense, commented that "the port at Jebel Ali is managed by Dubai Ports, so we rely on them frankly, for the security of our forces. There were 75 coalition partner ships there [last year]."[129] At this time Jebel Ali and Port Rashid were the only Gulf harbors that were members of the Container Security Initiative, which allowed US Customs officers to be stationed at these ports to handle containers directly bound for the United States.

Deborah Cowen captures the new spatiality of security when she writes that "The stretching of logistics systems across borders into 'pipelines of trade' means that supply chain security recasts not only the object of security but its logistics and spatial forms as well."[130] US military presence coupled with a host of private logistic operations meant that Washington could alternatively claim that by sending bombers, submarines, warships, and customs officials into the Gulf, they were defending US national interests, stabilizing the region, or facilitating global trade. These tangled economic and geostrategic webs, or confederation of interests, found a welcoming host in Jebel Ali.

CONCLUSIONS

FTZs are associated with footloose capitalism and globalization. In conjunction with global commodity chains, integrated financial markets, multinational firms, high-speed intercontinental travel, and flexible labor regimes, zones are part of the set of forces that are said to smash state borders and the flatten space. While recognized as enclaves, zones stand in for a homogenizing process driven by market forces to enhance mobility and speed by whittling away friction deriving from the particularities of place. This vision of what FTZ can achieve was advocated by international organizations for more than a half century and across the political spectrum. Executives and legislatures have been inundated by plenty of external compulsion coming from experts, firms, and lenders.

By narrating the genealogies of Kish and Jebel Ali, this chapter offers a different interpretation that argues that zones are better understood as political projects re-spatializing accumulation and enhancing control by political economic elites. What may be viewed as a contradiction between projecting state sovereignty and creating spaces of de-regulation were in fact palatable, even necessary, attempts to moor the authority of postcolonial states within geoeconomic entailments at the global scale. Therefore, the concrete historical process of coupling territory and sovereignty explored in the previous chapter did not end with the founding of sovereign nation-states but were ongoing practices and assertions of sovereignty vis-à-vis neighboring states.

States relaxed customs, labor, and investment regulations, hoping to enhance the liberties of capital and limit them for labor. Government agencies diverted public assets, such as land, for private benefit. By constructing these places with material infrastructures and specialized authorities unaccountable to the public, decisionmakers folded "far-off" islands and "remote" landscapes into productive national space and sought to make them meaningful to investors, engineers, capitalists, and vacationers. The free zones examined in this chapter became technologies harnessing economic value and consolidating political power. Thus, in contrast to conventional accounts of globalization that rest on ideas of modernization, westernization, and liberalism, global processes need to be seen as multiple in origin, some of which are compatible with and require illiberalism. Rather than begin with the idea of the FTZ as a western-inspired form resulting from the application of the neoliberal project, we need to understand them as responses combining local and global imperatives stretching back to the moment of decolonization. Iran and the UAE are another reminder that many of the policies associated with neoliberalism emerged in the processes of building midcentury developmental states.[131] The FTZ became redeployed and repurposed as capital mobility, liberalization of trade, and a check on the overly "interventionist" state in recent years that experts describe as the era of neoliberalism.

Kish and Jebel Ali, however, were not perfect spatial fixes. The shah's desire to retire to his self-created liminal Gulf space was overrun by the political will of revolutionaries, as was the plan to hold Khomeini in a Kish-shaped safe house. Shaykh Rashid's attempts at building autonomy for Dubai were confounded by every round of boom-bust cycles when Dubai had to turn to Abu Dhabi, Kuwait, and Qatar for financial rescue and confront the US Congress for its port acquisitions. As an aspiration, globalism is never complete and finished or without limits and contradictions.

Kish, Jebel Ali, and other zones are spaces of and for globalization. They mediate the internal and the external, the offshore and the mainland, and they also intercede between federal law and administrative provisions. They are deployments of geography to capture profits and bend supply chains so that they can function as intermediaries between "the global factory" and the final consumers across the world. Representationally and in practice, the Gulf is opened up to marshal global circulations, not simply as "flows" but as organized "systems" and "networks."[132] But the value of these spatio-legal zones is not just what lies within the zone but their status as beachheads for secondary ports, markets on the mainland, or hinterlands. This strategic porousness is what marks Kish and Jebel Ali as early endeavors in what has become supply-chain capitalism or logistics space.

What sort of regionalism is invoked by this globalism? It is a highly variegated Gulf which leverages its multiple and functionally different parts as geoeconomic seams. In the half century since the plans for Kish and Jebel Ali were drawn up, enclaves and administrative divisions have combined with technological innovations in shipping to fragment, rather than integrate, Gulf space through new hierarchies and monopolies.[133] Because of the requirement that ports provide dedicated terminals and infrastructure for loading and unloading containers and the high costs of ever larger container ships, companies want to limit port calls on their "mainline service." Terminal management arrangements and partnerships allow Jebel Ali and DP World to offer discounted port fees and other preferential terms and dominate shipping in the Gulf. Thus, there has emerged the possibility for a single port to become *the* entrepôt for the entire region. Due to a number of local and international interests and contingencies, such as wars, sanctions, and collaboration with the US Navy, Dubai's Jebel Ali port and logistical hub was able to take advantage of this possibility. Whereas in 1982 Saudi's Dammam outpaced Dubai, by 1986 Jebel Ali had overtaken this rival; in the intervening decades it has not relinquished its status as the leading maritime facility in the Gulf in terms of TEUs handled. Notably, Dubai's dominant position is in spite of attempts by the GCC countries to limit the rise of a single regional hub.[134] This dominance, however, is too contingent to be permanent. The ability of the Qatari economy to withstand the Saudi-UAE blockade emphasizes that Jebel Ali's preeminent role is not without limit.

Over the last two hundred years, connections between locations on the Gulf have not diminished but have become more unevenly distributed than in the era when merchants, diasporas, empires, and small wind- and coal-powered ships wove the port cities together. This is reflected in supertankers and mammoth container ships existing in the Persian Gulf alongside a steady traffic of goods via wooden dhows. This gray economy, and even illicit trade, that has encompassed commercial activities to and from Iran and Iraq typically must remain small-scale to avoid detection and is not suitable or profitable for container ships and large terminal operators.[135] Thus, these circulations are externalized by this shipping system and placed behind a veil of illegality and informality. This is yet another instance of how internationalization tears down certain boundaries and obstacles to exchange but must also create new barriers to maintain hierarchies and surplus.

If the FTZs were a means to establish distinct economic jurisdictions and regulatory regimes, another feature of the zones has been to generate a legally gray penumbra through which taxes can be avoided, illicit goods can be diverted, and unlawfully begotten assets can be laundered by shell companies. Kish's open borders and tax havens have facilitated the circulation of a host of "parachuters" with import-export licenses and well-worn smuggling routes, migrant laborers from Dubai on visa runs taking advantage of the porous boundary between mainland and offshore to renew their work status, and even a former FBI agent who has disappeared after visiting the island. The blurring of licit and illicit, inside and outside, has cognates in the UAE's zones. A steady drip of reports describe how FTZs in the Emirates are enmeshed in shadowy arms deals, nuclear technology transfers, money laundering, and movements of secret service operatives from a wide spectrum of countries. For some this has meant that Jebel Ali is a "threat to global trade security," and for others it has marked Dubai as an Achilles heel for sanctions regimes against Iraq, Iran, and elsewhere.[136] The customs regimes provide front companies, businessmen, and governments "automatic deniability" as the transshipment pathways are obfuscated by the relaxed reporting requirements of these economic zones.[137]

FIVE

URBANISM REBOUNDED

THE TERM *GULF CITIES* is used to bring a regional space and urban form together. It has been deployed in contemporary popular discussions of Dubai, Doha, and Abu Dhabi to identify them as a particular type of city consisting of opulent architecture, spectacular skylines, and an outward-looking approach often referred to as "globalism." These characteristics distill current trends and differentiate these places from the rest of the Arab world and the Middle East.[1] For some of their most avid cheerleaders, "Gulf cities" are "brand new" cultural centers "filling in the leadership vacuum" left by the stagnant capitals of Cairo, Beirut, and Damascus.[2] This exceptionalizing tendency is often coupled with an exclusionary one. *Gulf cities* is reserved for urban centers that materialized only after the 1970s oil boom, with Dubai becoming "the fantastically photogenic city of skyscrapers, seven-star hotels, and city-sized special economic zones and residential-entertainment enclaves."[3] Even the city's detractors, such as Mike Davis, point to its uniqueness, to how "Dubai has become the new global icon of imagineered urbanism" and "a hallucinatory pastiche of the big, the bad and the ugly."[4] David Harvey opts for describing the mega-urbanization projects as "astonishing if not criminally absurd."[5] Kuwait and Manama are sometimes referenced as earlier or less successful versions of Gulf cities, while Doha and Abu Dhabi have picked up the mantle from Dubai when the economic recession of 2008 deflated Dubai's market and aspiring rulers and consultants took the logic to these two newer frontiers. This leaves places such as Muscat and Sharjah as the latecomers or poor imitators of this Dubai consensus. Other urban centers on the coast—Basra, Bandar Abbas, Dhahran—drop out entirely, as do discussions of Gulf cities and neighborhood variations; the inequalities of urban segmentation are glossed over quite readily.

The ideological function and analytical thrust of the notion of a Gulf city abstracts these places away from their historical and, ironically, regional context, which has contributed to Kuwait and Dubai emerging alongside oft-forgotten competitors such as Basra and Lengeh. As Alex Boodrookas and I have argued, Gulf cities are not simply defined by an objective position on a Cartesian map, the presence of oil, or membership in the Gulf Coopera-tion Council.[6] Rather, we consider these uneven urban geographies to share a genus because of their historical place in transnational systems of capitalism and political control. By acknowledging this, we recognize Gulf urbanism as central to global capitalism and the very development of modern urban plan-ning. Urbanism is constitutive of twentieth-century capitalism because it ab-sorbs excess surplus and labor, and as capital cities they are nerve centers of state power. This chapter uncovers the highly negotiated process in which the social practices of urbanists (i.e., architects, urban planners, and real estate developers), the ruling elites, and denizens of all sorts collide and sometimes challenge logics of accumulation and sovereignty. These cities are the result of historical trajectories that predate the hydrocarbon windfalls of the last fifty years. Gulf cities should be placed in conversation with a history of "mobile urbanism" for architects and engineers who learned from their experiences planning and engineering cities in the Gulf and transferred those lessons to a global marketplace for urbanism.[7]

In this chapter, I reflect on this history to explore how it has aligned and intersected with regionalism in ways that produce neither a uniform and tran-shistorical "Gulf city" nor a single bounded Gulf region. The focus of this chapter will be the cities of the small Arab Gulf states, but reference will be made to cities in Iran, Saudi Arabia, and Iraq. I trace urban shifts across three historical eras: from the development of port cities to the emergence of na-tionalizing cities in the mid-twentieth century, and from there to the current conjuncture when globalizing cities are economic developmental. In explain-ing these dynamic developments since the beginning of the twentieth cen-tury, this chapter shows that urbanism, or the way people live in and organize cities, is a multiscalar process depending on social networks extending beyond the limits of city and into rural areas and internationally. Such landscapes are built and maintained by people drawn from many places across the world, who occupy distinct places in the urban social terrain and legal-political architecture. The process of demographic and economic urbanization, therefore, lays the groundwork for a contested regional formation and variegated urban terrain.

Approaching the urban as a continual and unbounded (although not unconstrained) process, rather than a territorial unit, resonates with the socio-spatial approach of the book. It sheds light on a history in which the production of cities required connectivity between places and unleashed a dialectic of inclusion and exclusion, making and unmaking, differentiating and homogenizing. If the urban is not an object but a process of socio-spatial organization mediated by capitalist accumulation and related modes of political control, Gulf cities are a lens to decipher the political economy of space-making.

PORT CITIES, IMMIGRATION UNITS

The port city was the reigning urban form on the shores of the Persian Gulf until the collapse of the pearling economy, the global depression of the 1930s, and the advent of company towns built to extract, refine, and transport oil. Urbanism in late nineteenth and the early twentieth centuries created interlocking port cities surrounding the Persian Gulf tethered to places and processes on an oceanic, even planetary, scale. The specificities of the pearling trade, caravan routes, credit systems, ecological conditions, and trade winds make it impossible to understand these places in isolation and, as discussed in chapter 1, define Gulf regionalism at this historical juncture as boundless and centered around the waterway.

During the *fin de siècle* there was a whole host of locales along the coastline of the Persian Gulf that grew rapidly from fishing villages of a few hundred people into port towns and cities of tens of thousands. Manama and Bandar Lengeh grew from 8,000 in the 1860s to approximately 20,000 in 1900,[8] while the population of the town of Kuwait ballooned from 6,000 in 1840s to 35,000 at the start of the twentieth century.[9] Some cities, such as Manama and Bushehr, saw more trade and attained a more enduring status as maritime centers. Others declined or grew in stature during this era—Bandar Lengeh's waning and the ascent of Dubai captures this interconnected dynamic. Contributing to these variations were distinctions among these harbors. The quality and safety of these "natural harbors" and anchorage facilities were a critical matter that benefited ports such as Bandar Lengeh and Kuwait but hindered the growth of Doha, Abu Dhabi, and Basra. As steamships entered the fray, the location of coal depots and the specificities of shipping schedules became consequential. These speedier and larger vessels increased scale of trade but also privileged some ports over others. Regardless of technology, through the circulation of people, goods, information, credit, disease, and ideas, port cities and towns acquired a character of being an "entrepôt," or a place "between ports," or, to go to the original Latin meaning, "between places."[10]

As wealth was being accumulated, a significant portion of capital fed back into the urban economies and accounts of ship-builders, shopkeepers, and landlords as much as rulers and traders.[11] The older mud walls, city gates, and defensive forts were gradually overrun by new demands and aspirations. Labor-intensive and grueling, pearl fishing required a substantially larger work force than the coastal towns alone could provide, and these port cities profited from labor migration and burgeoning consumerism in many ways. Speaking to anthropologist Peter Lienhardt in the 1950s, one Kuwait merchant based in Dubai reflected on the boom years of the first quarter of the twentieth century: "Those were times when the poor had money; prosperity comes from the poor, not from the rich."[12] This generalized and growing prosperity was reflected in the built environment. Wealthy merchants and members of the ruling families constructed elaborate compounds from more durable materials, with Iranian and Indian businessmen commissioning architecture with eclectic designs inspired by their places of origin. Meanwhile, the expanding urban population, drawn from across the peninsula, Iraq, and Iran, was housed in tents and thatched huts (*barastis*) made from mud and palm tree fronds and trunks. As the population became more permanent and savings swelled, masonry structures built out of coral, gypsum, and imported timber proliferated in the tightly bound quarters and labyrinthine alleys.

Migrants from many directions and backgrounds fed into the existing cultural, social, and economic diversity of these littoral societies (see chapter 1). People arrived from different places, lifeworlds, and possibilities—some were members of tribes, some were not; some spoke Arabic, Persian, and Swahili;

some were enslaved and others owned humans along with properties across the Indian Ocean. They encountered one another at work, in markets, and before judges and religious leaders, yet sustained themselves through particularistic relations and forms of patronage-based identities. These mixed-use neighborhoods and dense alleys weren't a melting pot, however. Nelida Fuccaro observes that "the heterogenous make-up of the urban population did not generate a processes of cultural osmosis between different urban groups. Dress, taste and material culture continued to distinguish members of individual communities regardless of their social status."[13] Meanwhile, those not tapped into the tribal system or with other social constellations remained isolated and relegated to shantytowns that grew in areas of neglect on the edge of towns.

Not only was the population diverse, but it was socially and spatially differentiated. Besides the overarching distinction between neighborhoods built around the seafaring economy and those urban neighborhoods focused on overland trade and the products of pastoralists, a "segmentary urban system" was built around neighborhoods.[14] As "immigration units," quarters or clusters of alleys were inscribed with the intensity of regional networks on the urban landscape.[15] When migrants arrived to Bushehr, Lengeh, Kuwait, Manama, and Dubai, they headed to specific neighborhoods, often named after their places of origin or kin. To give just one example, Lengeh and Dubai were both home to communities of people from the small Zargos mountain town of Bastak and therefore both had quarters named after them; the same is true for Evazis, who had quarters in Manama and Lengeh. It was at this neighborhood level that migrants were channeled into employment, housing, and relations of all sorts by affinities based on tribes, ethnicity, or ancestral hometowns. Coffee shops, houses of worship, and other institutions socialized people by class, religion, and, most importantly place of birth but also brought them together through public encounters. Large segments of urban society were organized through communally organized or "voluntary" associations to absorb immigrant populations and peripatetic workforces. In this respect these port cities were more like city-societies than city-states governed from the top down.[16]

Beyond urban space, social categories with varying degrees of precision were developed to parse out differences. For instance, in Kuwait, a central marker of distinction was between townspeople reliant on maritime livelihoods (*hadar*) and bedouin and pastoral communities (*badu*). These terms resonated and were evoked throughout the *longue durée*.[17] In the twin cities of Manama and al-Muharreq, inequalities between Sunni tribesmen and Arab Shia cultivators (*baharna*) were reflected in how urban space was organized by guild. Meanwhile, the significant numbers of Sunni and Shia laborers, peddlers, shopkeepers, and wealthy merchants from Iran to the coastal town of Arabia complicated the categories of "Persian" and "Arab" or Sunni and Shia and splintered class distinctions and ethnolinguistic categories.[18]

Up through the first third of the twentieth century, merchant families played the role of custodians of this segmented city-society structure. The provision of welfare and public resources (such as drinking water and religious ceremonies) was managed at the neighborhood level and came from the largesse of merchants, who patronized people drawn from their own ethnic, cultural, or geographic backgrounds. As these neighborhoods or "immigration units" blurred the distinction between home and abroad, they also filled the organizational and welfare vacuum left by representatives of central authorities or members of the ruling family. It was pearl merchants and others who funded some of the first networks of schools that helped galvanize ideas about constitutionalism, religious reform, and modernism in Bahrain, Dubai, Jeddah, Mecca, and Mumbai.[19] To the dismay of many locals. Britain's colonial role never translated into development spending, which was kept to a minimum.[20]

The relative neglect of public services by both rulers and colonial officers was the root of much discontent after the 1920s, when the pearling economy fell on meager times (see chapter 3). Merchants confronted rulers and agitated to create municipalities and councils as fora for elites to defend their propertied interests by institutionalizing their authoritative position in society and overseeing the finances of the palace. Workers in new sectors of the economy flexed their economic muscle to call for better work conditions and pay. Former pearl divers who had become porters were one group enjoying leverage at a time when the fisheries were being abandoned and shipping and trade dominated the maritime economy. Another set of locations for claim-making were new company towns.[21] These were places where former laborers broke the bonds of the pearling and date sectors to become wage-earning oil workers. As they rubbed shoulders with migrants from the hinterlands of Dhofar, Yemen, and tribal western Iran and encountered recruits from colonial outposts in South Asia, they confronted a whole new political economic complex and an urban landscape set adrift from the port cities and oriented toward what would become a global energy market.

COMPANY TOWNS, NATIONALIZING CITIES

In recent years, dissident voices inside and outside of the region have deployed this historiography of port cities to lament "the demise of the pluralistic civic tradition and cosmopolitan culture of port towns as a symbol of the violation of cities and urban lives by oil and modernity."[22] Despite the romanticizing tendencies inherent in this move, it helpfully encourages us to grapple with the reorientation of urban processes toward oil extraction and reinvestment of revenues by the ruling families, both of which were bolstered by British interests and an emergent set of state institutions. Ports and maritime lives still mattered, merchants were still powerful, and migrants continued to be recruited and even become majorities, but as the demography and size of urban areas grew at dizzying rates cities were designed as investment opportunities and tools for political control in an era of social agitation. This was consequential for how people related to one another and conceived of political community increasingly in national terms. The cities reflected and contributed to new regionalization projects mediated by sovereign territorial states, citizenship regimes, and rentier capitalism.

If the twentieth century started with the shores of the Persian Gulf ringed by a series of port cities, by midcentury these "brides of the sea" were accompanied by company towns or oil cities, which competed for labor and resources but also offered a new model for urban organization and social differentiation. As British and American oil firms assembled oil towns in the deserts of Arabia and barren mountains of Iran's Khuzestan, they ushered in an era of urban living that displaced densely woven port towns. Along with the revenue from the sale of crude oil, these company towns bestowed upon rulers and their allies models for the massive urban "modernization" of newly independent states. Urbanism was no longer a connective tissue bridging coastal communities but a malleable terrain to include and exclude residents as a means to build political power and bind nationhood.

A critical distinction developed between Gulf cities in the 1950s. One set became capital cities. Kuwait, Manama, Abu Dhabi, and Doha were seats of government, centers of political power, and locations for public sector investment and employment. They were the only or the primary cities before and after independence. The Gulf cities of Iran, Iraq, and Saudi Arabia, such as Bandar Abbas, Bushehr, Basra, Qatif and Dhahran, in contrast, were not capitals of their countries or necessarily important places in a demographic or economic sense. In these contexts the expansion of public education systems and the swelling employment opportunities in newly minted ministries took place in booming metropolises—Tehran, Baghdad, and Riyadh—far from the littoral. Basra, Bandar Abbas, and Dhahran may have been valued as the nation's gateway to the sea and oil fields, but they were increasingly positioned as provincial cities, geographically and politically distant from rapidly developing population centers, industrial heartlands, and national decision-making bodies. They even had to contend with alternative trade corridors and hubs being built along other borders, along other borders, as Saudi Arabia was doing in the Red Sea. They were part of state territory and the nation, but they were on its edge, and as such their denizens increasingly felt and expressed their marginality.[23]

Extractive Enclaves

As pearling, date farming, and boat building gave way to hydrocarbon extraction during the early twentieth century, new urban spaces were created and the compact old city centers were repurposed. This was initially exemplified by the segregated enclaves designed and built by oil companies, most notably Abadan in present-day southwestern Iran, Ahmadi in Kuwait, and Awali in Bahrain. Taking the form of "the colonial city" or the "garden city," these company towns represented the cutting edge of colonial urbanism.[24] Abadan provides a useful example. Like Ahmadi, its later counterpart in Kuwait, Abadan was designed by James Wilson, who served as the assistant to Sir Edwin Lutyens during the planning of colonial New Delhi during World War I and founded and directed the Iraqi Public Works Department from 1920 to 1926.[25] Wilson helped transport the urban forms of the Raj to the Gulf, replicating and updating their symbolic hierarchies in a new context in which the Anglo-Persian Oil Company had full control over industrial and residential quarters. They helped introduce urban planning and functional zoning to the region at the same time they were being devised and implemented in the metropole and colonial outposts.

Despite being located in different countries and run by multiple firms, all these company towns were designed to address the specific concern of

managing large numbers of workers in a remote region.[26] With roots in corporate paternalism, Fordism, and colonial uplift, these oil towns provided
housing, education, recreation, and transportation facilities for their employees. To protect the autonomy of the oil firms, they were strategically isolated from preexisting urban areas, which were often labeled "native towns."
These company towns became sites of new infrastructure and construction
of houses, roads, hospitals, schools, shops, churches, and venues for sport
and entertainment. Most importantly, these services and spaces were deeply
unequal. From the quality of the construction material and size of the housing to the quality of the drinking water and transportation, the cleavage between Anglo-American managers and Persian, Arab, and Indian working
classes was etched into the built environment. Blending imperial strategies
of governing through difference and corporate techniques of fragmenting
workers, the facilities and spaces of company towns reflected a strict racial
and economic hierarchy.[27] Indeed, many were inspired by Jim Crow or plan-
tation systems.[28]

"Senior" employees—meaning, with few exceptions, "white" employees—
enjoyed the amenities of lush suburbs and bungalows. Housing for senior
managers and engineers was based on the contemporary housing patterns,
architectural forms, and landscaping practices being adopted at the same
time in Anglo-American suburbs and garden cities. In Ahmadi, urban space
"replicated the company's policy of ethnic segregation," down to the minutest
details.[29] When the anthropologist Peter Lienhardt visited the Kuwaiti company town, he noted that even "the domestic furniture provided for each family correspond to the householder's grade of employment in the company.
Any wife invited out for a cup of coffee would be reminded by the furniture
how much higher or lower than her own hostess's husband rated."[30] Backed
by public relations campaigns, gendered civilizing missions, and the rhetoric of corporate paternalism, oil companies embraced the role of urban space
as a mechanism for consumption and civilization—but also division and
differentiation.[31]

The oil companies had opened up new frontiers for the expansion of
Anglo-American corporate capital along with its consumerist tendencies
and culturalist forms of control. The company "construed and popularized two contrasting profiles: that of the expatriate housewife of suburban
Awali as shopper and the urbanite oil worker as the accomplished company

employee."[32] Nathan Citino perceptively recounts that the idealized suburban life in the compounds overseen by the Arabian-American Oil Company (Aramco) represented the "abundance of American society brought to the Middle East" even as their exclusions caused disenchantment among many of their American and Arab employees and their spouses.[33] Other tensions broke through these pristine projections. For instance, in the late 1940s on the Saudi oil frontier, Italian workers turned to industrial action to demand pay and housing equal to Americans of the same rank, rather than the rotten conditions they found themselves in—akin to "concentration camps," according to an Italian government minister who visited the labor camp.[34] Even though Aramco relented and housed the workers in an improved "Italian quarter," these workers were outraged at having to live with "Orientals" instead of with Americans in the Senior Camp. Rather than integrate the Italians, Aramco terminated their contracts and sent them home. As chapter 3 documents, this did not put an end to workplace mobilization in the company oil towns as a new working class identity was being forged out of old ethnicities and kinship groupings.

Although the managerial class was the focal point of this "enclave preservation strategy," it represented only a small slice of the workforce and was separated out from the majority who built and operated the oil installations— the workers who were paid a fraction of the wages and lived in squalor and with whom the Italians did not want to reside.[35] These were people drawn from the immediate Gulf region (pastoralists, bedouins, former pearl divers, and the enslaved) and were recruited from South Asia. These workers lived in labor camps, "Arab villages," and the "intermediate staff camp," for those classified as "semi-skilled." In Abadan, "native" labor, consisting mostly of an Iranian workforce (some with experience in the oilfields of Baku), was housed originally in tents and self-built huts that were set apart from neighborhoods reserved for British managers and located on the alternate side of the mammoth refinery. Nader Ardalan, who became a field architect for the National Iranian Oil Company, recalls that "in residential areas, buses, clubs, and cinemas, an almost complete segregation was imposed between the Company people and the 'natives,' who barely survived in what was derogatorily names Kaghazabad (Paper City)."[36] In between the housing for British and American managers and quarters for native workers was intermediary lodging for clerical and technical staff from South Asia, whose presence varied depending on the location. In Abadan where the Anglo-Persian Oil Company recruited almost four thousand men from the subcontinent by 1922, the neighborhood originally named "Coolie Lane" was renamed "Indian Lane."[37]

Since the opening decades of the twentieth century, the company towns' built environments were implicated in producing "migrant" workers as temporary and valuable primarily for their labor, despite their central role in the social and political history of the region. Corporations sought to cut costs by framing workers as part of a temporary "construction phase" that they kept claiming would soon be over. They claimed that creating livable housing and worker training programs would be unnecessary and wasteful.[38] Many of the labor camps were unplanned, emerging as shanty towns for workers who came to be seen as both foreign and transient. Indeed, their very ramshackle informality reinforced perceptions of their occupants as transient interlopers who would be removed once the project was "finished."[39] As opposed to the orderly "single-family housing" of the managerial class, these camps were some of the earliest instances in which "bachelor" accommodations and mobility were associated with moral degradation and social pathology. This legacy has persisted for decades and invited repeated state regulation of these populations in the name of confronting "demographic imbalances" and triggering moral panics around the figure of the single foreign man or highly sexualized foreign woman (see below). Women, families, and the nation needed protection from these necessary, yet rootless bachelor populations that were positioned spatially, culturally, and politically apart from those living in the city center.[40]

Scaling Up from Company Towns to Master Plans

Oil companies built these towns in order to ratchet up production for the emerging global oil market and manage labor relations, but they were also models for urbanism in the Gulf as well as the metropole. In their separate studies of company towns in Kuwait and Iran, Farah al-Nakib and Kaveh Ehsani arrive at this conclusion.[41] Ehsani describes the oil towns in Khuzestan as laboratories for experimenting with urban planning before and after oil nationalization, while al-Nakib shows that Ahmadi was an attractive model for Kuwaitis and an exemplar for segregating communities. As state coffers were boosted by oil revenue generated by these oil towns, the Gulf's port cities were radically rebuilt to emulate these enclaves.

Because of and in spite of their discriminatory roots, as Iranians, Kuwaitis, Bahrainis, Saudis, and others organized and broke down the barriers to promotion and ultimately nationalized the companies, the towns and their homes were valorized as epitomes of modern living and paternalistic welfare. Town planners and developers modeled urban design beyond the oil frontier after the company towns as they adopted their standards for roads, plot demarcations, and construction regulations to expand urban centers of the mid-century era. In some cases, the company towns became springboards for the careers of young architects, including in consort with European consultants.[42]

The spillover effect of company towns on the rest of society also took a less direct but more pervasive dimension. The revenue generated from the extraction of oil and the improved agreements with the oil companies empowered governments to plow greater sums into a new era of urban growth in the quarter century after World War II. Major investments in infrastructure—power stations, desalination plants, airports, and road systems—and housing programs energized real estate markets and transformed urban life by rerouting migration and consumption patterns. Urban growth played a key role in accumulation through appropriation, dispossession, and market transactions. Spearheading this were the rulers, who held almost all the cards: hectares of publicly owned land, the planning regime, and public subsidies. The precise speed and timing of this urban expansion depended on when oil exports came online and the whims and quirks of any given ruler. For instance, Abu Dhabi's Shaykh Shakhbout was both notoriously skeptical of developmentalism and frugal; it wasn't until he was unseated in a British-backed coup and his brother, Zayed, took over in 1966 that Abu Dhabi took these initial steps.[43]

To realize these projects, a variety of workers needed to be recruited. The 1950s and 1960s witnessed the arrival of an increasing number of migrants, not so much to labor in the maritime world or the oil installations as to build and service new housing settlements, expand transportation networks, and underpin whole new service sectors and ways of living that pivoted around nuclear families with heads of households who were increasingly likely to become state employees. As early as the 1950s, the census revealed that the number of foreign-born residents was rising. In Kuwait's first post-independence census of 1965, Kuwaiti-born residents were already a minority.[44] At the same time British officials in Dubai concluded that "the economy . . . depends on a supply of cheap labour, and the logic of taking this labour in the form of illegal immigrants, especially from India, Pakistan, and Iran."[45] This pattern and appetite for the "supply of cheap labor" was established well before the 1970s oil revolution.

Ruling families, working under British tutelage, established land registry offices to issue and record title deeds. The initial beneficiaries of this national regimes of property ownership were the ruling families themselves. They expropriated "unused" or "unclaimed" customary-owned land and divided it up widely and strategically across branches of the ruling family. As pastoral and nomadic people were dispossessed, land was abstracted and constituted as real estate; it was parceled, sold, or transferred as gifts which incentivized investments in construction of all sorts. This process first took place in the Upper Gulf and then closer to mouth of the waterway. Oil surplus was invested in desert outskirts of towns as road systems and electric grids to draw with it residential housing and private capital. New land was literally manufactured through dredging schemes in which land was reclaimed from the sea and swamps. Using rubbish, coral, and rocks, land was reclaimed by states from the sea and became government property that could in turn be allocated to public-private conglomerates. This played an important role in the Bahraini archipelago's midcentury urban development now that the island of Muharreq today was four times its original size.[46] In more recent decades land reclamation has been enhanced to conjure up man-made islands in the shape of palms, oysters, and more in Dubai and Doha.

This property rights regime enriched rulers and their families, but it also went a long way to solidifying a social base for the emerging nation-states. Transaction and registration fees became a means for state and municipal revenue. More important, as land became the main destination for surplus capital, urban development became critical for building class power and aligning merchant capital with the ruling families. In the 1950s, constitutionalist, nationalist, and anti-imperial protest movements across the region demonstrated that merchant capital still had significant social power (see chapter 3). Rulers and their colonial allies realized that they would have "to buy the merchants out of politics rather than simply drive them out."[47] As land ownership became an asset for speculation and a lever for accumulation, it became the resource that ruling families shared with well-positioned merchant capitalists. Land grants were always a common means for rulers to curry favor and elicit loyalty, but at this critical conjuncture in which economic and population growth coincided with political contestation to drive up the stakes of loyalty to the nation-state as well as to the ruler. In the harried building booms beginning in the 1950s, early critiques of the rentier state showed that land speculation and construction became so profitable that they crowded out other investments and disincentivized economic diversification, compounding the deleterious monetary effects of oil exporting.[48] Land purchasing soon became the single largest expenditure in the Kuwaiti government budget, as elites with access to municipal bodies and land registration departments leveraged information and political influence to seize unprecedented profits.[49] This real estate economy kept housing scarce and therefore profitable for owners and investors. As land prices increased, smaller firms and construction operations were crowded out or absorbed by larger and better-resourced companies. Across the region, real estate augmented pre-oil channels of rentier wealth, including raiding at sea and on caravan trails, fishing licenses, and air landing fees from nascent commercial airlines and the military British air force.

Besides the commodification of land, population growth informed the tacit bargain between the old trading houses and palace. This mixture of migration and rising fertility rates drove up consumption that benefited property owners, importers, and retailers. In Kuwait, population growth rates averaged 9 percent between 1957 and 1975 and were over 20 percent in Abu Dhabi and Dubai.[50] All these new residents needed places to live, work, and eat; they were the merchant families' employees, tenants, and consumers. Along with bequeathing land and offering other subsidies, governments in eastern Arabia allocated the provision of public services, such as electricity and telephones, to the private sector, rather than creating public enterprises.[51] By the advent of the oil boom of the 1970s, the merchant capitalist class in eastern Arabia had traded away their political freedom to protect their accumulated wealth, a portfolio that included increasing shares of the valuable urban landscape.

While it is tempting to see oil as the force that transformed land into a creator of value, it was the imposition of unitary sovereignty that enabled both the creation of a market in land and the dominance of ruling families and their allies (see chapter 3). The urban space was the means through which this took place. As Farah al-Nakib demonstrates, at the turn of the twentieth century, Sheikh Mubarak of Kuwait freely distributed land, only to turn around several years later and demand that occupants repurchase their own plots, with prices determined by the ruler's own appraisers.[52] Thus, it was Mubarak's political power secured by his compact with the British Empire, that enabled the Kuwaiti ruling family to secure the land that became its primary source of income in the pre-oil era. In Saudi Arabia, the state expropriated massive tracts of land from its nomadic population in a nationalization program that was legitimated by international development consultants and models of urbanization that valorized automobiles.[53] But, as Toby Jones notes, the state did not "follow through on the promise of land ownership," instead using the access to land as another means of exerting control over its population.[54] Finally, in Iran's province of Khuzestan, the Anglo-Persian Oil Company's intervention eventually enabled the centralized state to sweep away its local competitors. Thus, while oil certainly raised the stakes of land ownership, the commodification of both oil and land relied on the imposition of totalizing territorial sovereignty, a process that predated the hydrocarbon age and was intimately interwoven with empire.

These urban development projects were folded into master plans giving an added sense of comprehensive vision and control of urban futures. Often drafted by British architects and engineering firms, these plans, which were ostensibly descriptive devices, were heavily prescriptive too. They drew on practices that had become standard in "new town" planning, using ring roads and functional zoning laws to contain and separate urban space into functional zones. In his meticulous study of Dubai's urban development in the second half of the twentieth century, Todd Reisz comments, "A master plan is typically commissioned to convey a sense of stability and to plot a city's bounded form. It gives geographical and spatial expression to administrative order and signals additional services to come (ring roads, public transit, financial districts, marinas, public parks)."[55] During the transition from British tutelage to independence and the dislocations brought on by the early waves of oil wealth, stability and control were prized by ruling families.

Yet Reisz and others have shown that master plans drawn up for Dubai, Kuwait, Manama, Basra, and elsewhere were rapidly outstripped by population growth, boom-bust cycles in the oil market, and engineering challenges of massive planning and construction. The plans were also subject to shifting interests among the allied merchant capital and ruling families. With their hold on land secure, this small coterie jockeyed to profit through every phase of the development process. As soon as plans were announced, speculators with inside information (many of whom were ruling family members) appeared to buy up empty or unclaimed property to resell to the government. In other cases, after learning that a planning scheme would increase the value of their land, owners would hold onto their plots until they could sell at astronomical prices. Some of the largest profits were realized before anything had been physically built. "[T]he building boom in Kuwait went beserk [*sic*] during the period 1954 to 1962," summarized the chief architect of the Ministry of Public Works, Saba George Shiber. "So careless have been the many sectors of the bureaucratic technical corps and their expensive outside 'support'—the 'private,' 'consultative,' and 'expert' echelons—that land and land-use planning has been economically wasteful, architecturally and aesthetic design visually dubious and master-planning and programming an orphan in the most challenging urbanization operation in history."[56] In the case of Dubai, planning and land laws were growth strategies that were schematic, flexible, and never fully implemented, as Stephen Ramos has uncovered.[57] New proposals and large infrastructural projects, such as the Jebel Ali man-made port or land reclamation schemes (especially in Manama and Muharreq), could thus be proposed and implemented by the monarch, his mercantile allies, and a cadre of advisors from international firms. While these cities functioned, in the words of Harvey Molotch, as "growth machines," they often did so despite, rather than because of, plans and planners.[58] Ultimately, property values and demographic realities superseded and overwhelmed plans and rendered their order obsolete.[59] But there always seemed to be another firm or consultant waiting in the wings to draft a newer plan. Unhampered by democratic participation or technocratic adherence to "the plan," these blueprints became known as "visions" (so Dubai, Qatar, and Saudi each have a Vision 2030). They took on the quality of a branding campaign, showcasing the ambition of the state, rather than planning the engineering of specific cities.

Spatializing Citizenship

Besides this strategic distribution of land rent, housing also became one of the cornerstones of the post-1950s development of social welfare systems, especially in the Arab Gulf states. To counteract the churning waters of economic dislocations as well as challenges to the legitimacy of ruling families from anticolonial and left-oriented movements, part of this early oil revenue was diverted to address social demands for welfare. Urged by technocrats, union organizers, and ordinary citizens, distributive programs were designed across the region. This included the building of medical facilities and the provision of education and public housing.

The delivery of housing was a cornerstone of these new "contradictory" relations between states and citizens in which "welfare planning . . . vacillated between modern reform and patriarchal authority."[60] Beginning in Kuwait and spreading to other countries, a series of housing schemes were devised to build residential neighborhoods for specific groups (such as civil servants or members of the military) or for the general population of citizens.[61] Located primarily in the outskirts of the urban core, these compounds found inspiration in the bungalows and single-family homes of oil towns and US suburbs. The state sectioned off undeveloped land or repurposed existing wards for constructing roads, clinics, schools, and highly ordered residential zones. This was the start of the polycentrism of Gulf cities and the proliferation of thinly connected enclaves.

This reordering of urban space did not make it socially homogeneous and introduced new distinctions. Wealthier citizens lived in villas and gated communities designed to keep out noncitizens, except servants and other help. In some cases governments extended low-interest loans to citizens, and in other instances former homes were purchased by the state at overvalued rates to facilitate the relocation of citizens to these suburbs. Over time the value of these affluent spaces was maintained by keeping working-class residents out. On the one hand, townspeople were relocated from the neighborhoods in the old cities to outlying regions; on the other hand, bedouin communities were settled and introduced to "modern" life closer to towns. In 1959 over a quarter of all houses in Manama were huts made from palm leaf. But after demolishing and replacing them with more permanent structures, six years later these *barasti*s only amounted to 8 percent of housing.[62] Yet, social hierarchies remained visible at the scale of the city, with ring roads, differences in size and quality of construction, and unequal social amenities spatializing distinctions.

This was the beginning of a turn away from the sea. Various technological developments ranging from automobile lifestyles to building out of coastlines through land reclamation schemes to port expansions resulted in relocating home, work, and public spaces away from the waterfront. The Palestinian scholar Saba George Shiber observes that "land was being devoured by streets" as "cars became the dominant factor of planning the city."[63] Contemporaneous urban planners such as Shiber, the Greek architect George Candilis, and a set of architects from communist Poland all anticipated recent scholarship by pointing out that as these metropolises grew, they disrupted a form of urbanism in which people encountered and acknowledged differences and instead hardened social boundaries.[64] In the shadow of the megaprojects, some of these architects experimented with designs, materials, and conceptions of neighborhood to combat the Gulf becoming "a dumping ground for alien landmarks."[65]

To discuss midcentury Gulf urbanism is to confront the gradations of citizenship and its manifold inequalities. Public welfare—housing, education, and health—became generous but was directed only to citizens. Those who could not claim citizenship were barred from owning property in the Arab Gulf states as well as in Iran. Just as the early oil era was remaking port cities, newly minted laws defined who belonged in the category of citizen and noncitizen. With British support, the first nationality laws stipulated that eligible citizens must demonstrate proof of residence within the specific territory at a certain foundational moment. For instance, Kuwait's 1959 nationality law defined "originally Kuwaiti" as someone who lived within the city walls in 1920 or descended from someone who did.[66] It marked a specific time and place in which people were required to dwell in the country in order to be considered a full member of the nation. It excluded those who came after but also those who remained outside the city walls or wandered beyond it. With only limited possibilities for naturalization (especially for women and their descendants), the remaining population fell into three administrative categories: noncitizens needing a sponsor to remain and work in the country; a select few naturalized citizens, who had certain political rights curtailed; and over one hundred thousand stateless people, or *bidun*. Nationality laws in other Arab Gulf states followed similar principles to limit access to the citizenship and the material benefits that come with it.

Noncitizens, meanwhile, now the growing majority of residents, were left vulnerable to economic exploitation and bureaucratic obstacles. When these laws were initially articulated in Kuwait and Bahrain in the 1930s they even posed predicaments to propertied individuals.[67] Merchants, shopkeepers, and other people living in Bahrain and Kuwait who hailed from Iran, and to a lesser extent Iraq, were forced to choose between acquiring Iranian or Iraqi citizenship and losing their property in Manama and Kuwait City or retaining their property to become citizens of Bahrain or Kuwait.[68]

Over time, the form of citizenship based on residency was replaced in eastern Arabia with a strong sense of patrilineal kinship and shared dissent. In these "ethnocracies," where belonging is based on real or fictive kinship and naturalization is almost completely foreclosed, being a citizen opened up the possibility of owning land or property and therefore of being recipients of future streams of revenue from these assets.[69] With little difference between citizens and noncitizens in terms of taxation and political rights, the ability to own property versus being relegated to the rental market became one of two key differences between rights-bearing citizens and noncitizen "guest workers." The other was one's rights in the labor market. Alex Boodrookas's astute reading of citizenship and property in relation to labor struggles in Kuwait shows that at the exact moment in which unions were forming and labor struggles were unfolding in the 1950s, rulers, firms, and colonial advisors embedded national distinctions into labor law and social rights to splinter labor mobilization.[70] It is at this juncture that the bulk of labor was carved out as "migrant labor" and those who were citizens were extended protections and avenues for upward mobility. These laws dealing with citizenship capture attitudes toward class, defining who is allowed to accumulate wealth and power and who is not.

The boundary between citizens and noncitizens or nationals and foreigners has been policed by a blend of state and markets. Noncitizens have been physically and spatially divided by class. Depending on their incomes, they were dispersed into various zones that were dominated by rental properties or were housed in remote labor camps. Housing in the older city core gradually fell into disrepair and became dominated by "bachelor" housing owned by citizens that was rented out to migrant workers living several to a room. Some citizens made substantial sums from renting accommodations directly or indirectly to the pool of millions of migrant workers. As people were sorted into discrete neighborhoods and housing markets, some as landlords and others as renters, the integrative port city "immigration units" unraveled. These neighborhoods continued to be tightly packed and shaped by cultures and practices of communities from many parts of Asia. Established businessmen from India or southern Iran continued to function as patrons and helped migrant workers acquire and maintain work visas and structure repayment of debts.[71] Increasingly, however, this role was played parasitically (sometimes quite cruelly) by recruiters, subcontractors, and moneylenders in both the sending and receiving countries. These different layers of companies and individuals that mediate the relationship between migrants and the city along with the disinterest of GCC bureaucracies and legal systems has made it close to impossible to hold anyone accountable for abuses.

Despite noncitizen labor becoming a present absence legally, bureaucratically, and even physically, they are also an absent present. The combination of aspiration and despair that drew workers to the Gulf cities has ensured that as they live and toil they leave their mark on the urban fabric. This is despite having very limited non-working hours, as well as a legal and social environment reminding them that they are temporary, monitored, and expendable. The use of spaces such as malls, parks, and beaches by working-class noncitizens are regulated by a mixture of unaffordability, physical distance from their residents, and various forms of security (private security forces, CCTV).[72] Instead, specific neighborhoods and spatial practices, such as playing cricket or sharing cooking duties and meals, become moments in which claims on the city and lives are made (see Image 8). Despite repression and these layers of segmenting space, tensions and contradictions can't be fully ironed out. Strikes have always been a feature of work sites and labor camps.[73] Meanwhile, the welfare of citizens depends on an ever-increasing foreign majority for most intimate aspects of their lives—caring for children and the elderly, cooking and cleaning homes, managing finances, and so much more.[74]

In addition to the growing number of migrants and the new ways they were being divvied up, the midcentury era saw a shift in the range of places migrants came from and the diversity of jobs they performed. Until the 1950s, migration happened through well-worn socially imbricated networks following historic sea lanes and inland trade routes. People from specific places along the Tigris and Euphrates rivers, Nejd, southern Arabia, the Persian plateau, the coastal subcontinent, and eastern Africa were drawn to the Gulf coast. With the exponential growth of oil revenue and formal institutions of the state after World War II, planes full of doctors, teachers, engineers, bankers, and civil servants arrived from Palestine, Jordan, Egypt, Syria, Sudan, and other Arab states.[75] While some of these migrants, especially from Egypt, competed with migrants from older migratory pathways for jobs in

IMAGE 8: *Dubai, 2015, View from Al Satwa* by Michele Nastasi. Reprinted with permission of Michele Nastasi.

construction and retail, many of these recruits from Arab countries were educated professionals who spoke the same language and shared much with Gulf Arab culture. This allowed Arab noncitizens, whom nationals often did *not* label as "foreign," to be more integrated into local societies and "under the banner of pan-Arabism locals and migrants could identify themselves as 'brothers' with similar interests."[76] As these communities situated themselves in the suburbanizing landscape, Anh Nga Longva writes that noncitizen Arabs "create[d], in a literal sense, a replica of the world from which they originate, and this replica finds substantive resonance" with citizens.[77] In some select cases, such as exiled Palestinians who arrived in large numbers in Kuwait and elsewhere in the Gulf after 1948 and 1967, their contributions were recognized with citizenship. These migration flows came at a juncture in which these nascent states needed their expertise and sought to station themselves within a politically meaningful regional imaginary, "the Arab world." The ruling al-Sabah family in Kuwait, who had to contend with vocal advocates of Arab nationalist causes in the Parliament, took the greatest steps to demonstrate solidarity with Arabism—Kuwait became home to approximately four hundred thousand Palestinians, and the family established the Kuwait Fund for Arab Economic Development in 1961 to distribute aid and investments across the Arab world totaling one-sixth of the state's oil revenue.[78] The other monarchies in the region neither faced the organized advocacy that Kuwait's relatively participatory political system ensured nor took similar steps to support their Arab brethren.[79] Unlike Kuwait, which gained independence in 1961, Sharjah and Abu Dhabi were marked by British suspicion of rulers having Arab nationalist sympathies leading to coups.

The ambivalent position of Arabs from outside of the Gulf region points to the centrality of statecraft in the urban process of the midcentury era. These port cities became more properly city-states in which the seat of government sought to order society and intervene between all residents, regardless if they were citizens or not. Despite the complicating case of UAE as a confederation, these were capital cities that stood in for the whole nation, both demographically and metaphorically. The previously scattered and ambulatory population became anchored on these metropoles. Over three-quarters of the population lived in these capitals, and the webs of connectivity (roads, power grids, markets) were centered on them to integrate people and commodities, ranging from food to cement production, into what was for the first time a *national* economy.[80] Supporting this was the proliferation of organizations and laws that segmented and socialized people as nationals and foreigners. As the examples above illustrate, this national space was not homogenizing, nor was it the same as a public space in which people interact despite their differences and address matters of social importance. Instead it was national in that it turned the scale of politics and markets away from the neighborhood, port city, or diasporic societies toward something understood as Kuwaiti, Bahraini, Emirati, and so forth.

This nationalizing of the Gulf cities had its cognate in how international experts thought about and measured the urban. In the 1950s demographers, policymakers, and social scientists on the world stage, including at the United Nations, began to conceive of and represent urbanization quantitatively.[81] A group of academics and UN-based policymakers developed a universal method and metric for measuring urbanization, which is to say, how urban, and by implication how modern and industrialized, a given country was. In academic studies and UN data panels, they measured how much of the population of every country was "urban," as distinct from the non-urban (or "rural") in any national territory. Today these measurements tell us that that Kuwait, Bahrain, UAE, Iran, and Iraq are 100, 89, 87, 76, and 71 percent urbanized. These are some of the highest rates in the world. With rates likes these the societies of the Persian Gulf are indicative of what the United Nations and others have described as a new "urban age" in which all *nations* follow a similar urbanizing trajectory.

GLOBALIZING CITIES, EXTENDING GULF URBANISM

The urban, however, can be coupled with the supra-national. Kuwait's 1951 master plan optimistically declared that once it was implemented it would be "the best planned and most socially progressive city in the Middle East."[82] Seventy years later the webpage for Saudi Arabia's Neom "smart city," or The Line, declared that its 105-mile horizontal city "is a civilizational revolution that puts humans first, providing an unprecedented urban living experience while preserving the surrounding nature. It redefines the concept of urban development and what cities of the future should look like."[83] In between these proclamations directed to the whole world are countless plans, visions, blueprints, and slide shows anticipating a planetary future through the remaking of cities in the Gulf. Almost always framed as lodestars for all of humanity, these proposals promise cities of spectacle and superlatives, full of technological wonders and attention-grabbing architecture that are abstracted from local particularities and therefore transportable elsewhere. For a brief moment a decade ago Abu Dhabi's Masdar city promised a zero-carbon city, which used oil revenues to attract the Massachusetts Institute of Technology and host of companies to live out their fantasies in the desert.[84] Renderings and video presentations of such projects situate the viewer far above the fray, detached from the human scale and reinforcing this urbanism's other-worldly possibilities.[85]

If midcentury urbanization in practice and theory assumed the territorial boundedness of cities and placed them squarely within the container of nation-states, this began to be challenged empirically, analytically, and normatively by the notion of world or global cities. The roots of this concept go back to the 1980s when scholars observed that a set of processes in the world economy enhanced the role of cities in capitalism.[86] Increased mobility of capital combined with fiber-optic communications, containerized transportation, and large-scale data analysis created new demands and opportunities for corporate control of production, services, and investments. In the context of a new international division of labor, where deindustrialization in North America and Europe was coupled with the relocation of manufacturing to Asia where labor was cheap and weak, a few major cities, or "global cities," played the role of "command centers" overseeing other urban nodes of the global economy.

The first generation of scholarship on global cities theory explored the world-spanning hierarchy of cities through which corporate managers coordinated production and finance, primarily in London, New York, Tokyo, and a few other centers. As municipal budgets were hit by austerity and government regulations were whittled away one state after another, the privatization of services and public spaces was one means by which capital more directly turned cities into sites of investment and accumulation. Researchers have examined how these urban policies and class strategies, described as neoliberalism, have been adopted and imposed on what was becoming known as the Global South. A host of consultants and conferences circulated ideas about "best practices" that self-conscious practitioners of global urbanism needed to adopt to make their cities more market-friendly. Only with these steps could cities be classified as global and improve their place in surveys and rankings.[87] Indices were designed to measure the extent to which cities had the urban forms and financial structures necessary to become centrally located in global and regional networks. In this way global cities theory became a market-led development model to emulate. The question became, which cities are the most global? Hence, these shimmering "central business districts" hosting multinational corporations became the expression and medium for neoliberal globalization and its simultaneous elimination of barriers (de-territorialization) and construction of new landscapes for accumulation (re-territorialization). In the hands of some of the more excitable writers, the rise of global cities implied the demise of nation-states and scalar shifts to supra-national organizations or subnational authorities, but this did not necessarily follow from the early theoretical work. Equally problematic in these more ideological works was the suggestion that global cities and the urban age were bound to homogenize all the of these top-ranking cities and leave their nonglobal or ordinary stepsisters in their wake. While no city or place, urban or rural, has been untouched by the constellation of processes described as globalization, divergence in outcomes and the difference in the kinds of involvement in these global processes is what is telling. "Globalizing cities," using the gerund form of the verb that suggests an ongoing dynamic, is a more appropriate term if we want to grapple with these multifarious processes and variegated ends.[88]

Gulf Urbanism's New Geographies

As in the case of company towns and mid-twentieth-century urban planning, the Persian Gulf, no stranger to trends in urbanism, adopted and adapted the global city form. While heavily focused on the experience of advanced industrial countries, the global cities paradigm and its emphasis on postindustrial production and knowledge economies were compelling to economies with plenty of capital but limited labor forces. (In this respect, it can be argued that the global cities model is less suited to Iran, Iraq, and Saudi Arabia than their neighbors with smaller populations and less pressure to generate employment.) As we saw in the previous chapter, as early as the 1970s policymakers embraced the language of connectivity and transregionalism as they positioned the Gulf as a critical global seam for transshipments and circulations. Already at this juncture investors and planners considered Gulf cities and their associated FTZs as key nodes of global commodity chains and a pivotal gateway to new markets. This theory had the added attraction of aligning with specific predicaments facing oil exporters. "Global cities" spoke to one of the main challenges facing the region—diversification away from fossil fuels before they ran out or were replaced with an alternative energy source. Political leaders and policymakers have long understood that being dependent on the export of fossil fuels comes with a number of drawbacks, including vulnerability to the vicissitudes of global energy markets, exposure to the perverse effects of overvalued domestic currencies, and the limited employment generated by these enclave industries. It is in this context that oil-poor Dubai led the charge in approaching urbanization as a key feature of diversifying the economy away from oil and gas and toward a host of place-specific service sectors ranging from tourism to transshipment.[89] Finally, by advocating for "urban entrepreneurism" and flexible accumulation, the global cities theory had affinities with a history of merchant capitalism playing a leading role in ruling coalitions.

To the praise of advocates and horror of critics, Dubai and, more recently, Doha and Abu Dhabi have adopted policies to situate themselves as key nodes in global circulations and potential regional command centers, recruiting a fleet of "starchitects" liberated to experiment with their visions and unburdened by financial handcuffs or municipal regulations.[90] "It's an amazing opportunity for the university to seed the urban fabric the way we would like it," commented Hilary Ballon, associate vice chancellor of New York University-Abu Dhabi.[91] Ballon, who is also an architectural historian, added, "Where else would you basically get to operate on a tabula rasa?" While retaining all decision-making powers in the grips of a small circle of royals, fund managers, and merchant capitalists, Gulf Arab states liberalized financial and ownership rules to attract foreign and local private investment. Initially these were implemented in FTZs, but over time some governments have chosen to loosen property ownership laws and have devised ways for some noncitizens, and even nonresidents, to own property. This has been a valuable opportunity for professional and wealthier Arab, South Asian, Iranian, and other resident noncitizens, many of whom have been long-term and sometimes multigenerational denizens with a sense of belonging and entitlement.[92] Meanwhile, FTZs, ranging from those in vicinity or airports to sector-specific enclaves such as Dubai's Media City and International Financial Center, relax visa restrictions as well as ownership and taxation laws to allow foreign companies to open regional headquarters and offices. Most of these development projects have been led by sovereign wealth funds and construction conglomerates partially owned by states and their aligned private interests. Creating these new state-owned or backed investment authorities and addressing the demands of noncitizen investors have driven new developments in other sectors, especially financial markets. Mergers and acquisitions have led to the formation of ever larger conglomerates, sometimes with interlocking directorships spanning across GCC states with the UAE and Saudi playing the central role.[93] While real estate bubbles have periodically collapsed, notably during the 2008 oil crash and global recession, states have utilized their reserves to support private and public firms and shift the burden onto migrant workers whose contracts had ended and who had been sent home or left in legal limbo.

When we speak of twenty-first-century Gulf urbanism, the sites of its enactment have also occurred far away from the Persian Gulf and been tethered to a new "Arab urban scale," as Adam Hanieh describes it.[94] Gulf cities were a place where urbanism converged on as well as fanned out from eastern

Arabia. Investments in real estate and related sectors have been profitable for a swath of Gulf firms and have enabled and driven economic and consequent social realignments across many Arab countries and beyond. By seizing opportunities created by structural adjustment in other counties and deepening the processes in its own image, in the past quarter century "Gulf capital" has become an integral part of class relations and the production of urban space in Egypt, Palestine, Lebanon, Morocco, and elsewhere in the Middle East. Gulf investment authorities and state-backed contractors have their fingerprints all over gargantuan projects across the region: Amman's Abdali and Marsa Zayed projects, Beirut's postwar urban renewal venture known as Solidere, Rawabi City outside Ramallah, and Egypt's still-unnamed new administrative capital being built beyond Cairo's second ring road. Emirati, Saudi, and Qatari firms have stepped into the fray as housing and banking sectors were privatized and property and rental regimes were de-regulated in one country after another. Between 2008 and 2017, GCC-related ventures accounted for over 44 percent of Egypt's large-scale real estate projects, while in Morocco and Jordan the figures were 67 percent and 90 percent, respectively. Meanwhile, GCC-based financial institutions helped create and expand mortgage markets in these same Arab countries to encourage housing acquisition and household borrowing.[95] Investors in skyscrapers, owners of gated communities, and underwriters of debt in cash-strapped Arab states combined to stimulate their own political geographies that extended Gulf urbanism into these new urban frontiers. Although concentrated in the Arab world, GCC economic portfolios included real estate, telecommunications, port facilities, and commercial banking assets in eastern Africa and South Asia. Not only did this help restructure the economies in Pakistan, Turkey, Eritrea, and elsewhere but it formed a profitable and major share of GCC portfolios. Simultaneously, Gulf capital's investment in farmland and agrobusiness in Egypt, Jordan, Yemen, Ethiopia, and Indonesia doubles as an important conduit for feeding urban populations in the Gulf as well as reaping massive profits for their agrarian sector.[96]

This recycling of Gulf urbanism into Arab capitals and even farmlands has created new opportunities for the Gulf urbanist coalition to reproduce itself at a new regional scale, one that is unmoored from its historic oceanic roots and parallels other geoeconomic endeavors in the twenty-first century. A steady stream of investments by GCC firms and sovereign wealth funds has been designed to both diversify financial portfolios and give the image that the region is more than a political repressive energy depot. Gulf oil exporters have been an important source of capital since the 1970s (see chapter 2) but have added a series of high-profile investments since the early 2000s oil boom. The list includes investments in Deutsche Bank, Citigroup, P&O, the London Stock Exchange Group, British Airways, Twitter, and many more major multinational firms across different sectors. Some of these dealings had a public relations dimension. Operating as advertising billboards for states and royal families, hosting major sports events (e.g., Qatar hosting the 2022 World Cup or Bahrain being the home to Formula One races) or purchasing and bankrolling what some would describe as lesser sports teams, who have bought up players, play fast and loose with the rules, and skyrocket up the league tables.

Although GCC purchases of North American companies is far less than Chinese, Brazilian, Russian, and Indian investments, their high-profile ventures in European and North American cultural, educational, and sport institutions are more than what international relations scholars have called "soft power"; some critics have described it as crass lobbying or "washing."[97] For the ruling families, these economic spectacles have played the added political role of dislodging themselves from existing regional patterns and cultivating alliances with capitalists and politicians in various powerful countries. This is in part a lesson drawn from the now-forgotten post-9/11 moment when anti-Muslim and -Arab xenophobia had whipped up hysteria in the United States and Europe against "Arab money." A rich pool of orientalist and racialized imagery was (and continues to be) evoked to criticize legitimate political and ethical questions about Saudi Arabia purchasing Newcastle United, Qatar hosting US universities in Doha's Education City, and Abu Dhabi attracting the Louvre and Guggenheim to Saadiyat Island. The branding campaigns that the UAE, Saudi, and Qatar have invested in are an insurance policy against this endemic racism abroad as well as the looming shadow of an energy transition away from fossil fuels. It is unclear, however, if these mega-projects manufacture popular support for rulers among their own citizens. They very well may. Yet it is critical to recall that in all of these cases, citizens have no oversight or opportunity to voice concerns about how these opaque and often secretive projects are designed in their own countries or how public wealth is invested abroad. This is not a glitch or an oversight but a feature of

Gulf globalism that requires the demos to be absent and decision-making to be insulated from the masses—from citizens as well as noncitizens. In the one GCC country where parliamentary oversight, greater press freedom, and party-competition exists, Kuwait, these sorts of mega-projects and flexibility for foreign capital are inhibited.[98]

Regional "Hauntings"

Some political leaders in the Arab Gulf and their economic and technocratic allies sought to move on from the twentieth-century formulation of Gulf regionalism built around the waterway by reaching for the global horizon. This did not come with either a fully developed new regional organizations or erasure of past formations. These efforts to globalize Gulf cities and turn their firms into instruments to remake urbanism elsewhere was accompanied with an indifference to inter-Gulf city collaboration and connectivity. Despite its original mandates to encourage economic and social integration among its members, the GCC has been famously under-institutionalized and has been uninterested and incapable of coordinating infrastructural projects, let alone creating a platform to generate collaboration among the member states. Instead of the sorts of amalgamation that may come with the formation of a Gulf mega-urban region or city-regionalism, there in fact has been growing replication of projects and competition between Dubai, Doha, Abu Dhabi, and other cities.[99] The 2017–21 Saudi- and UAE-led blockade of Qatar and its ultimate inability to grind Qatar's economy to a halt, for instance, is a testament to deep divisions in the GCC and the growing lack of interdependence between Qatari, UAE, and Saudi transportation and logistical networks. Despite Qatar's earlier reliance on Jebel Ali for transshipments of goods, it was able to restructure its trade patterns and enhance its ports to withstand the blockade.[100]

Instead, traces of past regional circulations and channels continue to matter and are etched on the urban terrain. These are the "hauntings" that theorist Ash Amin refers to in his advocacy for a relational rather than abstract understanding of space. He writes: "So, if we are to see cities and regions as spatial formations, they must be summoned up as temporary placements of ever moving material and immanent geographies, as 'hauntings' of things that have moved on but left their mark . . . , as situated moments in distanciated networks, as contoured products of the networks that cross a given place. *The sum is cities and regions without prescribed or proscribed boundaries."*[101] As powerful actors have conjured up new transnational entanglements, there are patterns that expose an incongruence between the GCC's urban and investment strategies and the actually existing circuits of capital and labor that sustain Gulf urbanism.

A highly original study of property ownership in Dubai in 2020 has shown the persistence of historical social cartographies.[102] Foreign investment in the Dubai housing and property markets has been an important lever in its post-oil-growth model. This has paid dividends too. The total foreign investment in Dubai's property ownership is twice as much as the real estate held in London by foreigners through shell companies. But these investments have a distinct pattern. Out of the $146 billion in foreign investment in Dubai's property ownership, over 47 percent of it comes from countries of the immediate littoral region—India (20%), Pakistan (7.3%), Saudi Arabia (6.7%), Iran (4.8%), Kuwait (2.4%), Iraq (1.8%), Oman (1.5%), Qatar (1.4%), and Bahrain (1.0%). If we add the United Kingdom (10.1%), the colonial ruler of Dubai until 1971, that would bring the total to 57 percent. The owners, investors, and sometimes residents of these properties are disproportionately wealthy South Asians, Arabs from neighboring countries, and Iranians. They are not necessarily representative of historical communities who traveled to or worked in Dubai, for they can afford to purchase apartments, villas, commercial properties, and labor camps as well as pay the required fees and taxes. However, in making these purchases, they are sketching a far more defined geography than that suggested by the branding campaigns projecting Dubai as a global city open to all corners of the world or narrowly defined by strategic policies in the Arab World. This pattern also suggests a far stickier or historically grounded geography than is allowed for by Amin's notion of spatial formations as temporary and ever-moving. It also reminds us that "the global" is shaped in particular places.

These same regional connections are preserved through migrant laborers, a topic on which the global cities paradigm has little to say and when it does focuses on human capital and managerial labor.[103] To contend with this almost century-long discourse of demographic threat, governments have implemented regularized labor nationalization campaigns (i.e., Emiritization or Saudization) that seek to restrict foreign laborers and replace them with citizens, especially in the private sector, where citizens have been highly underrepresented. To address the "problem" of citizens being more expensive to hire and private-sector employment being highly depressed, all countries in the GCC have adopted employment quotas, training programs, and financial incentives for corporations to increase labor market participation by nationals. These policies have been consistently ineffective and unappealing for firms wanting the sort of cheap and enfeebled labor that the set of laws and practices that kafala system provides. It has been a system that labor rights organizations, investigate journalists, and academic writers have regularly documented as being rife with opportunity for abuse, neglect, and the disavowal of responsibility. If replacing foreign workers with nationals has proved difficult, compounding the centrality of noncitizens in the economy is their role in a growth model predicated on commodified real estate markets. As various housing and urban projects have been enacted at more feverish pace and grander scale in Dubai, Abu Dhabi, Doha, and other smaller cities, one of the key markets for buyers has been professional expatriate communities, some of whom have had long and multigenerational lives in eastern Arabia. By reforming laws to enable internationalized property ownership, some strata of noncitizens have in fact become vital to the urban economy in new ways.

As Gulf capital went chasing contracts and aligning with elites at the Arab Urban scale, the circulation of workers from Egypt, Palestine, Jordan, Syria, and Yemen to the Gulf has been impeded, if not fully blocked. In 1975 non-GCC Arabs continued to make up the vast majority of expats in Saudi and Kuwait, but in Bahrain, the UAE, Qatar, and Oman had already plummeted to less than a third.[104] With the US-led 1990–91 Gulf War and the expulsion of almost a million Yemeni from Saudi Arabia and about half a million mostly Palestinian and Jordanians from Kuwait and Saudi, Arab expats became a minority and were systematically replaced by workers from Asia. Economic and political considerations encouraged these trends. Plasterers, drivers, and accountants from South Asia and Southeast Asia could be recruited at lower wages than their Egyptian, Palestinian, and Jordanian counterparts. They were also less able to integrate into the national society and "incite" and "agitate" opposition, as Arab laborers had been able to do through Arab nationalist, Islamist, leftist, or simply antimonarchical movements. As early as 1929, Syrian teachers organized a student-teacher strike in Bahrain.[105] Between 1940 and 1970, the height of anti-imperial Arab nationalism, politicized workers from Yemen, Egypt, and Dhofar were involved in everything from industrial action to rallies in support of Palestinian dispossession. This politics of fear led to contracts for Egyptians, Syrians, Yemenis, and other Arabs to be cancelled in the wake of the Arab uprisings in 2011. Even if strikes and labor resistance have not disappeared, South and Southeast Asian workers have been less embedded in society and therefore more contained and exploitable.

Although citizenship and noncitizenship entail important social, legal, and economic inequalities, there are other social and legal categories differentiating populations in the Gulf. Increasingly, this has become expressed spatially within the built environments of the globalizing Gulf cities. As elsewhere in the world, working-class citizens are the economic beneficiaries of racialized labor and the noncitizen underclass as well as being socially promoted above them by their status as citizens. Yet the stark differentiation of citizen and noncitizen occludes other struggles, specifically those related to the gradated nature of citizenship in Arab Gulf states and the presence of stateless people and tribally or ethically marked communities occupying an interstitial position in social hierarchies. Claire Beaugrand discusses two such communities in the context of Kuwait and Bahrain's projects for urban renewal.[106] Stateless people in Kuwait have been unable to gain recognition by the state as citizens. As an "administrative label," *bidun* marks them as "non-Kuwait," but due to their historic presence and residence in these societies they do not occupy the same place in the citizenship regime or labor market as foreign or guest workers. In Kuwait, this social marginality has been doubled since the midcentury housing programs and forced settlement of nomadic peoples. Stateless families have been physically located in cheaply made public housing in geographically remote areas on the outskirts of cities, including on the edge of the old Ahmadi oil company town. While Kuwait's *bidun* have had different experiences and treated by the state in a highly individualized fashion, this pattern of housing is a catalyst that unifies them. Through a close reading of various sources, Beaugrand shows that many stateless Kuwaitis have internalized a sense of shame and stigma in direct association with their residential surroundings.

Meanwhile, in Bahrain the term *village* and *villagers* has come to evoke a sense of humiliation born of living in degraded areas, often in the shadows of financial hubs and sleek high-rise blocks. Largely drawn from the majority Shia community—although not exclusively so—these communities have not received the same investments as other Bahrainis. Given that the state has been commanded by the Sunni Khalifa family, this material inequality has acquired a sectarian dimension, with Shia systematically discriminated against within Bahrain's political economy. In parallel, Manama's signature globalizing projects entailed reclaiming land from the sea and expanding road systems that erected barriers between farmers and their pastures and between fishermen and the sea. All the while, the Bahraini government acknowledges that there is a thirty-thousand-unit shortage of low-income housing.[107]

These globalizing urban Gulf regimes have remade cities across the Arab world, reached out to farmlands in Africa, and turned to recruiters to enlist dispossessed Asians to furnish the capital, calories, and labor needed to re-build their own cities. As such, neoliberalism has been deeply embedded in the Gulf's iteration of becoming global cities. These cities are clear examples of an urbanism that cannot be restricted to what takes place within them. This is an urbanism "without an outside," one that has generated new cartog-raphies and combined them with past segmentary forms to create a patch-work in which markets are differentiated by citizenship and class, in which regulations and laws shift based on borders of special economic zones, and in which the urban fabric is carved up by urban entrepreneurs' propensity for discrete socio-spatial niches.[108] Residents and visitors of Dubai, Doha, Abu Dhabi, Kuwait, and Bahrain are left moving between malls, sports clubs, and gated residential communities that operate as autonomous spaces with exclu-sionary practices differentiating in terms of disposable income or between "families" and "bachelors" or the matrix of subjective racial, gendered, and classed categories. These are not neighborhood immigrations units or func-tional zones within master plans from earlier decades but a series of priva-tized cities within the city, sometimes having their own private security or administrative authorities.

Built into this development strategy are real risks. For their profitability, speculative capital investments in fixed assets require continued flows of commodities, capital, and labor. If the flows fail to materialize due to eco-nomic recession, war, revolution, or cartel-like behavior by competitors, then fixed capital stands to be devalued and lost through bankruptcy, ma-terial decay, and technological obsolescence. In their extreme this leads to depopulation, dereliction, and decline. The result is that destruction of value is tied to the ruin of communities. The old "brides of the sea," such as Bander Lengeh, became tuckered-out towns anchoring grey economies or satellite towns, such as Sharjah. In the past half-century there were many instances of this that left their imprint on the region's urban terrain. The 2008–09 global recession wreaked havoc on Dubai, tarnishing its glistening image and giving investors from Abu Dhabi and elsewhere the opportunity to sweep in.[109]

Within this monumental urban scale exist interstices—vacant plots, parking lots, and grassy knolls—that become spaces for subaltern sociability and even subcultures.[110] Laborers organize strikes and protests, even if they are rarely covered by media.[111] That working-class action is typically cloistered in labor camps and construction sites and marginalized communities in Bahrain and Kuwait mobilize in "villages" and low-income housing areas are indications of how struggles are inscribed into the urban geography of the Gulf.

In February 2011 when "villagers" joined other Bahrainis to mobilize around their decades-long demands for constitutional rule, political rights, and social justice they marched on Manama's GCC Roundabout, popularly known as the Pearl Roundabout. Built on reclaimed land and serving as an intersection to a waterfront commercial center known as Bahrain Financial Harbor, the traffic roundabout hosted a three-hundred-foot-tall cement monument depicting sails of dhow ships holding up a pearl. Drawing inspiration from Egyptians, Tunisians, and Yemenis, young activists organized and occupied the city's most visible traffic roundabout and erected a tent city on the grass surrounding the massive statue. Those who encamped in the roundabout were building their own place in order to summon a different life, a life different from what the ruling family and economic elites had prescribed and constructed in Manama. In response, the Bahrain government turned to its GCC allies, the Saudi and UAE military, to drive out the encamped protesters. This resulted in at least four civilians being killed; in retaliation against the protestors authorities demolished several Shia mosques. Reports circulated of Bahrainis targeting migrant workers who had accused them of working for the security forces. A few weeks later, authorities tried to physically eradicate the uprising by tearing down the Pearl statue, the symbolic tribute to an era of national unity and Bahraini authenticity. In the hastily organized and televised demolition of the large monument depicting sails of dhow ships holding up a pearl, a migrant laborer was crushed to death by the tumbling edifice.[112] This tragedy captures how power can redraw urban space with little regard for the powerless.

CONCLUSION

Over the past century and a half, multitudes of people made their way to Gulf cities, drawn by opportunities and the needs of others or pushed by social

forces and personal aspiration. Upon arrival they encountered existing social formations and spatial politics that benefited from these new arrivals—
but were also threatened by them. This admixture of the powerful and the
enslaved, the well-financed and the indebted, the strategic and the aimless
were etched into the built environment through urban plans, architectural
forms, and housing polices. At the beginning of this time, a dozen port cities
were nodal points in a web of oceanic and land-based exchanges and circulations. Their growth took place through neighborhoods and diffuse but hierarchical relationships responding to economic opportunities far from the
city boundaries. As economic and political power became concentrated in
the hands of rulers, extractive firms, and a smaller array of merchants, these
cities had to situate themselves in relation to a new political container, the
nation-state. The built environment of capital cities, or provincial towns, or
company towns was a means to manage social relations and distribute surplus. A thicket of social boundaries hived off communities spatially, legally,
and functionally but also subordinated them in relations to increasingly
centralized forms of national power. By the end of the twentieth century urbanism was conscripted into projects ensuring liberties for capital mobility
and infrastructures for commodity circulation. Gulf cities expanded through
their own financial deregulation and investments in transportation networks
but also by private and public investments in other parts of the world, which
became key sites of sustaining the economies and reproduction of Gulf urbanism. *Dubaization* is the term used to deride how one's favorite city gets
transformed, but Dubai was never just a single origin. Across these decades,
what counted as "the hinterland" changed as technologies advanced and new
resources and people become exploitable. The contours and content of re-
gionhood shape-shifted and sometimes reappeared in new forms, but they
never completely disappeared with the turn to discourses of nationhood or
globalism.

SPATIAL FRICTIONS

BETWEEN 2000 AND 2017 I visited several places along the Persian Gulf coast. These were mostly short stays—for personal travel, research visits, to attend conferences, or as transit stops between destinations. My mixed social networks of Iranian businessmen, academic researchers, family, friends, and young hyphenated artists and students became gateways to circulate in the disparate social worlds of the UAE, Iran, Qatar, and Bahrain. They conditioned my thinking about how the Persian Gulf has been enveloped by imperfect and incomplete geopolitical and geoeconomic projects. My crisscrossing into and out of the Gulf continually made me aware of the limits of my knowledge and the differential positions that are entailed in the "power geometries"[1] involved in movement and belonging in the Gulf. These visits showed me how territorialization is lived, how it affects people's daily lives. I saw the gaps between the grand visions of strategists and the realities of everyday life. I saw the ambiguities in the way that regionalism was inhabited but also reoriented and rebuffed.

What helped me make out the tensions of region-making was being prevented from going to the UAE to teach at New York University-Abu Dhabi in the fall of 2017. The full texture and scope of what Doreen Massey describes as how "social groups and different individuals are placed in very distinct ways in relation to these flows and connections" became clear.[2] I was ensnared in one of the seams of twenty-first-century "global" higher education, or NYU's initiative to have faculty and students circulate through a series of branch campuses. Embracing a theological understanding of globalization as "a new Axial Age" defined by the timeless "joy of discovery of new worlds" and epochal shift in acceleration, NYU president and former law professor John Sexton envisioned the university as a web of affiliated "portals" and "nodes" enjoying discrete "locational advantages."[3] Internalizing older "study-abroad programs," NYU's Global Network University was marketed as an exciting opportunity for some to teach, learn, and conduct research in cities such as Florence, Madrid, and Accra. For others these campuses were a rare opportunity for academic employment in a tightening job market or a means for applicants to gain admission into NYU and credential-conscious students to mark themselves as being globally connected. From the budget-conscious perspective of trustees and administrators, the portal campuses are attractive not only in that they enhance endowments but also expand tuition receipts without the financial constraints of New York city's real estate market or its regulatory safeguards, including labor and nonprofit laws. For decision-makers in Abu Dhabi, hosting NYU and other university branch campuses was part of cultivating the globalizing city brand, using education to turn financial surplus into "human capital." It was also a means of currying favor from elites beyond its borders, while producing future ones. Abu Dhabi assumed all expenses in planning, designing, and building the campus as well as operations, which initially included substantial fellowships for all students and significant salaries and subsidies for employees. But the Abu Dhabi government maintained tight control. Khaldoon al-Mubarak, who was the founding chairman of one of the leading decision-making bodies in Abu Dhabi (the Executive Affairs Council) and the director of the quasi-state Mubadala that built the campus, joined NYU's Board of Trustees.[4] NYU-AD is not alone; Doha has created a whole Education City. NYU is also not unique, with Sciences Po, Northwestern University, Texas A&M, Georgetown University, and many other US and European universities opening campuses in recent years.[5] Experiences are varied, and I make no claim that mine is representative.

Shortly after NYU received its original $50 million gift from the Abu Dhabi government and the latter had begun to build the campus on the donated land earmarked for a cultural district that would include branches of the Louvre and Guggenheim museums, I had the opportunity to meet with one of its founding administrators. I casually inquired about the possibility of combining teaching and research on the Gulf region. NYU's initial statement spoke of the Middle East as a "crucial part of the world" and being an "entrepot of world politics and culture" with "Abu Dhabi itself as a cultural and intellectual center in the region."[6] I thought I was tapping into this sensibility by referencing a recent publication and list of past research visits to emphasize that my interests in the UAE were "genuine" since they predated NYU's new project. This faculty administrator, an expert on urbanism in New York who was the point person on academic matters, responded that the Abu Dhabi campus was "not set up for local research." I did not pursue the possibility further. In the initial discussions at the New York campus and in the marketing campaigns, references to the Middle East, the Arab world, or the Gulf region were conspicuously thin, if not totally absent. Nonetheless, a couple of years later the same administrator consulted with me about the possibility of Persian being taught at NYU-AD. I responded with my own recommendation—it would be exciting to offer language courses in Hindi and Urdu, enabling students to contemplate shared pasts and presents. This suggestion was met with silence. I don't know if the administrator's silence stemmed from indifference, unease, or willful amnesia, but I did learn that Chinese and Arabic were the two non-European languages taught on the campus, not any of the languages of the over 4 million South Asians—approximately 50 percent of the UAE population—who reside there.

In the meantime, it seemed that it was difficult to ignore that the global was operating in a specific place. Faculty and students contacted me, asking about "the region" or inquiring about the possibilities of traveling to Iran while teaching and studying in Abu Dhabi. Students from NYU-AD registered for my courses on Middle East politics in New York. Some of my students from NYU-AD were majoring in Arab Crossroads—a term coined to distinguish it from Middle East Studies but maintain an ethnicized anchor.

Yet, geography and region were overwritten by identity and national sovereignty. In 2017, nearly a decade after I began teaching at NYU, I approached a different faculty administrator at NYU-AD, one who was in charge of recruiting NYU faculty to the Emirates. I mentioned my continued interest in teaching in Abu Dhabi. This time I was greeted with enthusiasm and plans were drawn up for me to teach there in the next academic year. When it came time for me to apply for my residency visa, I was anxious because of the growing securitization of politics in the UAE and across the GCC after the 2011 Arab uprisings. Gulf royal families bristled at the possibility of the political status quo being disrupted, let alone democratization gaining a foothold in the Arab world. NYU's administrators assured me that my file for security clearance and residency would be shepherded along by their team of consultants. Yet my doubts grew when in an email exchange with another administrator, a much-read scholar of postcolonialism, he wondered if "sometimes people's last names makes [sic] their religious identity clear. Is that the case with yours?" This was in response to my request to leave blank the questions about my religion and sect on the NYU-AD human resources and UAE immigration forms. I was told that I must answer all the questions.

Several weeks later, I was informed by the same administrator that my application for a residency visa had not been approved. The Emirati authorities, often referred to by NYU administrators as "our partners," denied my security clearance without explanation and shut down the pathway to obtaining a work visa and residency. In a short phone conversation, it was shared with me that I was not alone in being refused.[7] While I was exhorted to keep the matter between us, the administrator tried to console me with the reassurance that I was not rejected in any personal sense, it was just that my application was not approved. I asked if they would follow up on this and appeal the decision. Despite saying that NYU-AD would do so, nothing happened and no explanation was offered by NYU or its partners. Rather than having me enter the UAE and engage in bordering practices used to regulate the movement and organizational capacity of citizens and noncitizens alike, it was easier to keep me at bay. However much globalization had become the organizing principle for the project, national sovereignty defined it—it was "transnationally framed, but nationally enacted."[8]

The UAE's bordering practice spilled over into the bureaucratic forms and organizational structures of the university. Questions about my place of birth, religion, sect, and my father's name, designed to reveal my roots, were duplicated on NYU human resource forms. As a US citizen and tenured faculty member who is also a person born in Iran into a Shia Muslim family and the author of works on politics in the Middle East, I was a bureaucratic inconvenience for NYU. It wasn't supposed to happen to me; but implicit is that it was meant to happen to someone else.

The manner in which these "mobility" issues were framed exposed the ways that even with NYU-AD's confident and abstracted version of a horizonless global, there persisted uncertainty and nagging doubts about the reality of unfettered markets and the "flat world." Was it possible to both sustain the global aspirations and maintain the partnership with "stakeholders" in Abu Dhabi and New York? This is a question less about the limits of liberalism and academic freedom than about the fallout from the collaboration between powerful actors selectively shifting the playing field to maintain power and privilege. Along with the others who have been denied entry, or who were forced into "workarounds" to enter and remain working at the university, or those who left NYU-AD under mysterious circumstances, I trace the boundaries of possibilities.[9] We expose the border-filled contradictions of the global imaginary that permeate the contemporary world and an increasingly market-oriented approach to education.[10] NYU's Global Network University was premised on the promise that "faculty and students [would] . . . move seamlessly through the [NYU] network" and prospects of cosmopolitanism built from a "kaleidoscopic interaction with deep connectivity."[11] The initiators of this ambitious project imagined that they were transcending the politics of what is actually a friction-laden world. This transcendence is easier articulated in glossy brochures and in polite conversations than enacted at border crossings.

Before one enters and after one arrives in the UAE, immigration laws and procedures are deployed to recruit and channel workers as temporary, but productive, residents. This happens with very different consequences, depending on one's class and place in a racialized social hierarchy. People are exposed to different levels of harm depending on their passport and ancestry. The kafala system, which ties entry and exit to employment, has gone through different iterations, even reform, since it was established in the twilight of the pearl economy and through the high-octane years of oil explorations and construction booms. The specter of deportation or the denial of entry has always essential to calibrate markets and discipline labor. But the bureaucratic management of residency is opaque and allows for Gulf states to balance labor needs with assessments of risk—potential for strikes, over-staying visas, political activism, or religious strife. Much blunter instruments can of course be deployed against dissident voices such as human rights activist Ahmad Mansoor Al Shehhi languishing in prison or researchers such as Matthew Hedges, the British doctoral student sentenced to life after a summary trial.[12]

NYU-AD's patronage by the UAE's ruling family and its hereditary and sectarian conceptions of nationhood were baked into the forms that I was required to fill out. And when I questioned this practice and its relationship to discrimination and academic freedom, administrators and faculty invoked "immigration laws of an independent sovereign state" as being incontrovertible. I don't know what explanations they offered when I was not present. I do know that the university president bristled at my request to make a public statement.[13] Similar to a century ago, sovereignty was invoked to deny responsibility as much as to seize it. Without drawing a false equivalence, the regulation of mobility of American university professors rhymed with the matrix of factors deployed by firms, colonial officers, and Gulf states to regulate labor that has been in place for dozens of years. Deference to local laws was again the alibi when it predictably surfaced that labor and immigration violations had taken place in the building of NYU-AD's campus on an island named Saadiyat, or happiness. The campus became home to sordid affairs, including broken promises, unpaid wages, worker strikes, and the deportations of laborers, all of which NYU trustees and the UAE government tried to ignore or blame on subcontractors and individuals.[14] Although brushed off as an isolated aberration, NYU's decision to set roots in Abu Dhabi did not take place in spite of the labor regime and collaboration with politically repressive forces but because of them.

In between the dizzying chatter of the global, genealogical mapping of identity, and the defensive resort to sovereignty, all notions of regionalism disappeared. Initially I was told that "local" research was not compatible with the mission of a "global" campus. In Sexton's original vision, "the regional" was always associated with the local, with confinement, and with defensive and failing "gating strategies."[15] But nationality and religious community mattered then, too, as my personal and family roots were documented to evaluate if I belonged in Abu Dhabi and if I could teach, work, and live there. Then when laborers went unpaid and were deported or my entry was denied, officials would invoke the sovereignty of the UAE or the responsibilities of recruitment agencies. The intention here was to obscure the process or to imply that the rules were the result of agreements between unanswerable university administrators and members of the ruling family. In none of this did the Gulf region figure—it did not stand in for a supra-national government or formal set of institutions, nor did it cement an imaginary, but agreed upon, historical cultural affinity. Meanwhile, rhetorically the Gulf, Persian or Arab, was conspicuously absent, or more precisely obscured and difficult to grasp. In the

United States, "the Gulf" stands in for many things, foremost among them war and bloodshed. These are not what university administrators want associated with places for young men and women to study and come of age. "The Arab Crossroads" program adopted a name that distanced itself from more conventional names (the Middle East) or a decolonizing geography (Southwest Asia). "Crossroads" worked well with Sexton's discourse of a new era of global connectivity and hinted at interactions and diversity. But at the same time, it was grounded in nationality (Arab) and describes the program as "an invitation to investigate the historical and contemporary religious, cultural, and ethnic diversity of the Arabic speaking world," while differentiating "the Arab World" from "its neighbors."[16] One study of both NYU-Abu Dhabi and NYU-Shanghai concluded that "area studies is not part of the curriculum," with courses and "the structure of the campuses tend[ing] towards non-area specific location, and a world that can be studied from anywhere (and therefore from nowhere in particular)."[17] The whole affair—both my visa rejection and NYU's response to it—pivoted around questions of belonging and bordering or socializing people into a bounded sense of place. What was elided was the politics of movement and how differences preclude the sharing of space.

* * *

I conclude this book in this intimate tone using my intended and unintended research because it offers a proximate view of the Persian Gulf. It is not the bird's-eye view privileged by most discussions but a multiplex lens that exposes the constellation of ways people have related to the same place. The human scale also introduces a different, shorter temporality of personal memory alongside longer processes of accumulation and state-building, let alone geological formations and fossil fuels deposits. By focusing on social fault lines we transcend simple binaries projected onto the Gulf. However specific my experience to try to teach at NYU-AD was, it underpins that region-making is practiced and enacted in addition to being planned and imagined. This multitude makes the regional elusive and sits at the heart of contestations over the Gulf. While aspiring to turn the Gulf region into well-ordered imperial, nationalist, or globalized space, these political projects inevitably simplify, exclude, and generate particularistic interests. These unintended or unforeseen outcomes as well as unequal social realities breed tensions and crystallize into what Greg Grandin calls "the absurdity of human efforts to force the concrete to conform to the abstract."[18]

To come to terms with the Persian Gulf belonging to many different and differently positioned peoples, *Making Space for the Gulf* began with the concrete ecological and social forms of the nineteenth century. Monsoons, trade, enslavement, and more brought people and places together as a littoral society hugging the coast but reaching far and wide via caravan routes, Indian Ocean seafarers, and even global markets for pearls and dates. The mix of mobility, interconnectedness, and cultural plasticity materialized in the port city form and shaped a class system built around debt as much as production.

Portuguese, Dutch, and, ultimately, British encounters did not completely displace these networked relations but introduced new hierarchies through imperial relations and concessionary commercial arrangements. A host of technologies bankrolled by finance capitalism transformed the geography of the sea-centered society. Telegraph lines, steamships, and the Suez Canal compressed distances and combined with new surveying methods and cartographic projections to catalyze an abstracted, bounded, geopoliticized Gulf molded for capital, a regional zone that was necessary for imperial stability and, later, "securing the free world." Yet, as soon as the Gulf was conceived as a homogeneous whole, it was dissected by state boundaries, Cold War rivalries, and clashes between sovereignty understood as fully-developed self-determination or mere international recognition of native rulers. Just as a more territorialized imperialism conditioned regionalism at the beginning of the twentieth century, internationalism carried with it nation-states as the dominant political container. With this spatialization came the challenging task of defining who belonged and could make claims in these emerging polities. The roots of the laws and categories that blocked my entry into the UAE extend back to the midcentury policies drawn up by colonial officers, oil firms, and rulers operating with a system of dual sovereignty. Time and again this model ran up against complex realities and ideological convictions about who did and did not merit inclusion and what profits channeled to which factors of production. Solutions were found by carving out exceptional spaces, as in FTZs, and using property and public welfare benefits to differentiate among nationalities as well as between classes. All this generated more, not fewer, borders and spatial distinctions. Despite the Carter Doctrine being steeped in classical geopolitical conceptions of enclosed, homogeneous space, what ensued in its repelling of "outside" forces from "the Persian Gulf region" was an assortment of bases, extraterritorial agreements, and logistics enclaves, rather than a duplication of Britain's absolute geography or a regional bloc of allied nation-states.

For something so tangible and vivid, the Persian Gulf evokes a vague and imprecise entity as a region. This book has argued that this is not due to some innate characteristic of the people or place but a product of historical struggles over the multiple ways regionalism is conceived and perceived. The Persian Gulf region has been treated at once as a unified whole, a contested frontier, a global seam, and an urban laboratory. It is for this reason that Persian Gulf history can be many things; it can be a mirror reflecting the histories of empires, capitalism, states, urbanism, commodities, and more. This book contends that the Persian Gulf allows us to see the world better. And therein lies the centrality of approaching regionalism relationally and the Gulf as a world of a region in which the inland sea is caught up in the world and vice versa.

* * *

The smell of gasoline burned my nose as I clambered into a rickety motorboat heading to Kish in December 2000. It was a stinging reminder that a third of the global oil trade passes through the nearby Strait of Hormuz.[19] As the handful of passengers and I bobbed up and down in the vessel and saw hazy outlines of container ships and tankers on the horizon, I remember telling myself that this scene must be what a chokepoint looks like. Almost two decades before my plans to teach at NYU-AD were scuttled, I was heading to Kish in the midst of its rejuvenation as a tourism destination for wealthier Iranians. As one of several stepping stones for the transshipment of commodities to "the mainland," the networks between islands and ports had become a sort of brokerage system for liberalizing trade and consumerism after more than a decade of revolution, war, and rationing. Improved roads and expanded airports made travel from Tehran to the southern shore far quicker and easier than during midcentury. And conversely, internal Iranian migration and commercial patterns stitched together what policymakers in the Islamic republic refer to as "deprived" areas on Iran's geographic periphery. Iranian society and economy were more national even if not homogeneous. Mobility was everywhere even if it was never costless.

My two companions and I had traveled from Tehran to Shiraz by plane and automobile to the shores of the Gulf. We parked our car at Charak, one of the many small port towns close to Bandar Abbas. As we waited for the motorboat to push off for the short ride to Kish, I noticed a long line of men, women, and children huddled under limited shade. It was a December morning, and the sun was not yet as hot as it would become, but the way they had spread out near the dock suggested that they were preparing for a long, drawn-out process. Their time seemed to be controlled by someone or something else. I knew that "locals" living in "the border region" were allotted special import licenses to bring goods from economic zones, so I interpreted this scene as a journey to Kish to bring small electrical appliances, clothing, and other consumer goods back to the mainland without paying any duties. I could not make out anyone organizing their excursion, but their large numbers suggested that they and their national ID cards were conscripted into a coordinated operation to take advantage of this regulatory loophole. "Smuggling" is how frustrated government officials in Tehran would describe it in countless media reports.[20]

I never found out if my speculation was correct or how long the two dozen would-be passengers had to wait to make the short trip to Kish, but when we approached the island, we saw another congregation of people with a hodgepodge of boxes and bags, obediently waiting to eventually board a boat back to Charak. This was a sort of just-in-time system in which one set of locals crossed into the free trade zone to enable another set to return with their bounty. I was left wondering if they were farmers from local villages or part of the wave of migrants settling in and around Bandar Abbas from both the border with Pakistan or the war zone near Iraq.[21] It is likely that many of the commodities being ferried across to the coast were produced in China, an early indicator of the shifting geoeconomics landscape, if not a looming geopolitical struggle. Exactly how profitable all this was for borderland residents was unclear, but profits and consumer goods were channeled to places far beyond the villages and neighborhoods targeted by the state's program.

My visit to Kish turned out to be unremarkable, except for the seafood meal at a restaurant run by a family from the Caspian Sea region. In the sparsely stocked malls or on the bike path encircling the island, I did not encounter any Filipinos who travel the short distance from Dubai to Kish Island to renew their work permits in the UAE. On webpages they created, these men and women document for their co-nationals and other migrants the steps needed to get to Kish and then back to the UAE. These "visa-run" experiences have been checkered, with some practitioners being stranded for weeks on end and others describing Iran's first FTZ as a paradise resort.[22]

Neither migrant workers nor residents of the southern coast, many of whom are Arabic-speakers, were what the planners of Kish had in mind when they initiated the project in the 1960s, but Kish was still a node for transnational encounter and circulation.

After we returned to the small jetty in desolate Charak, we set off for Shiraz via a circuitous route through rugged mountain passes. I knew little about Bastak, Lar, and Evaz; they were notable merely as towns having immaculate blacktop roads, well-stocked groceries, newly constructed buildings, and clean bathrooms. I learned that this was the fruit of decades of remittances and investments from the "Gulf-goers" who labored and lived on the Arabian coast and maintained households and "homes" of one sort or another on both coasts.[23] I only came to grasp the historical texture and scope in subsequent years, and when I sat down to write chapter 1 and read the descriptions of the Gulf as a littoral society.

As we drove through the parched, striated Zagros Mountains dotted with cisterns, we slowed down to pass through the occasional unassuming checkpoint, where we showed our national IDs. We had prepared ourselves for tense conversations with the security guards with the potential for small bribes or something more dire. Despite the exuberance of the reformist era under President Khatami, researchers and dual-national citizens were intimidated and arrested on scant charges without due process. But none of this happened. Instead, I recall spotting a few shrines (*imamzadeh*), one of which Fariba Adelkhah documents as patronized by "smugglers" heading north from the coast.[24] Persons labeled as "parachuters" or "suitcase traders" marked their successful navigation through a gauntlet of customs restrictions and traffic police by resting, praying, and making donations to saints in thanks for their protection. The riches funded two minarets, an electric water dispenser, and a drive-up donation box designed to ease the giving of alms. Several years after she published her ethnography of the Iranian borderlands, Adelkhah was arrested by Iranian authorities. She was one of many academics who have been detained and arrested on false charges by Iran, while receiving little or no support from their home countries in North America and Europe.

Four months later I visited Dubai for the first time. I recall that the airport was bustling, nothing like the tranquil jetty in Charak but possibly akin to Gulf harbors in the era of port cities. My US and Iranian passports didn't raise red flags at border control, as passport switching while entering Dubai was common, even if it was a luxury that few Iranians or others enjoyed. Crossing through customs felt seamless. Even though I did not know how differently the process would unfold in New York, I was anxious. The memories of my years of navigating passport checks with only a maroon-colored Iranian passport were still fresh.

Yet it felt that the bulk of travelers in the airport were napping as they passed their time in transit halls. They lingered before being siphoned off into other sections of the sprawling airport to have their travel documents scrutinized, before receiving their work permits or being returned home. The jagged edges of globalism that intentionally snag and slow down some and not others is acute at all ports. I assumed that most were heading to construction sites, "temporary" labor camps, or the old city center now emptied of its residents and converted into dormitory-like residences for "bachelors," even if they left wives, children, and obligations back home.

Seeing people clustered and waiting in orderly lines brought to mind the people anchored by the dock waiting to go to Kish. In the earlier instance the backdrop was the wind-chiseled mountains, in Dubai it was the bright lights festooned on duty-free stores, but neither scene was natural or free of compulsion. In both instances, a blend of hope and desperation was the catalyst for these movements, these passages that were monetized by brokers of all sorts. Their waiting also took place at territorial boundaries that were access points for some people or some things. The gauntlet of borders played a filtering role in which some were forced to wait. For others the airport was a gateway.

The people waiting at Charak and those in the lower reaches of Dubai International Airport manifested in the human labor necessary for globalism, or the regulated movement of people and things. Of humanity as things. But they also entrenched the idea that mobility is about having control over one's movement and not merely traversing space; that circulation is as much about moving (socially) up and down as (geographically) here and there, or that social hierarchies are reinforced while the possibility of upward mobility fuels risk-taking. Meanwhile, boundaries are not limited to questions of territorial demarcation and obstructing people in their tracks but rather a zone in which the legal and the illegal intersect. Borders function as membranes through which some people and objects are internalized by making them legitimate, legal, and authentic, while others are externalized by either obstructing entry or marking these entrants so that what is deemed contraband can be confiscated and that those labeled as foreigners can be expelled.

In 2001, Dubai's spectacular skyline and opulent architecture were beginning to stand in for "the Gulf" but still only in an embryonic state. But the hive of activity contrasted sharply with what I had witnessed in the tuckered-out port towns in Iran's Hormozgan Province or neighboring Sharjeh, which I visited during my two-week stay. The creek was lined with a medley of vessels, including box-laden dhows and sleek yachts. Wealth and consumption were conspicuous even if their sources seemed invisible.

The edges of my understanding began to sharpen a little when I stumbled upon an almost empty neighborhood at the mouth of Dubai's S-shaped creek and discovered that it was called Bastakiyya. While the city had grown inland, near Port Rashed, a cluster of small buildings with wind towers evoked the Bastak beyond the sea, the town that I briefly visited on my drive back from Kish. By the time I arrived, however, Bastakiyya was set back from the Gulf waters by land reclamation and a highway, and my brief visit was an invitation to think of the connected histories and codependencies that straddled the Gulf. Architectural forms, building materials, kinship ties, and concentrations of wealth echoed on multiple shores, leaving their imprint on the built environment of port cities and hinterland towns. This shared history was evoked when Emiratis switched into Persian to talk to me, a gesture that I found as charming as when they explained that they spoke a Persian "insider-language" (*khodemuni*) at home. Physical distance, meanwhile, was traversed genealogically by their recounting of family lineages stretching to the towns along Iran's coast and the mountains in Fars Province. A few years later, Bahrainis born in the 1960s shared memories of family holidays to Khuzestan and Fars to comment on my research and maintain our conversations.[25] These were moments, creative but easy to miss, in which we were building a sense of place that was mutual and not based on rootedness and authenticity. These mental maps are the relics of and an alternative socialization, and as such are seeds for developing ethical responsibilities and more edgeless spatializations of the Gulf.[26]

The vestiges of these earlier Gulf histories were simultaneously disavowed when a decade after my visit to Bastakiyya, it was renamed the Fahidi Historical Neighborhood. "The oldest residential neighborhood in Dubai" was now a "Heritage Village" and firmly fixed in the past.[27] Refurbished wind towers and buildings that signaled an earlier littoral society were now recruited into the language of national belonging and nostalgia—"a Gateway to Dubai's past and national identity" is one of its slogans.[28] Not unlike the Pearl Round-about in Bahrain, which "affirmed the Al Khalifa regime with symbols of an idealized Bahraini past," the enclosed heritage village "obviates the culturally diverse and heterogenous history of the Persian Gulf."[29]

These two Bastaks—one in Iran on the highway from Shiraz to the Gulf and the other in Dubai cloistered as an open-air museum—were severed by the reworking, if not outright silencing, of history. The different ways that these Bastaks were bridged or kept apart illustrates the importance of thinking about physical proximity and remoteness as relative and mutable. In other words, the importance of thinking of space-time, rather than only one or the other. Both places were products of channels carved in the past and the present. Even if Dubai's historical neighborhood was designed in op-position to the present, the agitated fascination with the past as heritage is only necessary because being Emirati or being permanent cannot be taken for granted. The nostalgia of the old neighborhood, in Dubai and elsewhere, was pressed into service at the same time that the global cities paradigm was on the march, threatening to erase all particularities from Dubai's landscape. Anxieties about cultural loss and the breakdown of the boundary between rightful citizens and temporary foreigners had been high for decades, but now they are reaching a fever pitch. In this sense the romanticized notion of place is reactionary and a withdrawal from the world, quite different from the exchanges I was having with some about a more open-ended and shared sense of place.

A second irony is that when this neighborhood in Dubai was built more than a century ago, it was done by fundamentally unrooted or uprooted people—polyglot families from southern Iran transplanted barely a hundred years ago. They enjoyed resources and had a desire to combine wood imported from India and eastern Africa with coastal coral, mud brick, and stone to con-struct buildings kept cool by methods deployed in the Iranian plateau. The di-rection and itineraries of flows heading to Iran's Bastak in the early twenty-first century are quite different, but they retain a set of regional horizons involving FTZs. This unbounded regionalism was sidelined by the heritage village's cel-ebration of the foresight of the Maktoum family and the entrepreneurial spirit of traders as an essential characteristic of Dubai. Bastakiyya, just like Bastak, neither has a single root nor is rootless; instead it is multi-rooted.

This book has tried to chart the passage from the nineteenth-century Bastak in the Zargos mountains to the early twentieth-century Bastakiyya in the port city on the Gulf to the one that is now situated as a heritage site within a self-identifying global city. It has sought to make sense of how discrete places and geographies have been cleaved from and connected to one another. It is my hope that by tracing the vectors of ships, imperial ambitions, and debts, by attending to the negotiations and motivations of kings and firms, immigrants and policymakers, this book has offered readers a new understanding of this multilayered region and the depth of its histories. In trying to summon up the Persian Gulf's past, I came to regard it anew. I had to sit with the binary interpretations imposed by the powerful in Tehran, Abu Dhabi, Washington, and London but tried to insist on the multitude of histories and conceptions of space and belonging. To make this intellectual journey and imagine alternative pathways, we must grapple with the notion that region-making stretches back over decades and may run in many directions, both geographic and political. To understand the real dynamism of what "the Gulf"—a flattening term—has been, we must embrace an understanding of space that is fundamentally social and therefore shared and multiple. If regions are always under construction, they carry with them possibilities. If regions can't escape the contradictions of containment and flow, we shouldn't shy away from the possibility of borders being gateways and friction being a root of creativity. It is only then can regionalism become a project for ethical responsibility and empathy.

Notes

INTRODUCTION

1. I use the term *Persian Gulf* for the body of water because it has been adopted by the United Nations, which implies a degree of common international acceptance; for brevity I will use the term *the Gulf*. On the political debates surrounding the name, see Kamyar Abdi, "The Name Game: The Persian Gulf, Archaeologists, and the Politics of Arab-Iranian Relations," in *Selective Remembrances: Archaeology in the Constriction, Commemoration, and Consecration of National Pasts,* ed. Philip L. Kohl, Mara Kozelsky, and Nachman Ben-Yehuda (Chicago: University of Chicago Press, 2008). The US government officially states that the Persian Gulf is "the only 'conventional' name" for the body of water, but lists "14 unofficial 'variants.'" Martin H. Levinson, "Mapping the Persian Gulf Naming Dispute," *ETC: A Review of General Semantics* 68, no. 3 (2011): 279–87.

2. Benedict Anderson, *Long Distance Nationalism: World Capitalism and the Rise of Identity Politics* (Amsterdam: CASA, 1992).

3. Daftar-e Motale'at Siyasi va Bayn-ol-Melali, *Gozideh-ye asnad- Khalij-e Fars,* vol. 1 (Tehran: Ministry of Foreign Affairs of the Islamic Republic of Iran, 1368), 134.

4. Ameen Rihani, *Around the Coasts of Arabia* (1930), quoted in James Onley, *The Arabian Frontier of the British Raj* (Oxford: Oxford University Press, 2007), 1.

5. Thomas Metcalf, *Imperial Connections: India in the Indian Ocean Arena, 1860–1920* (Berkeley: University of California Press, 2007), 9.

6. Quoted in Kristian Coates Ulrichsen, *The United Arab Emirates: Power, Politics, and Policymaking* (London: Routledge, 2017), 57.

7. "Excerpts From Weinberger Statement on Military Budget Outlay," *New York Times*, March 5, 1981.

8. Edward Said, *Orientalism* (New York: Vintage Books, 1978); Derek Gregory, "Imaginative Geographies," in *The Dictionary of Human Geography*, ed. Derek Gregory, Ron Johnston, Geraldine Pratt, Michael J. Watts, and Sarah Whatmore (Chichester, U.K.: Wiley-Blackwell, 2009); Michael J. Watts, "Collective Wish Images: Geographical Imaginaries and the Crisis of National Development," in *Human Geography Today*, ed. D. Massey, J. Allen, and P. Sarre (Cambridge: Polity Press, 1999), 85–107.

9. "Excerpts From Weinberger Statement on Military Budget Outlay."

10. Nicholas J. Spykman, "Geography and Foreign Policy, II," *American Political Science Review* 32, no. 2 (1938): 236.

11. Gearóid Ó Tuathail, *Critical Geopolitics: The Politics of Writing Global Space* (Minneapolis: University of Minnesota Press, 1996); Gerry Kearns, "Geopolitics," in *The Sage Handbook of Geographical Knowledge*, ed. John Agnew and David Livingston (London: Sage Publishing, 2011), 610- 622.

12. John Agnew, *Geopolitics: Re-visioning World Politics* (London: Routledge, 1998), 15–32.

13. Henri Lefebvre, *Production of Space* (Oxford: Blackwell, 1991), 410.

14. Edward W. Soja, "The Socio-Spatial Dialectic," *Annals of the Association of American Geographers* 70, no. 2 (June 1980): 210.

15. Raimo Väyrynen, "Regionalism: Old and New," *International Studies Review* 5, no. 1 (March 2003): 5–51.

16. Kristian Coates Ulrichsen, *Insecure Gulf: The End of Certainty and the Transition to the Post-Oil Era* (New York: Columbia University Press, 2011); Mehran Kamrava, *Troubled Waters: Insecurity in the Persian Gulf* (Ithaca, NY: Cornell University Press, 2018); Lenore Martin, *The Unstable Gulf: Threats from Within* (Lexington, MA: Lexington Books, 1984).

17. Behzad Sarmadi, "Transmigration, Proximity, and Sociopolitical Disconnection: Iranians in the United Arab Emirates," in *The Iranian Diaspora: Challenges, Negotiations, and Transformations*, ed. Mohsen Mostafavi Mobasher (Austin: University of Texas Press, 2018), 125–49.

18. Phillip E. Steinberg, *The Social Construction of the Ocean* (Cambridge: Cambridge University Press, 2001), 23, emphasis in the original.

19. Much of this work has been inspired by Henri Lefebvre, who offers the pithy statement that space is "not a thing but rather a set of relations" between objects and products. Lefebvre, *Production of Space*, 73. See also David Harvey, "Space as a Keyword," in *David Harvey: A Critical Reader*, ed. Noel Castree and Derek Gregory (Malden, MA: Blackwell Publishing, 2006), 270–93.

20. David Harvey, "Globalization and the 'Spatial Fix,'" *Geographische Revue* 2 (2001): 23–30.

21. On critical geopolitics, see Ó Tuathail, *Critical Geopolitics*; Agnew, *Geopolitics*; and Virginie Mamadouh, "Reclaiming Geopolitics: Geographers Strike Back," in *Geopolitics at the End of the Twentieth Century: The Changing World Political Map*, ed. Nurit Kliot and David Newman (London: Frank Cass, 2000), 118–38. One of the first works to explicitly engage with critical geopolitics to explore the Persian Gulf and the Middle East is Waleed Hazbun, *Beaches, Ruins, and Resorts: The Politics of Tourism in the Arab World* (Minneapolis: University of Minnesota Press, 2008).

22. Doreen Massey, "Power-Geometry and a Progressive Sense of Place," in *Mapping Futures: Local Cultures, Global Change*, ed. Jon Bird, Barry Curtis, Tim Putnam, George Robertson, and Lisa Tickner (London: Routledge, 1993), 60–70.

23. James Ferguson, *Global Shadows* (Durham, NC: Duke University Press, 2006), 25–49.

24. Neil Smith, "Scale Bending and the Fate of the National," in *Scale and Geographic Inquiry: Nature, Society, and Method*, ed. Eric Sheppard and Robert B. McMaster (Oxford: Blackwell, 2004), 192–212.

25. Ash Amin, "Placing Globalization," *Theory, Culture, and Society* 14, no. 2 (1997): 133.

26. Ayşe Çağlar and Nina Glick Schiller, *Migrants and City Making: Dispossession, Displacement, and Urban Regeneration* (Durham, NC: Duke University Press, 2018), 8.

27. See, among others, Fred Halliday, *Arabia without Sultans* (London: Saqi Books, 2002 [1974]); R. I. Lawless, *The Gulf in the Early 20th Century: Foreign Institutions and Local Responses*, Occasional Papers 31, Center for Middle Eastern and Islamic Studies, University of Durham, 1986; Alvin J. Cottrell, general editor, *The Persian Gulf States: A General Survey* (Baltimore: Johns Hopkins University Press, 1980). I thank Michael Fischer for bringing I Cottrell volume to my attention. Important recent works that abide by this more inclusive approach include David Commins, *The Gulf States: A Modern History* (New York: I. B. Tauris, 2012) and Lawrence Potter's series of edited volumes and projects that treat the Persian Gulf inclusively, for example, Lawrence G. Potter, ed., *The Persian Gulf in History* (New York: Palgrave Macmillan, 2009).

28. David F. Winkler, *Amirs, Admirals, and Desert Sailors: Bahrain, the U.S. Navy, and the Arabian Gulf* (Annapolis, MD: Naval Institute Press, 2007), x.

29. John Agnew, "Territorial Trap: The Geographical Assumptions of International Relations Theory," *Review of International Political Economy* 1, no. 1 (1994): 53–80.

30. Marc Lynch, ed., *The Arab Monarchy Debate: Arab Uprisings*, POMEPS Briefing 16 (December 19, 2012); F. Gregory Gause III, *Oil Monarchies: Domestic and*

Security Challenges in the Arab Gulf States (New York: Council on Foreign Relations Press, 1994); Michael Herb, *The Wages of Oil: Parliaments and Economic Development in Kuwait and the UAE* (Ithaca, NY: Cornell University Press, 2014).

31. Sheila Carapico, "Arabia Incognita: An Invitation to Arabian Peninsula Studies," in *Counter-Narratives: History, Contemporary Society, and Politics in Saudi Arabia and Yemen*, ed. Madawi al-Rasheed and Robert Vitalis (New York: Palgrave Macmillan, 2004), 22.

32. Sunil Amrith, *Crossing the Bay of Bengal: The Furies of Nature and the Fortunes of Migrants* (Cambridge: Harvard University Press, 2013), 285.

33. Some of this recent scholarship is discussed in Alex Boodrookas and Arang Keshavarzian, "The Forever Frontier of Urbanism: Historicizing Persian Gulf Cities," *International Journal of Urban and Regional Research* 43, no. 1 (January 2019): 14–29. See also Fahad Bishara, *A Sea of Debt: Law and Economic Life in the Western Indian Ocean, 1780–1950* (Cambridge: Cambridge University Press, 2017); Kaveh Ehsani, "Social Engineering and the Contradictions of Modernization in Khuzestan's Company Towns: A Look at Abadan and Masjed-Soleyman," *International Review of Social History* 48, no. 3 (2003): 361–99; Nelida Fuccaro, *Histories of City and State in the Persian Gulf: Manama since 1800* (Cambridge: Cambridge University Press, 2009); Andrew Gardner, *City of Strangers: Gulf Migration and the Indian Community in Bahrain* (Ithaca, NY: Cornell Press, 2010); Adam Hanieh, *Capitalism and Class in the Gulf* (New York: Palgrave Macmillan, 2011); Natasha Iskander, *Does Skill Make Us Human? Migrant Workers in 21st-Century Qatar and Beyond* (Princeton, NJ: Princeton University, 2021); Laleh Khalili, *Sinews of War and Trade: Shipping and Capitalism in the Arabian Peninsula* (London: Verso, 2020); Johan Mathew, *Margins of the Market: Trafficking and Capitalism across the Arabian Sea* (Berkeley: University of California Press, 2016); Matthew Hopper, *Slaves of One Master: Globalization and Slavery in Arabia in the Age of Empire* (New Haven: Yale University Press, 2015); Pascal Menoret, *Joyriding in Riyadh: Oil, Urbanism, and Road Revolt* (Cambridge: Cambridge University Press, 2014); Neha Vora, *Impossible Citizens: Dubai's Indian Diaspora* (Durham, NC: Duke University Press, 2013).

34. See Jarius Banaji, *A Brief History of Commercial Capitalism* (Chicago: Haymarket Books, 2019).

35. Doreen Massey, *For Space* (London: Sage, 2005), 141.

36. Lefebvre, *Production of Space*, 164, also 229.

37. Claire Beaugrand, "The Absurd Injunction to Not Belong and the *Bidun* in Kuwait," *International Journal of Middle East Studies* 52, no. 4 (2020): 726–32.

38. Reinhart Koselleck, *Sediments of Time: On Possible Histories*, trans. and ed. Sean Franzel and Stefan-Ludwig Hoffmann (Stanford: Stanford University Press, 2018).

39. Michael Pearson, "Littoral Society: The Concept and the Problems," *Journal of World History* 17, no. 4 (November 2006): 353–73.

40. Deborah Cowen and Emily Gilbert, "The Politics, War, and Territory," in *War, Citizenship, and Territory,* ed. Deborah Cowen and Emily Gilbert (New York: Routledge, 2008), 16–20; Steinberg, *Social Construction of the Ocean.*

41. Deborah Cowen, *The Deadly Life of Logistics: Mapping Violence in Global Trade* (Minneapolis: University of Minnesota Press, 2014).

42. Noora Lori, *Offshore Citizens: Permanent Temporary Status in the Gulf* (Cambridge: Cambridge University Press, 2019).

43. David Harvey, *Justice, Nature, and the Geography of Difference* (Oxford: Blackwell Publishers, 1996), 310.

CHAPTER ONE

1. Michael J. Watts, "Reflections on Circulation, Logistics, and the Frontiers of Capitalist Supply Chains." *Environment and Planning D: Society and Space* 37, no. 5 (October 2019): 945. The quote is from S. Markoff, "Afterword," in *States of Violence,* ed. F Coronil and J Skurski (Ann Arbor: University of Michigan Press, 2006), 33–75.

2. Michael Pearson, "Littoral Society: The Concept and the Problems," *Journal of World History* 17, no. 4 (November 2006): 356.

3. Including the region surrounding Basra, the coastal region near Muscat, and a few other locations, the Gulf possessed half of the world's date palms in the nineteenth century. Matthew Hopper, *Slaves of One Master: Globalization and Slavery in Arabia in the Age of Empire* (New Haven: Yale University Press, 2015), 23. On the date trade, see Yacoub Yusuf al-Hijji, *Kuwait and the Sea: A Brief Social and Economic History,* trans. Fahad Ahmad 'Isa Bishara (London: Arabian Publishing, 2010).

4. Farah Al-Nakib, *Kuwait Transformed: A History of Oil and Urban Life* (Stanford: Stanford University Press, 2016), 51.

5. Peter Lienhardt, *Disorientations, A Society in Flux: Kuwait in the 1950s,* ed. Ahmed Al-Shahi (Reading, U.K.: Ithaca Press, 1993), 46.

6. This is despite political tensions between Iran and the GCC countries. See Kamran Taremi, "The Role of Water Exports in Iranian Foreign Policy Towards the GCC," *Iranian Studies* 38, no. 2 (2005): 311–28.

7. Hala Fattah, *The Politics of Regional Trade in Iraq, Arabia, and the Gulf, 1745–1900* (Albany: State University of New York Press, 1997).

8. Abdul Sheriff, "The Persian Gulf and the Swahili Coast: A History of Acculturation over the *Longue Durée,*" in *The Persian Gulf in History,* ed. Lawrence G. Potter (New York: Palgrave Macmillan, 2009), 173–88.

9. Alan Villiers, *Sons of Sinbad* (London: Arabian Publishing, 2006 [1949]), 58; Willem Floor, *The Persian Gulf: The Rise and Fall of Bandar-e Lengeh: The Distribution Center for the Arabian Coast, 1750–1930* (Washington, DC: Mage Publishers, 2010), 15.

10. Janet Abu Lughod, *Before European Hegemony: The World System A.D. 1250–1350* (Oxford: Oxford University Press, 1989), 203; Phillip E. Steinberg, *The Social Construction of the Ocean* (Cambridge: Cambridge University Press, 2001), 41–52.

11. Villiers, *Sons of Sinbad*, 300.

12. Jill Crystal, *Oil and Politics in the Gulf: Rulers and Merchants in Kuwait and Qatar* (Cambridge: Cambridge University Press, 1990), 40.

13. H. J. Whigham, *The Persian Problem: An Examination of the Rival Positions of Russia And Great Britain In Persia With Some Account of the Persian Gulf And the Bagdad Railway* (New York: Scribner's, 1903), 47; Floor, *The Persian Gulf*, 18.

14. Villiers, *Sons of Sinbad*, 300–303; on Indian Ocean World connections to central Arabia, see Rosie Bsheer, *Archive Wars: The Politics of History in Saudi Arabia* (Stanford: Stanford University Press, 2020), 30–59.

15. Crystal, *Oil and Politics in the Gulf*, 24.

16. Villiers, *Sons of Sinbad*, 208, 318–19.

17. On Barak, "Outsourcing: Energy and Empire in the Age of Coal, 1820–1911," *International Journal of Middle East Studies* 47, no. 3 (2015): 425–45.

18. Karl Marx, *Grundrisse: Foundations of the Critique of Political Economy* (Harmondsworth, U.K.: Penguin Books, 1973), 524. See David Harvey's discussion of time-space compression in *The Condition of Postmodernity: An Enquiry into the Origins of Cultural Change*. Cambridge, MA: Blackwell, 1990), chs. 15–17.

19. Tony Ballantyne and Antoinette Burton, "Empires and the Reach of the Global," in *A World Connecting, 1870–1945*, ed. Emily S. Rosenberg (Cambridge: Belknap Press, 2012), 354.

20. Michael Pearson, *The Indian Ocean* (London: Routledge, 2003), 211.

21. Frank Broeze, "Dubai: Creek to Global Port City," *Harbours and Havens: Essays in Port History in Honour of Gordon Jackson* (St. John's, Canada: International Maritime Economic History Association 1999), 165.

22. Hopper, *Slaves of One Master*, 51–79.

23. Laleh Khalili, *Sinews of War and Trade: Shipping and Capitalism in the Arabian Peninsula* (London: Verso, 2020), 29.

24. Frauke Heard-Bey, *From Trucial States to United Arab Emirates: A Society in Transition* (London: Longman, 1982), 250; al-Hijji, *Kuwait and the Sea*, 13, 74–75.

25. Nelida Fuccaro, *Histories of City and State in the Persian Gulf: Manama since 1800* (Cambridge University Press, 2009), 59. See also Johan Mathew, *Margins of the Market: Trafficking and Capitalism across the Arabian Sea* (Berkeley: University of California Press, 2016).

26. Discussion of the pearling sector is drawn primarily from Hopper, *Slaves of One Master*; Floor, *The Persian Gulf*; al-Hijji, *Kuwait and the Sea*; Robert Carter, *Sea of Pearls: Arabia, Persia, and the Industry That Shaped the Gulf* (London: Alfardan, 2012).

27. David Commins, *The Gulf States: A Modern History* (New York: I. B. Tauris, 2012), 120. Hopper estimates that in 1915 there were 64,000 men on 3,400 boats engaged in pearl fishing in the entire Persian Gulf. Hopper, *Slaves of One Master*, 23.

28. Floor, *The Persian Gulf*, 9.

29. Nelida Fuccaro, "Pearl Towns and Early Oil Cities: Migration and Integration in the Arab Coast of the Persian Gulf," in *The City in the Ottoman Empire: Migration and the Making of Urban Modernity*, ed. Ulrike Freitag, Malte Fuhrmann, and Nora Lafi (New York: Routledge, 2011), 101; Al-Nakib, *Kuwait Transformed*, 28.

30. Carter, *Sea of Pearls*, 162.

31. Floor, *The Persian Gulf*, 12.

32. Members of the ruling family were often involved in commerce and money-lending, with the boundary between merchant and rulers was not as stark as some analytical discussion imply (see chapter 3).

33. Hopper, *Slaves of One Master*, 92–95.

34. Robert Carter, "The History and Prehistory of Pearling in the Persian Gulf," *Journal of the Economic and Social History of the Orient* 48, no. 2 (2005): 157, 179. See Villiers, *Sons of Sinbad*, 342.

35. Lorimer states that divers make as many as fifty dives a day. J. G. Lorimer "Appendix C: The Pearl and Mother-of-Pearl Fisheries of the Persian Gulf," *Gazetteer of the Persian Gulf, Oman, and Central Arabia*. Online edition by Brill, 2015, http://dx.doi.org/10.1163/2405-447X_loro_COM_001303, accessed January 22, 2020. Villiers states that it was about 120 dives per day or an equivalent of two hours underwater, *Sons of Sinbad*, 342.

36. Peter Lienhardt, *Sheikhdoms of Eastern Arabia* (New York: Palgrave, 2001), 29.

37. al-Hijji, *Kuwait and the Sea*, 138.

38. Lienhardt, *Sheikhdoms of Eastern Arabia*, 152.

39. Lienhardt, *Disorientations*, 99.

40. Nels Johnson, "Ahmad: A Kuwaiti Pearl Diver," in *Struggle and Survival in the Modern Middle East*, Second Edition, ed. Edmond Burke III and David N. Yaghoubian (Berkeley: University of California Press, 2006), 80–87.

41. Heard-Bey, *From Trucial States to United Arab Emirates*, 86, 111.

42. Victoria Penziner Highwater, "Pearling and Political Power in the Trucial States, 1850–1930: Debts, Taxes, and Politics," *Journal of Arabian Studies* 3, no. 2 (2013): 215–31.

43. Penziner Highwater, "Pearling and Political Power in the Trucial States," 226.

44. Enslaved people from the Swahili coast were used to construct and maintain irrigation systems necessary for date cultivation in Oman as early as the late seventeenth century. Sheriff, "The Persian Gulf and the Swahili Coast," 183; Thomas Ricks,

"Slaves and Slave Traders in the Persian Gulf, 18ᵗʰ and 19ᵗʰ Centuries: An Assessment," *Slavery and Abolition* 9, no. 3 (1998): 60–70.

45. Africans made up between 11 and 18 percent of the population of the main towns in Eastern Arabia in the first decade of the twentieth century. Hopper, *Slaves of One Master*, 9. But not all Africans were enslaved, and not all slaves were African. Men and women from Baluchistan and Southeastern Iran also experienced slavery, especially in the early twentieth century.

46. Karl Marx, *Capital: A Critique of Political Economy, Volume I* (London: Penguin Books, 1976), 926.

47. Among others, Sugata Bose, *A Hundred Horizons: The Indian Ocean in the Age of Global Empire* (Cambridge, MA: Harvard University Press, 2006), 79–97.

48. James Onley, "Transnational Merchants in the Nineteenth-Century Gulf," in *Transnational Connections and the Arab Gulf*, ed. Madawi al-Rasheed (London: Routledge, 2005), 59–89.

49. Fahad Bishara, *A Sea of Debt: Law and Economic Life in the Western Indian Ocean, 1780–1950* (Cambridge: Cambridge University Press, 2017); Adam Hanieh, *Capitalism and Class in the Gulf Arab States* (New York: Palgrave Macmillan, 2011), 78–82.

50. Fattah, *The Politics of Regional Trade*.

51. James Onley, *The Arabian Frontier of the British Raj* (Oxford: Oxford University Press, 2007), 162.

52. Behnam, *Zelzelah*, 82–83.

53. Pearson, "Littoral Society," 354.

54. Fariba Adelkhah references *saheli* (pl. *sawaheli*) as being used by coastal dwellers in Iran. Adelkhah, *The Thousand and One Borders of Iran: Travel and Identity*, trans. Andrew Brown (London: Routledge, 2016), 36.

55. However, this Arabic term references the Gulf in a more abstract manner and over time has come to refer to all people living in the Arabian Peninsula, regardless to their proximity to the shores or their relationship to the sea.

56. Fuccaro, *Histories of City and State in the Persian Gulf*, 63.

57. George N. Curzon. *Persia and the Persian Question*, 2 vols. (London: Frank Cass Co. Ltd., [1892]1966), 468.

58. Abdul Sheriff, "The Persian Gulf and the Swahili Coast," 176–77.

59. Ibid., 182.

60. Ibid., 179–82.

61. Samieh Nourinejad, "Batt Guran: ma'bad-e henduha dar bandar abbas," *Jelveh Honar* 12 (Fall and Winter 1393): 19–32. In a personal communication Ali Karjoo-Ravary kindly shared with me his observation that the zurkhaneh had Sikh iconography.

62. Onley, "Transnational Merchants in the Nineteenth-Century Gulf"; Frederick Anscombe, "An Anational Society: Eastern Arabia in the Ottoman Period," in *Transnational Connections and the Arab Gulf*, ed. Madawi al-Rasheed (London: Routledge, 2005), 21–38; Fuccaro, *Histories of City and State in the Persian Gulf*; Sheriff, "The Persian Gulf and the Swahili Coast," 176.

63. With the term *connectivity* I am referencing Peregrine Horden and Nicholas Purcell, *The Corrupting Sea: A Study of Mediterranean History* (London: Blackwell, 2000). On connected histories see Sanjay Subrahmanyam, "Connected Histories: Notes towards a Reconfiguration of Early Modern Eurasia." *Modern Asian Studies* 31, no. 3 (1997): 735–62. On a horizontal or weblike approach to imperial history, see Thomas Metcalf, *Imperial Connections: India in the Indian Ocean Arena, 1860–1920* (Berkeley: University of California Press, 2007).

64. Heard-Bey, *From Trucial States to United Arab Emirates*, 212; Villiers, *Sons of Sinbad*, 289.

65. Floor, *The Persian Gulf*, 71.

66. Crystal, *Oil and Politics in the Gulf*, 15.

67. Commins, *The Gulf States*, 36.

68. James D. Tracy, "Dutch and English Trade to the East: The Indian Ocean and the Levant, to about 1700," in *The Cambridge World History*, ed. J. Bentley, S. Subrahmanyam, and M. Wiesner-Hanks (Cambridge: Cambridge University Press, 2015), 240–62.

69. K. N. Chaudhuri, *Trade and Civilization in the Indian Ocean* (Cambridge University Press, 1985).

70. Bishara, *Sea of Debt*.

71. Ahmed Almaazmi, "Oman as an Empire: Transoceanic Mobilities and Legacies in the Western Indian Ocean," MESA Annual Conference, November 2019.

72. On long history of migration across the Gulf and the ideational valances and struggles in the modern Iran, see Ahmed al-Dailami, "'Purity and Confusion': The Hawala between Persians and Arabs in the Contemporary Gulf," in *The Persian Gulf in Modern Times: People, Ports, and History*, ed. Lawrence G. Potter (New York: Palgrave Macmillan, 2014), 299–26.

73. Heard-Bey, *From Trucial States to United Arab Emirates*, 113.

74. Crystal, *Oil and Politics in the Gulf*, 4.

75. Fuccaro, *Histories of City and State in the Persian Gulf*, 14.

76. Floor, *The Persian Gulf*, 101; Fatma al-Sayegh, "Merchants' Role in a Changing Society: The Case of Dubai, 1900–90," *Middle Eastern Studies* 34, no. 1 (January 1998): 87–102.

77. Crystal, *Oil and Politics in the Gulf*, 24–25; Farah Al-Nakib, *Kuwait Transformed*, 31–32.

78. Onley, *The Arabian Frontier of the British Raj*, 44–45; Sulṭān ibn Muḥammad al-Qāsimī, *The Myth of Arab Piracy in the Gulf* (London: Croom Helm, 1986).

79. Floor, *The Persian Gulf*, 42.

80. Curzon, *Persia and the Persian Question. In Two Volumes*, vol. 2, 398.

81. J. G. Lorimer, "Bahrain Principality," in *Gazetteer of the Persian Gulf, Oman and Central Arabia Online*, Volume 2, edited by Brill. Consulted online on 24 October 2019, http://dx.doi.org/10.1163/2405-447X_loro_COM_040079.

82. Carter, *Sea of Pearls*, 273.

83. Hopper, *Slaves of One Master*, 193–94.

84. Ibid., 194. This happened in Dubai as well. See Carter, *Sea of Pearls*, 262.

85. Fuccaro, *Histories of City and State in the Persian Gulf*, 127.

86. Carter, *Sea of Pearls*, 260.

87. al-Hijji, *Kuwait and the* Sea, 13.

88. Bose, *Hundred Horizons*, 87.

89. al-Hijji, *Kuwait and the Sea*, 137–66.

90. Bose, *Hundred Horizons*, 89.

91. Carter, *Sea of Pearls*, 267.

92. Hopper, *Slaves of One Master*.

93. Bose, *Hundred Horizons*, 91.

94. Omar Hesham AlShehabi, "Policing Labour in Empire: The Modern Origins of the Kafala Sponsorship System in the Gulf Arab States," *British Journal of Middle Eastern Studies* 48, no. 2 (2021): 291–310.

95. Lienhardt, *Sheikhdoms of Eastern Arabia*, 8, 162.

96. Hopper, *Slaves of One Master*, 80.

97. Lienhardt, *Sheikhdoms of Eastern Arabia*, 123.

98. On enslaved people in the oil sector in Qatar see Natasha Iskander, *Does Skill Make Us Human? Migrant Workers in 21st-Century Qatar and Beyond* (Princeton, NJ: Princeton University, 2021), 54–55. British officials and the Qatari ruler explicitly earmarking oil revenue to compensate slaveholders in order to ban it; Crystal, *Oil and Politics in the Gulf*, 144.

99. Bose, *Hundred Horizons*, 6.

CHAPTER TWO

1. The transcript of the speech can be found at The American Presidency Project, https://www.presidency.ucsb.edu/documents/address-the-nation-the-soviet-invasion-afghanistan and the video of the address is available at https://millercenter.org/the-presidency/presidential-speeches/january-4-1980-speech-afghanistan.

2. Ann Stoler, "Imperial Formations and the Opacities of Rule," in *Lessons of Empire: Imperial Histories and American Power*, ed. Craig Calhoun, Frederick Cooper,

and Kevin W. Moore (New York: The New Press, 2006), 54–55, emphasis in the original.

3. Ann Stoler, "Imperial Formations and the Opacities of Rule," 52.

4. The term *covert empire* comes from Priya Satia, *Spies in Arabia: The Great War and the Cultural Foundations of Britain's Covert Empire in the Middle East* (New York: Oxford University Press, 2008); *Arabian frontier* and *informal empire* are used in James Onley, *The Arabian Frontier of the British Raj* (Oxford: Oxford University Press, 2007).

5. Gearóid Ó Tuathail, *Critical Geopolitics: The Politics of Writing Global Space* (Minneapolis: University of Minnesota Press, 1996), 2.

6. Gary Fields, *Enclosure: Palestinian Landscapes in a Historical Mirror* (University of California Press, 2017), 8–10.

7. Peter Katznstein, *A World of Regions: Asia and Europe in the American Imperium* (Ithaca, NY: Cornell University Press, 2005).

8. Deborah Cowen and Neil Smith, "After Geopolitics? From the Geopolitical Social to Geoeconomics," *Antipode* 41, no. 1 (January 2009), 23. Leslie Hepple's definition also stresses the multiplicity of scales: "'Geopolitics' serves as an umbrella term, encapsulating the interaction of global and regional issues with economic and local structures." "The Revival of Geopolitics." *Political Geography Quarterly*, Supplement to 5, no. 4 (1986): 29.

9. On military history preceptive on the ocean see Phillip E. Steinberg, *The Social Construction of the Ocean* (Cambridge: Cambridge University Press, 2001), 16–20.

10. Nicholas J. Spykman, *The Geography of the Peace* (New York: Harcourt Brace & Co, 1944), 24–25, 54.

11. Alvin Cottrell and Michael Moodie, *The United States and the Persian Gulf: Past Mistakes, Present Needs* (New York: National Strategy Information Center, 1984), 16, emphasis added.

12. Ó Tuathail, *Critical Geopolitics*; Gerry Kearns, *Geopolitics and Empire: The Legacy of Halford Mackinder* (Oxford: Oxford University Press, 2009).

13. Ó Tuathail, *Critical Geopolitics*, 19.

14. Richard Peet shows that environmental determinism functioned to legitimize both ideological claims of imperialism and scientific basis of geography and race. See Peet, "The Social Origins of Environmental Determinism," *Annals of the Association of American Geographers* 75, no. 3 (September 1985): 309–33. See also Kearns, *Geopolitics and Empire*; Ó Tuathail, *Critical Geopolitics*, 1996.

15. Paul A. Kramer, "Empires, Exceptions, and Anglo-Saxons: Race and Rule between the British and United States Empires, 1880–1910," *Journal of American History* 88, no. 4 (March 2002): 1315–1353.

16. Reza Zia-Ebrahimi, "'Arab Invasion' and Decline, or the Import of European Racial Thought by Iranian Nationalists," *Ethnic and Racial Studies* 37, no. 6 (2014): 1043–61.

17. Percy Sykes, *A History of Persia in two volumes* (London: Routledge and Kegan Paul, 1969), vol. 1, 369.

18. Stephanie Jones, "British India Steamers and the Trade of the Persian Gulf, 1862–1914." *The Great Circle* 7, no. 1 (1985): 23–44; Johan Mathew, *Margins of the Market: Trafficking and Capitalism across the Arabian Sea* (Berkeley: University of California Press, 2016), 47–40.

19. On Barak, "Outsourcing: Energy and Empire in the Age of Coal, 1820–1911," *International Journal of Middle East Studies* 47, no. 3 (2015): 425–45.

20. H. J. Mackinder, "The Geographical Pivot of History," *The Geographical Journal* 23, no. 4 (April 1904): 421.

21. Ibid., 422.

22. Halford John Mackinder, *Britain and the British Seas* (London: William Heineman, 1902), 180–84. See also Kearns, *Geopolitics and Empire*, 68–78.

23. Mackinder, "The Geographical Pivot of History," 437. The parallels between Mackinder's essay and Lenin's theory of imperialism have been drawn by Neil Smith in *American Empire: Roosevelt's Geographer and the Prelude to Globalization* (Berkeley: University of California Press, 2003). On Mackinder's support for tariffs and party politics, see Kearns, *Geopolitics and Empire*, 50–55. Kearns also traces Mackinder's influence on Nazi geopolitics, American cold war policies of containment, and writing about American-led unipolarism.

24. Robert J. Blyth, "Britain Versus India in the Persian Gulf: The Struggle for Political Control, *c.* 1928–48," *Journal of Imperial and Commonwealth History* 28, no. 1 (2000): 90–111.

25. Briton Cooper Busch, *Britain and the Persian Gulf, 1894–1914* (Berkeley: University of California Press, 1967), 6–10.

26. John Darwin, *The Empire Project: The Rise and Fall of the British World-System, 1830–1970* (Cambridge: Cambridge University Press, 2014), 3.

27. Daniel Foliard, *Dislocating the Orient: British Maps and the Making of the Middle East, 1854–1921* (Chicago: University of Chicago Press, 2017).

28. Thomas P. Brockway, "Britain and the Persian Bubble, 1888–92," *Journal of Modern History* 13, no. 1 (March 1941): 39; See also John S. Galbraith, "British Policy on Railways in Persia, 1880–1900," *Middle Eastern Studies* 25, no. 4 (1898): 480–505.

29. Busch, *Britain and the Persian Gulf.*

30. Henry James Whigham, *The Persian Problem: An Examination of the Rival Positions of Russia and Great Britain in Persia with Some Account of the Persian Gulf and the Bagdad Railway* (New York: Scribner's, 1903), 67.

31. Peter Cain and Anthony Hopkins, *British Imperialism* (London: Longman Publisher, 1993), 351–59; Brockway, "Britain and the Persian Bubble."

32. Kearns, *Geopolitics and Empire*, 57.

33. George Nathaniel Curzon, *Persia and the Persian Question. In Two Volumes* (Frank Cass & Co Ltd., 1892), vol. 1, 3.

34. Ibid., 3–4.

35. George Nathaniel Curzon, *Frontiers* (Oxford: Clarendon Press, 1908), 54–55. At this point of his lecture, Curzon pivots away from his pursuit of a "scientific" approach to frontiers by evoking US history and "modern school of historians in America" that tie the expanding US frontier to "the evolution of national character" and the birth of the American nation and "virile democracy" in the midst of "ardours" and "savagery."

36. Ibid., 57–58.

37. Whigham, *The Persian Problem*, 44.

38. Ibid., 1.

39. Curzon, *Persia and the Persian Question*, vol. 1, 587.

40. Whigham, *The Persian Problem*, 72. Alfred Thayer Mahan was an American naval officer and long-time president of the Naval War College in Rhode Island. He was the author of *The Influence of Sea Power upon History, 1660–1783* (Boston: Little Brown Company, 1894 [1890]), which that posited "sea power" as the explanation for British global superiority and advocated it for the United States at the turn of the century. His advocacy was most directly consequential on Theodore Roosevelt, the then assistant secretary of the Navy, who put Mahan's ideas into practice in the Spanish-American war and the establishment of US bases in Cuba, Puerto Rico, Hawaii, and the Philippines.

41. Curzon, *Persia and the Persian Question*, vol. 2, 634.

42. Ibid., vol. 1, 5.

43. John Agnew, *Geopolitics: Re-visioning World Politics* (London: Routledge, 1998), 19.

44. Foliard, *Dislocating the Orient*, 266.

45. Ibid., 24, 31–37, 100–109. For examples, see "Part of the Cast of Arabia in the Gulf of Persia Surveyed by Lieut.ts J. M. Guy and G. B. Brucks assisted by Lieut.t R. Cogan, H. C. Marine. 1822. Engraved by John Bateman. Sheet 1st," British Library: Map Collections, IOR/X/3630/20/1, in Qatar Digital Library, https://www.qdl.qa/archive/81055/vdc_100024174406.0x000012, accessed May 15, 2023.

46. Matthew Edney, *Mapping an Empire: The Geographical Construction of British India, 1769–1843* (Chicago: University of Chicago Press, 1997).

47. Foliard, *Dislocating the Orient*, 37.

48. Jordan Branch, *The Cartographic State: Maps, Territory, and the Origins of Sovereignty* (Cambridge: Cambridge University Press, 2014), 14.

49. Foliard, *Dislocating the Orient*, 117.

50. On the longer trajectory of cartography and modern political formations and how cartographic techniques were first developed in European colonies after the sixteenth century and then reimported to Europe, see Branch, *The Cartographic State*.

51. Foliard, *Dislocating the Orient*, 192; see also the book's webpage https://dislocatingtheorient.parisnanterre.fr/chapter-6/#jp-carousel-919

52. Ibid., 181; see also the book's webpage https://dislocatingtheorient.parisnanterre.fr/chapter-6/

53. Ibid.,188.

54. Ibid., 266.

55. Curzon, *Persia and the Persian Question*, vol. 2, 451.

56. Curzon, *Frontiers*, 42.

57. Clayton R. Koppes, "Captain Mahan, General Gordan, and the Origins of the Term 'Middle East,'" *Middle Eastern Studies* 12, no. 1 (1976): 95–98, Alfred Mahan, "The Persian Gulf and International Relations," *National Review*, September 1902, 27–45, Roger Adelson, *London and the Middle East: Money, Power, and War, 1902–1922* (New Haven and London: Yale University Press, 1995), 22–26. Whigham deploys the term when he claims that Britain had "no policy in the Middle East." Whigham, *The Persian Problem*, 2.

58. Quoted in Busch, *Britain and the Persian Gulf*, 256.

59. Saleh Hmad al-Sagri, "Britain and the Arab Emirates, 1820–1956: A Documentary Study," PhD dissertation, University of Kent, July 1988, 63–65.

60. *The Spectator*, May 9, 1903; *The Railroad Men*, February 1904; *The New York Times* May 8, 1903, 8.

61. Daniel Yergin, *The Prize: The Epic Quest for Oil, Money, and Power* (New York: Simon and Schuster, 1991), 142.

62. Curzon, *Frontiers*, 55–57.

63. G. Lorimer "Appendix P: Cruise of His Excellency Lord Curzon, Viceroy of India, in the Persian Gulf," *Gazetteer of the Persian Gulf, Oman, and Central Arabia*. Online edition by Brill, 2015, accessed January 15, 2020.

64. Curzon, *Persia and the Persian Question*, vol. 2, 605, emphasis added.

65. Foliard, *Dislocating the Orient*, 206.

66. Soli Shahvar, "Iron Poles, Wooden Poles: The Electric Telegraph and the Ottoman: Iranian Boundary Conflict, 1863–1865," *British Journal of Middle Eastern Studies* 34, no. 1 (2007): 23–42.

67. Willem Floor, *The Persian Gulf: The Rise and Fall of Bandar-e Lengeh: The Distribution Center for the Arabian Coast, 1750–1930* (Washington, DC: Mage Publishers, 2010), 100.

68. Farah Al-Nakib, *Kuwait Transformed: A History of Oil and Urban Life* (Stanford: Stanford University Press, 2016), 23.

69. Frederick Anscombe, *The Ottoman Gulf: The Creation of Kuwait, Saudi Arabia, and Qatar* (New York: Columbia University Press, 1997), 114; Gabriel Young, "Infrastructures of Empire and Sovereignty: The Port of Basra in Interwar Iraq," *Journal of Arabian Studies* 9, no. 2 (2019): 123–44.

70. Andrea Rugh, *The Political Culture of Leadership in the United Arab Emirates* (New York: Palgrave, 2007), 105.

71. Anscombe, *The Ottoman Gulf*, 116–17.

72. Firoozeh Kashani-Sabet, *Frontier Fictions: Shaping the Iranian Nation, 1804–1946* (Princeton, NJ: Princeton University Press, 1999), 47–74; Zeinab Azarbadegan, "Imagined Geographies, Reinvented Histories: Ottoman Iraq as Part of Iran," *Journal of Ottoman and Turkish Studies Association* 5, no. 1 (2018): 115–41.

73. Camile Lyans Cole, "The Ottoman Model: Basra and the Making of Qajar Reform, 1881–1889," *Comparative Studies in Society and History* 64, no. 4 (2022): 1024–54.

74. Richard Schofield, "States Behaving Badly? The Unique Geopolitics of Island Sovereignty Disputes," Environment, Politics, and Development Working Paper Series, Department of Geography, King's College London, Paper no. 65 (2014), 27. Gesturing to how these maps were snapshots of a particular instance of time, a former British Political Resident and mediator in the Persian Gulf Island dispute between Iran and the UAE "mutter[d] in a moment of obvious exasperation" that "[t]he Persians took Sirri while we weren't looking in 1887. I sometimes wish they had taken the Tunbs and Abu Musa as well" (24).

75. Wilson Jacob, *For God or Empire: Sayyid Fadl and the Indian Ocean World* (Stanford: Stanford University Press, 2019).

76. Ashley Jackson, *Persian Gulf Command: A History of the Second World War in Iran and Iraq* (New Haven: Yale University Press, 2018); Steven Ward, *Pocket Guide to Iran: Instructions for American Servicemen in Iran during World War II* (North Charleston, SC: CreateSpace, 2012).

77. Roy Mottahedeh, *Mantle of the Prophet: Religion and Politics in Iran* (New York: Pantheon Books, 1985), 114–15.

78. Steven G. Galpern, *Money, Oil, and Empire in the Middle East: Sterling and Postwar Imperialism, 1944–1971* (New York: Cambridge University Press, 2009), 150.

79. G. Krozewski, *Money and the End of Empire: British International Economic Policy and the Colonies, 1947–1958* (Basingstoke, U.K.: Palgrave Macmillan, 2001); Galpern, *Money, Oil, and Empire in the Middle East*, 142–97. For a discussion of the historiographic debate the British withdrawal East of Suez and the variety of ways that economic retrenchment and foreign policy considerations worked in tandem,

see Shohei Sato, "Britain's Decision to Withdraw from the Persian Gulf, 1964–68: A Pattern and a Puzzle," *Journal of Imperial and Commonwealth History* 37, no. 1 (March 2009): 99–117.

80. Galpern, *Money, Oil, and Empire in the Middle East*, 150.

81. Ibid., 196–67 and 202–3. See also National Security Council report NSC 5820/1, "U.S. Policy Toward the Near East," November 4, 1958, FRUS 1958–1960, vol. 12, document 51.

82. Simon Smith, *Britain's Revival and Fall in the Gulf: Kuwait, Bahrain, Qatar and the Trucial States, 1950–1971* (London: Routledge, 2004).

83. Galpern, *Money, Oil, and Empire in the Middle East*, 203, footnote 10.

84. Mohammad Reza Shah was both distrustful and strategic and at various moments in his reign would turn to the Soviet Union to extract concessions and leverage it against the United States.

85. William Roger Louis, *Ends of British Imperialism: The Scramble for Empire, Suez, and Decolonization: Collected Essays* (London: Tauris, 2006), 643–64.

86. Ibid., 645.

87. Center for Strategic and International Studies, *The Gulf: Implications of British Withdrawal* (Washington, DC: Center for Strategic and International Studies, Georgetown University, 1969).

88. Sato, "Britain's Decision to Withdraw from the Persian Gulf, 1964–68," 108.

89. Ibid., 109.

90. R. K. Ramazani, *The Persian Gulf and the Strait of Hormuz* (Alphen aan den Rijn, the Netherlands: Sijthoff & Noordhoff, 1979), 88–104.

91. Rouhollah K. Ramazani, *Iran's Foreign Policy, 1941–1973* (Charlottesville: University Press of Virginia, 1975), 173.

92. "Floated to Victory on a Wave of Oil," *New York Times*, November 23, 2018.

93. Amitav Acharya, *U.S. Military Strategy in The Gulf* (London: Routledge, 1989), Timothy Mitchell, *Carbon Democracy: Political Power in the Age of Oil* (New York: Verso Press, 2011); Roger J. Stern, "Oil Scarcity Ideology in US Foreign Policy, 1908–97," *Security Studies* 25, no. 2 (2016): 214–57. European industrial recovery after World War II included transitioning away from coal and to oil, much of which was imported from the Middle East and North Africa.

94. Toby C. Jones, "America, Oil, and War in the Middle East," *Journal of American History* 99, no. 1 (June 2012): 208–218, Roger J. Stern, "Oil Scarcity Ideology in US Foreign Policy"; Robert Vitalis, *Oilcraft: The Myths of Scarcity and Security That Haunt U.S. Energy Policy* (Stanford: Stanford University Press, 2020). On the connection between weapons sales, wars, and profitability of oil firms, see Jonathan Nitzan and Shimshon Bichler, *The Global Political Economy of Israel* (London: Pluto Press, 2002).

95. Acharya, *U.S. Military Strategy in The Gulf,* 5.

96. Ibid., 11.

97. See sources in footnote 94; Barry Rosen, *Restraint: A New Foundation for U.S. Grand Strategy* (Ithaca, NY: Cornell University Press, 2015), 106–13; Christopher Dietrich, *Oil Revolution: Anticolonial Elites, Sovereign Rights, and the Economic Culture of Decolonization* (Cambridge: Cambridge University Press, 2017).

98. Brandon Wolfe-Hunnicutt, "Oil Sovereignty, American Foreign Policy, and the 1968 Coups in Iraq," *Diplomacy and Statecraft* 28, no. 2 (2017): 235–53.

99. Henry Kissinger, *White House Years* (Boston: Little, Brown, 1979), 1264.

100. Roham Alvandi, who is committed to presenting the shah as "an architect, not an instrument, of the Nixon Doctrine in the Persian Gulf" (372), references several US officials who describe Nixon's policy as a "one pillar policy," with the other possible pillar being Israel, not Saudi Arabia (359). "Nixon, Kissinger, and the Shah: The Origins of Iranian Primacy in the Persian Gulf," *Diplomatic History* 36, no. 2 (April 2012): 337–72. In addition, to sending troops to Oman, the Shah also transferred military equipment to Pakistan and Zaire. British military presence in the Gulf did not disappear and the counterrevolutionary war in Oman is a case in point. Fred Halliday observed that suppressing the Omani revolution ushered in a new form of counter-insurgency where the British government sent weapons and facilitate the recruitment of British soldiers as paid contractors to defend the Sultan came to power in a British backed coup in 1970. Fred Halliday, *Mercenaries: "Counter-Insurgency" in the Gulf* (Nottingham, U.K.: Spokesman, 1977).

101. David E. Spiro, *The Hidden Hand of American Hegemony: Petrodollar Recycling and International Markets* (Ithaca, NY: Cornell University Press, 1999), Peter Gowan, *The Global Gamble: Washington's Faustian Bid for World Dominance* (London: Verso, 1999).

102. Daniel Sargent, *A Superpower Transformed: The Remaking of American Foreign Relations in the 1970s* (New York: Oxford University Press, 2017), 5.

103. The oil price revolution is covered succinctly in F. Gregory Gause III, *The International Relations of the Persian Gulf* (Cambridge: Cambridge University Press, 2010), 25–34; Dietrich, *Oil Revolution.*

104. Nathan J. Citino, "Defending the 'Postwar Petroleum Order': The US, Britain, and the 1954 Saudi-Onassis Tanker Deal." *Diplomacy and Statecraft* 11, no. 2 (2000): 137–60.

105. Melani Macalister, *Epic Encounters Culture, Media, and U.S. Interests in the Middle East since 1945,* 2nd ed. (Berkeley: University of California Press, 2005).

106. Adam Hanieh, "Petrochemical Empire: The Geo-Politics of Fossil-Fuelled Production," *New Left Review* 130 (July–August 2021): 25–51.

107. Adam Hanieh, *Money, Markets, and Monarchies: The Gulf Cooperation Council and the Political Economy of the Contemporary Middle East* (Cambridge: Cambridge University Press, 2018), 30–34.

108. Spiro, *The Hidden Hand of American Hegemony*.

109. Alice Amsden, *Escape from Empire: The Developing World's Journey through Heaven and Hell* (Cambridge: MIT Press, 2007), 13.

110. Nathan Citino, *From Arab Nationalism to OPEC: Eisenhower, King Sa'ud, and the Making of US-Saudi Relations* (Bloomington: Indiana University Press, 2002), 163. Military training in Iran and Saudi Arabia dates back to years immediately after World War II. James A. Bill, *The Eagle and the Lion: The Tragedy of American Iranian Relations* (New Haven: Yale University Press, 1988); Thomas Ricks, "U.S. Military Missions to Iran, 1943–1978: The Political Economy of Military Assistance," *Iranian Studies*, vol. 12, no. 3/4 (1979): 163–193; Laleh Khalili, "The Infrastructural Power of the Military: The Geoeconomic Role of the U.S. Army Corps of Engineers in the Arabian Peninsula," *European Journal of International Relations* 24, no. 4 (2018): 911–33.

111. Andrew L. Johns, "The Johnson Administration, the Shah of Iran, and the Changing Pattern of U.S.-Iranian Relations, 1965–1967: 'Tired of Being Treated like a Schoolboy,'" *Journal of Cold War Studies* 9, no. 2 (2007): 78–79. Also, Iran's arms sales were "considered in Washington as 'a boost to the sagging United States balance of payments.' Senator J. W. Fulbright, chairman of the Foreign Relations Committee, was quoted as saying that the United States had become an 'arms salesman' in order to stop Communism but was now continuing in the role in order to enhance its balance of payments." Ramazani, *Iran's Foreign Policy*, 369; *New York Times*, February 25, 1973; *Washington Post*, February 25, 1973.

112. Vincent Bevins, *The Jakarta Method: Washington's Anticommunist Crusade and the Mass Murder Program That Shaped Our World* (New York: Public Affairs, 2020), Stuart Schrader, *Badges without Borders: How Global Counterinsurgency Transformed American Policing* (Berkeley: University of California Press, 2019).

113. Ramazani, *Iran's Foreign Policy*, 367. On the contracts signed and joint ventures created between Iran and US companies and government entities, see also Bill, *The Eagle and the Lion*, 200–15.

114. Joe Stork, "The Carter Doctrine and the US bases in the Middle East," *MERIP Reports* 90 (September 1980): 4.

115. Acharya, *U.S. Military Strategy in The Gulf*, 11.

116. Jahangir Amuzegar, "Persian Gulf Oil and the World Economy," in *The Persian Gulf and Indian Ocean in International Politics*, ed. Abbas Amirie (Tehran: Institute for International Political and Economic Studies, 1975), 325.

117. Interview with Archie Bolster, Oral History Project of the Foundation for Iranian Studies, part 8, p. 152.

118. Bill, *The Eagle and the Lion*, 201; Jeffrey Kimball, "The Nixon Doctrine: A Saga of Misunderstanding," *Presidential Studies Quarterly* 36, no. 1 (2006): 59–74.

119. Robert Graham, *Iran: The Illusion of Power* (London: Crom Helm, 1979), 187.

120. Shah made statements against US naval bases for public consumption, but not in private discussions with US officials. Interview with Jack Miklos, Oral History Project of the Foundation for Iranian Studies, part 7, p. 144.

121. Steven Ward, *Immortal: A Military History of Iran and its Forces* (Washington, DC: Georgetown University Press, 2009), 198; Drew Middleton, "Shah of Iran Due in U.S. to Seek Weapons," *New York Times*, July 22, 1973, 1.

122. Joe Stork and Jim Paul, "Arms Sales and the Militarization of the Middle East," *MERIP Reports*, no. 112 (February 1983): 8.

123. Andrew Friedman, *Covert Capital: Landscapes of Denial and the Making of the U.S. Empire in the Suburbs of Northern Virginia* (Berkeley: University of California Press, 2013), 220–93.

124. Bernard Weinraub, "The U.S. Policy on Arms Has a Life of Its Own: Rhetoric and Guilt," *New York Times*, September 18, 1977.

125. Christopher Dietrich, "'We Must Have a Defense Build-Up': The Iranian Revolution, Regional Security, and American Vulnerability," in *Global 1979: Geographies and Histories of the Iranian Revolution*, ed. Arang Keshavarzian and Ali Mirsepassi (Cambridge: Cambridge University Press, 2021), 248.

126. David Crist, *The Twilight War: The Secret History of America's Thirty-Year Conflict with Iran* (New York: Penguin Press, 2012), 36.

127. Quoted in Stern, "Oil Scarcity Ideology in US Foreign Policy, 1908–97," 243–44. See also Sargent, *Superpower Transformed*, 137.

128. In *The Persian Gulf and the Strait of Hormuz*, R. K. Ramazani recounts Soviet ambitions in the 1970s (50–52) but concludes that by 1979 Moscow had failed to accomplish its goals (52) and at two potential moments of conflict the Soviet Union pushed for negotiated settlement—the Iraqi-Kuwaiti border dispute of 1973 and the Iranian-Iraqi border dispute of 1974-7-5 (52–53).

129. "Reflections on the Soviet Intervention in Afghanistan," Memo to President Carter from Zbigniew Brzezinski, December 26, 1979 http://www.temple.edu/history/immerman/291/syllabus/BrzezinskiToCarterAfghanistan.htm, accessed September 23, 2013. See also Brzezinski's *The Grand Chessboard* in which he continues to think within Mackinder's terminology of a chessboard and the Euroasian heartland. Brzezinski, *The Grand Chessboard: American Primacy and its Geostrategic Imperatives* (New York: Basic Books, 1997). On the US role and provocations immediately prior to the Russian invasion of Afghanistan, see the National Security Archive, "The Soviet Invasion of Afghanistan, 1979: Not Trump's Terrorists, nor Zbig's Warm Water Ports," January 29, 2019, https://nsarchive.gwu.edu/briefing-book/

afghanistan-russia-programs/2019-01-29/soviet-invasion-afghanistan-1979-not
-trumps-terrorists-nor-zbigs-warm-water-ports.

130. Stern, "Oil Scarcity Ideology in US Foreign Policy, 1908–97," 243.

131. "The Crescent of Crisis: Iran and a Region of Rising Instability," *Time*, January 15, 1979, 18. This view is supported and shared by Henry Kissinger in the same issue. See "An Interview with Kissinger: Détente Should Not Become a Tranquilizer," *Time*, January 15, 1979, p. 29. Note that Brzezinski made similar statements two weeks earlier in *The New York Times Magazine*, December 31, 1978.

132. Academics instead recouped many of the ideas of geopolitics as "security" and "grand strategy" by international relations theorists and practitioners. A rare exception of someone who continued to use the term was Ladis Kristof, a political scientist and father of *New York Times* columnist Nicholas Krisstof. Hepple, "Revival of Geopolitics," 22–23.

133. This perception of a Soviet threat was central to the Committee on the Clear and Present Danger formed in 1976 and many of its members staffed Ronald Reagan's administration including George H. W. Bush and Jean Kirkpatrick. Midcentury American intellectuals gravitated to geopolitical ideas with people from different political persuasions such as Spykman, Kennan, Lattimore, and Kissinger tapping into ideas about land and sea power as well as frontiers to envisage the role of the United States in the world or regions, international legal institutions, and ideological struggles with communism.

134. Soviet vessels also visited Iran's Bandar Abbas in the 1970s. *Foreign Relations of the United States 1969–1976*, volume E-4, Documents on Iran and Iraq, 1969–1972, Telegram 76 From the Embassy in Iran to the Department of State Tehran, January 6, 1971, 1300Z.

135. Fred Halliday, "The Arc of Revolutions: Iran, Afghanistan, South Yemen, Ethiopia," *Race and Class* 20, no. 4 (April 1979): 373–90.

136. "The Crescent of Crisis: Iran and a Region of Rising Instability," *Time*, January 15, 1979, 18. In the struggle to present this swath of the globe in crisis, the article mentions India and Egypt's overpopulation as being the cause for impoverishment and urban unrest, while in the same breath Saudi Arabia's small population is flagged as a weakness.

137. In 1979 R. K. Ramazani describes the Persian Gulf as "the International oil highway" (22) and the Strait of Hormuz as "the global chokepoint." *Persian Gulf and the Strait of Hormuz*, 23.

138. Quoted in Crist, *Twilight* War, 12.

139. "The Crumbling Triangle," *The Economist*, December 9, 1978, p. 11. Instead of an arc, *The Economist* adopted a triangle to represent the argument. The corners of the triangle were Kabul in the East, Istanbul in the North, and Addis Ababa in the South.

140. "The Crescent of Crisis," *Time*, 18; note that the article also offers the decline of Soviet oil reserves as a reason for their expansionist plans within the region. The article claims that the USSR will run out of oil "within a decade"!

141. Cottrell and Moodie, *The United States and the Persian Gulf*, xi.

142. Ibid., x. At another point they write that "generally the Soviets would prefer to manipulate rather than march their way to the Gulf," Cottrell and Moodie, *The United States and the Persian Gulf*, 1.

143. *Time*, January 15, 1979.

144. Ó Tuathail, *Critical Geopolitics*, 40.

145. The transcript of the speech can be found at the American Presidency Project (https://www.presidency.ucsb.edu/documents/address-the-nation-the-soviet-invasion-afghanistan).

146. http://www.presidency.ucsb.edu/ws/?pid=33079#axzz2g6k6M2Cp.

147. Yergin, *The Prize*, 702.

148. W. Taylor Fain, "Conceiving the 'Arc of Crisis' in the Indian Ocean Region," *Diplomatic History* 42, no. 4 (2018): 694–719. Fain analyzes the Carter Doctrine from the perspective of how new "mental maps" in the 1970s were adopted by US officials that made the Indian Ocean a distinct security space.

149. Chandra Kumar, "The Indian Ocean: Arc of Crisis or Zone of Peace?" *International Affairs* 60, no. 2 (Spring 1984): 234.

150. Sargent, *A Superpower Transformed*, 289.

151. Crist, *The Twilight War*, 40. US involvement in Diego Garcia dates back to the early 1970s but expanded dramatically as a result of the strategic vision. One of the justifications for building the base in Diego Garcia was as a role resupplying and reinforcing Israel in case of another Arab-Israeli war and the fear that the US may not have access to the Azores. Alvin J. Cottrell and Walter F. Hahn, *Indian Ocean Naval Limitations: Regional Issues and Global Implication* (New York: National Strategy Information Center, 1976), 28.

152. David Vine, *Island of Shame: The Secret History of the U.S. Military Base on Diego Garcia* (Princeton, NJ: Princeton University Press, 2009).

153. Ibid., 10.

154. Cottrell and Moodie, *The United States and the Persian Gulf*, 3.

155. Crist, *The Twilight War*, 35.

156. Huntington's study was known as PRM-10 Net Assessment and characterized the Persian Gulf as Southwest Asia as probable theaters for conflict with the USSR. See Stern, "Oil Scarcity Ideology in US Foreign Policy, 1908–97," 28–29. Note that the State Department and the Treasury pushed back against Brzezinski and the NSC fearmongering.

157. Jones, "America, Oil, and War in the Middle East."

158. Andrew J. Bacevich, "Ending Endless War: A Pragmatic Military Strategy," *Foreign Affairs* 95, no. 5 (September/October 2016).

159. The best overview of the international relations of the Persian Gulf that covers this history in great detail and with a fair amount of critical appraisal is Gause, *The International Relations of the Persian Gulf.*

160. Toby Jones, "Energy and America's Long War in the Persian Gulf," Workshop on New Directions in Political Economy, Kevorkian Center for Near Eastern Studies, New York University, 2014.

161. Brzezinski, *The Grand Chessboard,* 53.

162. Ó Tuathail, *Critical Geopolitics,* 15.

163. Susan Strange, "Cave! Hic Dragones: A Critique of Regime Analysis," *International Organization* 36, no. 2 (1982): 479–96.

164. Beverly J. Silver and Giovanni Arrighi, "The End of the Long Twentieth Century," in *Business as Usual: The Roots of the Global Financial Meltdown,* ed. Craig J Calhoun and Georgi Derluguian (New York: New York University Press, 2011); J. Go, "Waves of Empire: US Hegemony and Imperialistic Activity from the Shores of Tripoli to Iraq, 1787–2003," *International Sociology* 22, no. 1 (January 2007): 5–40.

165. Deborah Cowen and Neil Smith, "After Geopolitics?" 31.

166. Quoted in Sargent, *Superpower Transformed,* 7.

167. Daniel Immerwahr, *How to Hide an Empire: A History of the Greater United States* (New York: Farrar, Straus and Giroux, 2019).

168. Ellis Goldberg and Robert Vitalis, "The Arabian Peninsula: Crucible of Globalization," working paper, European University Institute, Robert Schuman Centre for Advanced Studies, 2002.

169. *New York Times,* March 5, 1981.

170. Steinberg, *The Social Construction of the Ocean,* 156–57, 164–65; Michael Klare, "Mahan Revisited: Globalization, Resource Diplomacy, and Maritime Security," in *Maritime Strategy and Global Order: Markets, Resources, Security,* ed. Daniel Moran and James A. Russell (Washington, DC: Georgetown University Press, 2016), 261–81.

171. United States Navy, "A Cooperative Strategy for 21st Century Seapower: Forward, Engaged, Ready," March 2015, 1; available at: https://www.navy.mil/local/maritime/150227-CS21R-Final.pdf.

172. Smith, *American Empire,* 8.

CHAPTER THREE

1. Homa Katouzian, "The Campaign against the Anglo-Iranian Agreement of 1919," *British Journal of Middle Eastern Studies* 25, no. 1 (May 1998): 5–46.

2. "Veiled British Protectorate" is typically used to describe Britain's relationship with Egypt but Christopher Ross adopts the phrase to cover the case of Iran. Ross,

"Lord Curzon and E. G. Browne Confront the 'Persian Question.'" *Historical Journal* 52, no. 2 (2009): 408. See also Ervand Abrahamian, *The Coup: 1953, the CIA, and the Roots of Modern U.S.-Iranian Relations* (New York: The New Press, 2013), 25–27; N. S. Fatemi, "Anglo-Persian Agreement of 1919," *Encyclopædia Iranica*, II/1, pp. 59–61, available online at http://www.iranicaonline.org/articles/anglo-persian-agreement-1919, accessed December 30, 2012.

3. Glenda Sluga, *Internationalism in the Age of Nationalism* (Philadelphia: University of Pennsylvania Press, 2013).

4. Aiwha Ong, *Neoliberalism as Exception: Mutations in Citizenship and Sovereignty* (Durham, NC: Duke University Press, 2006), 100.

5. On the multiple models of sovereignty, see Stephen D. Krasner, *Sovereignty: Organized Hypocrisy* (Princeton, NJ: Princeton University Press, 1999), 9–25. He identifies four ideas of sovereignty: Westphalian sovereignty or the norm of non-interference and mutual recognition of states (sometimes known as negative sovereignty); domestic sovereignty or the ability of the state to have effective control within its borders; interdependence sovereignty or control of cross-border matters, and international legal sovereignty or international recognition of territory and authority.

6. Sovereignty can be thought of as the production of power over human bodies through laws and social institutions. This chapter does not explore this, but for a rich discussion of this process in the modern Iraq, see Sara Pursley, *Familiar Futures: Time, Selfhood, and Sovereignty in Iraq* (Stanford: Stanford University Press, 2018).

7. C. U. Aitchison, *A Collection of Treaties, Engagements, and Sanads Relating to India and Neighbouring Countries* (Calcutta: Govt. of India Central Publication Branch, 1933), 256. The 1839 Maritime Truce that banned maritime conflict during pearling seasons that was extended and then transformed into a Treaty of Perpetual Peace in 1853.

8. Frauke Heard-Bey, *From Trucial States to United Arab Emirates: A Society in Transition* (London: Longman, 1982), 212–16.

9. In 1878, the Gulf Resident and Fars Counsel-General based in Bushehr also represented the Foreign Office and Government in London. Thus, it came under the authority both the Government in Calcutta and London, which led to disputes and complications through the 1940s. See Robert J. Blyth, "Britain Versus India in the Persian Gulf: The Struggle for Political Control, c. 1928–48," *Journal of Imperial and Commonwealth History* 28, no. 1 (2000): 90–111.

10. James Onley, *The Arabian Frontier of the British Raj* (Oxford: Oxford University Press, 2007).

11. This coincides with Curzon's implementation of his forward policy in 1900 at which point the native agency system declined. Onley, *The Arabian Frontier of the British Raj*, 214. On Curzon Forward policy, see Briton Cooper Busch, *Britain and*

the Persian Gulf, 1894–1914 (Berkeley: University of California Press, 1967), 114–53, 235–69.

12. Muhammad Morsy Abdullah, *The United Arab Emirates: A Modern History* (London: Croom Helm), 250–55.

13. Onley describes these polities as protected state. Onley, *The Arabian Frontier of the British Raj*, 21–26. Anscombe describes the 1899 Anglo-Kuwaiti treaty a "concession bond" or a "quasi-protectorate." On the distinction between "protected states" and "protectorates," see Frederick Anscombe, *The Ottoman Gulf: The Creation of Kuwait, Saudi Arabia, and Qatar* (New York: Columbia University Press, 1997), 3, 111, 113. Anscombe argues that a "bond" is the term for a secret agreement, while protectorate is for a public treaty. Anscombe shows that Kuwait's treaty became public in 1912 although in the Anglo-Turkish agreement of 1913, the British named Kuwait as part of the Ottoman empire, which contravened the content of the 1899 agreement with Mubarak. The Ottoman Empire did not formally renounce its claims on controlling Kuwait until 1913.

14. Quoted in Abdulkhaleq Abdulla, "Political Dependency: The Case of the United Arab Emirates," PhD dissertation, Georgetown University, 1984, 88–89.

15. Anscombe explains that the flying of flags was a major sticking point because "the Ottomans based much of their tribal (and geopolitical) strategy upon the sovereignty implied by payment of tribute and flying flags." Anscombe, *The Ottoman Gulf*, 72. In the nineteenth century, slave ships took to flying the Persian Flag instead of flags from the sheikhdoms of the Arabian peninsula because the Anglo-Persian Treaty of the time did not allow British patrols to search for and seize slaves from Persian vessels. David Commins, *The Gulf States a Modern History* (New York: IB Tauris, 2012), 82; see also Johan Mathew, *Margins of the Market: Trafficking and Capitalism across the Arabian Sea* (Berkeley: University of California Press, 2016), 34–38.

16. Onley, *The Arabian Frontier of the British Raj*, 21–24; Tétreault, *Stories of Democracy*, 55. On the connection between British colonial practices in the Arabian protected states and in India, see John M. Willis, "Making Yemen Indian: Rewriting the Boundaries of Imperial Arabia," *International Journal of Middle East Studies* 41, no. 1 (February 2009): 22–38.

17. On Basra, see Reider Visser, *Basra, the Failed Gulf State: Separatism and Nationalism in Southern Iraq* (New Brunswick, NJ: Transaction Publishers, 2005); and Reider Visser, "Britain and Basra: Past Experiences and Current Challenges," http;//historiae.org, July 11, 2006. On the last two cases, see Andrea Rugh, *The Political Culture of Leadership in the United Arab Emirates* (New York: Palgrave, 2007), 193–216.

18. Treaties prohibited the import or export of arms (1902), gave British officials exclusive power to grant concessions on pearling, fishing, and other related activities (1911). Heard-Bey, *From Trucial States to United Arab Emirates*, 117; Aitchison,

A Collection of Treaties, Engagements, and Sanads Relating to India and Neighbouring Countries, 257, 263. In the next decade similar treaties were signed regarding concessions for oil explorations and landing rights. Political Residents were meant to be neutral in commercial negotiations, but as one of them acknowledged, they did "put word in when any matter of political importance crops up." Rupert Hay, *The Persian Gulf States* (Washington, DC: Middle East Institute, 1959), 67.

19. Abdulla, "Political Dependency," 132–35.

20. Abdullah, *The United Arab Emirates*, 99; Chelsi Mueller, *The Origins of the Arab-Iranian Conflict: Nationalism and Sovereignty in the Gulf between the World Wars* (Cambridge: Cambridge University Press, 2020).

21. Donald Hawley, *The Trucial States* (London: George Allen and Unwin Ltd., 1970), 161.

22. Frauke Heard-Bey, "The Beginning of the Post-Imperial Era for the Trucial States from World War I to the 1960s," in *United Arab Emirates: A New Perspective*, ed. Ibrahim Al-Abed (London: Trident Press, 2001), 119.

23. The seminal article on this topic is John Gallagher and Ronald Robinson, "The Imperialism of Free Trade," *Economic History Review* 6, no. 1 (1953): 1–15; Karuna Mantena, *Alibis of Empire: Henry Maine and the Ends of Liberal Imperialism* (Princeton, NJ: Princeton University Press, 2010).

24. Anscombe, *The Ottoman Gulf*, 3.

25. Ibid., 126.

26. Mary Ann Tetreault, "Autonomy, Necessity, and the Small State: Ruling Kuwait in the Twentieth Century," *International Organization* 45, no. 4 (Autumn 1991): 572–74.

27. Rugh, *The Political Culture of Leadership in the United Arab Emirates*, 103, 113.

28. Ibid., 13, 73, 77–78; Abdel Razzeq Takriti, "Colonial Coups and the War on Popular Sovereignty," *American Historical Review* 124, no. 3 (June 2019): 878–909.

29. Mahmood Mamdani, *Citizen and Subject: The Making of Citizen and Subject in Contemporary Africa* (Princeton, NJ: Princeton University Press, 1996); Toby Dodge, *Inventing Iraq: The Failure of Nation Building and a History Denied* (New York: Columbia University Press, 2003); Peter Lienhardt, *Sheikhdoms of Eastern Arabia* (New York: Palgrave, 2001).

30. Rugh, *The Political Culture of Leadership in the United Arab Emirates*, 40.

31. Abdulla, "Political Dependency," 80–83.

32. Anscombe, *The Ottoman Gulf*, 113–42.

33. Rugh, *The Political Culture of Leadership in the United Arab Emirates*, 13.

34. Alex Boodrookas, "The Making of a Migrant Working Class: Contesting Citizenship in Kuwait and the Persian Gulf, 1925–1975," PhD dissertation, New York University, 2019.

35. Christopher M. Davidson, "Arab Nationalism and British Opposition in Dubai, 1920–66," *Middle Eastern Studies* 43, no. 6 (November 2007): 880.

36. Hay, *The Persian Gulf States*, 20.

37. Omar Hesham AlShehabi, "Policing Labour in Empire: The Modern Origins of the Kafala Sponsorship System in the Gulf Arab States," *British Journal of Middle Eastern Studies* 48, no. 2 (2021): 291–310. On the situation on the Trucial States, see Hawley, *The Trucial States*, 178–81; Noora Lori, *Offshore Citizens: Permanent Temporary Status in the Gulf* (Cambridge: Cambridge University Press, 2019).

38. Commins, *The Gulf States*, 141.

39. Boodrookas, "The Making of a Migrant Working Class," chapter 2.

40. Lori, *Offshore Citizens*.

41. Boodrookas, "The Making of a Migrant Working Class."

42. Peter Lienhardt, *Disorientations, A Society in Flux: Kuwait in the 1950s*, ed. Ahmed Al-Shahi (Reading, U.K.: Ithaca Press, 1993), 56–57. See also Hay, *The Persian Gulf States*, 22.

43. This section draws on the historiography and discussion found in Jill Crystal, *Oil and Politics in the Gulf: Rulers and Merchants in Kuwait and Qatar* (Cambridge: Cambridge University Press, 1990); Nelida Fuccaro, *Histories of City and State in the Persian Gulf: Manama since 1800* (Cambridge University Press, 2009); Fatma al-Sayegh, "Marchants' Role in a Changing Society: The Case of Dubai, 1900–90," *Middle Eastern Studies* 34, no. 1 (January 1998): 87–102; Michael Herb, *The Wages of Oil: Parliaments and Economic Development in Kuwait and the UAE* (Ithaca, NY: Cornell University Press, 2014); Mary Ann Tétreault, *Stories of Democracy: Politics and Society in Contemporary Kuwait* (New York: Columbia University Press, 2000), 62–67; Heard-Bey, *From Trucial States to United Arab Emirates*, 255–58; Abdullah, *The United Arab Emirates*.

44. Al-Sayegh, "Merchants' Role in a Changing Society," 92–93; Eran Segal, "Merchants' Networks in Kuwait: The Story of Yusuf al-Marzuk," *Middle Eastern Studies* 45, no. 5 (Summer 2009): 715; Sheila Carapico, "Arabia Incognita: An Invitation to Arabian Peninsula Studies," in *Counter-Narratives: History, Contemporary Society, and Politics in Saudi Arabia and Yemen*, ed. Madawi al-Rasheed and Robert Vitalis (New York: Palgrave Macmillan, 2004), 22. News of majles uprisings in the Gulf spread across Indian ocean basin to Zanzibar. Alan Villiers, *Sons of Sinbad* (London: Arabian Publishing, 2006 [1949]), 232.

45. Al-Sayegh, "Merchants' Role in a Changing Society," 94–96; Rosemarie Said Zahlan, *The Making of the Modern Gulf States* (London: Unwin Hyman, 1989), 151–52.

46. Mathew, *Margins of the Market*, 82–142.

47. Abdullah, *The United Arab Emirates*, 126.

48. Davidson, "Arab Nationalism and British opposition in Dubai, 1920–66," 882–83; Rugh, *The Political Culture of Leadership in the United Arab Emirates*, 108–9.

49. Nelida Fuccaro, *Histories of City and State in the Persian Gulf.*

50. Omar Hesham AlShehabi, "Contested Modernity: Divided Rule and the Birth of Sectarianism, Nationalism, and Absolutism in Bahrain," *British Journal of Middle Eastern Studies* 44, no. 3 (2017): 352.

51. Tétreault, *Stories of Democracy*, 65.

52. Michael Herb, *All in the Family: Absolutism, Revolution, and Democracy in the Middle Eastern Monarchies* (Albany: State University of New York Press, 1999).

53. Abdullah, *The United Arab Emirates*, 131.

54. For a comparative analysis between the 1930s and 1950s protest movements and across different countries see Herb, *The Wages of Oil*, 60–106. On Kuwait, see Boodrookas, "The Making of a Migrant Working Class."

55. Talal al-Rashoud, "Icon of Defiance and Hope: Gamal Abdel Nasser's Image in Gulf History," *Mada*, November 28, 2020.

56. On oil towns see Kaveh Ehsani, "The Social History of Labor in the Iranian Oil Industry: The Built Environment and the Making of the Industrial Working Class (1908–1941)," PhD dissertation, Leiden University, 2014; Robert Vitalis, *America's Kingdom: Mythmaking on the Saudi Oil Frontier* (London: Verso, 2009). Many years ago Fred Halliday made the connection between Omani politics and migrants on the oil fields. Halliday, *Mercenaries: "Counter-insurgency" in the Gulf* (Nottingham, U.K.: Spokesman, 1977), 47.

57. Davidson, "Arab Nationalism and British Opposition in Dubai," 888; Mueller, *The Origins of the Arab-Iranian Conflict*, 185–88, 230–31.

58. Davidson "Arab Nationalism and British Opposition in Dubai," 884; Abdullah, *The United Arab Emirates*, 130–33.

59. Steven G. Galpern, *Money, Oil, and Empire in the Middle East: Sterling and Postwar Imperialism, 1944–1971* (New York: Cambridge University Press, 2009), 213.

60. Miriam Joyce, "The Bahraini Three on St. Helena, 1956–1961," *Middle East Journal* 54, no. 4 (Fall 2000): 613–23.

61. Heard-Bey, "The Beginning of the Post-Imperial Era," 118.

62. Jeff Eamon, "Policing the Bahrain Islands: Labor, Race, and the Historical Origins of Foreign Recruitment," master's thesis, Program in Near Eastern Studies, New York University, 2015.

63. Crystal, *Oil and Politics in the Gulf*, 1.

64. Many of the merchants involved in these political movements were the beneficiaries of agencies to represent foreign firms as well as the first rounds of real estate investments. To name just a few: al-Ghurair and al-Futtaim in Dubai and Fakhroo in Bahrain.

65. Boodrookas, "The Making of a Migrant Working Class," 107.

66. Heard-Bey, *From Trucial States to United Arab Emirates*, 259–60.

67. *Inter alia* Paul Dresch, "Foreign Matter: The Place of Strangers in Gulf Society," in *Globalization and the Gulf,* ed. John W. Fox, Nada Mourtada-Sabbah, and Mohammed al-Mutawa (London: Routledge, 2006), 200–222; Lori, *Offshore Citizens.*

68. Madawi al-Rasheed, *A History of Saudi Arabia,* 2nd ed. (Cambridge: Cambridge University Press, 2010), 37–46.

69. Toby C. Jones, *Desert Kingdom: How Oil and Water Forged Modern Saudi Arabia* (Cambridge: Harvard University Press, 2010), 11.

70. Daniel Foliard, *Dislocating the Orient: British Maps and the Making of the Middle East, 1854–1921* (Chicago: University of Chicago Press, 2017), 184.

71. Vitalis, *America's Kingdom.*

72. Ibid., 34. Jones's *Desert Kingdom* also identifies state-building as being intimately woven with management of technological projects and attempt to master nature to ensure political survival.

73. Rosie Bsheer, *Archive Wars: The Politics of History in Saudi Arabia* (Stanford: Stanford University Press, 2020).

74. This does not mean that ideas about Iran did not predate the Qajar Dynasty. See Mana Kia, *Persianate Selves: Memories of Place and Origin before Nationalism* (Stanford: Stanford University Press, 2020); Firoozeh Kashani-Sabet, *Frontier Fictions: Shaping the Iranian Nation, 1804–1946* (Princeton, NJ: Princeton University Press, 1999).

75. Vanessa Martin, *The Qajar Pact: Bargaining, Protest and the State in Nineteenth-Century Persia* (London: I. B. Tauris, 2005), 29–47.

76. Larry Potter, "The Consolidation of Iran's Frontier on the Persian Gulf in the Nineteenth Century," in *War and Peace in Qajar Persia: Implications Past and Present,* ed. Roxane Farmanfarmaian (London: Routledge, 2008), 125–48; Peter Brobst, "Sir Frederic Goldsmid and the Containment of Persia, 1863–73," *Middle Eastern Studies* 33, no. 2 (April 1997): 197–215.

77. Heshmatollah Azizi, Dariush Rahmanian, Houshang KhosroBaygi, and Mohammad Rostami, "Chegooneh shek giri 'hokmrani banader va jazaer Khalij-e Fars' be markaziyat-e Bushehr dar 'asr Naseri," *Pajhouheshnameh-ye Tarikhha-ye Mahali Iran* 7, no. 1 (Fall–Winter 1397): 171–90.

78. Shiva Balaghi, "Nationalism and Cultural Production in Iran, 1848–1906," PhD dissertation, University of Michigan, 2008, 201–6. An official gazette in Iran described Curzon's voyage as follows: "We congratulate the Viceroy in the part of the Persian nation on his arrival on our frontier, we expect good results from his visit, and we pray The Almighty for the continuation and consolidation of friendship and union between Persia and her old friend Great Britain, who rules today over millions of our coreligionists in the East whose prosperity and welfare we desire" (201).

79. Yadullah Shahibzadeh, *The Iranian Political Language: From the Late Nineteenth Century to the Present* (New York: Palgrave Macmillan, 2015), 79–82.

80. Abdullah, *The United Arab Emirates*, 226–27.

81. Willem Floor, *The Persian Gulf: The Rise and Fall of Bandar-e Lengeh: The Distribution Center for the Arabian Coast, 1750–1930* (Washington, DC: Mage Publishers, 2010), 59–60, 137.

82. Floor, *The Persian Gulf*, 60–71.

83. Friedrich Kratochwil, "Of Systems, Boundaries, and Territoriality: An Inquiry into the Formation of the State System," *World Politics* 39, no. 1 (October 1986): 39–40.

84. Mostafa Elm, *Oil, Power, and Principle: Iran's Oil Nationalization and its Aftermath* (Syracuse: Syracuse University Press, 1992), 17.

85. Phillip E. Steinberg, *The Social Construction of the Ocean* (Cambridge: Cambridge University Press, 2001), 152–53.

86. Stephanie Cronin, "Reform from Above, Resistance from Below: The New Order and its Opponents in Iran, 1927–29," in *The State and the Subaltern: Modernization, Society, and the State in Turkey and Iran*, ed. Touraj Atabaki (New York: I. B. Tauris, 2007), 71–95.

87. R. W. Ferrier, *The History of the British Petroleum Company*, vol. 1, p. 387. On Kha'zal's importance to the Anglo-Persian Oil Company's projects see Ehsani, "The Social History of Labor in the Iranian Oil Industry."

88. Shahbaz Shahnazaz, "Kaz'al Khan", *Encyclopeadia Iranica*, vol. 16, 188–97.

89. Elm, *Oil, Power, and Principle*, 27.

90. Ehsani, "The Social History of Labor in the Iranian Oil Industry," chapter 6.

91. The hiring of workers who were not subjects of the Shah violated the D'Arcy concession. I. J. Seccombe and R. I. Lawless, "Foreign Worker Dependence in the Gulf, and the International Oil Company," *International Migration Review* 20, no. 3 (1986): 558.

92. Chelsi Mueller, "Anglo-Iranian Treaty Negotiations: Reza Shah, Teymurtash and the British Government, 1927–32," *Iranian Studies* 49, no. 4 (2016): 577–92; Stephanie Cronin, *The Army and the Creation of the Pahlavi State in Iran, 1910–1926* (London: Tauris Academic Studies), 206–7.

93. Stephanie Cronin, "Popular Politics, the New State, and the Birth of the Iranian Working Class: The 1929 Abadan Oil Refinery Strike," *Middle East Studies* 46, no. 5 (September 2010): 711; Kaveh Bayat, "With or Without Workers in Reza Shah's Iran: Abadan, May 1929," in *The State and the Subaltern: Modernization, Society, and the State in Turkey and Iran* (London: I. B. Tauris, 2007), 111. On labor in the oil sector prior to World War II, see also Touraj Atabaki, "Far from Home, But at Home:

Indian Migrant Workers in the Iranian Oil Industry," *Studies in History* 31, no. 1 (2015): 85–114; Kaveh Ehsani, "Social Engineering and the Contradictions of Modernization in Khuzestan's Company Towns: A Look at Abadan and Masjed-Soleyman," *International Review of Social History* 48, no. 3 (2003): 361–99.

94. Gregory Brew, "In Search of 'Equitability': Sir John Cadman, Rezā Shah, and the Cancellation of the D'Arcy Concession, 1928-33," *Iranian Studies* 50, no. 1 (2017): 125–48.

95. Abdullah, *The United Arab Emirates*, 246–73; Richard Schofield, "States Behaving Badly? The Unique geopolitics of island Sovereignty Disputes," Environment, Politics, and Development Working Paper Series, Department of Geography, King's College London, Paper no. 65 (2014), 40.

96. Mueller, *The Origins of the Arab-Iranian Conflict*, 50–53, 63.

97. Cronin, *The Army and the Creation of the Pahlavi State in Iran*, 137.

98. Elm, *Oil, Power, and Principle*, 28–40.

99. Quoted in Brew, "'In Search of 'Equitability,'" 130.

100. Mosaddeq held that a state can only independent if it can bring all residents under its jurisdiction. H. E. Chehabi, "Muhammad Mosaddeq and 'the Standard Civilization,'" Association for Iranian Studies Biannual conference, Salamanca Spain, August 30–September 2, 2022.

101. Christopher R. W. Dietrich, *Oil Revolution: Anticocnonial Elites, Sovereign Rights, and the Economic Culture of Decolonization* (Cambridge: Cambridge University Press, 2017); Ervand Abrahamian, *The Coup: 1953, the CIA, and the Roots of Modern U.S.-Iranian Relations* (New York: The New Press, 2013); Gregory Brew, "The Collapse Narrative: The United States, Mohammed Mossadegh and The Coup Decision of 1953," *Texas National Security Review* 2, no. 4 (August 2019): 38–59.

102. Kenneth Rodman, *Sanctity vs. Sovereignty: The United States and the Nationalization of Natural Resource Investments* (New York: Columbia University Press, 1988).

103. On the World Bank refusing to extend Iran a loan due to lack of assurances that it could repay it, see https://history.state.gov/historicaldocuments/frus1951-54Iran/d313.

104. Bill A. James, *The Eagle and the Lion: The Tragedy of American Iranian Relations* (New Haven: Yale University Press, 1988), 156; see also Rouhollah K. Ramazani, *Iran's Foreign Policy, 1941–1973* (Charlottesville: University Press of Virginia, 1975), 361–63.

105. Sayyed Ruhollah Khomeini, "The Granting of Capitulatory Rights to the U.S.," in *Islam and Revolution. Writings and Declarations of Imam Khomeini*, translated and annotated by H. Algar (Berkeley: Mizan Press, 1981), 182.

106. Pursley, *Familiar Futures*, 13–23.

107. Dodge, *Inventing Iraq*; Prya Satia, "Developing Iraq: Britain, India, and the Redemption of Empire and Technology in World War I," *Past and Present* 197 (November 2007): 211–55.

108. Charles Trip, *A History of Iraq*, 3rd ed. (Cambridge: Cambridge University Press, 2010), 43.

109. Phebe Marr, *The Modern History of Iraq*, 3rd ed. (Boulder, CO: Westview Press, 2012), 22–24; Dodge, *Inventing Iraq*.

110. Priya Satia, *Spies in Arabia: The Great War and the Cultural Foundations of Britain's Covert Empire in the Middle East* (New York: Oxford University Press, 2008); Pursley, *Familiar Futures*, 33.

111. Mueller, *The Origins of the Arab-Iranian Conflict*, 58–59; Pursley, *Familiar Futures*, 63.

112. Marr, *The Modern History of Iraq*, 26.

113. Steven G. Galpern, *Money, Oil, and Empire in the Middle East*, 210.

114. Susan Pedersen, *The Guardians: The League of Nations and the Crisis of Empire* (New York: Oxford University Press, 2018), 263, 271.

115. Dodge, *Inventing Iraq*, xxxii. Dodge also calls the Iraqi states at its founding a "quasi state."

116. Pedersen, *The Guardians*, 283.

117. Pursley, *Familiar Futures*, 58–61.

118. Zainab Saleh, "On Iraqi Nationality: Law, Citizenship, and Exclusion," *Arab Studies Journal* 21, no. 1 (Spring 2013): 48–78. Stefan Tetzlaff, "The Turn of the Gulf: Empire, Nationalism, and South Asian Labor Migration to Iraq, c. 1900 -1935," *International Labor and Working-Class History* 79 (Spring 2011): 7–27.

119. Timothy Mitchell, *Carbon Democracy: Political Power in the Age of Oil* (New York: Verso, 2011), 144–51.

120. Dietrich, *Oil Revolution*, 231, 252.

121. Antony Anghie argues that the recognition doctrine developed in the nineteenth century and was critical for decolonization for it was the mechanism through which non-European societies could be recognized as a legal entity in international law. Anghie, *Imperialism, Sovereignty, and the Making of International Law* (Cambridge: Cambridge University Press, 2005).

122. Anghie, *Imperialism, Sovereignty, and the Making of International Law*, 54–93.

123. Ibid., 67.

124. Emily McIntire, "Migrants and Bureaucrats: Social Mobility in an Iranian Town," PhD dissertation, Harvard University, 1984; Mohammad Taghi Razvani, "Iranian Communities in the Persian Gulf: A Geographical Analysis," PhD dissertation, University of London, 1975. On tensions between non-southern Iranians who

migrated to Dubai after the 1979 Revolution and the long-standing communities (many of whom were Arabic-speakers) that bridged southern Iran and Dubai, see Amin Moghadam, "Iranian Migrations to Dubai: Constrains and Autonomy of a Segmented Diaspora," Working Paper No. 2021/3, Ryerson Centre for Immigration and Settlement and the CERC in Migration and Integration at Ryerson University.

125. McIntire, "Migrants and Bureaucrats," 63. Shahnaz Nadjmabadi references droughts in the 1940s as one cause of farmers leaving southern Iran for the Arab Gulf cities. "Cross-Border Networks: Labour Migration from Iran to the Arab Countries of the Persian Gulf," *Anthropology of the Middle East* 5, no. 1 (Spring 2010): 23.

126. McIntire, "Migrants and Bureaucrats," 67–73.

127. Lori, *Offshore Citizens*, 81-–82.

128. Ahmed al-Dailami, "'Purity and Confusion': The Hawala between Persians and Arabs in the Contemporary Gulf," in *The Persian Gulf in Modern Times: People, Ports, and History*, ed. Lawrence G. Potter (New York: Palgrave Macmillan, 2014), 301.

129. Neil Brenner, Bob Jessop, Martin Jones, and Gordon MacLeod, eds., *State/Space: A Reader* (Malden, MA: Blackwell, 2003).

130. Ronen Polan, *The Offshore World: Sovereign Markets, Virtual Places, and Nomad Millionaires* (Ithaca, NY: Cornell University Press, 2003).

CHAPTER FOUR

1. Priya Satia, *Spies in Arabia: The Great War and the Cultural Foundations of Britain's Covert Empire in the Middle East* (Oxford: Oxford University Press, 2008),137–64, 239–62.

2. Christopher M. Davidson, *The United Arab Emirates: A Study in Survival* (Boulder, CO: Lynne Rienner, 2005), 34–37.

3. Muhammad Morsy Abdullah, *The United Arab Emirates: A Modern History* (London: Croom Helm, 1978), 294.

4. The Iraqi Petroleum Company was itself a subsidiary of the Anglo Persian Oil Company (later Anglo Iranian Oil Company, British Petroleum, and BP).

5. Glen Balfour-Paul, *The End of Empire in the Middle East: Britain's Relinquishment of Power in Her Last Three Arab Dependencies* (Cambridge: Cambridge University Press, 1991), 114.

6. Donald Hawley, *The Trucial States* (London: George Allen and Unwin Ltd., 1970), 224.

7. The development Bank was owned by 100 percent by the Pahlavi Foundation and was the fifth largest bank in Iran and considered as the Royal family's personal bank. Robert Graham, *Iran: The Illusion of Power* (London: Croom Helm, 1979),

158–59; "Ladbroke to Manage Persian Gulf Casinos," *The Financial Times*, December 13, 1977.

8. Marziyeh Amiri, "Matrudan-e Kish," *Maydan*, 26 Azar 1398. https://meidaan .com/archive/66082

9. Nasrin Tabatabai and Babak Afrassiabi, *Kish: An Island Indecisive by Design* (Rotterdam: Nai Publishers, 2012), 68.

10. Neil Brenner, "Beyond State-Centrism? Space, Territoriality, and Geographical Scale in Globalization Studies," *Theory and Society* 28, no. 1 (February 1999): 39–78; Waleed Hazbun and Arang Keshavarzian, "Re-Mapping Transnational Connections in the Middle East," *Geopolitics* 15, no. 2 (May 2010): 203–9.

11. Ronen Palan, *The Offshore World: Sovereign Markets, Virtual Places, and Nomad Millionaires* (Ithaca, NY: Cornell University Press, 2003), 8.

12. Deborah Cowen, *The Deadly Life of Logistics: Mapping Violence in Global Trade* (Minneapolis: Minnesota Press, 2014), 53–90.

13. Jean-Pierre Singa Boyenge, "ILO Database on Export Processing Zones (Revised)," Working paper, International Labour Office, Geneva, Switzerland, April 2007.

14. Kishore Rao mentions that free trade zones are important in the contemporary US economy. See Rao, "Free Zones in the Middle East: Development Patterns and Future Potential," in *Trade Policy Developments in the Middle East and North Africa*, ed. Bernard Hoekman and Hanaa Kheir el-Din (Washington, DC: The World Bank, 2000), 246;, Josh Martin, "Gateways for the Global Economy," *Management Review* 87, no. 11 (December, 1998): 22.

15. Ananda Shakespeare, "GCC Free Zones," *MEED*, November 27, 2014.

16. Keller Easterling, *Extrastatecraft: The Power of Infrastructure Space* (London: Verso, 2014).

17. Palan, *The Offshore World*; Vanessa Ogle, "'Funk Money': The End of Empires, the Expansion of Tax Havens, and Decolonization as an Economic and Financial Event," *Past and Present* 249, no. 1 (2020): 213–249.

18. Patrick Neveling, "The Global Spread of Export Processing Zones, and the 1970s as a Decade of Consolidation," in *Changes in Social Regulation—State, Economy, and Social Protagonists since the 1970s*, ed. Knud Andersen and Stefan Müller (Oxford: Berghahn Books, 2017), 23–40. Patrick Neveling, "Export Processing Zones and Global Class Formation," in *Anthropologies of Class: Power, Practice, and Inequality*, ed. James Carrier and Don Kalb (Cambridge University Press, 2015), 164–82.

19. Ronen Palan, "International Financial Centers: The British-Empire, City-States, and Commercially Oriented Politics." *Theoretical Inquiries in Law* 11, no. 1 (2010): 149–76.

20. The standard label of "export processing zone" came about out of the work in UNIDO. See also Megan Maruschke, "Zones of Reterritorialization: Indian Free Trade Zones, 1947–1980s," *Journal of Global History* 12 (2017): 410–32.

21. David Harvey, "Globalization and the 'Spatial Fix,'" *Geographische Revue* 2 (2001): 23–30.

22. Neveling, "Global Spread of Export Processing Zones," 29.

23. Najmeh Bozorgmehr, "Iran Eyes Iraq Trade Decades after War," *Financial Times*, October 15, 2015.

24. Kish FTZ is one of six free currently active trade zones in Iran that have been founded by 2004; they are Qeshm Island (est. 1990) in the Persian Gulf, Chabahar, a seaport on the Sea of Oman (est. 1991), Aras in the northwest near the border (est. 2003), Anzali near the Caspian Sea in Gilan (2003), and Arvand in Khuzistan (2004).

25. Alan Villiers, *Sons of Sinbad* (London: Arabian Publishing, 2006 [1949]), 275; Iraj Afshar-Sistani, *Jazireh-ye Kish: morvarid-e Khalij-e Fars* (Tehran: Entesharat-e Hirmand), 54.

26. Ministry of Interior, *Census District Statistics of the First National Census of Iran* (Aban 1335 (November 1956)), vol. 99: Bandar Langeh Census District (Tehran: Ministry of Interior, Public Statistics, 1956), 1.

27. Mariam Behnam, *Zelzelah: A Woman before Her Time* (Dubai: Motivate, 1994); Frauke Heard-Bey, *From Trucial States to United Arab Emirates: A Society in Transition* (London: Longman, 1982), 243–45.

28. Maryam al-Sadat Malihi, *Radepa-ye amvaj: tarikh-e tawseh-ye jazireh-ye Kish 1300–1377* (Tehran: Sazman-e Mantaqeh-ye Azad-e Kish, n.d.), 17.

29. Mohamad-Reza Haydarzadeh, "Az Asouliyeh ta Kish: barressi tarikhcheh ijad-e manteq-e azad tejari dar Iran," *Mahnameh-ye Manateq-e Azad* 1 (Esfand, 1369 [1990]): 7. It seems that he began raising the possibility of creating a free trade zone in the southern Gulf and was inspired in part by Dubai's growing role as a transshipment hub.

30. ʿAbbas Masʿudi, *Didar az shaykh nishinha-yi Khalij-i Fars* ([Tehran]: Iran Chap, 1345 [1966]), 76–78.

31. "Kish dar aʾeyneh ruydad-ha," *Majalleh Manteq-e Azad* 2 (Farvardin 1370): 53–56.

32. Sazman-e Barnameh va Budjeh-ye Ostan-e Bushehr, *Barresi vazʿiyat-e banader-e ostan-e Bushehr*, 1372 [1993], 42. Haydarzadeh, "Az Asouliyeh ta Kish," 6. In 1961, there was a conversation between the Shah, David Lilienthal, and Jean Monnet to secure funding from World Bank for building "an international" port in Bandar Abbas complete with railroad links to southern Afghanistan and Pakistan. While it is not clear what exactly was meant to be an "international port" it seems that they were imagining a free trade port that would facilitate regional trade to Afghanistan and

Pakistan. David Lilienthal and Helen M. Lilienthal, *The Journals of David E. Lilienthal, Vol. V* (New York: Harper & Row, 1964), 174, 256.

33. Malihi, *Radepa-ye amvaj*, 20–21.

34. Manouchehr Hashemi, *Davari: Sokhani dar karnameh-ye Savak* (London: Aras Publishers, 1984), 269–80.

35. Taliesin Associated Architects of the Frank Lloyd Wright Foundation, *Minoo and Kish Islands: Potentially Important Resorts for Modern Iran, Tourist Feasibility Study for the Imperial Government of Iran, Ministry of Interior, Stage II*, vol. 1 (November 1967), TTA, 9.

36. Ibid., J-2.

37. Kimbal Thompson, "Nezam Amery: Architect Nezamedin Khazal Kabi al Ameryu," *Journal of the Taliesin Fellows* 31 (2008): 20–21; "Zendeginameh: Nezam 'Ameri (1305–1395)," *Hamshahri* 14 Tir, 1395, https://www.hamshahrionline.ir/news/339002/-۱۳%عامری-نظام-نامه‌گیندزDB%Bo۵-۱۳۹۵.

38. Wright's son-in-law, William Wesley Peters, and Amery had designed a palace for the Shah's elder sister, Princess Shams.

39. Taliesin Associated Architects of the Frank Lloyd Wright Foundation, *Minoo and Kish Islands: Potentially Important Resorts for Modern Iran, Tourist Feasibility Study for the Imperial Government of Iran, Ministry of Interior, Stage I* (November 1967), 98, 11. Evan Ward kindly brought this study to my attention. His own analysis of the plans by the Frank Lloyd Foundation and Iran's touristic plans are documented in Evan R. Ward, "Before Dubai: The Frank Lloyd Wright Foundation and Iranian tourism development, 1967–1969," *Journal of Tourism History* 11, no. 1 (2019): 46–62.

40. Taliesin Associated Architects of the Frank Lloyd Wright Foundation, *Minoo and Kish Islands: Potentially Important Resorts for Modern Iran, Tourist Feasibility Study for the Imperial Government of Iran, Ministry of Interior, Stage I, Vol. 1* (November 1967), 9. The study also concluded that Minu was appropriate for a free port or trade zone (16).

41. Interview with Nezam and Shenda Amery, September 13, 1989, and October 7, 1996. Frank Lloyd Wright Foundation Archives: oral histories, 1980s–2000s. The Frank Lloyd Wright Foundation Archives, The Museum of Modern Art, Avery Architectural and Fine Arts Library, Columbia University, New York. I am grateful to Pamela Casey for bringing these interviews to my attention.

42. Abbas Milani, *The Shah* (New York: Palgrave Macmillian, 2011), 354.

43. Asadollah Alam, *The Shah and I: The Confidential Diary of Iran's Royal Court, 1969–1977* (New York: I. B. Tauris, 1991), 103.

44. Mohamad-Reza Haydarzadeh, "Az Kish 53 ta Kish 73," *Mahnameh-ye Manateq-e Azad* 2 (Farvardin 1370 [1990]): 8.

45. Habib Ladjevardi, ed., *Khaterat -e 'Abd ol-Majid Majidi* (Cambridge: Iranian Oral History Project, Center for Middle Eastern Studies, Harvard University, 1998). PO would withdraw from projects that it did not like and were highly corrupt (this was the case of Kish); see Homa Katouzian, "The Pahlavi Regime in Iran," in *Sultanistic Regimes*, ed. H. E. Chehabi and Juan J. Linz (Baltimore: Johns Hopkins University Press, 1998), 200–201.

46. Khosrow Mi'tazed, "Kish: vilaha-ye bara-ye hezar nur-e chashmi," *Manataq-e azad*, no. 187 (2007): 46–51. On the British attempt to sell Concorde plans to Iran, see The National Archive, Prem 16/1513: "The PM agreed to see the Iranian Minister of Commerce, Mr. Mahdavi, during his visit to London in December, 1975." Tabatabai and Afrassiabi, *Kish*, 30.

47. Ladjevardi, ed., *Khaterat -e 'Abd ol-Majid Majidi*, 161.

48. Tabatabai and Afrassiabi, *Kish*, 55.

49. Denis Wright, in an interview recorded by Habib Ladjevardi, October 11, 1984, Haddenham, England, Tape 6, Iranian Oral History Collection, Harvard University.

50. Houshang Nahavandi, in an interview recorded by Shahrokh Meskoob, April 11, 1986, Paris, France, Tape 14, Iranian Oral History Collection, Harvard University

51. Behnam, *Zelzelah*, 202.

52. Desmond Harney, *The Priest and the King: Eyewitness Account of the Iranian Revolution* (London: I. B. Tauris, 1999), 104.

53. Jonathan Randal, "Corruption in Iran," *Washington Post*, November 19, 1978. See also Radio Zamaneh, https://www.zamaaneh.com/revolution/2008/10/print _post_126.html. On his wife, Virginia Monsef, see Haydarzadeh, "Az Kish 53 ta Kish 73," 8; Sistani, *Jazireh-ye Kish*, 54.

54. Hashemi, *Davari*, 275–76.

55. 'Abbas Mas'udi, *Didari-yi tazih az shaykh-nishinha-ye Khalij-i Fars pas az khuruj-i niruha-ye ingilis* ([Tehran]: Intisharat-i Mu'assasah-i Ittila'at, 1969), 60–69.

56. Mas'udi, *Didar az shaykh nishinha-yi Khalij-i Fars*; Mas'udi, *Didari-yi tazih az shaykh-nishinha-yi Khalij-i Fars pas az khuruj-i niruha-ye ingilis*.

57. William Roger Louis, *Ends of British Imperialism: The Scramble for Empire, Suez, and Decolonization* (London: I. B. Tauris, 2006), 877–903; Balfour-Paul, *End of Empire in the Middle East*; "The Gulf: Implications of British Withdrawal," Special Report Series: No. 8, The Center for Strategic and International Studies, Georgetown University, Washington, D.C., February 1969.

58. Alam, *The Shah and I*, 103; Rouhollah K. Ramazani, "Emerging Patterns of Regional Relations in Iranian Foreign Policy," *Orbis* 18, no. 4 (Winter 1975): 1043–69.

59. James F. Goode, "Assisting Our Brothers, Defending Ourselves: The Iranian Intervention in Oman, 1972–75," *Iranian Studies* 47, no. 3 (2014): 441–62. Fred

Halliday describes the war on Oman as a "counter-insurgency." Halliday, *Mercenaries: "Counter-insurgency" in the Gulf* (Nottingham, U.K.: Spokesman, 1977).

60. Naghmeh Sohrabi, "Where the Small Things Are: Thought on Writing Revolutions and Their Histories," *Jadaliyya* May 21, 2020, https://www.jadaliyya.com/Details/41154.

61. Gan Island was used as a military base by the British military in World War II and the subsequent decolonization struggles. Its use by the British air force and navy was scaled back after 1971. The National Archive, FCO 8/2740 NBP 063/548/1 "Iranian Interest in R.A.F. Gan (Maldive Islands)," 1976.

62. Mas'ud Kouhestaninejad, *Jazayer Irani-e Khalij-i Fars* (Tehran: Enteshar-e Dunya Eqtesad, 1393).

63. R. K. Ramazani, *The Persian Gulf and the Strait of Hormuz* (Alphen aan den Rijn, Sijthoff & Noordhoff, 1979), 100.

64. Manuchehr Hashemi, Harvard Oral History Project, Tape 2, https://sds.lib.harvard.edu/sds/audio/457650619.

65. Mas'udi, *Didari-yi tazih az shaykh-nishinha-yi*; 'Abbas Mas'udi, *Khalij-i Fars dar dawrin-i sarbulandi va shukuh* ([Tehran], Intisharat-i Mu'assasah-yi Ittila'at, 1973). The shah's diplomacy was lauded by the Nixon administration. See "75. Memorandum From the President's Assistant for national Security Affairs (Kissinger) to President Nixon, June 25, 1970," *Foreign Relations of the United States, 1969–1976, Volume E-4, Documents on Iran and Iraq, 1969–1972.*

66. Goode, "Assisting Our Brothers, Defending Ourselves," 449.

67. Cowen, *Deadly Life of Logistics*; Rafeef Ziadeh, "Transport Infrastructure and Logistics in the Making of Dubai Inc.," *International Journal of Urban and Regional Research* 42, no. 2 (2018): 182–97; Laleh Khalili, *Sinews of War and Trade: Shipping and Capitalism in the Arabian Peninsula* (London: Verso, 2020).

68. Milani, *Shah*, 354.

69. Tabatabai and Afrassiabi, *Kish*, 70–71. See also Sistani, *Jazireh-ye Kish*, 52–53.

70. In addition, the High Council of Free Trade-Industrial Zones was established in 1992 and was charged with the overseeing and management of all current and future zones. As stipulated by the law passed by the Majles on June 21, 1993 (Article 5), each free trade zone is managed and operated by its own authority. Vahe Petrossian, "Free Trade Zones Open to Foreigners," *Middle East Economic Digest,* July 2, 1993.

71. Musa Pajoohan, "Regional Development or Regional Policies? A Review of 60 Years of Regional Planning and Development in Pre and Post Islamic Republic Iran," *Journal of Regional and City Planning* 30, no. 2 (August 2019): 102–22.

72. Qualitative and quantitative information in government reports, journalistic accounts, interviews with officials, and a few academic studies make it clear that in

terms of foreign investment, creation of jobs, and exports, Iran's free trade zone have performed poorly and not met the expectations at the time of their founding. For discussion of the economic performance of Kish Island, see Hassan Hakimian, "Iran's Free Trade Zones: Back Doors to the International Economy?" *Iranian Studies* 44, no. 6 (2011): 851–874.

73. Narges Erami and Arang Keshavarzian, "When Ties Don't Bind: Smuggling Effects, Bazaars, and Regulatory Regimes in Postrevolutionary Iran," *Economy and Society* 44, no. 1 (2015): 110–39; Fariba Adelkhah, *The Thousand and One Borders of Iran: Travel and Identity*, trans. Andrew Brown (New York: Routledge, 2016); Nidhi Mahajan, "Dhow Itineraries: The Making of a Shadow Economy in the Western Indian Ocean," *Comparative Studies of South Asia, Africa, and the Middle East* 39, no. 3 (2019): 407–19.

74. William H. Sullivan, *Mission to Iran* (New York: Norton, 1981), 190.

75. Drew Middleton, "The Shah of Iran Due in U.S. to Seek Weapons," *New York Times*, July 22, 1973. In Behnam's telling, the shah was going to live at the naval barracks in Bandar Abbas. Behnam, *Zelzelah*, 206.

76. Neta Fenigar and Rachel Kallus, "Building a 'New Middle East': Israeli Architects in Iran in the 1970s," *Journal of Architecture* 18, no. 3 (2013): 381–401; Neta Fenigar and Rachel Kallus, "Israeli Planning in the Shah's Iran: A Forgotten Episode," *Planning Perspectives* 30 (2015): 231–51; "132. Telegram From the Embassy in Iran to the Department of State, June 2, 1975," *Foreign Relations of the United States, 1969–1976, Volume E-4, Documents on Iran and Iraq, 1969–1972.*

77. Embassy Tehran to Department of State, Telegram 01118, January 23, 1979, 1979TEHRAN01118, Central Foreign Policy Files, 1973–79/ Electronic Telegrams, 1979: General Records of the Department of State, National Archives, accessed August 8, 2018. I thank Mohammad A. Tabaar for helping me locate this file.

78. For instance, in late 1973, 40 rebellious clerics in Qom were banished to Bandar Lengeh for up to three years. Graham, *Iran*, 147. British officials also exiled people by sending them to islands, such as Hormuz. Basidu on Qeshm island was a place that people were sent when they were banished by the central government. Willem Floor, *The Persian Gulf: The Rise and Fall of Bandar-e Lengeh: The Distribution Center for the Arabian Coast, 1750–1930* (Washington, DC: Mage Publishers, 2010), 60.

79. Kaveh Ehsani, "The Social History of Labor in the Iranian Oil Industry: The Built Environment and the Making of the Industrial Working Class (1908–1941)," PhD dissertation, Leiden University, 2014; Alexander Boodrookas, "The Making of a Migrant Working Class: Contesting Citizenship in Kuwait and the Persian Gulf, 1925–1975," PhD dissertation, New York University, 2020; Alex Boodrookas and Arang Keshavarzian, "The Forever Frontier of Urbanism: Historicizing Persian Gulf Cities," *International Journal of Urban and Regional Research* 43, no. 1 (January 2019): 14–29.

80. Essa Saleh al-Gurg, *The Wells of Memory: An Autobiography* (London: John Murray, 1980), 78–81.

81. Ole Bouman, Mitra Khoubbrou, and Rem Koolhaas, eds., *Al-Manakh*, special issue (2007), 154.

82. Heard-Bey, *From Trucial States to United Arab Emirates*, 262.

83. Michael Pacione, "City Profile: Dubai," *Cities* 22, no. 3 (2005): 260.

84. Gary Fields, *Enclosure: Palestinian Landscapes in a Historical Mirror* (University of California Press, 2017).

85. Hawley, *The Trucial States*, 148–49, 173; Heard-Bey, *From Trucial States to United Arab Emirates*, 301–2.

86. The National Archive, FO 1016/80, File 2056, "Arbitration in Dubai-Abu Dhabi Boundary Dispute from June 1948," 1948.

87. On the British decision to end its colonial relationship with the Arab sheikdoms of the Gulf and the various boundary disputes at that time, see Balfour-Paul, *End of Empire in the Middle East*, ch. 4.

88. Davidson, *The United Arab Emirates*, 199–208. From the perspective of the British, the Shaykh Rashid and Shaykh Zayed rivalry fueled tensions. See the National Archive, FCO 8/2887/NBE 014/1, U.A.E. Internal Political Affairs, 1977 and The National Archive, FCO 8/2888/NBE 014/3, U.A.E. Annual Review 1976, 1977.

89. Palan, *The Offshore World*, 59.

90. Stephen Ramos, *Dubai Amplified: The Engineering of a Port Geography* (Burlington, VT: Ashgate Publishers, 2010), 72–73, 96–97; K.B., "Ports," *Financial Times*, April 4, 1977.

91. Dubai's creek was dredged in the 1960 despite the British approving a loan from the British Bank of the Middle East. The project was ultimately financed by the Kuwaiti government. Sharjah's plans to dredge their own creek and port, but was less successful leaving Dubai as the key transshipment hub in the Trucial coast. On the dredging of the creek and the challenges of receiving funding for the project see Matthew MacLean, "Spatial Transformation and the Emergence of 'the National:' Infrastructures and the Formation of the United Arab Emirates, 1950–1980," PhD dissertation, New York University, 2017, 167–68.

92. Abdulkhaleq Abdulla, "Political Dependency: The Case of the United Arab Emirates," PhD dissertation, Georgetown University, December 1984, 144–45.

93. John Duke Anthony, *Arab States of the Lower Gulf: People, Politics, Petroleum* (Washington, DC: Middle East Institute, 1975), 164.

94. See Ramos, *Dubai Amplified*; Khalili, *Sinews of War and Trade*; Wouter Jacobs and Peter Hall, "What Conditions Supply Chain Strategies of Ports? The Case of Dubai," *GeoJournal* 68 (2007): 327–42.

95. For a comprehensive analysis of Jebel Ali and Dubai's larger array of infrastructural investments, see Ziadeh, "Transport Infrastructure and Logistics in the Making of Dubai Inc." All data on Jebel Ali comes from this article unless otherwise noted.

96. Graeme Wilson, *Rashid's Legacy: The Genesis of the Maktoum Family and the History of Dubai* (Dubai: Media Prima, 2006), 368. In his 1984 book, Michael Fields, who lauds Dubai as a *"leissez-faire* entrepot" (60), viewed the Jebel Ali port as having a "questionable commercial prospects" (65). Michael Fields, *Merchants: The Big Business Families of Arabia* (London: John Murray, 1984).

97. *Middle East Economic Digest* 23, no. 11 (March 1979): 47.

98. As early as 1974, the British consulate in Dubai reported discussions of creating a free trade zone. The National Archive, FCO 8/2362/NBT 6/548/1, Part B, "Commercial and Economic Relations between United Kingdom and United Arab Emirates (UAE)," 1974, folio 192.

99. Fatma al-Sayegh, "Merchants' Role in a Changing Society: The Case of Dubai, 1900–90," *Middle Eastern Studies* 34, no. 1 (January 1998): 87–102.

100. "Dubai Exports Continue to Accelerate," *Gulf News*, August 10, 2008, http://www.gulfnews.com/business/Trade/10236134.html, accessed August 28, 2008.

101. Rafeef Ziadeh points out that Jebel Ali FTZ attracts more than 20 percent of UAE's foreign direct investment. Ziadeh, "Transport Infrastructure and Logistics in the Making of Dubai Inc," 187.

102. Among others, Fields, *Merchants*, 60–61; Anthony, *Arab States of the Lower Gulf*, 154–60; Jeffrey Sampler and Saeb Eigner, *From Sand and Silicon: Achieving Rapid Economic Growth, Lessons from Dubai* (London: Profile Books, 2003); Thomas Friedman, "Holding Up Arab Reform," *New York Times*, December 16, 2004; Afshin Molavi, "Dubai Rising," *Brown Journal of World Affairs* 12, no. 1 (Summer/Fall 2005): 103–10. Similar arguments can be found about Shaykh Zayed bin Sultan Al-Nahyan. On "Zayidism," see Enver Koury, *The United Arab Emirates: Its Political System and Politics* (Hyattsville, MD: Institute of Middle Eastern and North African Affairs, 1980).

103. Intriguingly, even Dubai's economic growth at the turn of the last century is explained by "a liberal and farsighted ruler at the turn of the twentieth century . . . Sheikh Maktum bin Hasher, who ruled from 1894 to 1906." Al-Sayegh, "Merchants' Role in a Changing Society," 88.

104. Ibid. See also Michael Matly and Laura Dillon, "Dubai Strategy: Past, Present, Future," Harvard Business School, February 27, 2007.

105. I first presented this argument in Arang Keshavarzian, "Geopolitics and the Genealogy of Free Trade Zones in the Persian Gulf," *Geopolitics* 15, no. 2 (May 2010):

263–89. For the most thorough discussion of the planning and deviations for the original models for Jabel Ali, see Ramos, *Dubai Amplified*, 107–38. Ramos also highlights how Jebel Ali was a direct competitor to Saudi Arabia's own maritime project in Jubail, which was contracted to Halcrow (109).

106. Ibrahim al-Abed, "The Historical Background and Constitutional Basis to the Federation," in *United Arab Emirates: A New Perspective*, ed. Ibrahim al-Abed and Peter Hellyer (London: Trident Press, 2001), 121–44. See also Heard-Bey, *From Trucial States to United Arab Emirates*.

107. The UAE has oil reserves of about 98 billion barrels, 94 percent of which are in Abu Dhabi.

108. The National Archive, FCO 8/2660/NBE 014/2, Internal Political Situation: United Arab Emirates (UAE), 1976, folio 31–41.

109. The National Archive, FCO 8/2660/NBE 014/2, Internal Political Situation: United Arab Emirates (UAE), 1976, folio 34.

110. Abdulla, "Political Dependency," 241–42.

111. Wilson, *Rashid's Legacy*, 432–33. The decree was not implemented until January 1985. I cannot account for the delay in the implementation of the law, but we can speculate that it was part of the broader negotiation on constitutional structure of the UAE. Also, it is reasonable to assume that the decline in oil prices and subsequent economic downturn after 1983 added impetus for expanding trade to generate more revenue and attract investment.

112. Davidson, *The United Arab Emirates*, 232.

113. Other free zones in Dubai include: Dubai Airport Free Zone (1996), Dubai Cars and Automotive Zone (2000), Dubai Internet City (2000), Dubai Media City (2001), Gold and Diamond Park (2001), Dubai Knowledge Village (2003), and Dubai Health Care City (2003). Free trade zones in other emirates include: Fujairah Free Zone (1987), Ahmed Bin Rashed Free Zone in Umm al-Quwain (1988), Hamriyah Free Zone in Sharjah (1995), Sharjah Airport International Free Zone (1995), and Ajman Free Zone (1996).

114. Kathleen Bishtawi, "A Construction Bonanza," *Financial Times*, July 8, 1976.

115. Sophia Qasrawi, "Foreign Direct Investment in the UAE: Determinants and Recommendations," The Emirates Occasional Papers, No. 57, The Emirates Center for Strategic Studies and Research, 2004, 43. A general manager operating in the zone underlined this too (40–41).

116. The local business community was in fact hostile toward the influx for foreign firms during the oil boom years. Anthony, *Arab States of the Lower Gulf*, 160.

117. The National Archive: FCO 8/2623/ NB 065/1, "Anglo/US Talks on Defense Matters in Persian Gulf [American Position in the Gulf]," 1975. See also The National

Archive: FCO 8/2363, NBT 6/548/1 Part C. "Commercial and Economic Relations between United Kingdom and United Arab Emirates (UAE)," 1974.

118. See also The National Archive, FO 1016/838/1391/66C, "Dubai Harbour (Halcrow/Arabicon)," 1966 and The National Archive, FCO 8/2665/NBE 020/548/1, Part B, "U.K./U.A.E. joint Committee," 1976, folio 61.

119. Abdulla, "Political Dependency," 114–21.

120. The National Archive: FCO 8/2666/NBE 020/548/1, Part C, "UK-UAE Joint Committee," 1976. On British contractors and advisors in Dubai, see The National Archive, FCO 8/2361/NBT 6/548/1, Part A, "Commercial and Economic Relations between United Kingdom and United Arab Emirates (UAE)," 1974. This file examines bids for the Dubai aluminum smelter that was built in Jebel Ali and documents the critical role played by Saif Ahmed al-Ghurair in brokering the contract.

121. Kathleen Bishtawi, "A Construction Bonanza," *Financial Times*, July 8, 1976. Jebel Ali port was designed and built by a joint venture composed of an three private companies—the Emirati Dubai Transport Company, the Dutch the Stevin Construction Middle East, and Balfour Beatty Construction, a prominent British construction company involved in the construction of M25 Motorway (The London ring road) and the Channel tunnel, as well as various projects in the British Empire in the 1920s and 1930s, including in Mandate Palestine and Iraq. It is currently building the Burj Mall in Dubai. Other major British contractors active in Dubai at this time were Sir William Halcrow and Partners (Halcrow International Partnership), Costain Construction Company, and Taylor Woodrow International.

122. The National Archive, FCO 8/2660/NBE 014/2, Internal Political Situation: United Arab Emirates (UAE), 1976, folio 31.

123. Al-Sayegh, "Merchants' Role in a Changing Society," 100.

124. Kristian Coates Ulrichsen, *The United Arab Emirates: Power, Politics, and Policy-Making* (London: Routledge, 2017), 141–47.

125. Sean Foley, "What Wealth Cannot Buy: UAE Security at the Turn of the Twenty-first Century," in Barry Rubin, ed., *Crises in the Contemporary Persian Gulf* (London: Frank Cass 2002), 49. See also Jeffrey R. Marcus, "Between the Storms: How Desert Storm Shaped the U.S. Navy of Operation Iraqi Freedom," *White House Studies* 14, no. 2 (Spring 2004).

126. Michael Knights, "Southern Gulf Co-Operation Council Countries Brace for Terrorist Attacks," *Jane's Intelligence Review*, November 1, 2005. In 2006, the chief operating officer of DP World told a congressional committee that just in one year, US Navy vessels spent over 1,400 days the UAE ports of Dubai, Jebel Ali, Abu Dhabi, and Fujairah; "National Security Implications of the Dubai Ports World Deal to Take

Over Management of U.S. Ports," hearing before the Committee on Armed Services, House of Representatives, One Hundred Ninth Congress, 2nd session, March 2, 2006.

127. "Mina Jebel Ali," *Global Security*, http://www.globalsecurity.org/military/facility/jebel-ali.htm, accessed January 14, 2008. In a 2000 speech in Abu Dhabi, Secretary of Defense William Cohen also states that the "This is the port the that the United States Navy visits the most outside of the United States." http://www.defenselink.mil/transcripts/transcript.aspx?transcriptid=1187, accessed January 14, 2008.

128. This statement is based on data provided via personal communication with the U.S. Naval Forces Central Command, Department of the Navy, June 2, 2009.

129. Steve Negus and William Wallis, "An American Style Emirate? Dubai Sees a Future as Ally, Entrepot and Playground," *Financial Times*, May 8, 2006. The Fujairah to Jebel Ali land link is also the critical logistics pipeline for the Navy in case the Strait of Hormuz is closed.

130. Cowen, *Deadly Life of Logistics*, 55.

131. Amy Offner, *Sorting Out the Mixed Economy: The Rise and Fall of Welfare and Developmental States in the Americas* (Princeton, NJ: Princeton University Press, 2019).

132. Cowen, *Deadly Life of Logistics*.

133. Arang Keshavarzian, "From Port Cities to Cities with Ports: Towards a Multiscalar History of Persian Gulf Urbanism in the Twentieth Century," in *Gateways to the World: Port Cities in the Persian Gulf*, ed. Mehran Kamrava, (Oxford: Oxford University Press, 2016), 19–41.

134. Frank Broeze, "Dubai: Creek to Global Port City," in *Harbours and Havens: Essays in Port History in Honour of Gordon Jackson*, ed. Lewis R. Fischer and Adrian Jarvis (St. John's, Newfoundland: International Maritime Economic History Association, 1999), 184.

135. Erami and Keshavarzian, "When Ties don't Bind"; Ahmed Kanna, "Dubai in a Jagged World," *Middle East Report* 243 (Summer 2007): 22–29; Pete Moore, "Making Big Money on Iraq," *Middle East Report* 252 (Fall 2009): 22–29.

136. Bryan R. Early, "The Proliferation Threat from Free Trade Zones," *The Monitor* 12, no. 1 (2006): 3–6; Moises Naim, *Illicit: How Smugglers, Traffickers, and Copycats Are Hijacking the Global Economy* (New York: Anchor, 2005).

137. Gary Milholilin and Kelly Motz, "Nukes 'R' US," *New York Times*, March 4, 2004; Stefan Candea and Khadija Ismayilova, "Offshore Companies Provide Link between Corporate Mogul and Azerbaijan's President," *International Consortium of Investigative*

Journalists, April 3, 2013, https://www.icij.org/investigations/offshore/offshore -companies-provide-link-between-corporate-mogul-and-azerbaijans-president/.

CHAPTER FIVE

1. Abdulkhaleq Abdulla, "The Arab Gulf Moment," in *The Transformation of the Gulf: Politics, Economics, and the Global Order,* ed. David Held and Kristian Ul-richsen (London: Routledge, 2012), 106–24; Yasser Elsheshtawy, "Tribes with Cit-ies," *Dubaization Blog,* 2013, http://dubaization.com/post/66097171299/tribes -with-cities; Abbas Al-Lawati, "Gulf Cities Have Long Way to Go Before Leading Arab World," *Al-Monitor,* October 14, 2013, http://www.al-monitor.com/pulse/ originals/2013/10/gulf-dubai-abu-dhabi-doha-arab.html; Sultan Sooud al-Qassemi, "Thriving Gulf Cities Emerge as New Centers of Arab World," *Al-Monitor,* October 8, 2013, http://www.al-monitor.com/pulse/originals/2013/10/abu-dhabi-dubai -doha-arab-centers.html.

2. Abdulkhaleq Abdulla, "Khaleej Cities Are Present and Future," *Al-Monitor,* Oc-tober 20, 213, https://www.al-monitor.com/originals/2013/10/gulf-dubai-doha-abu -dhabi-center-arab-world.html, accessed June 9, 2016.

3. Ahmed Kanna, *Dubai: The City as Corporation* (Minneapolis: Minnesota Uni-versity Press, 2011), 5. On Gulf city type and the Dubai model, see Sulyaman Khalaf, "The Evolution of the Gulf City Type, Oil, and Globalization," in *Globalization and the Gulf,* ed. John W. Fox, Nada Mourtada-Sabbah, and Mohammed al-Mutawa (London: Routledge, 2006), 244–65; Martin Hvidt, "The Dubai Model: An Outline of Key Development-Process Elements in Dubai," *International Journal of Middle East Studies* 41, no. 3 (August 2009): 397–418; Yasser Elsheshtawy, "Resituating the Dubai Spectacle," in *The Superlative City: Dubai and the Urban Condition in the Early Twenty-First Century,* ed. Ahmed Kanna (Cambridge: Harvard University Graduate School of Design, 2013), 104–21.

4. Mike Davis, "Fear and Money in Dubai," *New Left Review* 41 (September–October 2006), 50, 54.

5. David Harvey, "The Right to the City," *New Left Review* 53 (September–October 2008), 30.

6. Alex Boodrookas and Arang Keshavarzian, "The Forever Frontier of Urban-ism: Historicizing Persian Gulf Cities," *International Journal of Urban and Regional Research* 43, no. 1 (January 2019): 14–29.

7. Eugene McCann and Kevin Ward, *Mobile Urbanism: Cities and Policymaking in the Global Age* (Minneapolis: University of Minnesota Press, 2011).

8. Willem Floor, *The Persian Gulf: The Rise and Fall of Bandar-e Lengeh: The Dis-tribution Center for the Arabian Coast, 1750–1930* (Washington, DC: Mage Publishers,

2010), 9; Nelida Fuccaro, *Histories of City and State in the Persian Gulf: Manama since 1800* (Cambridge: Cambridge University Press, 2009), 90).

9. Nelida Fuccaro, "Pearl Towns and Early Oil Cities: Migration and Integration in the Arab Coast of the Persian Gulf," in *The City in the Ottoman Empire: Migration and the Making of Urban Modernity*, ed. Ulrike Freitag, Malte Fuhrmann, and Nora Lafi (New York: Routledge, 2011), 101.

10. Todd Reisz, *Showpiece City: How Architecture Made Dubai* (Stanford: Stanford University Press, 2021), 34.

11. Fuccaro, *Histories of City and State in the Persian Gulf*, 150–64.

12. Lienhardt, *Sheikhdoms of Eastern Arabia*, 152.

13. Fuccaro, *Histories of City and State in the Persian Gulf*, 66.

14. Ibid., 110; on segmentation in Bushehr, see Vanessa Martin, *The Qajar Pact: Bargaining, Protest, and the State in Nineteenth-Century Persia* (London: I. B. Tauris, 2005), 29–30.

15. Farah Al-Nakib, *Kuwait Transformed: A History of Oil and Urban Life* (Stanford: Stanford University Press, 2016), 82.

16. Fuccaro, *Histories of City and State in the Persian Gulf*, 71. Here al-Muharraq's segmentation based on sect and economic specialization seems to be a noteworthy exception (29–41).

17. Al-Nakib, *Kuwait Transformed*.

18. Fuccaro, *Histories of City and State in the Persian Gulf*, 62–70.

19. Rosie Bsheer, *Archive Wars: The Politics of History in Saudi Arabia* (Stanford: Stanford University Press, 2020), 38.

20. Matthew MacLean, "Spatial Transformation and the Emergence of 'the National': Infrastructures and the Formation of the United Arab Emirates, 1950–1980," PhD dissertation, New York University, 2017.

21. Fatma al-Sayegh, "Marchants' Role in a Changing Society: The Case of Dubai, 1900–90," *Middle Eastern Studies* 34, no. 1 (January 1998): 95.

22. Fuccaro, *Histories of City and State in the Persian Gulf*, 4.

23. Gabriel Young, "Boundaries of the State: Basra, and the Making of an Iraqi Periphery, 1920–1963," PhD dissertation, New York University, 2024.

24. Anthony D. King, *Urbanism, Colonialism, and the World-Economy: Cultural and Spatial Foundations of the World Urban System* (London: Routledge, 1990).

25. Mark Crinson, "Abadan: Planning and Architecture under the Anglo-Iranian Oil Company," *Planning Perspectives* 12, no. 3 (1997): 348; Reem Alissa, "The Oil Town of Ahmadi since 1946: From Colonial Town to Nostalgic City. *Comparative Studies of South Asia, Africa, and the Middle East* 33, no. 1 (2013): 43; Al-Nakib, *Kuwait Transformed*, 134–38.

26. The size and population of the oil enclaves varied with the thinly populated island of Abadan's growing from 61,000 in 1934 to 226,000 in 1956, while Ahmadi was much smaller, but still reaching almost 13,000 in 1961. Richard Lawless and Ian J. Seccombe, "Impact of the Oil Industry on Urbanization in the Persian Gulf Region," in *Urban Development in the Muslim World*, ed. Houchang Amirahmadi and Salah S. el-Shakhs (New Brunswick, NJ: Rutgers University Press, 1993), 196, 203.

27. Alissa, "The Oil Town of Ahmadi"; Robert Vitalis, *America's Kingdom: Mythmaking on the Saudi Oil Frontier* (London: Verso Press, 2009); Kaveh Ehsani, "Social Engineering and the Contradictions of Modernization in Khuzestan's Company Towns: A Look at Abadan and Masjed-Soleyman," *International Review of Social History* 48, no. 3 (2003): 361–99.

28. Greg Grandin, *Fordlandia: The Rise and Fall of Henry Ford's Forgotten Jungle City* (New York: Metropolitan Books, 2009); Vitalis, *America's Kingdom*.

29. Alissa, "The Oil Town of Ahmadi," 45.

30. Peter Lienhardt, *Disorientations, A Society in Flux: Kuwait in the 1950s*, ed. Ahmed Al-Shahi (Reading, U.K.: Ithaca Press, 1993), 31.

31. Mona Damluji, "The Oil City in Focus: The Cinematic Spaces of Abadan in the Anglo-Iranian Oil Company's Persian Story," *Comparative Studies of South Asia, Africa, and the Middle East* 33, no. 1 (2013): 75–88; Alissa, "The Oil Town of Ahmadi"; Nelida Fuccaro, "Shaping the Urban Life of Oil in Bahrain: Consumerism, Leisure, and Public Communication in Manama and in the Oil Camps, 1932–1960s," *Comparative Studies of South Asia, Africa, and the Middle East* 33, no. 1 (2013): 59–74.

32. Fuccaro, "Shaping the Urban Life of Oil in Bahrain," 70.

33. Nathan Citino, "Suburbia and Modernization: Community Building and America's Post–World War Two Encounter with the Arab Middle East," *Arab Studies Journal* 13–14 (Fall 2005/Spring 2006), 44–45.

34. Ian J. Seccombe and Richard Lawless, "Work Camps and Company Towns: Settlement Patterns and the Gulf Oil Industry," working paper. University of Durham, Center for Middle Eastern and Islamic Studies, Durham, England, 1987, 72–74.

35. Robert Vitalis, "Black Gold, White Crude: An Essay on American Exceptionalism, Hierarchy, and Hegemony in the Gulf," *Diplomatic History* 26, no. 2 (2002): 205.

36. Nader Ardalan, "A Personal Reflection: On the Traditional, the Modern, and the Perennial in Iranian Architecture," in *Architecture Dynamics in Pre-Revolutionary Iran: Dialogic Encounter between Tradition and Modernity*, ed. Mohammad Gharipour (Bristol, U.K.: Intellect, 2019), 11.

37. Touraj Atabaki, "Far from Home, But at Home: Indian Migrant Workers in the Iranian Oil Industry," *Studies in History* 31, no. 1 (2015): 85–114.

38. Seccombe and Lawless, "Work Camps and Company Towns," 60; Kaveh Ehsani, "Social Engineering and the Contradictions of Modernization in Khuzestan's Company Towns: A Look at Abadan and Masjed-Soleyman," *International Review of Social History* 48, no. 3 (2003): 361–99.

39. Seccombe and Lawless, "Work Camps and Company Towns," 39, 42, 55–57.

40. Natasha Iskander, *Does Skill Make Us Human? Migrant Workers in 21st-Century Qatar and Beyond* (Princeton, NJ: Princeton University, 2021). Since the 1950s, Arab Gulf state have to construed the threat from Egyptians, Syrians, Palestinians and other non-GCC Arabs as political—they are vectors of Pan-Arabism, Nasserism, Baathism, Islamism, etc. Meanwhile the threat from the much larger South Asian and South East Asian populations has been depicted as cultural, moral, and sexual. See Anh Nga Longva, "Neither Autocracy nor Democracy but Ethnocracy: Citizens, Expatriates, and the Socio-Political System in Kuwait," in *Monarchies and Nations: Globalisation and Identity in the Arab States of the Gulf*, ed. Paul Dresch and J. Piscatori (London: I. B. Tauris, 2005), 122–25.

41. Al-Nakib, *Kuwait Transformed*; Ehsani, "Social Engineering and the Contradictions of Modernization in Khuzestan's Company Towns."

42. Ardalan, "A Personal Reflection," 11–12.

43. Yasser Elsheshtawy, "Cities of Sand and Fog: Abu Dhabi's Global Ambitions," in *The Evolving Arab City: Tradition, Modernity, and Urban Development*, ed. Yasser Elsheshtawy (London: Routledge, 2008), 258–304; MacLean, "Spatial Transformation."

44. Al-Nakib, *Kuwait Transformed*, 10.

45. Todd Reisz, *Showpiece City*, 169.

46. Dictaphone Group and Dia Saleh, "Bahrain: An Island without Sea البحرين جزيرة بلا بحر," *Artezine* Fall 2013, https://arteeast.org/quarterly/bahrain-an-island-without-sea/.

47. Jill Crystal, *Oil and Politics in the Gulf: Rulers and Merchants in Kuwait and Qatar* (Cambridge: Cambridge University Press, 1990), 57.

48. Hossein Mahdavy, "The Pattern and Problems of Economic Development in Rentier States: The Case of Iran," in *Studies in the Economic History of the Middle East*, ed. M. A. Cook. (Oxford: Oxford University Press, 1970), 428–67.

49. Ghanim Hamad al-Najjar, "Decision-Making Process in Kuwait: The Land Acquisition Policy as a Case Study," PhD dissertation, University of Exeter, 1984.

50. Michael Bonine, "The Urbanization of the Persian Gulf Nations," in *The Persian Gulf States: A General Survey*, ed. Alvin J. Cottrell (general editor) (Baltimore: Johns Hopkins University Press Baltimore 1980), 245, 261.

51. Al-Sayegh, "Marchants' Role in a Changing Society," 99.

52. Farah Al-Nakib, *Kuwait Transformed*, 38. For a discussion of this process in Dubai, see Stephen Ramos, *Dubai Amplified: The Engineering of a Port Geography* (Burlington, VT: Ashgate Publishers, 2010), 67–69. Toby Jones identifies land in rural Saudi Arabia as similarly a method of creating inequalities and political conflicts. *Desert Kingdom: How Oil and Water Forged Modern Saudi Arabia* (Cambridge: Harvard University Press, 2010).

53. Pascal Menoret, *Joyriding in Riyadh: Oil, Urbanism, and Road Revolt* (Cambridge: Cambridge University Press, 2014), 83.

54. Jones, *Desert Kingdom*, 81.

55. Reisz, *Showpiece City*, 237.

56. Saba George Shiber, *The Kuwait Urbanization: Being an Urbanistic Case-Study of a Developing Country—Documentation, Analysis, Critique* (Kuwait: Kuwait Government Printing Press, 1964), 2.

57. Ramos, *Dubai Amplified*.

58. Harvey Molotch, "The City as a Growth Machine: Toward a Political Economy of Place," *American Journal of Sociology* 82, no. 2 (1976): 309–32.

59. Reisz, *Showpiece City*, 237.

60. Asseel al-Ragam, "Negotiating the Politics of Exclusion: Georges Candilis, Housing, and the Kuwaiti Welfare State," *International Journal of Urban and Regional Research* 41, no. 3 (June 2017): 235.

61. Ibid., Al-Nakib, *Kuwait Transformed*; Fuccaro, *Histories of City and State in the Persian Gulf*, 205–6.

62. Mustapha Ben Hamouche, "Manama: The Metamorphosis of an Arab Gulf City," in *The Evolving Arab City: Tradition, Modernity, and Urban Development*, ed. Yasser Elsheshtawy (London: Routledge, 2008), 189.

63. Shiber, *The Kuwait Urbanization*, 2, 75.

64. Al-Ragam, "Negotiating the Politics of Exclusion"; Shiber, *The Kuwait Urbanization*; and Lukasz Stanek, "Mobilities of Architecture in the Global Cold War: From Socialist Poland to Kuwait and Back," *International Journal of Islamic Architecture* 4, no. 2 (2015): 365–98. Al-Nakib points out that Kuwait's old city quarters, which mixed Sunnis and Shias, Arabs and Persians, the poor and the wealthy, were reinvented through government policies that turned suburbs into more homogenous enclaves based on socioeconomic class. *Kuwait Transformed*, 135–36.

65. Quoted in Stanek, "Mobilities of Architecture in the Global Cold War," 372.

66. Anh Nga Longva, *Walls Built on Sand: Migration, Exclusion, and Society in Kuwait* (Boulder, CO: Westview Press, 1997), 47–52.

67. Alex Boodrookas, "The Making of a Migrant Working Class: Contesting Citizenship in Kuwait and the Persian Gulf, 1925–1975," PhD dissertation, New York

University, 2020; Lindsey R. Stephenson, "Rerouting the Persian Gulf: The Transnationalization of Iranian Migrant Networks, c. 1900–1940." PhD dissertation, Princeton University, 2018, 115–44; Firoozeh Kashani-Sabet, "Pandering in the Persian Gulf: Arabia, Iran, and Anglo-American Relations, 1900–71," in *American-Iranian Dialogues: From Constitution to White Revolution, c. 1890s–1960s,* ed. M. K. Shannon (London: Bloomsbury Academic, 2022), 82–83.

68. Tens of thousands of people living in Iran are considered stateless. Many are Afghan refugees or children of refugees or mixed marriages. However, there are significant numbers of undocumented Baluch, who face considerable impediments to accessing government services including schooling. As far as I am aware the provinces abutting the Gulf do not have significant numbers of stateless people.

69. Longva, "Neither Autocracy nor Democracy but Ethnocracy," 119.

70. Boodrookas, "Making of a Migrant Working Class."

71. Neha Vora, *Impossible Citizens: Dubai's Indian Diaspora* (Durham and London: Duke University Press, 2013); Emily McIntire, "Migrants and Bureaucrats: Social Mobility in an Iranian Town," PhD dissertation, Harvard University, 1984.

72. Noora Lori, "National Security and the Management of Migrant Labor: A Case Study of the United Arab Emirates," *Asian and Pacific Migration Journal* 20, nos. 3/4 (2011): 315–37.

73. Iskander, *Does Skill Make Us Human?*; Michelle Buckley, "Locating Neoliberalism in Dubai: Migrant Workers and Class Struggle in the Autocratic City," *Antipode* 45, no. 2 (2012): 256–74. Coalition for Fair Labor, *Forced Labor at NYU Abu Dhabi: Compliance and the Cosmopolitan University,* May 2018.

74. Attiya Ahmed, "Beyond Labor: Foreign Residents in the Gulf States," in *Migrant Labor in the Persian Gulf,* ed. Mehran Kamrava and Zahra Babar (New York: Columbia University Press, 2012), 21–40.

75. The seminal discussion of Arab migrants is Longva's *Walls Built on Sand,* 54–56. A recent thoughtful discussion of the circular migration of Egyptian workers to and from Qatar and the UAE is Samuli Schielke, *Migrant Dreams: Egyptian Workers in the Gulf States* (Cairo: American University in Cairo Press, 2020).

76. On not being labeled foreign, see Longva, *Walls Built on Sand,* 54–56. On being "brothers," see John Chalcraft, "Migration Politics in the Arabian Peninsula," in *The Transformation of the Gulf: Politics, Economics, and the Global Order,* ed. David Held and Kristian Ulrichsen (London: Routledge, 2012), 73.

77. Longva, "Neither Autocracy nor Democracy but Ethnocracy," 123.

78. Shiber, *The Kuwait Urbanization,* LXIII.

79. Michael Herb, *The Wages of Oil: Parliaments and Economic Development in Kuwait and the UAE* (Ithaca, NY: Cornell University Press, 2014).

80. MacLean, "Spatial Transformation and the Emergence of 'the National.'"

81. Neil Brenner and Christian Schmid, "The 'Urban Age' in Question," *International Journal of Urban and Regional Research* 38, no. 3 (2014): 731–55.

82. Al-Nakib, *Kuwait Transformed*, 92.

83. "The Line, New Wonders for the World," https://www.neom.com/en-us/regions/theline, accessed June 29, 2022.

84. Günel, Gökçe, *Spaceship in the Desert: Energy Climate Change and Urban Design in Abu Dhabi* (Durham, NC: Duke University Press, 2019), Gökçe Günel, "Masdar City 2020," *Middle East Report* 296 (Fall 2020).

85. Michele Nastasi, "A Gulf of Images: Photography and the Circulation of Spectacular Architecture," in *The New Arab Urban: Gulf Cities of Wealth, Ambition, and Distress*, ed. Harvey Molotch and Davide Ponzini (New York: New York University Press, 2019), 99–129.

86. John Friedmann, "The World City Hypothesis," *Development and Change* 17, no. 1 (January 1986), 69–83; Saskia Sassen, *The Global City: New York, London, Tokyo* (Princeton, NJ: Princeton University Press, 1991)

87. Ali Parsa and Ramin Keivani, "The Hormuz Corridor: Building a Cross-Border Region Between Iran and the UAE," in *Global Networks, Linked Cities*, ed. S. Sassen (New York: Routledge, 2002), 183–207; David Bassens, Ben Derudder, and Frank Witlox, "Searching for the Mecca of Finance: Islamic Financial Services and the World City Network," *Area* 42, no. 1 (March 2010): 35–46. See the Globalization and World Cities Network at http://www.lboro.ac.uk/gawc/. It has ranked Dubai's level of connectedness as increasing steadily since 2008.

88. Peter Marcuse and Ronald van Kempen, eds., *Globalizing Cities: A New Spatial Order?* (London: Blackwell, 2000).

89. Michelle Buckley and Adam Hanieh, "Diversification by Urbanization: Tracing the Property-Finance Nexus in Dubai and the Gulf," *International Journal of Urban and Regional Research* 38, no. (2014): 155–75. Omar Hesham Alshehabi and Saleh Suroor, "Unpacking 'Accumulation by Dispossession,' 'Fictitious Commodification,' and 'Fictitious Capital Formation': Tracing the Dynamics of Bahrain's Land Reclamation," *Antipode* 48, no. 4 (September 2016): 835–56.

90. Kanna's *Dubai* (77–104) offers an incisive discussion about the cultural assumptions adopted and political work done by architects in turning these "tabula rasa" into futuristic models.

91. Zvika Krieger, "The Emir of NYU," *New York Magazine*, April 10, 2008. https://nymag.com/news/features/46000/index2.html.

92. Ahmed, "Beyond Labor"; Amin Moghadam, "Iranian Migrations to Dubai: Constrains and Autonomy of a Segmented Diaspora," Working Paper No. 2021/3,

Ryerson Centre for Immigration and Settlement and the CERC in Migration and Integration at Ryerson University; Behzad Sarmadi, "'This Place Should Have Been Iran': Iranian Imaginings in/of Dubai," *Ajam Media Collective*, May 20, 2013; Vora, *Impossible Citizens*.

93. Adam Hanieh, *Capitalism and Class in the Gulf* (New York: Palgrave Macmillan, 2011); Adam Hanieh, *Money, Markets, and Monarchies: The Gulf Cooperation Council and the Political Economy of the Contemporary Middle East* (Cambridge: Cambridge University Press, 2018).

94. Hanieh, *Money, Markets, and Monarchies*, 146–73; see also Harvey Molotch and Davide Ponzini, eds., *The New Arab Urban: Gulf Cities of Wealth, Ambition, and Distress* (New York: New York University Press, 2019).

95. Hanieh, *Money, Markets, and Monarchies*, 183–85.

96. Ibid., 112–45.

97. Steffen Hertog, "A Quest for Significance: Gulf Oil Monarchies' International 'Soft Power' Strategies and Their Local Urban Dimensions," in *The New Arab Urban: Gulf Cities of Wealth, Ambition, and Distress*, ed. Harvey Molotch and Davide Ponzini (New York: New York University Press, 2019), 276–329.

98. Herb, *The Wages of Oil*.

99. Sami Moisio and Andrew E. G. Jonas, "City-Regions and City-Regionalism," in *Handbook on the Geographies of Regions and Territories*, ed. Anssi Paasi, John Harrison, and Martin Jones (Cheltenham, U.K.: Elgar, 2020), 285–97.

100. Kristian Coates Ulrichsen, *Qatar and the Gulf Crisis* (Oxford: Oxford University Press, 2020).

101. Ash Amin, "Regions Unbound: Towards a New Politics of Place," *Geografiska Annaler: Series B, Human Geography* 86, no. 1 (2004): 34, emphasis in the original.

102. Annette Alstadsæter, Bluebery Planterose, Gabriel Zucman, and Andreas Økland, "Who Owns Offshore Real Estate? Evidence from Dubai," EU Tax Observatory, EU Tax Observatory Working Paper, no. 1 (May 2, 2022).

103. For a critical reading of this this class in Dubai and how they creatively align Emirati and neoliberal values, see Ahmad Kanna's discussion of "flexible citizenship," *Dubai*, 135–70.

104. Andrzej Kapiszewski, "Arab versus Asian Migrant Workers in the GCC Countries," United Nations Expert Group on International Migration and Development in the Arab Region, May 22, 2006, 9.

105. Chalcraft, "Migration Politics in the Arabian Peninsula," 69.

106. Claire Beaugrand, "Urban Margins in Kuwait and Bahrain: Decay, Dispossession, and Politicization," *City* 18, no. 6 (2014): 735–45. On the bidun communities

in the UAE, see Noora Lori, *Offshore Citizens: Permanent Temporary Status in the Gulf* (Cambridge: Cambridge University Press, 2019).

107. Ben Hamouche, "Manama: The Metamorphosis of an Arab Gulf City."

108. Neil Brenner, "Introduction: Urban Theory without an Outside," in *Implosions/Explosions: Towards a Study of Planetary Urbanization*, ed. Neil Brenner (Berlin: Jovis, 2014), 14–31.

109. For some discussion on inter-city competition, see Khaled Adham, "Rediscovering the Island: Doha's Urbanity from Pearls to Urbanity," and Yasser Elsheshtawy, "Cities of Sand and Fog: Abu Dhabi's Global Ambitions," in *The Evolving Arab City: Tradition, Modernity, and Urban Development*, ed. Yasser Elsheshtawy (London: Routledge, 2008), 258–304.

110. Yasser Elsheshtawy, *Temporary Cities: Resisting Transience in Arabia* (New York: Routledge: 2019); Menoret, *Joyriding in Riyadh*; Laure Assaf, "Abu Dhabi Is My Sweet Home," *City* 24, no. 5–6 (2020): 830–41.

111. Iskander, *Does Skill Make Us Human?*; Buckley, "Locating Neoliberalism in Dubai," Coalition for Fair Labor, "Force Labor at NYU Abu Dhabi: Compliance and the Cosmopolitan University," May 2018.

112. Al Jazeera Documentary, "Shouting in the Dark," August 4, 2011, https://www.youtube.com/watch?v=xaTKDMYOBOU; Elizabeth Rauh, "An Enduring Monument: Bahrain's 2011 Pearl Roundabout Protests," *Middle Eastern Journal of Culture and Communication* 11 (July 2018): 141–73.

CONCLUSION

1. Doreen Massey, "Power-Geometry and a Progressive Sense of Place," in *Mapping Futures: Local Cultures, Global Change*, ed. Jon Bird, Barry Curtis, Tim Putnam, George Robertson, and Lisa Tickner (London: Routledge 1993), 60–70.

2. Ibid., 61.

3. John Sexton, "Global Network University Reflection," December 21, 2010, https://www.nyu.edu/about/leadership-university-administration/office-of-the-president-emeritus/communications/global-network-university-reflection.html. On the Catholic and theological roots of Sexton's vision for society, see Sean Salai, "Former NYU President John Sexton on Faith, Reason, and Free Speech on Campus," *America: The Jesuit Review*, September 3, 2019, https://www.americamagazine.org/politics-society/2019/09/03/former-nyu-president-john-sexton-faith-reason-and-free-speech-campus. A profile of Sexton approach to governance and faculty reactions is offered by Zvika Krieger, "The Emir of NYU: John Sexton's Abu Dhabi Debacle," *The Atlantic*, March 13, 2013.

4. Lucas Wyman, "The Mercenary University," *Jacobin*, June 2, 2016.

5. Neha Vora, *Teach for Arabia: American Universities, Liberalism, and Transnational Qatar* (Stanford: Stanford University Press, 2019).

6. John Sexton, "NYU Abu Dhabi, and Our Global Future," Correspondence from Fall 2007, https://www.nyu.edu/about/leadership-university-administration/office-of-the-president-emeritus/communications/nyu-abu-dhabi-and-our-global-future.html.

7. See Mohamad Bazzi's op-ed in the *New York Times* for his experience and interpretation of his security clearance denial that same year. Mohamad Bazzi, "N.Y.U. in Abu Dhabi: A Sectarian Bargain," *New York Times*, September 26, 2017, https://www.nytimes.com/2017/09/26/opinion/nyu-abu-dhabi.html.

8. Paul Silverstein, "The New Barbarians: Piracy and the North African Frontier," *CR: The New Centennial Review* 5, no. 1 (Spring 2005): 189.

9. Freedom House reports, "At least 10 faculty members from New York University (NYU) have been denied entry to teach or conduct research at NYU's Abu Dhabi campus. Students, staff, and support personnel have also been denied entry." https://freedomhouse.org/country/united-arab-emirates/freedom-world/2021, accessed May 18, 2023. Excel spreadsheets and personal testimonials shared with the author suggest that there have been a greater number of cases.

10. Isaac Komola, *Making the World Global: U.S. Universities and the Production of the Global Imaginary* (Durham, NC: Duke University Press, 2019).

11. Sexton, "Global Network University Reflection."

12. See letters written by Middle East Studies Association's Committee on Academic Freedom on the case of Ahmad Mansoor and Matthew Hedges, accessed May 23, 2023, https://mesana.org/advocacy/committee-on-academic-freedom/-/-/uae/Ahmed+Mansoor; https://mesana.org/advocacy/committee-on-academic-freedom/2018/11/25/british-phd-student-matthew-hedges-given-life-sentence; see also Shana Marshall, "Scholars, Spies, and the Gulf Military Industrial Complex," *Middle East Report Online*, September 4, 2019.

13. It was only after five months, many letters from departments, and an investigation by the Faculty Committee on the Global Network that Andrew Hamilton issued a public statement that included the phrase "It is unimaginable to me that either would pose a security threat based upon their writing and scholarship." See "Exchange of letters on Global Mobility at NYU Abu Dhabi (Faculty Committee on the Global Network)," January 24, 2018, https://www.nyu.edu/about/leadership-university-administration/office-of-the-president/communications/exchange-of-letters-on-global-mobility-at-nyu-abu-dhabi-faculty-committee.html.

14. Coalition for Fair Labor, "Force Labor at NYU Abu Dhabi: Compliance and the Cosmopolitan University," May 2018; Ariel Kaminer and Sean O'Driscoll,

"Workers at N.Y.U.'s Abu Dhabi Site Faced Harsh Condition," *New York Times*, May 18, 2014.

15. Sexton, "Global Network University Reflection."

16. "Arab Crossroads Studies Major," New York University-Abu Dhabi, https://nyuad.nyu.edu/en/academics/undergraduate/majors-and-minors/arab-crossroads-studies-major.html, accessed May 16, 2023.

17. Tom Looser, "The Global University, Area Studies, and the World Citizen: Neoliberal Geography's Redistribution of the 'World,'" *Cultural Anthropology* 27, no. 1 (2012): 103–4.

18. Greg Grandin, *The End of the Myth: From the Frontier to the Border Wall in the Mind of America* (New York: Metropolitan Books, 2019), 148.

19. In my first visit I drove to Bandar Abbas, Lengeh, and the free trade islands of Qeshm and Kish because I was curious how commercial activities worked at the edge of Iran's national economy. Shopkeepers, importers, and exporters in the Tehran bazaar repeatedly described "the ports" as being essential for, competitors to, or in partnership with trading interests in the capital city.

20. Narges Erami and Arang Keshavarzian, "When Ties Don't Bind: Smuggling Effects, Bazaars, and Regulatory Regimes in Postrevolutionary Iran," *Economy and Society* 44, no. 1 (2015): 110–39.

21. Pooya Alaedini, Uwe Deichmann, and Helen Shahrriari, "Land Markets and Housing Dynamics in Low Income Settlements in Iran: Examining Data from Three Cities," working paper, World Bank Symposium, 2007.

22. Pilipinos [*sic*] in Persian Limbo: My Experience with the OFWs of Kish Island, December 16, 2013, https://www.unipronow.org/oldblog/pilipinos-persian-limbo-experience-ofws-kish-island, accessed May 15, 2023; "Kish Island: A Haven for Hopeful OFWs," https://steemit.com/life/@plumandrain/kish-island-a-haven-for-hopeful-ofws, accessed May 15, 2023.

23. Emily Josephine Wells McIntire, "Migrants and Bureaucrats: Social Mobility in an Iranian Town," PhD dissertation, Harvard University, 1984; Mohammad Taghi Razvani, "Iranian Communities in the Persian Gulf: A Geographical Analysis," PhD dissertation, University of London 1975; Shahnaz R. Nadjmabadi, "Cross-Border Networks: Labour Migration from Iran to the Arab Countries of the Persian Gulf," *Anthropology of the Middle East* 5, no. 1 (Spring 2010): 18–33.

24. Fariba Adelkhah, *The Thousand and One Borders of Iran: Travel and Identity*, trans. Andrew Brown (London: Routledge, 2016), 73–74.

25. Evidence for Arab Gulf travelers and pilgrims to Iran in the 1960s is contained in Taliesin Associated Architects of the Frank Lloyd Wright Foundation, *Minoo and Kish Islands: Potentially Important Resorts for Modern Iran, Tourist Feasibility Study for*

the Imperial Government of Iran, Ministry of Interior, Stage I and II, vol. 1 (November 1967).

26. This was not something that I experienced in brief visits to southern Iran. In Iran officials and ordinary people mostly treated my belonging juridical question and one settled through documentation. Instead, as an Iranian raised primarily abroad and with only meager ties to southern and rural Iran, I experienced the discomforting mix of intimacy and existential estrangement.

27. Sulayman Khalaf, "Globalization and Heritage Revival in the Gulf: An Anthropological Look at Dubai Heritage Village," *Journal of Social Affairs* 19, no. 75 (Fall 2002): 14–40.

28. "Al Fahadi Historical Naighborhood," https://artsandculture.google.com/ story/al-fahidi-historical-neighborhood-dubai-culture-arts-authority/zAWRZ _j5CQugJw?hl=en, accessed May 15, 2023.

29. Elizabeth Rauh, "An Enduring Monument: Bahrain's 2011 Pearl Roundabout Protests," *Middle Eastern Journal of Culture and Communication* 11 (July 2018): 149.

Bibliography

Abdi, Kamyar. "The Name Game: The Persian Gulf, Archaeologists, and the Politics of Arab-Iranian Relations." In *Selective Remembrances: Archaeology in the Constriction, Commemoration, and, Consecration of National Pasts*, edited by Philip L. Kohl, Mara Kozelsky, and Nachman Ben-Yehuda, 206–43. Chicago: University of Chicago Press, 2008.

Abdulla, Abdulkhaleq. "The Arab Gulf Moment." In *The Transformation of the Gulf: Politics, Economics, and the Global Order*. Edited by David Held and Kristian Ulrichsen, 106–24. London: Routledge, 2012.

———. "Political Dependency: The Case of the United Arab Emirates." PhD dissertation, Georgetown University, 1984.

Abdullah, Muhammad Morsy. *The United Arab Emirates: A Modern History*. London: Croom Helm, 1978.

Abrahamian, Ervand. *The Coup: 1953, the CIA, and the Roots of Modern U.S.-Iranian Relations*. New York: The New Press, 2013.

Abu Lughod, Janet. *Before European Hegemony: The World System A.D., 1250–1350*. Oxford: Oxford University Press, 1989.

Acharya, Amitav. *U.S. Military Strategy in The Gulf*. London: Routledge, 1989.

Adelkhah, Fariba. *The Thousand and One Borders of Iran: Travel and Identity*. Translated by Andrew Brown. New York: Routledge, 2016.

Adelson, Roger. *London and the Middle East: Money, Power, and War, 1902–1922*. New Haven and London: Yale University Press, 1995.

Afshar-Sistani, Iraj. *Jazireh-ye Kish: morvarid-e Khalij-e Fars*. Tehran: Entesharat-e Hirmand, 1378/1999.

Agnew, John. *Geopolitics: Re-visioning World Politics.* London: Routledge, 1998.

———. "Territorial Trap: The Geographical Assumptions of International Relations Theory." *Review of International Political Economy* 1, no. 1 (1994): 53–80.

Ahmed, Attiya. "Beyond Labor: Foreign Residents in the Gulf States." In *Migrant Labor in the Persian Gulf,* edited by Mehran Kamrava and Zahra Babar, 21–40. New York: Columbia University Press, 2012.

Aitchison, C. U. *A Collection of Treaties, Engagements, and Sanads Relating to India and Neighbouring Countries.* Calcutta: Govt. of India Central Publication Branch, 1929.

Al-Abed, Ibrahim. "The Historical Background and Constitutional Basis to the Federation." In *United Arab Emirates: A New Perspective,* edited by Ibrahim al-Abed and Peter Hellyer, 121–44. London: Trident Press, 2001.

Alaedini, Pooya, Uwe Deichmann, and Helen Shahrriari, "Land Markets and Housing Dynamics in Low Income Settlements in Iran: Examining Data from Three Cities." Working paper, World Bank Symposium, 2007.

Alam, Asadollah. *The Shah and I: The Confidential Diary of Iran's Royal Court, 1969–1977.* New York: I. B. Tauris, 1991.

Al-Dailami, Ahmed. "'Purity and Confusion': The Hawala between Persians and Arabs in the Contemporary Gulf." In *The Persian Gulf in Modern Times: People, Ports, and History,* edited by Lawrence G. Potter, 299–326. New York: Palgrave Macmillan, 2014.

Al-Gurg, Essa Saleh. *The Wells of Memory: An Autobiography.* London: John Murray, 1980.

Al-Hijji, Yacoub Yusef. *Kuwait and the Sea: A Brief Social and Economic History.* Translated by Fahad Ahmad 'Isa Bishara. London: Arabian Publishing, 2010.

Alissa, Reem. "The Oil Town of Ahmadi since 1946: From Colonial Town to Nostalgic City." *Comparative Studies of South Asia, Africa, and the Middle East* 33, no. 1 (2013): 41–58.

Almaazmi, Ahmed. "Oman as an Empire: Transoceanic Mobilities and Legacies in the Western Indian Ocean." MESA Annual Conference, November 2019.

Al-Najjar, Ghanim Hamad. "Decision-Making Process in Kuwait: The Land Acquisition Policy as a Case Study." PhD dissertation, University of Exeter, 1984.

Al-Nakib, Farah. *Kuwait Transformed: A History of Oil and Urban Life.* Stanford: Stanford University Press, 2016.

Al-Ragam, Asseel. "Negotiating the Politics of Exclusion: Georges Candilis, Housing and the Kuwaiti Welfare State." *International Journal of Urban and Regional Research* 41, no. 3 (June 2017): 235–50.

Al-Rasheed, Madawi. *A History of Saudi Arabia.* 2nd ed. Cambridge: Cambridge University Press, 2010.

Al-Rashoud, Talal. "Icon of Defiance and Hope: Gamal Abdel Nasser's Image in Gulf History." *Mada,* November 28, 2020.

Al-Sagri, Saleh Hmad. "Britain and the Arab Emirates, 1820–1956: A Documentary Study." PhD dissertation, University of Kent, 1988.

Al-Sayegh, Fatma. "Merchants' Role in a Changing Society: The Case of Dubai, 1900–90." *Middle Eastern Studies* 34, no. 1 (January 1998): 87–102.

AlShehabi, Omar Hesham "Contested Modernity: Divided Rule and the Birth of Sectarianism, Nationalism, and Absolutism in Bahrain." *British Journal of Middle Eastern Studies* 44, no. 3 (2017): 333–55.

———. "Policing Labour in Empire: The Modern Origins of the Kafala Sponsorship System in the Gulf Arab States." *British Journal of Middle Eastern Studies* 48, no. 2 (2021): 291–310.

Alshehabi, Omar Hesham, and Saleh Suroor, "Unpacking 'Accumulation by Dispossession,' 'Fictitious Commodification,' and 'Fictitious Capital Formation': Tracing the Dynamics of Bahrain's Land Reclamation." *Antipode* 48, no. 4 (September 2016): 835–56.

Alstadsæter, Annette, Bluebery Planterose, Gabriel Zucman, and Andreas Økland, "Who Owns Offshore Real Estate? Evidence from Dubai." EU Tax Observatory, EU Tax Observatory Working Paper, no. 1, May 2, 2022.

Alvandi, Roham. "Nixon, Kissinger, and the Shah: The Origins of Iranian Primacy in the Persian Gulf." *Diplomatic History* 36, no. 2 (April 2012): 337–72.

Amin, Ash. "Placing Globalization." *Theory, Culture, and Society* 14, no. 2 (1997): 123–37.

———. "Regions Unbound: Towards a New Politics of Place." *Geografiska Annaler: Series B, Human Geography* 86, no. 1 (2004): 33–44.

Amrith, Sunil. *Crossing the Bay of Bengal: The Furies of Nature and the Fortunes of Migrants.* Cambridge: Harvard University Press, 2013.

Amsden, Alice. *Escape From Empire: The Developing World's Journey through Heaven and Hell.* Cambridge: MIT Press, 2007.

Amuzegar, Jahangir. "Persian Gulf Oil and the World Economy." In *The Persian Gulf and Indian Ocean in International Politics,* edited by Abbas Amirie, 321–45. Tehran: Institute for International Political and Economic Studies, 1975.

Anderson, Benedict. *Long Distance Nationalism: World Capitalism and the Rise of Identity Politics.* Amsterdam: CASA, 1992.

Anghie, Antony. *Imperialism, Sovereignty, and the Making of International Law.* Cambridge: Cambridge University Press, 2005.

Anscombe, Frederick. "An Anational Society: Eastern Arabia in the Ottoman Period." In *Transnational Connections and the Arab Gulf*, edited by Madawi al-Rasheed, 21–38. London: Routledge, 2005.

———. *The Ottoman Gulf: The Creation of Kuwait, Saudi Arabia, and Qatar*. New York: Columbia University Press, 1997.

Anthony, John Duke. *Arab States of the Lower Gulf: People, Politics, Petroleum*. Washington, DC: Middle East Institute, 1975.

Ardalan, Nader. "A Personal Reflection: On the Traditional, the Modern, and the Perennial in Iranian Architecture." In *Architecture Dynamics in Pre-Revolutionary Iran: Dialogic Encounter between Tradition and Modernity*, edited by Mohammad Gharipour, 3–55. Bristol, U.K.: Intellect, 2019.

Atabaki, Touraj. "Far from Home, But at Home: Indian Migrant Workers in the Iranian Oil Industry." *Studies in History* 31, no. 1 (2015): 85–114.

Azarbadegan, Zeinab. "Imagined Geographies, Reinvented Histories: Ottoman Iraq as Part of Iran." *Journal of Ottoman and Turkish Studies Association* 5, no. 1 (2018): 115–41.

Aziz Chaudhry, Kiren. *The Price of Wealth*. Ithaca, NY: Cornell University Press, 1997.

Azizi, Heshmatollah, Dariush Rahmanian, Houshang Khosro Baygi, and Mohammad Rostami. "Chegooneh shek giri 'hokmrani banader va jazaer Khalij-e Fars be markaziyat-e Bushehr dar 'asr Naseri." *Pajhouheshnameh-ye Tarikhha-ye Mahali Iran* 7, no. 1 (Fall/Winter 1397): 171–90.

Bacevich, Andrew J. "Ending Endless War: A Pragmatic Military Strategy." *Foreign Affairs* 95, no. 5 (September/October 2016): 36–44.

Balaghi, Shiva. "Nationalism and Cultural Production in Iran, 1848–1906." PhD dissertation, University of Michigan, 2008.

Balfour-Paul, Glen. *The End of Empire in the Middle East: Britain's Relinquishment of Power in Her Last Three Arab Dependencies*. Cambridge: Cambridge University Press, 1991.

Ballantyne, Tony, and Antoinette Burton. "Empires and the Reach of the Global." In *A World Connecting, 1870–1945*, edited by Emily S. Rosenberg, 285–434. Cambridge: Belknap Press, 2012.

Banaji, Jarius. *A Brief History of Commercial Capitalism*. Chicago: Haymarket Books, 2019.

Barak, On. "Outsourcing: Energy and Empire in the Age of Coal, 1820–1911." *International Journal of Middle East Studies* 47, no. 3 (2015): 425–45.

Bassens, David, Ben Derudder, and Frank Witlox, "Searching for the Mecca of Finance: Islamic Financial Services and the World City Network." *Area* 42, no. 1 (March 2010): 35–46.

Bayat, Kaveh. "With or Without Workers in Reza Shah's Iran: Abadan, May 1929." In *The State and the Subaltern: Modernization, Society, and the State in Turkey and Iran*, edited by Touraj Atabaki, 111–22. London: I. B. Tauris, 2007.

Beaugrand, Claire. "The Absurd Injunction to Not Belong and the *Bidun* in Kuwait." *International Journal of Middle East Studies* 52, no. 4 (2020): 726–32.

———. "Urban Margins in Kuwait and Bahrain: Decay, Dispossession, and Politicization." *City* 18, no. 6 (2014): 735–45.

Behnam, Mariam. *Zelzelah: A Woman before Her Time*. Dubai: Motivate, 1994.

Ben Hamouche, Mustapha. "Manama: The Metamorphosis of an Arab Gulf City." In *The Evolving Arab City: Tradition, Modernity, and Urban Development*, edited by Yasser Elsheshtawy, 184–217. London: Routledge, 2008.

Bevins, Vincent. *The Jakarta Method: Washington's Anticommunist Crusade and the Mass Murder Program That Shaped Our World*. New York: Public Affairs, 2020.

Bill, James A. *The Eagle and the Lion: The Tragedy of American Iranian Relations*. New Haven: Yale University Press, 1988.

Bishara, Fahad. *A Sea of Debt: Law and Economic Life in the Western Indian Ocean, 1780–1950*. Cambridge: Cambridge University Press, 2017.

Blyth, Robert J. "Britain Versus India in the Persian Gulf: The Struggle for Political Control, c. 1928–48." *Journal of Imperial and Commonwealth History* 28, no. 1 (2000): 90–111.

Bonine, Michael E. "The Urbanization of the Persian Gulf Nations." In *The Persian Gulf States: A General Survey*, edited by Alvin J. Cottrell (general editor), 225–78. Baltimore: Johns Hopkins University Press Baltimore, 1980.

Boodrookas, Alex. "The Making of a Migrant Working Class: Contesting Citizenship in Kuwait and the Persian Gulf, 1925–1975." PhD dissertation, New York University, 2020.

Boodrookas, Alex, and Arang Keshavarzian. "The Forever Frontier of Urbanism: Historicizing Persian Gulf Cities." *International Journal of Urban and Regional Research* 43, no. 1 (January 2019): 14–29.

Bose, Sugata. *A Hundred Horizons: The Indian Ocean in the Age of Global Empire*. Cambridge, MA: Harvard University Press, 2006.

Bouman, Ole, Mitra Khoubbrou, and Rem Koolhaas, eds. *Al-Manakh*, special issue (2007).

Branch, Jordan. *The Cartographic State: Maps, Territory, and the Origins of Sovereignty*. Cambridge: Cambridge University Press, 2014.

Brenner, Neil. "Beyond State-Centrism? Space, Territoriality, and Geographical Scale in Globalization Studies." *Theory and Society* 28, no. 1 (February 1999): 39–78.

―――. ed. *Implosions/Explosions: Towards a Study of Planetary Urbanization*. Berlin: Jovis, 2014.

Brenner, Neil, Bob Jessop, Martin Jones, and Gordon MacLeod, eds. *State/Space: A Reader*. Malden, MA: Blackwell, 2003.

Brenner, Neil, and Christian Schmid. "The 'Urban Age' in Question." *International Journal of Urban and Regional Research* 38, no. 3 (2014): 731–55.

Brew, Gregory. "The Collapse Narrative: The United States, Mohammed Mossadegh and the Coup Decision of 1953." *Texas National Security Review* 2, no. 4 (August 2019): 38–59.

―――. "In Search of 'Equitability': Sir John Cadman, Rezā Shah and the Cancellation of the D'Arcy Concession, 1928-33." *Iranian Studies* 50, no. 1 (2017): 125–48.

Brobst, Peter. "Sir Frederic Goldsmid and the Containment of Persia, 1863–73." *Middle Eastern Studies* 33, no. 2 (April 1997): 197–215.

Brockway, Thomas P. "Britain and the Persian Bubble, 1888–92." *Journal of Modern History* 13, no. 1 (March 1941): 36–47.

Broeze, J. Frank. "Dubai: Creek to Global Port City." In *Harbours and Havens: Essays in Port History in Honour of Gordon Jackson*, edited by L. R. Fisher and A. Jarvis, 159–90. St. John's, Canada: International Maritime Economic History Association, 1999.

Brzezinski, Zbigniew. *The Grand Chessboard: American Primacy and Its Geostrategic Imperatives*. New York: Basic Books, 1997.

Bsheer, Rosie. *Archive Wars: The Politics of History in Saudi Arabia*. Stanford: Stanford University Press, 2020.

Buckley, Michelle. "Locating Neoliberalism in Dubai: Migrant Workers and Class Struggle in the Autocratic City." *Antipode* 45, no. 2 (2012): 256–74.

Buckley, Michelle, and Adam Hanieh. "Diversification by Urbanization: Tracing the Property-Finance Nexus in Dubai and the Gulf." *International Journal of Urban and Regional Research* 38, no. 1 (2014): 155–75.

Busch, Briton Cooper. *Britain and the Persian Gulf, 1894–1914*. Berkeley: University of California Press, 1967.

Cain, Peter, and Anthony Hopkins. *British Imperialism*. London: Longman Publisher, 1993.

Çağlar, Ayşe, and Nina Glick Schiller. *Migrants and City Making: Dispossession, Displacement, and Urban Regeneration*. Durham, NC: Duke University Press, 2018).

Carapico, Sheila. "Arabia Incognita: An Invitation to Arabian Peninsula Studies." In *Counter-Narratives: History, Contemporary Society, and Politics in Saudi Arabia and Yemen*, edited by Madawi al-Rasheed and Robert Vitalis, 11–33. New York: Palgrave Macmillan, 2004.

Carter, Robert. "The History and Prehistory of Pearling in the Persian Gulf." *Journal of the Economic and Social History of the Orient* 48, no. 2 (2005): 139–209.

———. *Sea of Pearls: Arabia, Persia, and the Industry That Shaped the Gulf.* London: Alfardan, 2012.

Center for Strategic and International Studies. *The Gulf; Implications of British Withdrawal.* Washington, DC: Center for Strategic and International Studies, Georgetown University, 1969.

Chalcraft, John. "Migration Politics in the Arabian Peninsula." In *The Transformation of the Gulf: Politics, Economics, and the Global Order*, edited by David Held and Kristian Ulrichsen, 66–85. London: Routledge, 2012.

Chaudhuri, K. N. *Trade and Civilization in the Indian Ocean.* Cambridge: Cambridge University Press, 1985.

Chehabi, H. E. "Muhammad Mosaddeq and 'the Standard Civilization,'" Association for Iranian Studies Biannual conference, Salamanca, Spain, August 30–September 2, 2022.

Citino, Nathan. "Defending the 'Postwar Petroleum Order': The US, Britain, and the 1954 Saudi-Onassis Tanker Deal." *Diplomacy and Statecraft* 11, no. 2 (2000): 137–60.

———. *From Arab Nationalism to OPEC: Eisenhower, King Sa'ud, and the Making of US-Saudi Relations.* Bloomington: Indiana University Press, 2002.

———. "Suburbia and Modernization: Community Building and America's Post–World War Two Encounter with the Arab Middle East." *Arab Studies Journal* 13–14 (Fall 2005/Spring 2006): 39–64.

Coates Ulrichsen, Kristian. *Insecure Gulf: The End of Certainty and the Transition to the Post-Oil Era.* New York: Columbia University Press, 2011.

———. *Qatar and the Gulf Crisis.* Oxford: Oxford University Press, 2020.

———. *The United Arab Emirates: Power, Politics, and Policymaking.* London: Routledge, 2017.

Cole, Camile Lyans. "The Ottoman Model: Basra and the Making of Qajar Reform, 1881–1889." *Comparative Studies in Society and History* 64, no. 4 (2022): 1024–54.

Commins, David. *The Gulf States: A Modern History.* New York: I. B. Tauris, 2012.

Cottrell, Alvin J., and Walter F. Hahn. *Indian Ocean naval Limitations:Regional Issues and Global Implication.* New York: National Strategy Information Center, 1976.

Cottrell, Alvin J., ed. *The Persian Gulf States: A General Survey.* Baltimore: Johns Hopkins University Press, 1980.

Cottrell, Alvin J., and Michael Moodie. *The United States and the Persian Gulf: Past Mistakes, Present Needs.* New York: National Strategy Information Center, 1984.

Cowen, Deborah. *The Deadly Life of Logistics: Mapping Violence in Global Trade.* Minneapolis: Minnesota Press, 2014.

Cowen, Deborah, and Emily Gilbert, "The Politics, War, and Territory." In *War, Citizenship, and Territory*, edited by Deborah Cowen and Emily Gilbert, 16–20. New York: Routledge, 2008.

Cowen, Deborah, and Neil Smith. "After Geopolitics? From the Geopolitical Social to Geoeconomics." *Antipode* 41, no. 1 (January 2009): 22–48.

Crinson, Mark. "Abadan: Planning and Architecture under the Anglo-Iranian Oil Company." *Planning Perspectives* 12, no. 3 (1997): 341–59.

Crist, David. *The Twilight War: The Secret History of America's Thirty-Year Conflict with Iran.* New York: Penguin Press, 2012.

Cronin, Stephanie. *The Army and the Creation of the Pahlavi State in Iran, 1910–1926.* London: Tauris Academic Studies, 1997.

———. "Popular Politics, the New State, and the Birth of the Iranian Working Class: The 1929 Abadan Oil Refinery Strike." *Middle East Studies* 46, no. 5 (September 2010): 699–732.

———. "Reform from Above, Resistance from Below: The New Order and Its Opponents in Iran, 1927–29." In *The State and the Subaltern: Modernization, Society, and the State in Turkey and Iran*, edited by Touraj Atabaki, 71–95. New York: I. B. Tauris, 2007.

Crystal, Jill. *Oil and Politics in the Gulf: Rulers and Merchants in Kuwait and Qatar.* Cambridge: Cambridge University Press, 1990.

Curzon, George N. *Frontiers.* Oxford: Clarendon Press, 1908.

———. *Persia and the Persian Question.* 2 vols. London: Frank Cass Co. Ltd., 1892–1966.

Daftar-e motale'at siyasi va bayn-ol-melali. *Gozideh-ye asnad- Khalij-i Fars.* Vol. 1. Tehran: Ministry of Foreign Affairs of the Islamic Republic of Iran, 1368[1989].

Damluji, Mona. "The Oil City in Focus: The Cinematic Spaces of Abadan in the Anglo-Iranian Oil Company's Persian Story." *Comparative Studies of South Asia, Africa, and the Middle East* 33, no. 1 (2013): 75–88.

Darwin, John. *The Empire Project: The Rise and Fall of the British World-System, 1830–1970.* Cambridge: Cambridge University Press, 2014.

Davidson, Christopher M. "Arab Nationalism and British Opposition in Dubai, 1920–66." *Middle Eastern Studies* 43, no. 6 (November 2007): 879–92.

———. *The United Arab Emirates: A Study in Survival.* Boulder, CO: Lynne Rienner, 2005.

Davis, Mike. "Fear and Money in Dubai." *New Left Review* 41 (September–October 2006): 47–68.

Dietrich, Christopher R. W. *Oil Revolution: Anticolonial Elites, Sovereign Rights, and the Economic Culture of Decolonization*. Cambridge: Cambridge University Press, 2017.

———. "'We Must have a Defense Build-Up': The Iranian Revolution, Regional Security, and American Vulnerability." In *Global 1979: Geographies and Histories of the Iranian Revolution*, edited by Arang Keshavarzian and Ali Mirsepassi, 245–89. Cambridge: Cambridge University Press, 2021.

Dodge, Toby. *Inventing Iraq: The Failure of Nation Building and a History Denied*. New York: Columbia University Press, 2003.

Dresch, Paul. "Foreign Matter: The Place of Strangers in Gulf Society." In *Globalization and the Gulf*, edited by John W. Fox, Nada Mourtada-Sabbah, and Mohammed al-Mutawa, 200–222. London: Routledge, 2006.

Eamon, Jeff. "Policing the Bahrain Islands: Labor, Race, and the Historical Origins of Foreign Recruitment." Master's thesis, Program in Near Eastern Studies, New York University, 2015.

Early, Bryan R. "The Proliferation Threat from Free Trade Zones." *The Monitor* 12, no. 1 (2006): 3–6.

Easterling, Keller. *Extrastatecraft: The Power of Infrastructure Space*. London: Verso, 2014.

Edney, Matthew. *Mapping an Empire: The Geographical Construction of British India, 1769–1843*. Chicago: University of Chicago Press, 1997.

Ehsani, Kaveh. "Social Engineering and the Contradictions of Modernization in Khuzestan's Company Towns: A Look at Abadan and Masjed-Soleyman." *International Review of Social History* 48, no. 3 (2003): 361–99.

———. "The Social History of Labor in the Iranian Oil Industry: The Built Environment and the Making of the Industrial Working Class (1908–1941)." PhD dissertation, Leiden University, 2014.

Elm, Mostafa. *Oil, Power, and Principle: Iran's Oil Nationalization and Its Aftermath*. Syracuse: Syracuse University Press, 1992.

Elsheshtawy, Yasser. "Cities of Sand and Fog: Abu Dhabi's Global Ambitions." In *The Evolving Arab City: Tradition, Modernity, and Urban Development*, edited by Yasser Elsheshtawy, 258–304. London: Routledge, 2008.

———. ed. *The Evolving Arab City: Tradition, Modernity, and Urban Development*. London: Routledge, 2008.

———. "Resituating the Dubai Spectacle." In *The Superlative City: Dubai and the Urban Condition in the Early Twenty-First Century*, edited by Ahmed Kanna, 104–21. Cambridge: Harvard University Graduate School of Design, 2013.

———. *Temporary Cities: Resisting Transience in Arabia*. New York: Routledge: 2019.

Erami, Narges, and Arang Keshavarzian. "When Ties Don't Bind: Smuggling Effects, Bazaars, and Regulatory Regimes in Postrevolutionary Iran." *Economy and Society* 44, no. 1 (2015): 110–39.

Fain, W. Taylor. "Conceiving the 'Arc of Crisis' in the Indian Ocean Region." *Diplomatic History* 42, no. 4 (2018): 694–719.

Fattah, Hala. *The Politics of Regional Trade in Iraq, Arabia, and the Gulf, 1745–1900.* Albany: State University of New York Press, 1997.

Fenigar, Neta, and Rachel Kallus. "Building a 'New Middle East': Israeli Architects in Iran in the 1970s." *Journal of Architecture* 18, no. 3 (2013): 381–401.

Fenigar, Neta, and Rachel Kallus. "Israeli Planning in the Shah's Iran: A Forgotten Episode." *Planning Perspectives* 30, no. 2 (2015): 231–51.

Ferguson, James. *Global Shadows.* Durham, NC: Duke University Press, 2006.

Ferrier, R. W. *The History of the British Petroleum Company, Vol. 1 The Developing Years 1901–1932.* Cambridge: Cambridge University Press, 1982.

Fields, Gary. *Enclosure: Palestinian Landscapes in a Historical Mirror.* University of California Press, 2017.

Fields, Michael. *Merchants: The Big Business Families of Arabia.* London: John Murray, 1984.

Floor, Willem. *The Persian Gulf: The Rise and Fall of Bandar-e Lengeh: The Distribution Center for the Arabian Coast, 1750–1930.* Washington, DC: Mage Publishers, 2010.

Foley, Sean. "What Wealth Cannot Buy: UAE Security at the Turn of the Twenty-first Century." In *Crises in the Contemporary Persian Gulf,* edited by Barry Rubin, 33–74. London: Frank Cass, 2002.

Foliard, Daniel. *Dislocating the Orient: British Maps and the Making of the Middle East, 1854–1921.* Chicago: University of Chicago Press, 2017.

Friedman, Andrew. *Covert Capital: Landscapes of Denial and the Making of the U.S. Empire in the Suburbs of Northern Virginia.* Berkeley: University of California Press, 2013.

Friedmann, John. "The World City Hypothesis." *Development and Change* 17, no. 1 (January 1986): 69–83.

Fuccaro, Nelida. *Histories of City and State in the Persian Gulf: Manama since 1800.* Cambridge: Cambridge University Press, 2009.

———. "Pearl Towns and Early Oil Cities: Migration and Integration in the Arab Coast of the Persian Gulf." In *The City in the Ottoman Empire: Migration and the Making of Urban Modernity,* edited by Ulrike Freitag, Malte Fuhrmann, and Nora Lafi, 99–116. New York: Routledge, 2011.

———. "Shaping the Urban Life of Oil in Bahrain: Consumerism, Leisure, and Public Communication in Manama and in the Oil Camps, 1932–1960s."

Comparative Studies of South Asia, Africa, and the Middle East 33, no. 1 (2013): 59–74.

Galbraith, John S. "British Policy on Railways in Persia, 1870—1900." *Middle Eastern Studies* 25, no. 4 (1989): 480–505.

Gallagher, John, and Ronald Robinson. "The Imperialism of Free Trade." *Economic History Review* 6, no. 1 (1953): 1–15.

Galpern, Steven G. *Money, Oil, and Empire in the Middle East: Sterling and Postwar Imperialism, 1944-1971.* New York: Cambridge University Press, 2009.

Gardner, Andrew. *City of Strangers: Gulf Migration and the Indian Community in Bahrain.* Ithaca, NY: Cornell Press, 2010.

Gause, F. Gregory, III. *The International Relations of the Persian Gulf.* Cambridge: Cambridge University Press, 2010.

———. *Oil Monarchies: Domestic and Security Challenges in the Arab Gulf States.* New York: Council on Foreign Relations Press, 1994.

Go, Julian. "Waves of Empire: US Hegemony and Imperialistic Activity from the Shores of Tripoli to Iraq, 1787–2003." *International Sociology* 22, no. 1 (January 2007): 5–40.

Goldberg, Ellis, and Robert Vitalis. *The Arabian Peninsula: Crucible of Globalization.* EUI Working Papers. RSC Np. 2002/9. Mediterranean Program Series, European University Institute, Robert Schuman Centre for Advanced Studies, 2002.

Goode, James F. "Assisting Our Brothers, Defending Ourselves: The Iranian Intervention in Oman, 1972–75." *Iranian Studies* 47, no. 3 (2014): 441–62.

Goswami, Manu. *Producing India: From Colonial Economy to National Space.* Chicago: University of Chicago Press, 2004.

Gowan, Peter. *The Global Gamble: Washington's Faustian Bid for World Dominance.* London: Verso, 1999.

Graham, Robert. *Iran: The Illusion of Power.* London: Crom Helm, 1979.

Grandin, Greg. *The End of the Myth: From the Frontier to the Border Wall in the Mind of America.* New York: Metropolitan Books, 2019.

———. *Fordlandia: The Rise and Fall of Henry Ford's Forgotten Jungle City.* New York: Metropolitan Books, 2009.

Gregory, Derek. "Imaginative Geographies." In *The Dictionary of Human Geography,* edited by Derek Gregory, Ron Johnston, Geraldine Pratt, Michael J. Watts, and Sarah Whatmore, 369–71. Chichester, U.K.: Wiley-Blackwell, 2009.

Günel, Gökçe. "Masdar City 2020." *Middle East Report* 296 (Fall 2020).

———.*Spaceship in the Desert: Energy Climate Change and Urban Design in Abu Dhabi.* Durham, NC: Duke University Press, 2019.

Hakimian, Hassan. "Iran's Free Trade Zones: Back Doors to the International Economy?" *Iranian Studies* 44, no. 6 (2011): 851–74.

Halliday, Fred. *Arabia without Sultans*. London: Saqi Books, 2002 [1974].

———. "The Arc of Revolutions: Iran, Afghanistan, South Yemen, Ethiopia." *Race and Class* 20, no. 4 (April 1979): 373–90.

———. *Mercenaries: "Counter-Insurgency" in the Gulf*. Nottingham, U.K.: Spokesman, 1977.

Hanieh, Adam. *Capitalism and Class in the Gulf Arab States*. New York: Palgrave Macmillan, 2011.

———. *Money, Markets, and Monarchies: The Gulf Cooperation Council and the Political Economy of the Contemporary Middle East*. Cambridge: Cambridge University Press, 2018.

———. "Petrochemical Empire: The Geo-Politics of Fossil-Fuelled Production." *New Left Review* 130 (July–August 2021): 25–51.

Harney, Desmond. *The Priest and the King: Eyewitness Account of the Iranian Revolution*. London: I. B. Tauris, 1999.

Harvey, David. *The Condition of Postmodernity: An Enquiry into the Origins of Cultural Change*. Cambridge, MA: Blackwell, 1990.

———. "Globalization and the 'Spatial Fix.'" *Geographische Revue* 2 (2001): 23–30.

———. *Justice, Nature, and the Geography of Difference*. Oxford: Blackwell Publishers, 1996.

———. "Space as a Key Word." In *David Harvey: A Critical Reader*, edited by Noel Castree and Derek Gregory, 270–93. Oxford: Blackwell Publishing, 2006.

———. "The Right to the City." *New Left Review* 53 (September–October 2008): 23–40.

Hashemi, Manouchehr. *Davari: Sokhani dar karnameh-ye savak*. London: Aras Publishers, 1984.

Hawley, Donald. *The Trucial States*. London: George Allen and Unwin Ltd., 1970.

Hay, Rupert. *The Persian Gulf States*. Washington, DC: Middle East Institute, 1959.

Haydarzadeh, Mohamad-Reza. "Az Asouliyeh ta Kish: barressi tarikhcheh ijad-e manteq-e azad tejari dar Iran." *Mahnameh-ye Manateq-e Azad* 1 (Esfand, 1369 [1990]): 6–8.

———. "Az Kish 53 ta Kish 73." *Mahnameh-ye Manateq-e Azad* 2 (Farvardin 1370 [1990]): 5–9.

Hazbun, Waleed. *Beaches, Ruins, and Resorts: The Politics of Tourism in the Arab World*. Minneapolis: University of Minnesota Press, 2008.

Hazbun, Waleed, and Arang Keshavarzian. "Re-Mapping Transnational Connections in the Middle East." *Geopolitics* 15, no. 2 (May 2010): 203–9.

Heard-Bey, Frauke. "The Beginning of the Post-Imperial Era for the Trucial States from World War I to the 1960s." In *United Arab Emirates: A New Perspective*, edited by Ibrahim Al-Abed, 126–30. London: Trident Press, 2001.

———. *From Trucial States to United Arab Emirates: A Society in Transition.* London: Longman, 1982.

Hepple, Leslie W. "The Revival of Geopolitics." *Political Geography Quarterly,* Supplement to vol. 5, no. 4 (1986): 21–36.

Herb, Michael. *All in the Family: Absolutism, Revolution, and Democracy in the Middle Eastern Monarchies.* Albany: State University of New York Press, 1999.

———. *The Wages of Oil: Parliaments and Economic Development in Kuwait and the UAE.* Ithaca, NY: Cornell University Press, 2014.

Hertog, Steffen. "A Quest for Significance: Gulf Oil Monarchies' International 'Soft Power' Strategies and their Local Urban Dimensions." In *The New Arab Urban: Gulf Cities of Wealth, Ambition, and Distress,* edited by Harvey Molotch and Davide Ponzini, 276–329. New York: New York University Press, 2019.

Hopper, Matthew. *Slaves of One Master: Globalization and Slavery in Arabia in the Age of Empire.* New Haven: Yale University Press, 2015.

Horden, Peregrine, and Nicholas Purcell. *The Corrupting Sea: A Study of Mediterranean History.* London: Blackwell, 2000.

Hvidt, Martin. "The Dubai Model: An Outline of Key Development-Process Elements in Dubai." *International Journal of Middle East Studies* 41, no. 3 (August 2009): 397–418.

Immerwahr, Daniel. *How to Hide an Empire: A History of the Greater United States.* New York: Farrar, Straus and Giroux, 2019.

Iskander, Natasha. *Does Skill Make Us Human? Migrant Workers in 21st-Century Qatar and Beyond.* Princeton, NJ: Princeton University, 2021.

Jacob, Wilson. *For God or Empire: Sayyid Fadl and the Indian Ocean World.* Stanford: Stanford University Press, 2019.

Jacobs, Wouter, and Peter Hall, "What Conditions Supply Chain Strategies of Ports? The Case of Dubai." *GeoJournal* 68 (2007): 327–42.

Jackson, Ashley. *Persian Gulf Command: A History of the Second World War in Iran and Iraq.* New Haven: Yale University Press, 2018.

Johns, Andrew L. "The Johnson Administration, the Shah of Iran, and the Changing Pattern of U.S.-Iranian Relations, 1965–1967: 'Tired of Being Treated like a Schoolboy.'" *Journal of Cold War Studies* 9, no. 2 (2007): 78–79.

Johnson, Nels. "Ahmad: A Kuwaiti Pearl Diver." In *Struggle and Survival in the Modern Middle East,* edited by Edmond Burke III and David N. Yaghoubian, 80–87. 2nd ed. Berkeley: University of California Press, 2006.

Jones, Stephanie. "British India Steamers and the Trade of the Persian Gulf, 1862–1914." *The Great Circle* 7, no. 1 (1985): 23–44.

Jones, Toby C. "America, Oil, and War in the Middle East." *Journal of American History* 99, no. 1 (June 2012): 208–18.

———. *Desert Kingdom: How Oil and Water Forged Modern Saudi Arabia.* Cambridge: Harvard University Press, 2010.

———. "Energy and America's Long War in the Persian Gulf." Workshop on New Directions in Political Economy, Kevorkian Center for Near Eastern Studies, New York University, 2014.

Joyce, Miriam. "The Bahraini Three on St. Helena, 1956–1961." *Middle East Journal* 54, no. 4 (Fall 2000): 613–23.

Kapiszewski, Andrzej. "Arab versus Asian Migrant Workers in the GCC Countries." United Nations Expert Group on International Migration and Development in the Arab Region, May 22, 2006.

Kamrava, Mehra. *Troubled Waters: Insecurity in the Persian Gulf.* Ithaca, NY: Cornell University Press, 2018.

Kanna, Ahmed. "Dubai in a Jagged World." *Middle East Report,* no. 243 (Summer 2007): 22–29.

———. *Dubai: The City as Corporation.* Minneapolis: Minnesota University Press, 2011.

Kashani-Sabet, Firoozeh. *Frontier Fictions: Shaping the Iranian Nation, 1804–1946.* Princeton, NJ: Princeton University Press, 1999.

———. "Pandering in the Persian Gulf: Arabia, Iran, and Anglo-American Relations, 1900–71." In *American-Iranian Dialogues: From Constitution to White Revolution, c. 1890s–1960s,* edited by M. K. Shannon, 73–94. London: Bloomsbury Academic, 2022.

Katouzian, Homa. "The Campaign against the Anglo-Iranian Agreement of 1919." *British Journal of Middle Eastern Studies* 25, no. 1 (May 1998): 5–46.

———. "The Pahlavi Regime in Iran." In *Sultanistic Regimes,* edited by H. E. Chehabi and Juan J. Linz, 182–205. Baltimore: Johns Hopkins University Press, 1998.

Katzenstein, Peter. *A World of Regions: Asia and Europe in the American Imperium.* Ithaca, NY: Cornell University Press, 2005.

Kearns, Gerry. "Geopolitics." In *The Sage Handbook of Geographical Knowledge,* edited by John Agnew and David Livingston, 610–22. London: Sage Publishing, 2011.

———. *Geopolitics and Empire: The Legacy of Halford Mackinder.* Oxford: Oxford University Press, 2009.

Keshavarzian, Arang. "From Port Cities to Cities with Ports: Towards a Multiscalar History of Persian Gulf Urbanism in the Twentieth Century." In *Gateways to the World: Port Cities in the Persian Gulf,* edited by M. Kamrava, 19–41. Oxford: Oxford University Press, 2017.

———. "Geopolitics and the Genealogy of Free Trade Zones in the Persian Gulf." *Geopolitics* 15, no. 2 (May 2010): 263–89.

Khalaf, Sulayman. "The Evolution of the Gulf City Type, Oil, and Globalization." In *Globalization and the Gulf,* edited by John W. Fox, Nada Mourtada-Sabbah, and Mohammed al-Mutawa, 244–65. London: Routledge, 2006.

———. "Globalization and Heritage Revival in the Gulf: An Anthropological Look at Dubai Heritage Village." *Journal of Social Affairs* 19, no. 75 (Fall 2002): 14–40.

Khalili, Laleh. "The Infrastructural Power of the Military: The Geoeconomic Role of the U.S. Army Corps of Engineers in the Arabian Peninsula." *European Journal of International Relations* 24, no. 4 (2018): 911–33.

———. *Sinews of War and Trade: Shipping and Capitalism in the Arabian Peninsula.* London: Verso, 2020.

Khomeini, Sayyed Ruhollah. "The Granting of Capitulatory Rights to the U.S." In *Islam and Revolution: Writings and Declarations of Imam Khomeini.* Translated and annotated by H. Algar, Berkeley: Mizan Press, 1981.

Kia, Mana, *Persianate Selves: Memories of Place and Origin before Nationalism.* Stanford: Stanford University Press, 2020.

Kimball, Jeffrey. "The Nixon Doctrine: A Saga of Misunderstanding." *Presidential Studies Quarterly* 36, no. 1 (2006): 59–74.

King, Anthony D. *Urbanism, Colonialism, and the World-Economy: Cultural and Spatial Foundations of the World Urban System.* London: Routledge, 1990.

Klare, Michael. "Mahan Revisited: Globalization, Resource Diplomacy, and Maritime Security." In *Maritime Strategy and Global Order: Markets, Resources, Security,* edited by Daniel Moran and James A. Russell, 261–81. Washington, DC: Georgetown University Press, 2016.

Komola, Isaac. *Making the World Global U.S. Universities and the Production of the Global Imaginary.* Durham, NC: Duke University Press, 2019.

Koppes, Clayton R. "Captain Mahan, General Gordan, and the Origins of the Term 'Middle East.'" *Middle Eastern Studies* 12, no. 1 (1976): 95–98.

Koselleck, Reinhart. *Sediments of Time: On Possible Histories.* Edited and translated by Sean Franzel and Stefan-Ludwig Hoffmann. Stanford: Stanford University Press, 2018.

Kouhestaninejad, Mas'ud. *Jazayer Irani-e Khalij-i Fars.* Tehran: Enteshar-e Dunya Eqtesad, 1393 [2014].

Koury, Enver. *The United Arab Emirates: Its Political System and Politics.* Hyattsville, MD: Institute of Middle Eastern and North African Affairs, 1980.

Kramer, Paul A. "Empires, Exceptions, and Anglo-Saxons: Race and Rule between the British and United States Empires, 1880–1910." *Journal of American History* 88, no. 4 (March 2002): 1315–53.

Krasner, Stephen D. *Sovereignty: Organized Hypocrisy.* Princeton, NJ: Princeton University Press, 1999.

Kratochwil, Friedrich. "Of Systems, Boundaries, and Territoriality: An Inquiry into the Formation of the State System." *World Politics* 39, no. 1 (October 1986): 27–52.

Krozewski, G. *Money and the End of Empire: British International Economic Policy and the Colonies, 1947–1958.* Basingstoke, U.K.: Palgrave Macmillan, 2001.

Kumar, Chandra. "The Indian Ocean: Arc of Crisis or Zone of Peace?" *International Affairs* 60, no. 2 (Spring 1984): 233–46.

Ladjevardi, Habib, ed. *Khaterat -e 'Abd ol-Majid Majidi.* Cambridge: Iranian Oral History Project, Center for Middle Eastern Studies, Harvard University, 1998.

Lawless, Richard. *The Gulf in the Early 20th Century: Foreign Institutions and Local Responses, Occasional Papers 31.* Durham: Center for Middle Eastern and Islamic Studies, University of Durham, 1986.

Lawless, Richard, and Ian J. Seccombe. "Impact of the Oil Industry on Urbanization in the Persian Gulf Region." In *Urban Development in the Muslim World*, edited by Houchang Amirahmadi and Salah S. el-Shakhs, 183–202. New Brunswick, NJ: Rutgers University Press, 1993.

———. "Work Camps and Company Towns: Settlement Patterns and the Gulf Oil Industry." Working paper. Durham: University of Durham, Center for Middle Eastern and Islamic Studies, 1987.

Lefebvre, Henri. *Production of Space.* Oxford: Blackwell, 1991.

Levinson, Martin H. "Mapping the Persian Gulf Naming Dispute." *ETC: A Review of General Semantics* 68, no. 3 (2011): 279–87.

Lienhardt, Peter. *Disorientations, A Society in Flux: Kuwait in the 1950s.* Edited by Ahmed Al-Shahi. Reading, U.K.: Ithaca Press, 1993.

———. *Sheikhdoms of Eastern Arabia.* New York: Palgrave, 2001.

Lilienthal, David, and Helen M. Lilienthal. *The Journals of David E. Lilienthal, Vol. V.* New York: Harper & Row, 1964.

Longva, Anh Nga. "Neither Autocracy nor Democracy but Ethnocracy: Citizens, Expatriates, and the Socio-Political System in Kuwait." In *Monarchies and Nations: Globalisation and Identity in the Arab States of the Gulf*, edited by P. Dresch and J. Piscatori, 114–35. London: I. B. Tauris, 2005.

———. *Walls Built on Sand: Migration, Exclusion, and Society in Kuwait.* Boulder, CO: Westview Press, 1997.

Looser, Tom. "The Global University, Area Studies, and the World Citizen: Neoliberal Geography's Redistribution of the 'World.'" *Cultural Anthropology* 27, no. 1 (2012): 97–117.

Lori, Noora. "National Security and the Management of Migrant Labor: A Case Study of the United Arab Emirates." *Asian and Pacific Migration Journal* 20, no. 3/4 (2011): 315–37.

———. *Offshore Citizens: Permanent Temporary Status in the Gulf.* Cambridge: Cambridge University Press, 2019.

Lorimer, J. G. "Appendix C: The Pearl and Mother-of-Pearl Fisheries of the Persian Gulf." *Gazetteer of the Persian Gulf, Oman, and Central Arabia.* Online edition. Leiden: Brill, 2015. http://dx.doi.org/10.1163/2405-447X_loro_COM _001303.

Louis, William Roger. *Ends of British Imperialism: The Scramble for Empire, Suez, and Decolonization: Collected Essays.* London: I. B. Tauris, 2006.

Lynch, Marc, ed. *The Arab Monarchy Debate: Arab Uprisings.* POMEPS Briefing 16, December 19, 2012.

MacLean, Matthew. "Spatial Transformation and the Emergence of 'the National': Infrastructures and the Formation of the United Arab Emirates, 1950–1980." PhD dissertation, New York University, 2017.

McAlister, Melani. *Epic Encounters: Culture, Media, and U.S. Interests in the Middle East since 1945,* 2nd ed. Berkeley: University of California Press, 2005.

Mackinder, Halford John. *Britain and the British Seas.* London: William Heineman, 1902.

———. "The Geographical Pivot of History." *Geographical Journal* 23, no. 4 (April 1904): 421–37.

Mahan, Alfred. *The Influence of Sea Power upon History, 1660–1783.* Boston: Little Brown Company, 1894 [1890].

———. "The Persian Gulf and International Relations." *National Review,* September 1902, 27–45.

Mahajan, Nidhi. "Dhow Itineraries: The Making of a Shadow Economy in the Western Indian Ocean." *Comparative Studies of South Asia, Africa, and the Middle East* 39, no. 3 (2019): 407–19.

Mahdavy, Hossein. "The Pattern and Problems of Economic Development in Rentier States: The Case of Iran." In *Studies in the Economic History of the Middle East,* edited by M. A. Cook, 428–67. Oxford: Oxford University Press, 1970.

Malihi, Maryam al-Sadat. *Radepa-ye amvaj: tarikh-e tawseh-ye jazireh-ye Kish 1300–1377.* Tehran: Sazman-e Mantaqeh-ye Azad-e Kish, n.d.

Mamadouh, Virginie. "Reclaiming Geopolitics: Geographers Strike Back." In *Geopolitics at the End of the Twentieth Century: The Changing World Political Map,* edited by Nurit Kliot and David Newman, 118–38. London: Frank Cass, 2000.

Mamdani, Mahmood. *Citizen and Subject: The Making of Citizen and Subject in Contemporary Africa.* Princeton, NJ: Princeton University Press, 1996.

Mantena, Karuna. *Alibis of Empire: Henry Maine and the Ends of Liberal Imperialism.* Princeton, NJ: Princeton University Press, 2010.

Marcus, Jeffrey R. "Between the Storms: How Desert Storm Shaped the U.S. Navy of Operation Iraqi Freedom." *White House Studies* 14, no. 2 (Spring 2004): 153–71.

Marcuse, Peter, and Ronald van Kempen, eds. *Globalizing Cities: A New Spatial Order?* London: Blackwell, 2000.

Marr, Phebe. *The Modern History of Iraq.* 3rd ed. Boulder, CO: Westview Press, 2012.

Martin, Josh. "Gateways for the Global Economy." *Management Review* 87, no. 11 (December 1998): 22–26.

Martin, Lenore. *The Unstable Gulf: Threats from Within.* Lexington, MA: Lexington Books, 1984.

Martin, Vanessa. *The Qajar Pact: Bargaining, Protest, and the State in Nineteenth-Century Persia.* London: I. B. Tauris, 2005.

Maruschke, Megan. "Zones of Reterritorialization: Indian Free Trade Zones, 1947 to the 1980s." *Journal of Global History* 12, no. 3 (2017): 410–32.

Marx, Karl. *Capital: A Critique of Political Economy, Volume I.* London: Penguin Books, 1976.

———. *Grundrisse: Foundations of the Critique of Political Economy.* Harmondsworth: Penguin Books, 1973.

Massey, Doreen. *For Space.* London: Sage, 2005.

———. "Power-Geometry and a Progressive Sense of Place." In *Mapping Futures: Local Cultures, Global Change,* edited by Jon Bird, Barry Curtis, Tim Putnam, George Robertson, and Lisa Tickner, 60–70. London: Routledge 1993.

Mas'udi, 'Abbas. *Didar az shaykh nishinha-yi Khalij-i Fars.* [Tehran]: Iran Chap, 1345 [1966].

———. *Didari-yi tazih az shaykh-nishinha-yi Khalij-i Fars pas az khuruj-i niruha-ye ingilis.* [Tehran]: Intisharat-i Mu'assasah-i Ittila'at, 1348 [1969].

———. *Khalij-i Fars dar dawrin-i sarbulandi va shukuh.* [Tehran]: Intisharat-i Mu'assasah-yi lttila'at, 1352 [1973].

Mathew, Johan. *Margins of the Market: Trafficking and Capitalism across the Arabian Sea.* Berkeley: University of California Press, 2016.

McCann, Eugene, and Kevin Ward. *Mobile Urbanism: Cities and Policymaking in the Global Age.* Minneapolis: University of Minnesota Press, 2011.

McIntire, Emily. "Migrants and Bureaucrats: Social Mobility in an Iranian Town." PhD dissertation, Harvard University, 1984.

Menoret, Pascal. *Joyriding in Riyadh: Oil, Urbanism, and Road Revolt.* Cambridge: Cambridge University Press, 2014.

Metcalf, Thomas. *Imperial Connections: India in the Indian Ocean Arena, 1860–1920.* Berkeley: University of California Press, 2007.

Mi'tazed, Khosrow. "Kish: vilaha-ye bara-ye hezar nur-e chashmi." *Manataq-e azad*, no. 187 (1386 [2007]): 46–51.

Milani, Abbas. *The Shah*. New York: Palgrave Macmillan, 2011.

Mitchell, Timothy. *Carbon Democracy: Political Power in the Age of Oil*. New York: Verso Press, 2011.

Moghadam, Amin. "Iranian Migrations to Dubai: Constrains and Autonomy of a Segmented Diaspora." Working paper No. 2021/3, Ryerson Centre for Immigration and Settlement and the CERC in Migration and Integration at Ryerson University.

Moisio, Sami, and Andrew E. G. Jonas. "City-Regions and City-Regionalism." In *Handbook on the Geographies of Regions and Territories*, edited by Anssi Paasi, John Harrison, and Martin Jones, 285–97. Cheltenham, U.K.: Elgar, 2020.

Molavi, Afshin. "Dubai Rising." *Brown Journal of World Affairs* 12, no. 1 (Summer/Fall 2005): 103–10.

Molotch, Harvey. "The City as a Growth Machine: Toward a Political Economy of Place." *American Journal of Sociology* 82, no. 2 (1976): 309–32.

Molotch, Harvey, and Davide Ponzini, eds. *The New Arab Urban: Gulf Cities of Wealth, Ambition, and Distress*. New York: New York University Press, 2019.

Moore, Pete. "Making Big Money on Iraq." *Middle East Report*, no. 252 (Fall 2009): 22–29.

Mottahedeh, Roy. *Mantle of the Prophet: Religion and Politics in Iran*. New York: Pantheon Books, 1985.

Mueller, Chelsei. "Anglo-Iranian Treaty Negotiations: Reza Shah, Teymurtash, and the British Government, 1927–32." *Iranian Studies* 49, no. 4 (2016): 577–92.

———. *The Origins of the Arab-Iranian Conflict: Nationalism and Sovereignty in the Gulf between the World Wars*. Cambridge: Cambridge University Press, 2020.

Nadjmabadi, Shahnaz R. "Cross-Border Networks: Labour Migration from Iran to the Arab Countries of the Persian Gulf." *Anthropology of the Middle East* 5, no. 1 (Spring 2010): 18–33.

Naim, Moises. *Illicit: How Smugglers, Traffickers, and Copycats Are Hijacking the Global Economy*. New York: Anchor, 2005.

Nastasi, Michele. "A Gulf of Images: Photography and the Circulation of Spectacular Architecture." In *The New Arab Urban: Gulf Cities of Wealth, Ambition, and Distress*, edited by Harvey Molotch and Davide Ponzini, 99–129. New York: New York University Press, 2019.

Neveling, Patrick. "Export Processing Zones and Global Class Formation." In *Anthropologies of Class: Power, Practice, and Inequality*, edited by James Carrier and Don Kalb, 164–82. Cambridge: Cambridge University Press, 2015.

————. "The Global Spread of Export Processing Zones, and the 1970s as a Decade of Consolidation." In *Changes in Social Regulation—State, Economy, and Social Protagonists since the 1970s*, edited by Knud Andersen and Stefan Müller, 23–40. Oxford: Berghahn Books, 2017.

Nitzan, Jonathan, and Shimshon Bichler. *The Global Political Economy of Israel.* London: Pluto Press, 2002.

Nourinejad, Samieh. "Batt Guran: ma'bad-e henduha dar bandar abbas." *Jelveh Honar* 12 (Fall/Winter 1393 [2014]): 19–32.

Offner, Amy. *Sorting Out the Mixed Economy: The Rise and Fall of Welfare and Developmental States in the Americas.* Princeton, NJ: Princeton University Press, 2019.

Ogle, Vanessa. "'Funk Money': The End of Empires, the Expansion of Tax Havens, and Decolonization as an Economic and Financial Event." *Past and Present* 249, no. 1 (2020): 213–49.

Ong, Aiwha. *Neoliberalism as Exception: Mutations in Citizenship and Sovereignty.* Durham, NC: Duke University Press, 2006.

Onley, James. *The Arabian Frontier of the British Raj.* Oxford: Oxford University Press, 2007.

————. "Transnational Merchants in the Nineteenth-Century Gulf." In *Transnational Connections and the Arab Gulf*, edited by Madawi al-Rasheed, 59–89. London: Routledge, 2005.

Ó Tuathail, Gearóid. *Critical Geopolitics: The Politics of Writing Global Space.* Minneapolis: University of Minnesota Press, 1996.

Pacione, Michael. "City Profile: Dubai." *Cities* 22, no. 3 (2005): 255–65.

Pajoohan, Musa. "Regional Development or Regional Policies? A Review of 60 Years of Regional Planning and Development in Pre and Post Islamic Republic Iran." *Journal of Regional and City Planning* 30, no. 2 (August 2019): 102–22.

Palan, Ronen. "International Financial Centers: The British-Empire, City-States, and Commercially Oriented Politics." *Theoretical Inquiries in Law* 11, no. 1 (2010): 149–76.

————. *The Offshore World: Sovereign Markets, Virtual Places, and Nomad Millionaires.* Ithaca, NY: Cornell University Press, 2003.

Parsa, Ali, and Ramin Keivani, "The Hormuz Corridor: Building a Cross-Border Region Between Iran and the UAE." In *Global Networks, Linked Cities*, edited by Saskia Sassen, 183–207. New York: Routledge, 2002.

Pearson, Michael. *The Indian Ocean.* London: Routledge, 2003.

————. "Littoral Society: The Concept and the Problems." *Journal of World History* 17, no. 4 (November 2006): 353–73.

Pedersen, Susan. *The Guardians: The League of Nations and the Crisis of Empire.* New York: Oxford University Press, 2018.

Peet, Richard. "The Social Origins of Environmental Determinism." *Annals of the Association of American Geographers* 75, no. 3 (September 1985): 309–33.

Penziner Highwater, Victoria. "Pearling and Political Power in the Trucial States, 1850–1930: Debts, Taxes, and Politics." *Journal of Arabian Studies* 3, no. 2 (2013): 215–31.

Polan, Ronen. *The Offshore World: Sovereign Markets, Virtual Places, and Nomad Millionaires*. Ithaca, NY: Cornell University Press, 2003.

Posen, Barry. *Restraint: A New Foundation for U.S. Grand Strategy*. Ithaca, NY: Cornell University Press, 2015.

Potter, Lawrence G., "The Consolidation of Iran's Frontier on the Persian Gulf in the Nineteenth Century." In *War and Peace in Qajar Persia: Implications Past and Present*, edited by Roxane Farmanfarmaian, 125–48. London: Routledge, 2008.

———, ed. *The Persian Gulf in History*. New York: Palgrave Macmillan, 2009.

Pursley, Sara. *Familiar Futures: Time, Selfhood, and Sovereignty in Iraq*. Location: Stanford University Press, 2018.

Qasrawi, Sophia. "Foreign Direct Investment in the UAE: Determinants and Recommendations." *The Emirates Occasional Papers*, No. 57, The Emirates Center for Strategic Studies and Research, 2004.

Ramazani, Rouhollah K. "Emerging Patterns of Regional Relations in Iranian Foreign Policy." *Orbis* 18, no. 4 (Winter 1975): 1043–69.

———. *Iran's Foreign Policy, 1941–1973*. Charlottesville: University Press of Virginia, 1975.

———. *The Persian Gulf and the Strait of Hormuz*. Alphen aan den Rijn, the Netherlands: Sijthoff & Noordhoff, 1979.

Ramos, Stephan. *Dubai Amplified: The Engineering of a Port Geography*. Burlington, VT: Ashgate, 2010.

Rao, Kishore. "Free Zones in the Middle East: Development Patterns and Future Potential." In *Trade Policy Developments in the Middle East and North Africa*, edited by Bernard Hoekman and Hanaa Kheir el-Din, 245–64. Washington, DC: The World Bank, 2000.

Rauh, Elizabeth. "An Enduring Monument: Bahrain's 2011 Pearl Roundabout Protests." *Middle Eastern Journal of Culture and Communication* 11 (July 2018): 141–73.

Razvani, Mohammad Taghi. "Iranian Communities in the Persian Gulf: A Geographical Analysis." PhD dissertation, University of London, 1975.

Reisz, Todd. *Showpiece City: How Architecture Made Dubai*. Stanford: Stanford University Press, 2021.

Ricks, Thomas. "Slaves and Slave Traders in the Persian Gulf, 18th and 19th Centuries: An Assessment." *Slavery and Abolition* 9, no. 3 (1998): 60–70.

———. "U.S. Military Missions to Iran, 1943–1978: The Political Economy of Military Assistance." *Iranian Studies* 12, no. 3/4 (1979): 163–93.

Rodman, Kenneth. *Sanctity vs. Sovereignty: The United States and the Nationalization of Natural Resource Investments*. New York: Columbia University Press, 1988.

Rosen, Barry. *Restraint: A New Foundation for U.S. Grand Strategy*. Ithaca, NY: Cornell University Press, 2015.

Ross, Christopher N. B. "Lord Curzon and E. G. Browne Confront the 'Persian Question.'" *Historical Journal* 52, no. 2 (2009): 385–411.

Rugh, Andrea B. *The Political Culture of Leadership in the United Arab Emirates*. New York: Palgrave, 2007.

Said, Edward. *Orientalism*. New York: Vintage Books, 1978.

Said Zahlan, Rosemarie. *The Making of the Modern Gulf States*. London: Unwin Hyman, 1989.

Saleh, Zainab. "On Iraqi Nationality: Law, Citizenship, and Exclusion." *Arab Studies Journal* 21, no. 1 (Spring 2013): 48–78.

Sampler, Jeffrey, and Saeb Eigner. *From Sand and Silicon: Achieving Rapid Economic Growth, Lessons from Dubai*. London: Profile Books, 2003.

Sargent, Daniel. *A Superpower Transformed: The Remaking of American Foreign Relations in the 1970s*. New York: Oxford University Press 2017.

Sarmadi, Behzad. "'This Place Should Have Been Iran:' Iranian Imaginings in/of Dubai." *Ajam Media Collective*, May 20, 2013.

———. "Transmigration, Proximity, and Sociopolitical Disconnection: Iranians in the United Arab Emirates." In *The Iranian Diaspora: Challenges, Negotiations, and Transformations*, edited by Mohsen Mostafavi Mobasher, 125–49. Austin: University of Texas Press, 2018.

Saskia, Sassen. *The Global City: New York, London, Tokyo*. Princeton, NJ: Princeton University Press, 1991.

Satia, Priya. "Developing Iraq: Britain, India, and the Redemption of Empire and Technology in World War I." *Past and Present* 197 (November 2007): 211–55.

———. *Spies in Arabia: The Great War and the Cultural Foundations of Britain's Covert Empire in the Middle East*. New York: Oxford University Press, 2008.

Sato, Shohei. "Britain's Decision to Withdraw from the Persian Gulf, 1964–68: A Pattern and a Puzzle." *Journal of Imperial and Commonwealth History* 37, no. 1 (March 2009): 99–117.

Schielke, Samuli. *Migrant Dreams: Egyptian Workers in the Gulf States*. Cairo: American University in Cairo Press, 2020.

Schofield, Richard. "States Behaving Badly? The Unique Geopolitics of Island Sovereignty Disputes." Environment, Politics, and Development Working Paper Series, Paper no. 65, Department of Geography, King's College London, 2014.

Schrader, Stuart. *Badges without Borders: How Global Counterinsurgency Transformed American Policing*. Berkeley: University of California Press, 2019.

Seccombe, I. J., and R. I. Lawless. "Foreign Worker Dependence in the Gulf and the International Oil Company: 1910–50." *International Migration Review* 20, no. 3 (1986): 548–74.

Segal, Eran. "Merchants' Networks in Kuwait: The Story of Yusuf al-Marzuk." *Middle Eastern Studies* 45, no. 5 (Summer 2009): 709–19.

Shahibzadeh, Yadullah. *The Iranian Political Language: From the Late Nineteenth Century to the Present*. New York: Palgrave Macmillan, 2015.

Shahvar, Soli. "Iron Poles, Wooden Poles: The Electric Telegraph and the Ottoman: Iranian Boundary Conflict, 1863–1865." *British Journal of Middle Eastern Studies* 34, no. 1 (2007): 23–42.

Sheriff, Abdul. "The Persian Gulf and the Swahili Coast: A History of Acculturation over the *Longue Durée*." In *The Persian Gulf in History*, edited by L. G. Potter, 173–88. Palgrave Macmillan, New York, 2009.

Shiber, Saba George. *The Kuwait Urbanization: Being an Urbanistic Case-Study of a Developing Country—Documentation, Analysis, Critique*. Kuwait: Kuwait Government Printing Press, 1964.

Silver, Beverly J., and Giovanni Arrighi. "The End of the Long Twentieth Century." In *Business as Usual: The Roots of the Global Financial Meltdown*, edited by Craig J. Calhoun and Georgi Derluguian, 53–58. New York: New York University Press, 2011.

Silverstein, Paul. "The New Barbarians: Piracy and the North African Frontier." *CR: New Centennial Review* 5, no. 1 (Spring 2005): 179–212.

Singa Boyenge, Jean-Pierre. "ILO Database on Export Processing Zones (Revised)." Working paper, International Labour Office, Geneva, April 2007.

Sluga, Glenda. *Internationalism in the Age of Nationalism*. Philadelphia: University of Pennsylvania Press, 2013.

Smith, Neil. *American Empire: Roosevelt's Geographer and the Prelude to Globalization*. Berkeley: University of California Press, 2003.

———. "Scale Bending and the Fate of the National." In *Scale and Geographic Inquiry: Nature, Society, and Method*, edited by E. Sheppard and R. B. McMaster, 192–212. Oxford: Blackwell, 2004.

Smith, Simon. *Britain's Revival and Fall in the Gulf: Kuwait, Bahrain, Qatar, and the Trucial States, 1950–1971*. London: Routledge, 2004.

Sohrabi, Naghmeh. "Where the Small Things Are: Thoughts on Writing Revolutions and Their Histories." *Jadaliyya*, May 21, 2020.

Soja, Edward W. "The Socio-Spatial Dialectic." *Annals of the Association of American Geographers* 70, no. 2 (June 1980): 207–25.

Spiro, David E. *The Hidden Hand of American Hegemony: Petrodollar Recycling and International Markets.* Ithaca, NY: Cornell University Press, 1999.

Spykman, Nicholas J. "Geography and Foreign Policy, II." *American Political Science Review* 32, no. 2 (April 1938): 213–36.

———. *The Geography of the Peace.* New York: Harcourt Brace, 1944.

Stanek, Lukasz. "Mobilities of Architecture in the Global Cold War: From Socialist Poland to Kuwait and Back." *International Journal of Islamic Architecture* 4, no. 2 (2015): 365–98.

Steinberg, Phillip E. *The Social Construction of the Ocean.* Cambridge: Cambridge University Press, 2001.

Stephenson, Lindsey R. "Rerouting the Persian Gulf: The Transnationalization of Iranian Migrant Networks, c. 1900–1940." PhD dissertation, Department of Near Eastern Studies, Princeton University, 2018.

Stern, Roger J. "Oil Scarcity Ideology in US Foreign Policy, 1908–97." *Security Studies* 25, no. 2 (2016): 214–57.

Stoler, Ann. "Imperial Formations and the Opacities of Rule." In *Lessons of Empire: Imperial Histories and American Power,* edited by Craig Calhoun, Frederick Cooper, and Kevin W. Moore, 48–60. New York: The New Press, 2006.

Stork, Joe. "The Carter Doctrine and the US Bases in the Middle East." *MERIP Reports,* no. 90 (September 1980): 3–14, 32.

Stork, Joe, and Jim Paul. "Arms Sales and the Militarization of the Middle East." *MERIP Reports,* no. 112 (February 1983): 5–15.

Strange, Susan. "Cave! Hic Dragones: A Critique of Regime Analysis." *International Organization* 36, no. 2 (1982): 479–96.

Subrahmanyam, Sanjay. "Connected Histories: Notes towards a Reconfiguration of Early Modern Eurasia." *Modern Asian Studies* 31, no. 3 (1997): 735–62.

Sullivan, William H. *Mission to Iran.* New York: Norton, 1981.

Sykes, Percy. *A History of Persia in Two Volumes.* 2 Vols. London: Routledge and Kegan Paul, 1969.

Tabatabai, Nasrin, and Babak Afrassiabi. *Kish: An Island Indecisive by Design.* Rotterdam: NAi Publishers, 2012.

Takriti, Abdel Razzeq. "Colonial Coups and the War on Popular Sovereignty." *American Historical Review* 124, no. 3 (June 2019): 878–909.

Taremi, Kamran. "The Role of Water Exports in Iranian Foreign Policy Towards the GCC." *Iranian Studies* 38, no. 2 (2005): 311–28.

Tétreault, Mary Ann. "Autonomy, Necessity, and the Small State: Ruling Kuwait in the Twentieth Century." *International Organization* 45, no. 4 (1991): 565–91.

———. *Stories of Democracy: Politics and Society in Contemporary Kuwaiti.* New York: Columbia University Press, 2000.

Tetzlaff, Stefan. "The Turn of the Gulf: Empire, Nationalism, and South Asian Labor Migration to Iraq, c. 1900–1935." *International Labor and Working-Class History* 79 (Spring 2011): 7–27.

Tracy, James D. "Dutch and English Trade to the East: The Indian Ocean and the Levant, to about 1700." In *The Cambridge World History*, edited by J. Bentley, S. Subrahmanyam, and M. Wiesner-Hanks, 240–62. Cambridge: Cambridge University Press, 2015.

Tripp, Charles. *A History of Iraq*. 3rd ed. Cambridge: Cambridge University Press, 2010.

Väyrynen, Raimo. "Regionalism: Old and New." *International Studies Review* 5, no. 1 (March 2003): 25–51.

Villiers, Alan. *Sons of Sinbad*. London: Arabian Publishing, 2006 [1949].

Vine, David. *Island of Shame: The Secret History of the U.S. Military Base on Diego Garcia*. Princeton, NJ: Princeton University Press, 2009.

Visser, Reider. *Basra, the Failed Gulf State: Separatism and Nationalism in Southern Iraq*. New Brunswick, NJ: Transaction Publishers, 2005.

———. "Britain and Basra: Past Experiences and Current Challenges," historiae .org, July 11, 2006.

Vitalis, Robert. *America's Kingdom: Mythmaking on the Saudi Oil Frontier*. London: Verso Press, 2009.

———. "Black Gold, White Crude: An Essay on American Exceptionalism, Hierarchy, and Hegemony in the Gulf." *Diplomatic History* 26, no. 2 (2002): 185–213.

———. *Oilcraft: The Myths of Scarcity and Security That Haunt U.S. Energy Policy*. Stanford: Stanford University Press, 2020.

Vora, Neha. *Impossible Citizens: Dubai's Indian Diaspora*. Durham, NC: Duke University Press, 2013.

———. *Teach for Arabia: American Universities, Liberalism, and Transnational Qatar*. Stanford: Stanford University Press, 2019.

Ward, Evan R. "Before Dubai: The Frank Lloyd Wright Foundation and Iranian Tourism Development, 1967–1969." *Journal of Tourism History* 11, no. 1 (2019): 46–62.

Ward, Steven. *Immortal: A Military History of Iran and its Forces*. Washington, DC: Georgetown University Press, 2009.

———. *Pocket Guide to Iran: Instructions for American Servicemen in Iran during World War II*. North Charleston, SC: CreateSpace, 2012.

Watts, Michael J. "Collective Wish Images: Geographical Imaginaries and the Crisis of National Development." In *Human Geography Today*, edited by D. Massey, J. Allen and P. Sarre, 85–107. Cambridge: Polity Press, 1999.

Whigham, Henry James. *The Persian Problem: An Examination of the Rival Positions of Russia and Great Britain in Persia with Some Account of the Persian Gulf and the Bagdad Railway.* New York: Scribner's, 1903.

Willis, John M. "Making Yemen Indian: Rewriting the Boundaries of Imperial Arabia." *International Journal of Middle East Studies* 41, no. 1 (February 2009): 22–38.

Wilson, Graeme. *Rashid's Legacy: The Genesis of the Maktoum Family and the History of Dubai.* Dubai: Media Prima, 2006.

Winkler, David F. *Amirs, Admirals, and Desert Sailors: Bahrain, the U.S. Navy, and the Arabian Gulf.* Annapolis: Naval Institute Press, 2007.

Wolfe-Hunnicutt, Brandon. "Oil Sovereignty, American Foreign Policy, and the 1968 Coups in Iraq." *Diplomacy and Statecraft* 28, no. 2 (2017): 235–53.

Wyman, Lucas. "The Mercenary University." *Jacobin,* June 2, 2016.

Yergin, Daniel. *The Prize: The Epic Quest for Oil, Money, and Power.* New York: Simon and Schuster, 1991.

Young, Gabriel. "Boundaries of the State: Basra, and the Making of an Iraqi Periphery, 1920-1963." PhD dissertation, New York University, 2024.

———. "Infrastructures of Empire and Sovereignty: The Port of Basra in Interwar Iraq." *Journal of Arabian Studies* 9, no. 2 (2019): 123–44.

Zia-Ebrahimi, Reza. "'Arab Invasion' and Decline, or the Import of European Racial Thought by Iranian Nationalists." *Ethnic and Racial Studies* 37, no. 6 (2014): 1043–61.

Ziadeh, Rafeef. "Transport Infrastructure and Logistics in the Making of Dubai Inc." *International Journal of Urban and Regional Research* 42, no. 2 (2018): 182–97.

Index

1–4, 136–37, 205n1; oil as Western countries Achilles heel from, 74–75; oil production of, 67–68; pipelines of trade in, 126–27; power vacuum in, 62–66; regionalism of, 5–8, 11–12, 45–46; regionalization of, 5–7; relationships in, 14; satellite photo of, 2; security architecture of, 7; shallow waters of, 21; social arrangements of, 8; as social bridge, 16; social diversity of, 31–33; sovereign nation-states in, 88–89; as umbilical cord of industrial free world, 4–5; as unified territorial object, 5–6; United Nations term as, 205n1; U.S. actions in, 85; water's multiple functions of, 16; Weinberger on, 4. *See also* Arabian Gulf; Gulf states; Middle East; regionalism. *See also* Strait of Hormuz

Persian Gulf Command, 62

Persian Gulf Ports and Islands governorate, 109

The Persian Problem (Curzon and Whigham), 53

petrodollar recycling, 69–73, 148

photography, aerial, 123, 125

pirates, 50, 89–90

place, 125, 141–42, 151, 157, 184, 196–98, 202–3

Planning and Budget Organization (Iran), 133, 240n45

Point Four policies, 127

politics: Bahrain's ruling families, 100; closed systems of, 49; economics in, 38, 63; FTZs as projects for, 151–52; merchants in, 231n64; oil causing centralization inf, 103–4; power in, 6, 18, 38, 63, 161–62; power over

human bodies, 227n6; ruling families alliances in, 182; science of, 13–14

Popular Front for the Liberation of the Oman and the Arab Gulf, 101

population: of Africans, 212n45; of Dubai, 149; growth 27, 149, 157, 167–68, 169; of Kuwait, 27, 157–58, 168; low and declining, 22, 41, 69, 130, 189, 224n136; overpopulation and, 224n136; urbanism with, 158

port cities, 19–20, 24, 26, 30, 38, 82, 97, 130, 153, 157–61, 189, 200–201, 258n19

ports, 31–33, 127, 212n55; Bandar Abbas "international," 238n32; commercial activities of, 258n19; deep-water harbor, 145; at Jebel Ali, 124, 145–46, 246n121; Jebel Ali's man-made, 147; natural harbors, 158; U.S. investments of, 78; U.S. using Jebel Ali, 150, 247n127

Port Rashid, 145, 151, 202

Portuguese Empire, 35, 39

postcolonial states, 119, 193

power geometry, 10, 190

private-sector employment, 185

property ownership, 31, 111, 142, 159, 167–68, 172–73, 180, 184

protectorate agreements, 119, 228n13

protesters, in Bahrain, 188

protests, 101–2

public services and welfare, 51, 60, 166, 170–72, 197

Qajar Dynasty (r. 1789–1925), 59, 108, 111

qanat (irrigation systems), 22, 211n44

al-Qasimi, Saqr bin Sultan, 94

Qasimi dynasty, 59–61, 86, 108–11

Printed in the USA
CPSIA information can be obtained
at www.ICGtesting.com
JSHW022350100224
57094JS00001B/1

9 781503 638877